Military Politics and Democracy in the Andes

Military Politics and Democracy in the Andes

Maiah Jaskoski

The Johns Hopkins University Press
Baltimore

Printed in the United States of America on acid-free paper
9 8 7 6 5 4 3 2 1

The Johns Hopkins University Press
2715 North Charles Street
Baltimore, Maryland 21218-4363
www.press.jhu.edu

Library of Congress Cataloging-in-Publication Data
Jaskoski, Maiah, 1977–
Military politics and democracy in the Andes / Maiah Jaskoski.
p. cm.
Includes bibliographical references and index.
ISBN 978-1-4214-0907-8 (hbk. : alk. paper) — ISBN 978-1-4214-0908-5 (electronic) — ISBN 1-4214-0907-0 (hbk. : alk. paper) — ISBN 1-4214-0908-9 (electronic)
1. National security—Peru. 2. National security—Ecuador. 3. Peru—Military policy. 4. Ecuador—Military policy. 5. Peru. Ejército—Evaluation. 6. Ecuador. Ejército—Evaluation. 7. Internal security—Peru. 8. Internal security—Ecuador. 9. Peru—Politics and government—21st century. 10. Ecuador—Politics and government—21st century. I. Title.
UA637.J33 2013
322'.50985—dc23 2012036055

A catalog record for this book is available from the British Library.

Special discounts are available for bulk purchases of this book. For more information, please contact Special Sales at 410-516-6936 or specialsales@press.jhu.edu.

The Johns Hopkins University Press uses environmentally friendly book materials, including recycled text paper that is composed of at least 30 percent post-consumer waste, whenever possible.

With love, to
John Kaltenstein
and
the memory of David R. Jaskoski

Contents

Acknowledgments ix

Acronyms and Abbreviations xiii

1 Military Mission Performance in Latin America 1

Challenges to Security and Democratic Civil-Military Relations in the Andes 3

Explaining Military Mission Performance in Democratic Latin America 5

Case Selection: A Focus on the Army in Peru and Ecuador 18

The Data 20

Overview of the Analysis 20

2 Civil-Military Relations in Democratic Peru and Ecuador 23

High Constraints on Peru's Military 24

Low Constraints on Ecuador's Military 30

3 Army Mission Performance in Post-Transition Peru and Ecuador, 1980s–1990s 37

Sovereignty before Policing 37

Deviations: Contradictions in Missions and Sovereignty Neglect 50

Alternative Explanations 56

4 Mission Constraint and Neglect of Counterinsurgency: Peru since 2000 58

Staying in the Barracks 58

Insecurity in Sendero Zones 59

Predictions of the Legitimacy, Professionalism, and Resource Maximization Hypotheses 64

Army Inaction 73

Restrictions on Army Autonomy 83

Contradiction through Mission Constraint 83

The Source of the Senior Cohort's "Need" for Autonomy 92

Neglect of Counterinsurgency as a Way to Maintain Predictability for Patrols 97

Return to Assertive Counterinsurgency 102
Narrow Mission Beliefs and Minimal Police Work 105

5 Mission Overload and Neglect of Border Defense: Ecuador since 2000 115
Neglecting a Porous Border while Policing the Interior 116
Insecurity in Northern Ecuador 116
Predictions of the Legitimacy, Professionalism, and Resource Maximization Hypotheses 124
Assertive Policing 133
Overwhelming Security Responsibilities 140
Policing to Avoid Obsolescence 140
Contradiction through Mission Overload 150
Managing the Contradiction 155
The Contradiction Escalates 157
Alternative Explanations: Revisiting Legitimacy 161

6 Battalions for Hire: Private Army Contracts in Peru and Ecuador 165
Resource-Hungry Army Units 166
Local Client Influence 168
Limits to Client Influence 181

7 Comparative Perspectives on Military Mission Performance 184
Colombia: Tolerance of Policing amid Ongoing Insurgency 185
Venezuela: Mission Loss, Organizational Trauma, and Rejection of Police Work 194
Bolivia: Policing despite Organizational Trauma 198
Extreme Executive Control: Trends in Venezuela and Bolivia 202
Reflections on Assigning Militaries to Conduct Police Work 205

Appendix. Field Research Methodology 207
Notes 215
References 249
Index 281

Acknowledgments

I am grateful to the many individuals and institutions that helped with this project. The study began nearly nine years ago as a dissertation prospectus at the University of California, Berkeley, where my committee was highly supportive of the research. Ruth Berins Collier was a phenomenal guide on my journey from rough descriptions and causal models to the final version of the dissertation, "Mission Impossible? Military Politics in Peru and Ecuador." David Collier challenged me to stay true to the empirics of my cases while speaking to broader, pressing questions that emerged from scholarship and from Latin American political realities. Todd La Porte introduced me to public administration theory, which enabled me to organize the complex, and in many ways quite different, cases of Ecuador and Peru within a single framework. Kent Eaton's astute observations on the empirics, structure, and underlying argument of the research contributed to the project substantially, at all its stages. Mark Healey offered exceptional feedback, as well.

Within the community of scholars of Latin American militaries, David Pion-Berlin and Harold Trinkunas made valuable suggestions as the dissertation and then the book evolved. I am particularly indebted to Sam Fitch and Deborah Norden for the time they invested in critiquing the full manuscript in great detail.

I developed my central argument and drafted much of the empirics over the course of two semesters of Ruth Berins Collier's Latin American Politics writing seminar at UC Berkeley, an energizing arena for writing and for receiving insights from trusted colleagues and friends. Thank you Mauricio Benítez, Taylor Boas, Adam Cohon, Tasha Fairfield, Candelaria Garay, Sam Handlin, Veronica Herrera, Daniel Hidalgo, Neal Richardson, Mekoce Walker, and, of course, Ruth. Lindsay Rose Mayka provided indispensable feedback on the project during our time together at Berkeley and then again when she commented on multiple drafts of the manuscript.

I have been fortunate to work among colleagues in the Department of National Security Affairs at the Naval Postgraduate School who supported my focus on this book. I especially want to acknowledge Anne Clunan for helping me identify connections between the project and broader themes in research on security matters, and fellow junior faculty members Naazneen Barma, Erik Dahl, Scott Siegel, and Arturo Sotomayor for their suggestions on chapters.

Comments on elements of the analysis were also provided by Neil Abrams, Christopher Darnton, Jonathan Hartlyn, Jennifer Holmes, Cynthia McClintock, Stephanie McNulty, Marcos Robledo, Frederick Shepherd, Erica Turner, and Zach Zwald.

During my fieldwork in Ecuador and Peru, several people were unbelievably generous, sharing with me their expertise, contacts, and/or archives over the course of multiple, usually quite lengthy, communications: in Ecuador, Pablo Andrade, Dimitri Barreto, Santiago Basabe, César Duque, Gandhi Espinosa, Bertha García, Alexandra McDowall, Hernán Moreano, Cecilia Ortiz, Diego Pérez Enríquez, Fredy Rivera, Brian Selmeski, and Arturo Torres; and in Peru, Ciro Alegría, Hugo Cabieses, Jacqueline Fowks, Gustavo Gorriti, Enrique Obando, Ana Ortega, Ricardo Soberón, Ana María Tamayo, and John J. Youle. I also thank those who granted me interviews but whose names have been omitted from this book to protect their privacy, including the Ecuadorian and Peruvian army officers who candidly shared with me their views and experiences.

Many institutions granted me access to archives, databases, and other collections, including, in Ecuador, ACNUR, the Aurelio Espinosa Politécnica library, Casa de la Cultura, CEDHU, the Central Bank library, Colegio Militar Eloy Alfaro, Defence Systems Ecuador, the Democracia, Seguridad y Defensa foundation at the Catholic University, the Escuela Politécnica del Ejército, FLACSO, IAEN, Informe Confidencial, INREDH, the National Congress, and the San Francisco University; and in Peru, APOYO Opinión Mercado S.A., APRODEH, CAEN, the Catholic University, Centro de Estudios Históricos Militares, Centro de Información de la Defensoría del Pueblo, DESCO, ESG, IDL, IEP, and the National Congress. FLACSO-Ecuador and the Instituto de Estudios Peruanos extended to me institutional affiliations.

Funding for this study was provided by a National Security Education Program David L. Boren Graduate Fellowship, the Naval Postgraduate School Research Initiation Program, a Continuing Student Fellowship of the UC Berkeley Department of Political Science, and a Dean's Normative Time to Degree Fellowship and a Summer Grant from the UC Berkeley Graduate Division. At the Johns Hopkins University Press, I thank Suzanne Flinchbaugh for her commitment to this book, and Linda Strange for her exceptional assistance in preparing the manuscript. Of course, none of the individuals or institutions named here are responsible for the study's findings or errors, which are solely my responsibility.

Numerous people gave me encouragement while I researched and wrote this book. Above all, I thank my family. My husband, John Kaltenstein, has supported my intellectual and professional development since we met in Ken Sharpe's Latin American Politics class at Swarthmore College. John and our son, Samuel David, bring me immeasurable joy.

NOTE TO THE READER. Unless otherwise indicated, all quotations from interviews with Peruvians and Ecuadorians are the author's translation from Spanish, as are all quotations from Spanish-language written sources.

Acronyms and Abbreviations

GDP	gross domestic product
GNP	gross national product
IACHR	Inter-American Court of Human Rights
ICRC	International Committee of the Red Cross
IHL	international humanitarian law
NAS	Narcotics Affairs Section, U.S. Department of State
NGO	nongovernmental organization
OPEC	Organization of Petroleum Exporting Countries
UNOHCHR	United Nations Office of the High Commissioner for Human Rights
USAID	United States Agency for International Development

BOLIVIA

ADEPCOCA	Asociación Departamental de Productores de Coca
UMOPAR	Unidad Móvil Policial para Áreas Rurales
YPFB	Yacimientos Petrolíferos Fiscales Bolivianos

COLOMBIA

AUC	Autodefensas Unidas de Colombia
CINEP	Centro de Investigación y Educación Popular
CODHES	Consultoría para los Derechos Humanos y el Desplazamiento
ELN	Ejército de Liberación Nacional
FARC	Fuerzas Armadas Revolucionarias de Colombia

ECUADOR

AVC	Alfaro Vive ¡Carajo!
CACYF	Compañías de Acción Cívica y Forestación

CEDHU	Comisión Ecuménica de Derechos Humanos
CENAF	Centros de Atención y Control de la Frontera
CEPE	Corporación Estatal Petrolera Ecuatoriana
CONAIE	Confederación de Nacionalidades Indígenas del Ecuador
COSENA	Consejo de Seguridad Nacional
DINE	Dirección de Industrias del Ejército
FLACSO	Facultad Latinoamericana de Ciencias Sociales
FTC	Fuerza de Tarea Conjunta
GIAC	*grupos irregulares armados de Colombia*
INAGUE	Instituto Nacional de Guerra
OCP	Oleoducto de Crudos Pesados
OPIP	Organización de Pueblos Indígenas de Pastaza

PERU

APAVM	Asociación de Productores Agropecuarios del Valle de Monzón
APRODEH	Asociación Pro Derechos Humanos
CAD	*comité de autodefensa*
CAEM	Centro de Altos Estudios Militares
CAEN	Centro de Altos Estudios Nacionales
CGTP	Confederación General de Trabajadores del Perú
CNDDHH	Coordinadora Nacional de Derechos Humanos
CNI	Consejo Nacional de Inteligencia
CODHAH	Comité de Derechos Humanos Alto Huallaga
CONACS	Consejo Nacional de Camélidos Sudamericanos
CONPACCP	Confederación Nacional de Productores Agropecuarios de las Cuencas Cocaleras del Perú
CSJM	Consejo Supremo de Justicia Militar
CVR	Comisión de la Verdad y Reconciliación
DINCOTE	Dirección Nacional Contra el Terrorismo
DINI	Dirección Nacional de Inteligencia
DIRANDRO	Dirección Antidrogas
ELN	Ejército de Liberación Nacional
ESG	Escuela Superior de Guerra
GEIN	Grupo Especial de Inteligencia
IEP	Instituto de Estudios Peruanos

INRENA	Instituto Nacional de Recursos Naturales
MIR	Movimiento de Izquierda Revolucionaria
MIR-EM	Movimiento de Izquierda Revolucionaria–El Militante
MRTA	Movimiento Revolucionario Túpac Amaru
OCI	*oficina de control institucional*
PRODES	Programa Pro Descentralización
PSR-ML	Partido Socialista Revolucionario-Marxista-Leninista
RDR	*recursos directamente recaudados*
SIN	Servicio de Inteligencia Nacional
SNMPE	Sociedad Nacional de Minería, Petróleo y Energía
TC	Tribunal Constitucional
TGP	Transportadora de Gas del Perú
VAH	Valle del Alto Huallaga
VRAE	Valle del Río Apurímac y Ene

VENEZUELA

AD	Acción Democrática
COPEI	Comité de Organización Política Electoral Independiente
MBR-200	Movimiento Bolivariano Revolucionario 200
PCV/MIR	Partido Comunista de Venezuela Movimiento de la Izquierda Revolucionaria
PDVSA	Petróleos de Venezuela, S.A.

Source: Based on United Nations Map No. 3838 Rev. 3, May 2004

Source: Based on United Nations Map No. 3878 Rev. 3, June 2004

Military Politics and Democracy in the Andes

CHAPTER 1

Military Mission Performance in Latin America

Since military rule gave way to democracy in Latin America, the region's armed forces have been assigned missions that range from border defense to counterinsurgency to antinarcotics to protest control. With these orders in hand, militaries have prioritized some missions over others and refused to perform certain assignments altogether. What factors explain this varied propensity to take on different missions? This book explains why the Peruvian and Ecuadorian armies have done little to defend national sovereignty from organized, armed actors; why, in place of this sovereignty work, they differ in the degree to which they police; and who benefits from the armies' security efforts. It provides an empirical account of the armies' mission performance since democratization, explains it by drawing on insights from the field of organization theory, and then extends the analysis to the other Andean armed forces. Understanding military mission performance sheds light on the post-transition civil-military relations, the state's capacity to confront security challenges, and the fundamental question of the state's responsiveness to elected officials in Latin American democracies.

The armies of Ecuador and Peru challenge our expectations about military behavior. Ecuadorian security is tightly intertwined with the Colombian civil war, due to the porous nature of the Ecuador-Colombia border. Armed Colombian guerrilla fighters routinely cross into northern Ecuador, using the territory to resupply, train, and find respite from combat. The Ecuadorian government views these incursions as a threat to the country's basic security and, in a context of public alarm over the guerrillas, assigns the army to guard the border against them. Ecuadorian army officers at all levels of the hierarchy consider border defense to be their principal mission, and defending the northern border would be the most obvious way to attract more military spending. However, the army only minimally patrols the border and instead focuses on policing missions, such as protest control and antinarcotics, suggesting that the army is driven by something other than an interest in gaining public legitimacy, performing its most professional mission of defending national sovereignty, or maximizing budgetary resources.

Peru's army faces different security threats. The 1980s and 1990s saw major, violent insurrection from a Maoist insurgency, Sendero Luminoso (in English, "Shining Path"). Since 2000, remnants of the group have continued to threaten security in some remote areas of the country, and the government has supported defense spending to prevent guerrilla resurgence, a policy backed by many social actors. For their part, army officers believe that addressing the guerrilla threat is their most important ongoing assignment. Yet, like its Ecuadorian counterpart, the army has shown great reluctance to move into a counterinsurgency role, underperforming a highly professional, legitimate, profitable mission. The Peruvian army has also rejected available policing missions, with the result that it has done little work at all.

Why have the two armies not sought to protect against threats to the legal constitution of the state—in Ecuador, a border threat, and in Peru, an internal insurgency? Given that the two armies have neglected these missions, why have they differed in the extent to which they have taken on policing? That is, why has the Ecuadorian army turned to police work instead of protecting its borders, whereas the Peruvian army has remained in the barracks? This study explains the Peruvian and Ecuadorian armies' mission performance since democratization in the late 1970s and early 1980s. It challenges three prominent explanations of military behavior: (1) militaries, like other bureaucracies, try to maximize their budgets; (2) militaries will seek to perform missions deemed legitimate by the public; and (3) in the interest of maintaining professionalism, militaries will address sovereignty threats—external enemies and insurgents—rather than fulfill policing functions such as crime fighting or protest control. The comparison between the two countries also pushes us to go beyond the idea that militaries refuse missions as a way to pressure the government to grant them added prerogatives, in a civil-military power struggle.

This study finds that, first and foremost, the two armies have prioritized predictability for troops on patrol, who, to do their job, require clear instructions regarding goals and procedures for reaching those goals. At different moments, predictability has been challenged by a stark contradiction in each army's sovereignty assignment: the army has been ordered to combat a sovereignty threat but has also received a message incompatible with that order. In Peru, the government reduced the army's autonomy in the counterinsurgency arena to the point where officers found their counterinsurgency mission impossible. In contrast, in Ecuador, where the government did not challenge the army's autonomy, the contradiction can be traced to the army's overload in its security responsibilities. To manage that overload, army leaders sought to avoid the eruption of war with Colombian insurgents on the northern border by ordering northern army units, stationed in the north to patrol the border, not to fight the guerrillas. These units thus received contradictory orders: not to fight the very insurgents they were supposed to purge from the north. A patrol assigned a mission that contains a contradiction can hardly be expected to be effective in the field. The Peruvian and Ecuadorian armies have limited their participation in the sovereignty missions of counterinsurgency and border defense, respectively, as a means of maintaining predictability for patrols.

CHALLENGES TO SECURITY AND DEMOCRATIC CIVIL-MILITARY RELATIONS IN THE ANDES

Research on Latin American, especially Andean, military missions is timely. Working state institutions that provide citizens with some degree of protection, representation, and continuity are needed for building stable, competitive democracy in the region's post-transition setting (O'Donnell 1993, 2001; Yashar 2005; Mainwaring 2006; Hilbink 2007). Indeed, scholars of democratization have emphasized that democratic consolidation requires that the state bureaucracy be "usable" by democratic leaders (Linz and Stepan 1996, 10–11). With regard to the military in particular, usability is fundamentally about the elected government's ability to successfully command the military to perform security missions, as the armed forces' basic function is "the management of violence" (Huntington 1957).

The research presented in this book gets to the core of this issue, explaining different degrees to which Andean armed forces do their work in response to government orders. It places front and center military neglect of salient sovereignty missions, behavior that is disconcerting, given that the armed forces are generally the only state institution equipped to defend international borders and fight insurgents.

The actions of state security forces to provide security and maintain order arise as an especially critical dimension of state performance in the Andes, a region that stands out for its intense and complex insecurity and where governments have relied on both police and military force for providing security and establishing order. The global center of coca cultivation is the Andes (United Nations Office on Drugs and Crime 2007, 63–65), where both illegal drug production and trafficking are common. The drug trade is superimposed on and exacerbates an Andes-specific threat to security in post-transition Latin America: insurgency. Moreover, the Andean region has seen international warfare—rare in Latin America—on two occasions in the current democratic period (between Peru and Ecuador in 1981 and 1995). A final dimension of insecurity in the region is powerful protests, which have interrupted major government privatization efforts (e.g., Bolivia in 2000, Peru in 2002) and have prematurely removed sitting presidents in Ecuador (1997, 2000, 2005), in Bolivia (2003, 2005), and, briefly, in Venezuela (2002). To counter these security challenges, Andean militaries have been called upon for international border defense, counterinsurgency, and, given that police forces have been feckless in the region, multiple policing missions.

Functioning, active armed forces may help to achieve order and thus foster stable democracy, yet assigning certain missions to the military might politicize the institution, threatening democracy from a different direction. Internal roles such as economic development and counterinsurgency (as opposed to external defense) contributed to a military politicization so intense that it led to military coups and long-term military rule during the 1960s–1980s, as Alfred Stepan (1971, 1973, 1978) found in Brazil and Peru. Apprehensiveness has lingered that internal missions could cause Latin American armed forces' political influence to expand (e.g., Hunter 1994). Given normative concerns and scholarly questions about strengthening state capacity and responsiveness, reducing insecurity, and containing military political power, it is imperative to describe and systematically explain military mission performance—that is, what missions the different militaries perform and which missions are prioritized over others.

EXPLAINING MILITARY MISSION PERFORMANCE IN DEMOCRATIC LATIN AMERICA

Military missions, or tasks, differ from the much broader concept of military roles—that is, the armed forces' place in the state and society (Hunter 1996, 1; Pion-Berlin and Arceneaux 2000, 415–16). Security missions are tasks that involve physically controlling and/or confronting people—who may be insurgents, civilians, or members of another national military—for the purpose of protecting the physical well-being of other people or of property.[1] Security missions thus diverge from political intervention and are different from development work, such as road and bridge construction.

The book further distinguishes between two kinds of security missions: defense of sovereignty and policing. Border defense against the territorial expansion of neighboring countries and counterinsurgency are characterized as *sovereignty missions*, as they are conducted in the name of defending a country from organized, armed actors that seek to challenge the legitimacy of the state.[2] In contrast, other security missions—for example, protest control, crime fighting, and contraband interdiction—are referred to here as *policing*.

Since democratization in Latin America, experts on the region's militaries have concentrated on explaining the varied levels of civilian political control of the armed forces after they left government and returned to the barracks.[3] This research agenda has produced empirical, conceptual, and theoretical insights into how we think about the armed forces and their power vis-à-vis civilians in government. Yet the current literature has produced little analysis of security missions, the central functions that militaries are expected to serve from the barracks. In terms of militaries' mission neglect, analysis of military "shirking" in Latin America has been restricted to research on the refusal of militaries to repress antigovernment protests during the unique situation of a "constitutional crisis" that threatens to remove the sitting president from office (Pion-Berlin and Trinkunas 2010).[4] Other than this specific type of neglect, scholars generally have expected Latin American armed forces to perform their assigned missions.

Scholarship specific to Peruvian and Ecuadorian military security missions exemplifies these shortcomings. Chapter 3 draws on secondary analysis of the Peruvian army's laxity toward armed insurgents during the second half of the 1980s, but no prior in-depth analysis has sought to explain the mission performance of the Peruvian armed forces since the conclusion of the Alberto Fujimori government (1990–2000), which exhibited authoritarian tendencies and politicized the military. Studies of security in Ecuador since 2000 have observed that the army shifted from the south—where it had focused on guarding the border with Peru—to the northern provinces, attributing the move to the intensification of Colombia's internal conflict, just across the border (e.g., P. Andrade 2002, 208–11; Bonilla 2006, 121–22). Yet these studies do not describe or explain the army's actual neglect of the border after having moved north, nor do they analyze the army's balance of sovereignty work and policing in the north or elsewhere in the country. The Ecuadorian army's neglect of the northern border when Colombian insurgents first operated on the border, in the mid-1980s, has not received attention.

In spite of these limitations, from research on post-transition Latin American armed forces we can extract four hypotheses for military mission performance, all of which are grounded in armed forces' institutional interests. First, a military might more or less assertively conduct its assigned missions, depending on how much autonomy it enjoys relative to elected officials. Second, due to officers' desire to maintain professionalism, militaries are expected to focus, as much as possible, more on fighting sovereignty threats—work considered most professional within the armed forces—and less on police work. Third, scholars anticipate that militaries will eagerly take on security missions that are viewed as legitimate within society. Fourth, it is predicted that militaries will perform the missions likely to justify the most defense spending. The four hypotheses, drawn from research on post-transition Latin American militaries, have foundations in classic work on civil-military relations. The following discussion looks to Huntington's analysis of modern, professional military interests in his 1957 *The Soldier and the State: The Theory and Politics of Civil-Military Relations*, a defining work in the field of civil-military relations. The brief review of the literature, supported by evidence presented throughout this book, reveals shortcomings of the hypotheses for explaining mission performance in Peru and Ecuador. It then introduces the argument of this study, which is rooted in theories of organizations.

Autonomy

One factor that could influence whether or not the armed forces perform an assigned mission is their degree of autonomy in relation to civilians in government. From one perspective, a less autonomous military should be more likely to respond to government orders. This approach may not apply in Latin America, where civilian expertise in defense matters and thus government's capacity to monitor military mission performance are low overall (Pion-Berlin 2005; Pion-Berlin and Trinkunas 2007).

A different view on autonomy begins with the military's *preference* for autonomy to do its work without civilian interference. Huntington (1957, 83–85) posits that armed forces tend to demand an arrangement whereby they enjoy professional autonomy. Consistent with this idea, Latin American militaries might resent governments that challenge their autonomy, and in response they might reject their assigned missions. This power play would be a specific instance of two dimensions developed by Alfred Stepan (1988, 68, 93) to measure civilian control under democracy: (1) "military prerogatives," or powers—generally formalized in legal structures—that the military presumes it holds, and (2) "articulated military contestation," or protest against the government—such as lobbying or staging a coup—often in response to civilian challenges to military prerogatives. Stepan does not examine the degree to which the military performs missions, and yet we can extend the model: mission neglect could be a way in which armed forces contest government actions and, more specifically, government challenges to military autonomy.

This autonomy perspective goes far toward explaining the Peruvian army's mission performance. As we will see, reductions in military autonomy relative to the judiciary in human rights matters and, in guerrilla zones, relative to the national police and subnational political officials, led the army to resist counterinsurgency orders. When the government granted the armed forces autonomy once again, the army responded to government demands for counterinsurgency.[5] However, the same does not hold for Ecuador, where the military's autonomy has not been challenged significantly but the military still has underperformed its sovereignty mission. Moreover, across-time changes in the Peruvian army's autonomy do not match up with its steady rejection of police work since the 1990s. Because this study endeavors to develop a single theory to explain mission performance in both countries across time, in the sovereignty and policing arenas, we move on to other frameworks.

Professionalism

A different explanation for why militaries might perform some missions more than others is grounded in the idea that officers are motivated principally by an interest in maintaining their status as professional war fighters. Huntington (1957, 66–67) wrote of modern armed forces oriented toward the professional mission of international warfare: militaries were fixated on national security threats and the need to protect state security against those threats. For Latin American militaries, professional missions include both external defense and counterinsurgency. The professionalism hypothesis thus leads us to expect that, where possible, Latin American militaries will be more oriented toward these sovereignty missions than toward police work.

Although Latin America has seen little interstate violence,[6] the region's armed forces have a long history of prioritizing external defense. As discussed in this volume, in response to military defeat by Peru in 1981, the Ecuadorian military dedicated itself to revamping its educational curricula and training to improve its international war-fighting capacity. In the next armed conflict between the two countries, fourteen years later, Ecuador's armed forces won, prompting Peru's military to direct more resources toward external defense.

In addition to prioritizing external defense, when salient, Latin American militaries have also taken seriously counterinsurgency throughout the twentieth century, a period of intense internal violence. Leftist insurgencies arose throughout the region following the 1959 Cuban Revolution. From the military perspective, those guerrilla movements were a threat to the sovereignty of the nation and to the very existence of the armed forces.[7] In this period of widespread military concern about internal security threats—and little in the way of immediate international threats—armed forces shifted from an external-defense orientation ("old professionalism") to a focus on counterinsurgency and economic development ("new professionalism"), adding combat against guerrillas to the military's repertoire of professional missions (Stepan 1973). In most countries in the region, the armed forces responded to the insurgent threat, as well as to general economic and political turmoil, by staging coups and running government directly.[8]

Considering this historical orientation toward external defense and counterinsurgency, it should be no surprise that contemporary analyses of Latin American armed forces emphasize militaries' preference for sovereignty missions. For example, Brian Loveman (1999, 270; see also 271–74) writes that "maintaining national sovereignty" through external defense was still the "most traditional and legitimate role" of Latin American militaries. With regard to counterinsurgency, Perelli and Rial emphasize the great importance that Latin American militaries place on counterinsurgency, even after most of Latin America's guerrilla threats have faded.

> For the U.S. military, fighting insurgency means facing low-intensity disturbances; for the Latin American military, on the other hand, it is a question of

> high-intensity conflicts, inasmuch as these consume practically all available resources and jeopardize the stability and continued existence of affected countries' economic, social, and political systems. Insurgency, for the Latin American military, is not a peripheral conflict; it is often *the* conflict. (Perelli and Rial 1996, 72, emphasis in original)

If sovereignty missions are the most professional missions for militaries, then, logically, policing missions are less so. Indeed, Linz and Stepan (1996, 219–20) find that democratic consolidation in Brazil and the Southern Cone was limited by the lack of an attractive security mission for the armed forces, which disliked the available antinarcotics work for being unprofessional.

Some argue that if the armed forces have maintained a positive relationship with the civilian population, they will be more prone to reject police work, as it involves repressing their own countrymen. Illustrative of this dynamic is the Venezuelan army's response to being ordered to repress the famous 1989 "Caracazo" protests that led to hundreds and maybe thousands of deaths (Trinkunas 2005, 174); consequently, antigovernment sentiment expanded within segments of the army, which had operated economic development programs in impoverished Venezuelan communities (Norden 1996c).[9]

In the Peruvian and Ecuadorian cases, we will see that the professionalism hypothesis fails to explain military behavior. Both armies have neglected their most professional, salient missions: counterinsurgency in Peru and northern border defense in Ecuador. Insofar as the professionalism hypothesis predicts the degree to which a military unoccupied by sovereignty work will take on policing, the framework also falls short. The Ecuadorian army, which historically has enjoyed a relatively positive relationship with civilians, has conducted policing, whereas Peru's army, which in its recent past committed massive human rights abuses against the civilian population during a major counterinsurgency effort, has refused police work.

Public Legitimacy

Whereas the professionalism hypothesis is grounded in the premise that militaries themselves prefer certain missions, a different hypothesis calls attention to what *society* values. For Huntington, the modern professional officer corps seeks to employ force in a manner deemed legitimate within society. Specifically, the officer identifies legitimate behavior by looking to government officials for direction: "His behavior in relation to society is guided by an awareness that his skill can only be utilized for purposes approved by society through its political agent, the state" (Huntington 1957, 15). Consistent with Huntington, in post-transition Latin America we expect the armed forces to prioritize the missions that society supports. However, because Latin American militaries have been known to align with powerful social actors and remove elected governments from power, public legitimacy is not related solely to what the government, as the "political agent" of society, orders the military to do; it also rests on interests in society separate from government policy.

The military in Latin America has been pressured to seek out or accept new missions from the government so as to remain legitimate. With the military no longer running government or operating according to the logic of the Cold War, and now under democracy—which places exceptional demands on state institutions in terms of their social responsibility and accountability—pressures to redefine military roles have been considerable (Goodman 1996; Hunter 1996; Millett and Gold-Biss 1996; Norden 1996b; Rial 1996; Loveman 1999). In this context, militaries have performed different policing missions in the interest of being legitimate. For example, Hunter (1996, 25–26) examines cases in the mid-1990s in which the Brazilian army agreed to fight gang and drug-trafficking activities in Rio de Janeiro's slums (*favelas*), so as to prove relevant in a setting in which citizens and government were more concerned about these internal security challenges than they were about sovereignty threats.

Nonetheless, the public legitimacy hypothesis has limited power for predicting military mission performance in Latin America, including in Peru and Ecuador. First, work on post–Cold War military missions assumes that if a traditional mission—that is, border defense or counterinsurgency—were salient in a given country, then the national military would actively perform that most legitimate mission. The Peruvian and Ecuadorian armies' neglect of their sovereignty work obviously belies this assumption. Second, the public legitimacy argument does not explain why an army unoccupied by sovereignty work might choose to remain on base rather than tackle visible, legitimate policing assignments ordered by the executive, which has been the case in Peru during much of its democracy.

Third and finally, the public legitimacy perspective can lead us to muddied and even conflicting predictions. Although society- and government-backed military missions have been legitimate, because of the abuses that can come with those missions, security work has also reduced the armed forces' legitimacy.[10] For instance, armed forces worry that by bringing them into conflict with farmers, coca eradication may erode the military's reputation in society (Rial 1996, 55). The question of military conflict with civilians is crucial in this region haunted by appalling episodes of military abuses against civilian populations. In some cases, the past was so bloody that to maintain public legitimacy—or to achieve it in the first place—the military has had to pull out of police work altogether, most notably in Argentina in the aftermath of the "Dirty War" (1976–83), when a new national defense law narrowly defined the Argentine armed forces' role as external defense (Fitch 1998, 118–19).

In other countries, avoiding police work is not the clear choice of militaries that seek public legitimacy. In spite of significant military repression of protesters in Venezuela's Caracazo, still the armed forces enjoyed substantial popular support (see chapter 7). In the case of the Brazilian army's work in the *favelas*, society and the government continued supporting the mission, and the army's reputation remained positive despite its human rights violations during a major operation (Hunter 1996, 26). In Peru, though the government, courts, and many segments of society, including the country's main human rights organization, have demanded that the military respect human rights, those same actors have also called for more army efforts to eliminate the remnants of the country's armed insurgency.

Resource Maximization

Closely tied to the military's desire for public legitimacy are its budget interests: armed forces seeking state resources should perform missions deemed legitimate by the government, which doles out those resources. In Huntington's (1957, 67) analysis, professional officers seek to obtain as much as they can from the state to support their security missions: "Since the state normally is incapable of maintaining forces to meet all or most possible threats, the military man is usually required to establish a ladder of military priorities . . . His military instincts lead him to urge the state to go as far down the ladder as possible."

This resource maximization perspective would seem highly applicable in Latin America. Research on civil-military relations in Latin America has asserted that, with their missions in flux following democratization and the Cold War, the region's armed forces have seen cuts to their budgets—reductions that also have been part of the trend toward shrinking the size of the state through economic liberalization (e.g., Marcella 1994, 14–15; Hunter 1996; Norden 1996b; Rial 1996; Cruz and Diamint 1998; Loveman 1999, 258–60). We would thus expect militaries to perform government-assigned missions not only for the sake of legitimacy but also to attract funding, given that they must compete intensively with other state sectors for resources: "Latin American militaries are asked to justify their demands (a roundabout way of asking them to justify their very existence) in the face of more pressing needs in the health, education, housing, and social security sectors" (Perelli and Rial 1996, 77; similarly, Hunter 1996, 1997; Rial 1996). Hunter (1997) finds the military budget to be a topic so sensitive in Argentina, Brazil, Chile, and Peru that she uses defense budget cuts as an indicator of civilian control of the armed forces. Latin American officers are predicted to seek funds from sources other than the state, as well: experts on the U.S. drug war have argued that U.S. security support has brought Andean militaries into the specific mission of antinarcotics (e.g., Youngers and Rosin 2005). In short, the resource maximization perspective predicts that Latin American militaries would forcefully perform those missions likely to attract the most funds.

As I will show in this book, neither the Peruvian nor the Ecuadorian army has behaved so as to maximize its resource base, even amid cuts in national defense spending. Each army has neglected its most lucrative mission, taking into account both national state and U.S. resources: counterinsurgency in Peru, northern border defense in Ecuador. In place of counterinsurgency, for the most part the Peruvian army has withdrawn to train on its bases rather than perform assigned police work that would raise funds (though less than counterinsurgency work would generate) for the institution.

COMBINING THE PROFESSIONALISM, legitimacy, and resource maximization hypotheses, we arrive at the following prediction: militaries prefer sovereignty work when it is available, but in its absence, starved for resources and needing to seem valuable to society, these militaries may accept policing missions as a last resort. Hunter's (1996) comparative study of post-transition Argentina, Brazil, and Chile illustrates this dynamic nicely. Hunter argues that a military's political reputation and access to state resources explain military policing, external defense, and international peacekeeping efforts. She finds that with a strong reputation and secure resource base, the military has freedom to select its missions and will enthusiastically embrace external defense as the mission most tightly linked to national sovereignty. Only when undergoing budget reductions did militaries in her study reach out to policing, to demonstrate their importance.

The combination of the three hypotheses can also lead us to expect a different outcome. Like a "living organism subjected to hypothermia," a military with scarce resources might abandon "peripheral functions" and concentrate on sovereignty missions (Perelli and Rial 1996, 77–78, crediting Richard L. Millett). This dynamic is perhaps consistent with what Hunter (1996, 16–17) observes for Argentina: under President Menem (1989–99), the armed forces were "relatively quiescent" when their budget was cut, because the government "offered them at least the minimal amount of resources to satisfy their core institutional and professional interests."

Therefore, scholars disagree somewhat about whether resource-hungry militaries will limit their work to sovereignty defense or reach out to police work that, while less desirable, may be more visible and therefore more likely to secure public legitimacy and defense spending. However, both perspectives consistently put forth the idea that militaries will focus on those sovereignty missions that are salient.

The above hypotheses, then, cannot explain army neglect of sovereignty missions in Peru and Ecuador. In each country, the army has been assigned to a salient sovereignty mission that is supported politically and financially by the popularly elected government—and that attracts external funding—but the army has not always energetically performed this mission. In place of sovereignty defense, the Ecuadorian army has carried out extensive policing, whereas Peru's army has rejected policing missions and instead occupied itself mainly with on-base training.

The Importance of Predictability for Patrols

What most directly explains the mission performance of the Peruvian and Ecuadorian armies is their tendency to maintain predictability for officers and soldiers who conduct patrols. The armies have resisted work that challenges predictability, even when it means underperforming professional, legitimate, lucrative missions.

Mission Beliefs

A first step toward explaining mission performance is to analyze officers' "mission beliefs," conceived of here as rules for what missions the army should perform. Mission beliefs are thus a subset of "role beliefs," a well-established concept in studies of Latin American civil-military relations that captures officers' beliefs about appropriate military participation in security, economic development, and politics (e.g., Stepan 1971, 172–87; Fitch 1977, 129–33; 1998, 65–72;

2001, 67–78). More generally, research on Latin American politics has a long history of taking seriously actors' beliefs about their appropriate roles, as exemplified by Guillermo O'Donnell's work on "bureaucratic authoritarianism."[11]

Consistent with Stepan's (1971) research on military role beliefs, an army's mission beliefs are shaped by past experiences. It is here, in considering the formation of mission beliefs, that we gain insight from frameworks based on military interests in resources, legitimacy, and professionalism. As predicted by those hypotheses, in the democratic period, both armies initially put their sovereignty responsibilities ahead of their policing assignments. Also as expected, when in the 1990s the Ecuadorian army's main sovereignty mission—southern border defense against Peru—concluded, the army turned to policing and economic development work to prove its indispensability and to justify its budget. In contrast, in Peru, where the army's sovereignty mission of counterinsurgency has remained salient, the army has not developed a commitment to police work.

Yet the two cases teach us a lesson about mission beliefs that the resource maximization, legitimacy, and professionalism hypotheses do not predict: once formed, mission beliefs have a lasting influence on an army's behavior, a finding consistent with Stepan's (1971) research, which attributes causal weight to military role beliefs.[12] The Ecuadorian army has remained committed to balancing its policing and sovereignty work, even after it was again handed a salient sovereignty mission—northern border defense—that officers still deemed more professional than policing. In Peru, negative attitudes toward police work that developed in the 1990s have continued. Finally, the armies' behavior also demonstrates how, whereas the professionalism hypothesis emphasizes only militaries' preferences for their most professional, sovereignty missions, the mission beliefs framework allows for a continuum along which sovereignty work may be very professional and policing, less professional (as in Ecuador) or altogether unprofessional and inappropriate (as in Peru).

Predictability in an Uncertain Environment

Mission beliefs establish armies' preferences for different missions. However, contradictory orders can prevent an army from performing missions that its beliefs support. This next stage in the analysis explores how contradictions—real or perceived—in the armies' sovereignty missions have arisen and have kept the armies from vigorously performing those assignments. Drawing on theories of organizations, we can think of the contradictions as challenges to predictability for army patrols, the part of each army that performs its central function of security. In both countries, the army's response to this uncertainty has been to underperform sovereignty work as a way to maintain predictability for the patrols.

The contradictions and resulting mission neglect illustrate the more general proclivity of organizations to shield their key functions from uncertainty. Contingency theory tells us that the structure of an organization can be understood as responses and adaptations to the organization's environment (Scott 2003, 96–97).[13] Building on that insight, James D. Thompson's (1967) foundational *Organizations in Action* theorizes that an organization will protect its "technical core" from uncertainty in the environment in which the organization works, or in Thompson's study, the "task environment."[14] One archetypical example of this concept is the classroom, the technical core of a school where the core function of educating students takes place.[15]

The technical core in the present analysis consists of armed officers and soldiers assigned to security work, given that the Peruvian and Ecuadorian armies' missions have been mainly patrol-based, such as border defense operations, counterinsurgency, and urban anticrime work. In northern Ecuador and in Peru's guerrilla zones, patrols move on foot through dense jungle, and the young lieutenant or second lieutenant in charge is responsible for keeping the soldiers safe while leading operations against skilled, heavily armed insurgents. The work is inherently riddled with uncertainty for the officer and troops, who do not know whether they will come across armed insurgents or civilians, whether they will be able to distinguish between the two, or whether they will respond quickly enough to "successfully" execute their mission—that is, capture or kill the insurgents while protecting their men and, hopefully, not harming civilians. However, this challenging work is predictable insofar as army personnel can apply training protocols unambiguously in specific situations. Predictability is reduced when the patrol's orders contain contradictions. For instance, an army patrol will confront unpredictability if the patrol is both (1) sent into the jungle to eliminate insurgents and (2) discouraged from engaging in combat; it is ambiguous how the patrol should treat guerrillas that it encounters.

At different times in both Peru and Ecuador, a contradiction has arisen in the army's salient sovereignty mission. The contradiction has reduced predictability for patrols, thereby interfering with their work. In each country the contradiction developed by a distinct path. In Peru, it was caused by *mission constraint*: the government assigned the army to counterinsurgency while also reducing the army's autonomy in relation to the justice system, national police, and subnational political officials. For more senior officers, these reductions in autonomy introduced a contradiction into the counterinsurgency mission, because the army was supposed to fight insurgents but was denied the autonomy that those officers deemed necessary to do the work successfully. In Ecuador, by contrast, the contradiction emerged from *mission overload*. The army was overloaded with multiple missions, and officers thought that defending the northern border could spark a long-term counterinsurgency war that would drain army resources and prevent the army from carrying out its other missions. Committed to both sovereignty and policing, army leaders told commanders in the north not to fight the insurgents. Therefore, at the same time that the army was assigned to defend the border, it was not to confront the armed actors threatening that border.

In each country, army commanders have sought to protect patrols from the contradiction and thus unpredictable work, which has meant sending out fewer patrols and working in locations where patrols are less likely to find armed insurgents. In sum, a push to maintain immediate predictability for patrols more directly explains armies' mission performance in Peru and Ecuador than do officers' interests in resources, legitimacy, or professionalism.

When organizations face uncertainty, they can act to maintain predictability within the technical core through different structures and processes, depending on the range of possible changes in their environment. Contingency theorists Lawrence and Lorsch (1967) are credited with observing that organizations and organizational subunits that have more stable, more certain, and less complex environments tend to exhibit formal, hierarchical structures. In contrast, environmental instability, uncertainty, and complexity spawn more organic organizational forms (Scott 2003, 96–97). Similarly, in Thompson's (1967, 72) words, "When the range of task-environment variations is large or unpredictable, the responsible organization component must achieve the necessary adaptation by monitoring that environment and planning responses, and this calls for localized units."

In this study, army structure differs dramatically across the two cases, in accordance with the amount of multitasking required of army field units. Peruvian army units have been responsible for few routine missions—generally speaking, counterinsurgency in guerrilla zones and external defense training or border patrols elsewhere—and correspondingly, the army has been highly centralized. Therefore, in response to the contradiction in the army's counterinsurgency mission, officers at the uppermost echelons proved important in reducing the army's counterinsurgency work: army leaders decreased the overall army presence in guerrilla zones and halted major operations. At the lowest levels, officers in guerrilla zones refused to initiate counterinsurgency operations by insisting that they first receive specific orders from their superiors, thereby reinforcing the army's centralized structure.

Relative to the case of Peru, the Ecuadorian army has been decentralized. Battalion commanders have had significant discretion, enabling them to balance their units' many security responsibilities and respond to the ebb and flow of varying security challenges in their assigned zones. The army's structure also means that it has fallen primarily on northern battalion commanders to prevent patrol leaders from having to negotiate between the two contradictory goals in the north.

My application of Thompson's framework can be situated in relation to a rich literature that explores the extent to which organizational forces—generally construed as bureaucratic inertia resistant to change—shape the behavior of armed forces in the United States and Europe,[16] and more specifically to other treatments of Thompson's approach that have analyzed European military doctrine during the interwar period (Posen 1984, 2004) and growing organizational complexity in the U.S. military caused by adopting new equipment (Demchak 1991). The present study permits a hard test of Thompson's framework compared with the scholarship on the U.S. and European armed forces. Perhaps due in part to the low level of civilian control in Peru and Ecuador in security matters, my analysis shows how uncertainty can explain armies' mission performance[17]—an outcome more fundamental than doctrine or adaptation to new technology, which merely support missions that are taken as given. Most striking, the Peruvian and Ecuadorian cases reveal that the drive to maintain predictability within the technical core was sufficiently powerful that it took precedence over maximizing organizational resources and performing the armies' most legitimate, professional missions.

Resources and Beneficiaries

While neither army's behavior can be explained wholly by the resource maximization hypothesis, resources still have affected the armies' security work. As mentioned above, the Ecuadorian army's sudden loss of its southern border defense mission in the late 1990s caused it to take on police work, partly to justify defense spending. In addition, there is a second way in which resources have affected the army's behavior, in both countries. Even when resource interests have not influenced the amount of sovereignty work and/or policing that the armies have undertaken, paying third parties—that is, actors outside the central government—have nevertheless procured a significant amount of services that the armies are willing to offer. These clients, especially private companies in the extractive industries, have purchased the Peruvian army's limited counterinsurgency services and the Ecuadorian army's policing services through local deals with army unit commanders, ensuring that the army does more client-preferred activities than work for the public.

The analysis contributes to a small body of research on third-party influence on Latin American militaries and its alarming implications for civilian control of the armed forces and, more broadly, state accountability in Latin America (Cruz and Diamint 1998, 118–19; Ferreyra and Segura 2000, esp. 29–30). The analysis of client influence on the Peruvian and Ecuadorian armies also brings to the fore the overlooked question of *who benefits* from military missions.

CASE SELECTION: A FOCUS ON THE ARMY IN PERU AND ECUADOR

This book focuses on a single branch of the armed forces, the army, to facilitate an in-depth analysis of military organizational dynamics. In Latin America, and certainly in Peru and Ecuador, the army is the most influential branch in the military and in society. For instance, the army generally has led the government during episodes of military rule (Lowenthal 1976, 5). Under the current democracies, armies remain dominant relative to the air force and navy, based on budget and manpower. In 2007, between 54 and 85 percent of all military personnel in South American countries served in the army, and the army's budget made up between 44 and 72 percent of the total budget devoted to the three branches (Red de Seguridad y Defensa de América Latina 2007).[18] Given that many of the region's security threats have been primarily land-based—including, for example, insurgencies, protests, border conflict, and crime in cities and remote regions—the army, as the military's major ground force, is more likely than the air force or the navy to be challenged to balance or choose among multiple security responsibilities, and it therefore proves ideal for this study.

Peru and Ecuador serve as an exceptional pair of countries for analyzing army missions, for several reasons. To begin, the comparison allows us to hold constant ideological tradition. In a time when military governments throughout Latin America sought to eradicate insurgency in line with their respective versions of the National Security Doctrine,[19] the Peruvian and Ecuadorian military regimes, led by the army, exercised low levels of repression relative to their

Southern Cone counterparts and were the most progressive military regimes of South America. These nationalist regimes—as evinced by their policies in the critical hydrocarbon and, in Peru, mining sectors[20]—protected freedoms of the political left, articulated critiques of dominant rural oligarchies, and even redistributed land through agrarian reform (Stepan 1978, 119; Conaghan 1988, 81–87, 94–97; Isaacs 1993, 35–65, 84–92; Conaghan and Malloy 1994, 47–69; Yashar 2005, 91–98, 114, 229–35, 241–44).[21]

In addition to this unique ideological history, another benefit of the Peru-Ecuador comparison is that, under democracy, the armies have been given multiple policing assignments, and the cases allow us to analyze both types of sovereignty missions: border defense and counterinsurgency. The two armies engaged in international combat (against each other) in 1981 and 1995. Increasingly since the 1980s, Colombian insurgents have threatened the integrity of Ecuador's international border, and in the current period of relative international peace in Latin America, the challenge posed by the cross-border spillover of insurgents from Colombia into neighboring countries is the only type of external armed threat in the region. Throughout its democratic period, Peru has experienced the region's second kind of sovereignty threat: internal insurgency.

That each army has underperformed its sovereignty assignment facilitates a close-up analysis of an understudied phenomenon (Collier and Mahoney 1996, 72–74)—military mission neglect in Latin America—and presents a strong test of the professionalism, legitimacy, and resource maximization hypotheses, because if Peruvian and Ecuadorian army leaders were the budget-maximizing, legitimacy-hungry professionals depicted in the literature, the armies would seem "most likely" (Eckstein 1975) to perform their sovereignty missions.

Peru and Ecuador also vary in ways helpful for the analysis. The marked differences in civilian control of the armed forces, explored in detail in the coming chapters, push us beyond the idea that some armed forces neglect their missions as a reaction to government attacks on their autonomy. From the vantage point of the legitimacy, professionalism, and resource maximization hypotheses, it is curious that the Peruvian army has not conducted more policing and that the Ecuadorian army has welcomed it—considering that police work would potentially bring resources and legitimacy to both armies and that the Peruvian army's recent experience in internal security, in the form of a major counterinsurgency effort, would make it seem more likely to accept policing assignments than its Ecuadorian counterpart.

THE DATA

In contrast to work on civil-military relations that approaches militaries as unitary actors, this book underscores how armed forces—and branches thereof—must be treated as complex organizations. Only by looking at the behavior of army officers of different ranks working in different capacities does the study identify the organizational dynamics surrounding the "technical core" (i.e., the patrols). Furthermore, the study identifies private companies' influence on who benefits from army services, by scrutinizing local resource transfers and their effects on army base commanders' decisions about operations within their zones of responsibility.

A close-up view of army behavior was made possible by my unique access to these two armies. I carried out the majority of research over the course of thirteen months during 2005 and 2006, supplemented by follow-up research in 2009. I conducted candid, semi-structured interviews with more than 150 army officers on several battalion and brigade bases and in the capital cities of Lima, Peru, and Quito, Ecuador. The resulting samples exhibit variation in specialty, rank, and most recent geographic and mission assignment. Outside the two armies, I interviewed more than 170 other subjects: journalists; academics; representatives of nongovernmental organizations; private-sector actors; navy, air force, and police officers; elected and appointed local, regional, and national political officials; and officials from the U.S. defense and state departments. In the interest of respecting the comfort and privacy of subjects and protecting the validity of my data, most interviews were not audio-recorded. The majority of the interview excerpts included in this book are therefore rough quotations based on handwritten notes taken during and immediately following interviews. Also in the interest of protecting subjects' privacy, I have chosen not to identify the base locations that I visited.[22] All quantitative presentations of interview data are based on data collected during 2005 and 2006.

My review of newspaper and government archives, army doctrinal materials, and secondary sources allowed me to triangulate and supplement data from interview responses. Analysis of the 1980s and 1990s is based primarily on these additional data sources.[23]

OVERVIEW OF THE ANALYSIS

To provide a foundation for the analysis of mission performance in this book, I first review, in chapter 2, civil-military relations in Peru and Ecuador since democratization. Chapter 3 then applies the study's predictability framework to army security work during the 1980s and 1990s in the two countries. It explains mission neglect in the second half of the 1980s, when the Peruvian army halted its counterinsurgency efforts, and the Ecuadorian army, which consistently put first its mission of defending the southern border against Peru, proved inattentive to the *northern* border, which became vulnerable to incursions by armed Colombian insurgents. I argue that each army underperformed its sovereignty mission so as to maintain predictability for the work of patrols on the ground, when a contradiction in the sovereignty mission challenged that predictability. In Peru, the contradiction arose through mission constraint, when the government ordered the army to conduct counterinsurgency while withholding autonomy, which senior officers believed the army needed to do the work. In Ecuador, the contradiction is traced to mission overload. To avoid becoming heavily entrenched in a war against Colombian insurgents, Ecuador's army sought not to fight the guerrillas. This decision introduced a contradiction in the border mission for patrols, which were to defend the border from external, armed actors but not clash with those same actors.

In chapters 4 and 5, I analyze army mission performance since 2000 in Peru and Ecuador, respectively, explaining why the armies have neglected sovereignty missions and why they differ in the extent to which they have engaged in policing. Echoing the discussion in chapter 3 of the Peruvian army's behavior in the late 1980s, chapter 4 shows that the human rights policy of Peru's government after 2000 limited the army's autonomy relative to the justice system and, in guerrilla zones, relative to the national police and political officials. Those restrictions created a contradiction in the counterinsurgency mission from the perspective of senior officers, who maintained that at the same time the army was given the counterinsurgency mission, it was denied the autonomy necessary to do the work effectively. Burdened with that contradiction, senior officers refused to abide by executive orders to pursue the insurgents, steering the army as a whole away from the mission. From the perspective of army leadership, in 2008 there was a return to predictability for troops in the counterinsurgency zone when the national congress approved rules of engagement that gave the army more autonomy in relation to the civilian judicial system. The army has responded by returning to more aggressive counterinsurgency. In terms of policing, I argue that the army has refused to take on that work—even under the new rules of engagement—principally because it has operated according to narrow mission beliefs that define policing as inappropriate.

Chapter 5 turns to the Ecuadorian case. It shows how, with the 2000 implementation of Plan Colombia, which targeted insurgents and pushed them south into Ecuador in mounting numbers, the army has been overloaded with security responsibilities. This overload has emerged even though its southern border responsibilities concluded with a 1998 Ecuador-Peru peace agreement, due to the army's broad mission beliefs—that is, its deep commitment to remaining active in the policing arena. The overload has introduced a contradiction into the Ecuadorian army's northern border mission. Its main mission has been to defend the northern border from incursions by Colombian guerrillas, but it has tried not to fight those same insurgents when they cross into Ecuador, lest skirmishes lead to a war that could absorb the army's resources indefinitely. Northern field commanders have contended with the two conflicting border assignments by limiting army patrols' exposure to the contradiction—that is, by ordering few, tentative border patrols. Because the army has done so little to defend the border, it has been available to police throughout the country, which it has done.

Chapter 6 moves on to the question of who has benefited from the armies' missions. Whereas mission beliefs and the predisposition to secure predictability for the troops have affected the amount of policing and sovereignty work that the two armies perform, clients have hired army units for that security work, with resources outside the national defense budget.

A concluding chapter places the Peruvian and Ecuadorian cases in comparative perspective. Chapter 7 draws on secondary sources on the armed forces in Bolivia, Colombia, and Venezuela to analyze how militaries' experiences under democracy have affected their mission performance, with an emphasis on military policing. I conclude the study by reflecting on challenges encountered by governments in the Andean region when they assign their armed forces to police work.

CHAPTER 2

Civil-Military Relations in Democratic Peru and Ecuador

An examination of civil-military relations in Peru and Ecuador since the transition to democracy is a crucial starting point for this analysis of the armies' mission performance. In this chapter, I show how civil-military dynamics have fostered the emergence of a contradiction in each army's sovereignty mission. For Peru, the chapter highlights significant structural and political constraints confronting the armed forces in the 1980s and then again in the post-2000 period, laying the groundwork for the finding that when the government has restricted the army's autonomy—especially in relation to the justice system—it has, in the view of army officers, generated a contradiction in the army's counterinsurgency mission.

In Ecuador, in contrast, the armed forces have encountered very few constraints. Instead, since democratization, Ecuador's government and societal actors have permitted—and even invited—the armed forces to perform a wide range of state, economic, and more broadly political functions. Subsequent chapters will show that the army's overload in security missions, in particular, has led to a contradiction in its mission to defend the northern border.

Beyond providing background for the contradictions in the armies' sovereignty missions, this chapter also helps to rule out one explanation for military mission neglect in Peru and Ecuador: the idea that armed forces refuse to perform their assigned missions in response to government efforts to subordinate the military. The comparison illuminates the Ecuadorian military's sweeping autonomy. That Ecuador's army nonetheless has neglected northern border defense motivates us to look beyond an autonomy-focused approach to explain the Peruvian and Ecuadorian cases within a single framework.

HIGH CONSTRAINTS ON PERU'S MILITARY

Civil-military relations in Peru since the country's transition to democracy can be organized into three time periods. First, in the 1980s, economic crisis and internal conflict reached high levels, and the government sought to hold the military accountable for human rights abuses. During that decade, and in response to those constraints, military political involvement took the form of opposition to government policies—especially with regard to internal security and the economy—culminating in the formation of a coup coalition within the armed forces. Second, the Alberto Fujimori government (1990–2000) granted the military autonomy to carry out security work while manipulating the armed forces, placing on them direct, personal controls. Third, the years following Fujimori's departure from office have been characterized as a period of democratization, partly due to government efforts to rein in the armed forces. Perhaps because their professionalism had suffered during the prior decade, the armed forces now seemed willing to step out of politics and did not actively contest the new constraints placed on them by the government. Rather, as we will see in later chapters, the Peruvian military has reacted to new reductions to its autonomy by withdrawing from the counterinsurgency effort.

The 1980s: Civil-Military Tensions amid Escalating Crises

In the 1980s, the Peruvian armed forces had declining resources to fight an overwhelming insurgent threat and were highly critical of the Fernando Belaúnde Terry (1980–85) and Alan García (1985–90) administrations for their failed efforts to defeat the Sendero Luminoso (Sendero) insurgency (McClintock 1989, 136). Overall poor communication between civilians in government and the armed forces exacerbated misunderstandings and civil-military conflict (Obando 1994; Rospigliosi 2000, 55, 59). Under García, constraints, including the government's measures to hold the armed forces accountable for human rights abuses, intensified to the point that they triggered a major military conspiracy against the government.

Belaúnde inherited armed forces that had a positive reputation in society. The military had exercised limited repression during military rule (1968–80) and looked professional relative to the police force, which had been brutal in its counterinsurgency efforts against Sendero in the first years of democracy. The armed forces' image was enhanced further when they defeated the Ecuadorian military in the brief 1981 conflict in the Condor mountain range (Gorriti 1999, 115–17). In the delicate post-transition years, the Belaúnde administration refrained from seriously challenging the institutional autonomy of the military, which was highly respected and thus had the potential for destabilizing the new regime. For example, the defense budget was "as large [as] or larger" than it had been under military rule, in spite of the economy's negative growth rates,[1] and "the acquisition program designed during the military regime was accepted in its entirety" by the government (Obando 1994, 108; see also McClintock 1998, 132–33). Furthermore, the government did not press the armed forces to share intelligence files from the outgoing military regime.[2] Belaúnde did, however, strive to contain the military's power by delaying the militarization of the state's counterinsurgency effort (see chapter 3).

The relatively tranquil civil-military relations under Belaúnde did not last. During García's first administration (1985–90), the insurgent threat expanded, and a deepening economic crisis resulted in reduced defense spending (Obando 1994, 111–13). The armed forces' resentment of the government grew when, after the most intense years of indiscriminate military violence against civilian populations, García sought to improve state security forces' respect for human rights (see chapter 3). In opposition to García's failed state-led economic policies, ineffectiveness in counterinsurgency, and human rights policies, and the military's dismal resource base, a coup coalition formed within the armed forces, starting in 1988 (Obando 1994, 111–13; Rospigliosi 2000, 53, 73–77, 81).[3]

The 1990s: Professional Autonomy and Politicization

President Alberto Fujimori (1990–2000) dissolved the coup impetus within the armed forces through neoliberal economic policies that stabilized the economy, and with hard-line policies against insurgents that included granting the military autonomy to conduct security operations.[4] Yet the government did constrain the military by manipulating and politicizing it.

These developments are best understood amid the larger political reality of the 1990s. Although Fujimori came to power in 1990 through free and fair elections, with military backing he staged a self-coup, or *autogolpe*, on April 5, 1992, when he dissolved the congress and closed the courts, marking the beginning of his "National Emergency and Reconstruction Government." Fujimori governed by decree for the next year. Confronted with international pressures to return democracy to Peru, in 1993 he held elections for a constituent assembly that produced a constitution that was approved by popular referendum (Levitsky 1999, 78; McClintock 2006a, 245–48). Yet there is consensus among experts on Peruvian politics that the Fujimori government's authoritarian tendencies did not end with installment of the new constitution. For instance, McClintock characterizes Peru under Fujimori after the 1992 *autogolpe* as "electoral authoritarianism," based on the following criteria: "(1) a record of assault against the constitutional order (such as a coup or coup attempt); (2) a record of constitutionally dubious attempts to extend presidential term limits; (3) a record of credible charges of manipulation of the playing field, of the vote count in previous elections, or both . . . (4) a substantial majority of citizens (and a larger percentage than during previous democratic eras) judging the regime authoritarian in opinion polls," and (5) "a state's or ruling party's use of political violence to punish, terrorize, or demoralize the opposition" (2006a, 243–44).[5]

In this regime setting, Fujimori's government granted the armed forces increased authority over counterinsurgency operations. The *autogolpe* enabled him to push through decrees that empowered the military, facilitating its aggressive fight against the guerrillas (see chapter 3). Yet politically, the military was controlled: Vladimiro Montesinos, Fujimori's intelligence advisor, used Peru's intelligence agency (Servicio de Inteligencia Nacional, SIN) to spy on military personnel to ensure their loyalty to Fujimori.[6] Furthermore, the military was used to promote the government. Army engineering units and "civic action battalions" performed politically targeted civic action work that included road-building projects.[7] Army personnel even disseminated pro-government propaganda, delivered political speeches, and contributed to campaign strategies during presidential campaigns (Conaghan 2005, 82, 164–65).

Under Fujimori, the military's professionalism was hurt both through such politicization and by the illegal cocaine trade. Corruption in the armed forces began in the 1980s but consolidated at all levels of the hierarchy only after the military began drug interdiction in the 1990s (Dreyfus 1999, 388–89; Rospigliosi 2000, 219), a mission analyzed in chapter 3. Corruption was "total" in the military high command and among personnel assigned to Peru's coca center, the Upper Huallaga Valley (Valle del Alto Huallaga, VAH) in the central highlands (Comisión de la Verdad y Reconciliación [CVR] 2003, 2:242).[8] At the regional and local levels, the military was so involved in the cocaine business that officers competed to be assigned to the VAH specifically to receive bribes (Dreyfus 1999, 389). Planes with drug cargos were permitted to depart from army counterinsurgency bases in exchange for drug monies.[9]

By November 2000, when the national congress formally removed Fujimori from office—while he was in exile in Japan[10]—Peru's armed forces had been thoroughly corrupted through their antinarcotics role and were top-heavy due to excessive promotions granted in exchange for loyalty to Fujimori and Montesinos, as explained by officers during my interviews. In addition, the armed forces had a stockpile of deficient war materials, obtained through shady arms deals that bought poor equipment for the military while lining the pockets of Montesinos (Páez 3/27/05, 11/14/05).[11]

Left alone to do its work, and yet with its loyalty to the government closely scrutinized, the military did little to oppose the Fujimori government or its policies. In particular, some public military opposition showed itself on two occasions. First, there was what Peruvian security experts refer to as the "November 13 Movement" that arose in response to (1) the April 1992 *autogolpe*; (2) a November 11, 1992, decree through which Fujimori gave himself the power to dismiss any military officer; and (3) the belief that Fujimori's government was planning to commit fraud in the upcoming November 22, 1992, constituent assembly elections. On the evening of November 12, 1992, approximately 250 soldiers, led by a small group of officers, gathered in front of the government palace. The leader (retired general Salinas Sedó) claimed that the group intended to capture Fujimori and immediately pass power to Máximo San Román—Peru's vice president and an opponent of the April coup—who planned to hold general elections within one year (*Latin America Weekly Report* 11/26/92). Fujimori learned of the coup plans, and the rebellion was called off with no armed confrontations. Approximately twenty-five officers were arrested for their involvement in the revolt (*New York Times* 11/14/92).

A second incident of military opposition to Fujimori was the October–November 2000 rebellion in southern Peru by a group of approximately four hundred army personnel headed by Lieutenant Colonel Ollanta Humala (president, 2011–present) and his younger brother, Antauro Humala, a retired army major (*La República* 11/6/00).[12] The military revolt succeeded an alarming sequence of events involving Montesinos that had begun when the press aired a now famous videotape (known in Peru as the "Vladivideo") of Montesinos offering an opposition congressperson $15,000 to join Fujimori's majority in the congress. After the airing, Fujimori fired Montesinos, who then fled to Panama for asylum. Montesinos returned to Peru immediately before the rebellion (*BBC News* 11/2/00; García Calderón 2001, 51, 54). The military rebels demanded the arrest of Montesinos for manipulating the military and Fujimori's resignation on the grounds that his recent, third consecutive election was fraudulent (*El Comercio* [Lima] 10/30/00a).[13]

After 2000: New Constraints on Military Autonomy and Limited Political Contestation

The armed forces encountered renewed constraints after Fujimori left office in late 2000, as subsequent administrations proved eager to introduce reforms that fostered transparency and civilian dominance of the armed forces. Perhaps because of interests within the military in regaining professionalism after Fujimori and Montesino's direct, personal control of the institution, since 2000 the armed forces have not actively contested the reforms. To complement the present analysis of reforms, in later chapters I analyze at length how judicial and executive decisions have made the military more accountable to the civilian justice system in matters of human rights and have reduced military authority in Sendero zones, where the armed forces are now responsible for providing security but no longer wield economic or political power.

A critical, early step in the reform process was a purge of Fujimori supporters. On taking his post in November 2000, Walter Ledesma—retired army general and interim defense minister under transitional president Valentín Paniagua (2000–2001)—removed twelve generals who were up for retirement that December (*New York Times* 11/26/00), as well as eighteen other generals, as a retired officer who had been involved in that process recounted during an interview.[14] Post-Fujimori purges extended to officers below the rank of general, in an effort to rebalance the top-heavy institution, according to that same retired officer and as reported by international news sources.[15]

Another area of reform is military education. Chapter 4 addresses the Peruvian military's instruction in human rights and international humanitarian law, one measure of civilian control of military education (Pion-Berlin 1992, 88; F. Agüero 2005). In addition, civilian instruction in Peru's army began in 2001, with an army project intended to increase the rigor of officers' education. As a result of the project, cadets receive a university degree on graduating from the officer formation school, the Escuela Militar de Chorrillos, where they study under both military instructors and civilian university professors.[16] Beyond the Escuela Militar, army majors now must study at civilian universities to advance to the rank of lieutenant colonel, according to a senior officer who had shaped the education reforms. Military education has been further civilianized through changes within the Center for Higher National Studies (Centro de Altos Estudios Nacionales, CAEN), which, since moving from the jurisdiction of the military joint command to that of the defense ministry in 1997, has widened its course offerings to attract journalists and civilian government officials (Hurtado 2005, 66).[17]

Another dimension of heightened government constraints on Peru's armed forces is expanded civilian influence in the defense ministry. President Alejandro Toledo (2001–6) selected the country's first civilian—that is, having no military service background—defense minister, and in his second term, President Alan García (2006–11) appointed only civilians to the post. Civilians and retired officers headed vice-ministries during the Toledo and García administrations.

At the same time that civilians have filled influential positions in the defense ministry, the ministry's institutional power has grown. The 2002 defense ministry law gave the minister more authority over the armed forces and enhanced organizational differentiation by establishing two vice-ministries—one for administrative and economic matters, a second to oversee logistics and personnel issues. The law was rewritten in 2007 (Law 29075), again increasing specialization within the ministry as well as executive power over the armed forces, for the first time defining the defense minister as "Supreme Head of the Armed Forces."

Increased civilian control has also taken the form of cuts to and increased transparency in military finances. The defense budget has shrunk steadily as a percentage of national spending since the late 1980s, from 14.4 percent in 1989 to 8 percent in 2006 (Palomino Milla 2004, 131; Ministerio de Economía y Finanzas, Perú, n.d.). Budget contraction since 2000 is of particular note, since previous reductions were offset somewhat by several supreme decrees and secret "urgency decrees" under Fujimori that channeled state funds from the government's privatization contracts and the external debt to the defense sector (Hernández Breña 2003, 85–87).[18]

As for transparency, corruption was drastically scaled back, with the removal of pro-Fujimori/Montesinos officers from the ranks, the opening of multiple corruption cases against military officers shortly after the democratic transition (Soberón Garrido 2001; *Economist* 1/11/03), and the military's reduced role in antinarcotics (see chapter 3). Another improvement in transparency is that military budget information is now available to the congress and the public in a format comparable to budgets of other ministries, making possible closer scrutiny of the budget (Hernández Breña 2003, 34–35; Otárola Peñaranda 2004, 176–77). According to a 2002 law governing Peru's national oversight system (Law 27785), each government sector, including the defense ministry and the individual military branches, is assigned an institutional control office (*oficina de control institucional*, OCI), dependent directly on the national audit office (Robles Montoya 2005, 139).

Some limitations to government oversight of military financial practices are worth noting. For instance, auditing is essentially internal to the armed forces, given that active-duty and retired officers head the military branch-level OCIs (Robles Montoya 2005, 140). Furthermore, the "defense fund," established in 2004 by Law 28455, channels profits from Peru's private natural gas conglomerate (Camisea) toward the military and police, for the acquisition and maintenance of equipment, without congressional oversight of the fund's allocation or spending (Supreme Decree 011-2005-DE).[19] Finally, as described in chapter 6, army units across the country earn unreported revenue through deals with actors outside the central government.

In spite of the reforms that have increased government control of the Peruvian military over the past ten years, there has been no major rebellion by the armed forces against government since Fujimori left office. The only fringe rebellion—staged in January 2005 by two hundred army reservists led by Antauro Humala—was a demand for President Toledo's resignation over corruption issues (*New York Times* 1/3/05), and not about reductions in military autonomy.

LOW CONSTRAINTS ON ECUADOR'S MILITARY

In contrast to the Peruvian case, Ecuador's military has contended with few structural or political constraints under democracy. Its political prominence—most evident in its role in effecting the premature removal of elected presidents, as analyzed below—is thus best understood not as a backlash against challenges to military prerogatives but rather as a logical extension of the military's roles in the state, economy, and society at large, welcomed by the government and by societal actors.

The analysis here emphasizes dynamic interactions between the military and civilians in government and an across-time increase in the military's political role under democracy. Yet one constant has been the military's exceptional influence in defense matters, with some exceptions in the mid- and late-2000s (see below). Civilian security experts have been lacking in both the defense ministry and the legislature. It has been the joint command and the service commanders—not the defense minister—that have served as the center of gravity in defense-related issues.[20] The military also enjoys power through the national security council (Consejo de Seguridad Nacional, COSENA), assigned to advise the executive on national security matters. Civilian members of COSENA include the president, presidents of the congress and of the supreme court, and the ministers of defense, government, finances, and foreign relations. In practice, the council's military members exercise the most influence, according to experts on defense and security matters whom I interviewed (see also Arízaga González and García Gallegos 2006, 56). The development of the defense ministry's 2002 "white book," a public statement of Ecuador's national defense policy, was a highly visible project that the ministry upheld as a momentous step toward making defense policy more transparent and civilian controlled. However, defense experts, including civilians who had participated in and scholars who conducted research on the endeavor, characterized the book as a product of military thinking (e.g., Pérez Enríquez 2003).

The Transition Years

Post-transition Peru and Ecuador looked very different, if we examine structural constraints on the armed forces. Whereas in the 1980s, Peru's military suffered from resource shortages amid severe economic crisis, oil-rich Ecuador did not experience hyperinflation (Fitch 1998, 81). Moreover, while Peru confronted an exploding insurgency threat, Ecuador's only insurgency was the small, urban group Alfaro Vive ¡Carajo! (AVC), active during the government of President León Febres Cordero (1984–88). Consequently, Ecuador's defense sector was not under strain. In fact, the military's loss to Peru in the 1981 conflict justified an increase in defense spending: the military budget jumped markedly in real terms following the defeat and then rose by another 30 percent under Febres Cordero (Fitch 1998, 80–81).

In those early years of Ecuador's democracy, the armed forces had exceptional autonomy, as shown by their intense reactions to the few government decisions in the defense arena that ran counter to military preferences. For example, in 1982 the Army Council of Generals blocked the proposal of President Osvaldo Hurtado (1981–84) to conclude peacefully the Peru-Ecuador border dispute and caused the defense minister who had supported the Hurtado proposal to resign

(Fitch 1998, 88). A high-profile case of military insubordination occurred in 1986, when air force general Frank Vargas Pazzos and five hundred military personnel took control of the Manta air force base on the central coast to protest corruption in Febres Cordero's government—specifically, purported government graft in an airplane purchase—and executive interference in military promotions. At Febres Cordero's request, the army recovered the base for the government and moved Vargas to the Quito air force base, where he was jailed. Vargas and his supporters responded by seizing that base as well, and the president again called on the army, this time to regain control of the Quito base and to move Vargas to a third base, outside the capital. When Febres Cordero refused to release Vargas from jail, elite paratroopers abducted the president, the defense minister, and other high-level officials, threatening to kill all of them if they did not release Vargas. The civil-military conflict was resolved only after Febres Cordero, "visibly shaken," promised on television that Vargas would be freed and the rebels would face no charges (Conaghan and Malloy 1994, 169–171).[21]

After Cenepa: Military Participation in the Early Removal of Presidents

Military political intervention increased markedly in Ecuador in the late 1990s, to the point where the armed forces contributed to the early removal of sitting presidents by withdrawing their support from the government (1997, 2005) and by joining with indigenous movement leaders to form a coup coalition (2000). These political interventions by the military were part of the latter's spread into multiple arenas—including civilian state bureaucracies and the economy—in the wake of the final armed conflict between Peru and Ecuador, the 1995 Cenepa War, when the Ecuadorian military underwent a budgetary and role crisis.[22] Perhaps the military's crises were best summed up by Colonel Fausto Cobo, a key player in the 2000 coup coalition, speaking shortly after the indigenous-military rebellion: "After the signing of the peace the army remained without leadership. The paradigm of war was withdrawn and the army remained in the air. No one had the ability to reorient it. Everyone spoke of the army that had won the war, but the soldiers felt frustrated, the officers unmotivated, the president took measures against the Armed Forces, reduced conscripts and budgets, and the strategic and operational capacity dropped to truly low levels" (Dieterich 2000, 120). Chapter 5 further explores the crisis as it has affected the army's mission performance, but the focus here is on expansion of the military's role in society and the state more broadly after the war.

After Cenepa, the armed forces' already large presence in the state and the economy grew. The Ecuadorian military has participated in a number of economic sectors, including the shrimp, flower, textile, and hotel industries. The army's Industrial Directorate (Dirección de Industrias del Ejército, DINE), created during the 1970s under military rule, remained active throughout the 1980s and 1990s as an owner of companies and a partner in joint public-private enterprises. Its investments have spanned the munitions, steel, ceramics, construction, and automobile industries (Vallejo 1991; Fitch 1998, 120–21; Diamint 2003, 57–58). When President Sixto Durán Ballén (1992–96) launched a series of privatization reforms, the armed forces passionately and successfully defended their presence in the economy (Fitch 1998, 122).

In addition to this economic power, the armed forces have administered important civilian state agencies, a role granted by the executive. In August 1996, the Abdalá Bucaram government (1996–97) temporarily ordered the army to run the national customs agency, as a means of reducing corruption (*El Comercio* [Quito] 1/21/03). President Fabián Alarcón (1997–98) also charged the armed forces with cleaning up customs, in February 1997, an assignment that lasted until mid-1999 (*El Comercio* [Quito] 2/13/97, 1/21/03). Between April 2003 and June 2005, now under President Lucio Gutiérrez (2003–5), the military again ran the agency (*El Comercio* [Quito] 4/2/03, 6/25/05; *Hoy* 4/8/03). The armed forces seemed willing to carry out the function: during the 2003–5 period, the number of active-duty military personnel administering the agency went from sixty-one—thirty-five from the army, six from the air force, and eleven from the navy—to eighty (*El Comercio* [Quito] 4/2/03, 6/25/05). Beyond customs, another civilian agency that the military has overseen is Petroecuador, the state oil company. Between December 2007 and March 2010, a series of consecutive executive emergency decrees placed the navy in control of Petroecuador for the purpose of enhancing the company's efficiency (Observatorio Político Defensa, Seguridad y Relaciones Civil-Militares [Observatorio Político] 1/08; *El Comercio* [Quito] 1/19/11).

As for the military's participation in premature executive turnover, this analysis follows the lead of other research on civil-military relations in Ecuador that has pointed to the military's loss of its raison d'être since the Cenepa War to help explain its participation in the early removal of elected presidents in 1997 and 2000 (García Gallegos 2000, 171; Lucero 2001, 65; Pérez Enríquez 2004).[23] The 1997, 2000, and 2005 events occurred during periods of intense antigovernment popular protest that opposed liberal economic reforms and stabilization efforts.[24] The first case was the removal of President Bucaram six months after he took office. Bucaram's government had received widespread criticism for siphoning monies to his party and family and for its unpopular neoliberal economic measures that deviated from campaign promises of populist spending to benefit the poor. Nationwide uprisings broke out in February 1997 when Bucaram announced price increases for essentials, including cooking gas and electricity (Jameson 1997). During the protests, significant political actors—including President Bucaram himself, Vice President Rosalía Arteaga, the U.S. ambassador, members of the United Workers' Front, and business sector leaders (*El Comercio* [Quito] 2/18/97)—approached the military either to plead with it to keep Bucaram in office or to demand that it withdraw its support from him, to force him to leave. The armed forces formally withdrew their support from Bucaram and coordinated the political transition: Arteaga was made president temporarily, on February 9, and two days later the congress named its head, Fabián Alarcón, as interim president (*El Comercio* [Quito] 2/10/97, 2/19/97).[25]

Another economic and political crisis precipitated the second event, in 2000, a military-indigenous coup that removed President Jamil Mahuad (1998–2000). Shortly after Mahuad took office, the first of many national banks failed. By the end of 1999, the government had transferred $6 billion, or about 23 percent of the gross national product (GNP), to the banking sector in an attempt to stabilize the economy (Lucero 2001, 62). The value of Ecuador's currency (the *sucre*) dropped, social spending was cut drastically, the minimum wage fell, and unemployment doubled. In January 2000, amid the economic crisis and a campaign finance scandal that linked the owner of one of the bailed-out banks to Mahuad's presidential campaign, Mahuad announced his unpopular dollarization plan, decreasing confidence in the president and the political system as a whole (Lucero 2001, 63).[26] On January 21, 2000, more than ten thousand indigenous people from several highland provinces amassed in Quito (Lucero 2001, 63). Colonel Lucio Gutiérrez and approximately four hundred army personnel, mainly officers (Dieterich 2000, 68), joined with indigenous protesters and occupied, nonviolently, the congressional building.[27] Gutiérrez, former head of the supreme court Carlos Solórzano, and Antonio Vargas—president of the national indigenous movement (Confederación de Nacionalidades Indígenas del Ecuador, CONAIE)—proclaimed themselves the Junta of National Salvation. The junta planned to run the country for five or six months before installing a civilian government, according to statements made by Gutiérrez in the aftermath of the coup (Dieterich 2000, 67). Shortly after the takeover of the congress, the military joint command demanded that Mahuad step down, which he did. That same night, General

Mendoza, head of the joint command and standing defense minister, replaced Gutiérrez as the military member of the junta. Within hours Mendoza handed over power to Gustavo Noboa, who had been vice president under Mahuad (Lucero 2001, 59).

Besides the military's role crisis and accumulation of functions in the state and economy, an additional factor helps to explain the armed forces' participation in the 2000 coup: their civic action efforts in the 1990s that involved military-indigenous contact (Selmeski 2002, 5–6). Although indigenous mobilizing in Ecuador has been traced to the 1960s, CONAIE's main entrance onto the political scene was its first major mobilization, which paralyzed entire provinces in June 1990 by blocking transit and taking over subnational government offices (Van Cott 2005, 111; Yashar 2005). In response, the army embarked on a new civic action effort, known as *apoyo al desarrollo*, or development aid, specifically as a strategy to deter indigenous mobilizing (Selmeski 2007, 158–59). The *apoyo al desarrollo* program brought army civic action to Ecuador's highlands for the first time, in the form of health, communications, agriculture, and education projects (Falconí Ramos 1991, 30–31; Vallejo 1991, 66; Selmeski 2002, 3; 2007, 159), and exposed many Ecuadorian army personnel to the country's indigenous population.[28]

The third case of premature executive turnover was the April 2005 removal of President (and now retired army colonel) Lucio Gutiérrez, who took office as Ecuador's democratically elected president in January 2003. There was an upsurge of opposition to Gutiérrez in November 2004, due to accusations that he had embezzled public resources and property to favor his party's candidates in the October 2004 local and provincial elections. That scandal paled in comparison to the unconstitutional replacement of the supreme court justices, carried out in December 2004 by Gutiérrez and his supporters in the congress. Gutiérrez's days were numbered when the new court dismissed charges against former president Bucaram in April 2005, at which point Bucaram returned to Ecuador, spurring massive protests (particularly in Quito). From April 15 to April 20, the national media asked when and how the armed forces would resolve the crisis, once again evincing the military's legitimate role in politics. On April 20 the congress made public its decision to remove Gutiérrez, and the armed forces, too, played their part: the military joint command formally withdrew its support from the Gutiérrez government (*El Comercio* [Quito] 4/21/05, 4/22/05).

Although this analysis of the Ecuadorian case has emphasized military autonomy throughout the post-transition period, there have been signs, starting with the administration of Alfredo Palacio (2005–7) and continuing under Rafael

Correa (2007–present), of some civilian participation in and power over defense matters. For the first time, civilians with no military service background have been appointed to the post of defense minister. Furthermore, civilians can now serve in the ministry as vice-minister, undersecretary, and advisor, in accordance with a 2007 organic law (*ley orgánica*), and by May 2007, five civilians were filling such senior staff positions (Fundación Democracia, Seguridad y Defensa 2007a, 2007b; Observatorio Político 4/08). Under the 2007 organic law and article 162 of the 2008 constitution, the armed forces can operate legally in (otherwise) private industries only insofar as the military companies directly relate to national defense (Fundación Democracia, Seguridad y Defensa 2007a; Observatorio Político 6/07, 1/08, 6/08; *Latin American Herald Tribune* 1/6/09). Correa achieved further control of military financial practices when he used his decree power to abolish the Junta de Defensa Nacional, a military body that until that point had used its budget to purchase weapons and equipment without congressional supervision (Observatorio Político 9/08, 12/08).[29] Nontheless, these measures to monitor military finances have been accompanied by other investments in the armed forces, resources that may have served to appease the armed forces. Throughout 2008, Correa and his defense ministers announced plans to modernize and replenish military equipment (Observatorio Político 1/08, 4/08, 6/08, 12/08),[30] and Correa used his decree power to speed up the process of military salary bumps: according to Correa's project, salaries were to increase by approximately 10 percent in 2006, 23 percent in 2007, 34 percent in 2008, and 34 percent in 2009, at which point generals would earn as much as ministers (Observatorio Político 2/08).

Overall, then, under democracy, the Ecuadorian military has enjoyed high levels of autonomy vis-à-vis civilians and, often backed by successive administrations, it has taken on many roles in the state and in society, to the point where it has been an increasingly powerful political player. This trajectory contrasts with the Peruvian case of constraints on the armed forces and accompanying military withdrawal from the political arena. As we will see in later chapters, these varied civil-military dynamics have implications for each army's mission performance, helping to explain how, in each case, a contradiction emerged in the army's salient sovereignty mission, but through a distinct path.

CHAPTER 3

Army Mission Performance in Post-Transition Peru and Ecuador, 1980s–1990s

In the first two decades of democracy, the different civil-military dynamics in Peru and Ecuador played out vividly in army mission performance. In spite of both armies' clear preference for sovereignty work—as predicted by hypotheses focused on military interests in professionalism, resources, and public legitimacy—in each country, a contradiction arose in the army's salient sovereignty mission that reduced predictability for the work of patrols, thereby causing the army to underperform its mission. In Peru, it was government constraints on the army's autonomy that led to the contradiction. Ecuador's army, free of those constraints, instead found itself overloaded with excessive security responsibilities, and the contradiction grew out of that overload.

SOVEREIGNTY BEFORE POLICING

To observe the origins and effects of the contradictions, I first analyze periods when that interference was not present. As I will show, the "status quo" behavior of the two armies was to prioritize salient missions that were highly legitimate, professional, and lucrative, both by aggressively performing salient sovereignty missions and by refusing police work that interfered with those efforts to defend sovereignty.

Peru: Border Defense and Counterinsurgency

For much of the 1980s and 1990s, Peru's army showed a deep commitment to sovereignty work. The army defended the northern border against Ecuador, performed counterinsurgency, and put those missions ahead of policing.

Assertive Border Defense against Ecuador

Since democratization, the Peruvian and Ecuadorian armed forces have engaged in armed combat at two moments, as part of a border dispute dating back to 1830, the year of Ecuadorian independence.[1] Peru's armed forces proved victorious in a 1981 conflict that lasted a few days (Rousseau 2005, 78). In the January 1995 Cenepa War, a series of skirmishes,[2] the Peruvian military lost on the battlefield. Cease-fire agreements were signed in February 1995, and by May 3, 1995, both sides had withdrawn their forces from the contested zone (Marcella and Downes 1999, 3; Herz and Pontes Nogueira 2002, 47). The longstanding border dispute was fully resolved when presidents Fujimori and Mahuad signed the Brasília Presidential Act on October 26, 1998 (Simmons 1999, 20).

The Peruvian army took its border mission seriously, mobilizing energetically for both the 1981 and 1995 conflicts and increasing its external defense focus after the 1995 defeat. The loss in the Cenepa War was devastating to the military, both because it created the need to improve the public's opinion of the armed forces and because it proved how "seriously affected" the military's professionalism was by the corruption that had accompanied its antinarcotics work (Rospigliosi 2000, 163–64). Given these grave concerns about professionalism and legitimacy, the military withdrew from antinarcotics (an action formalized through a 1996 legislative decree) and invested more in external defense (Loveman 1999, 278; Rospigliosi 2000, 163). The army reinforced the border by creating the sixth army region (comparable to a division, with a specific territorial jurisdiction), specifically to provide security in Peru's Amazonas department, which abuts Ecuador in the disputed territory.[3]

Major Insurgent Threat

Whereas the conflict with Ecuador led to armed combat only twice in the 1980s and 1990s, Peru's ongoing, salient sovereignty threat during that period was posed by two insurgencies: Sendero Luminoso and the smaller Movimiento

Revolucionario Túpac Amaru (MRTA). In 1969, in the southern highland department of Ayacucho, Sendero was born from a Maoist offshoot of Peru's communist party that had strong ties to the party's youth group and to the local University of Huamanga.[4] After spreading throughout Ayacucho and into neighboring departments during the 1970s, Sendero staged its first major violent attack the day before the general elections that precipitated Peru's democratic transition. On May 17, 1980, five hooded members of Sendero restrained the registrar of voters and burned the voter registry and ballot boxes in Chuschi, a town in Ayacucho (Gorriti 1999, 17).

University of Huamanga philosophy professor Abimael Guzmán led Sendero, which expanded beyond the student population to successfully recruit many peasant combatants by appealing to frustrations over socioeconomic conditions, serving as the law in a region of the country where the Peruvian state was absent, and coercing the peasantry into cooperating with the movement (Degregori 1996; McClintock 1998, 63–72, 271–81, 287–98). Cynthia McClintock vividly captures this brutality in the following excerpt from her in-depth research on the insurgency:

> For Sendero Luminoso, those who stood in its way were the enemy, and—even if they were unarmed civilians—should be assassinated . . . Whereas the military and police were the principal targets of . . . most previous Latin American guerrilla movements, only 17 percent of Shining Path's victims were members of the military or police; most victims were unarmed civilians . . .
>
> Sendero killed not only routinely, but savagely . . . One of the most common tactics was the beheading of victims. Also, eyes were gouged out; men were castrated; children were disemboweled; and human bonfires were set. Sendero socialized its young recruits to violence; children of five and six were taught to kill chickens so that they would be accustomed to blood, and by the age of nine were smashing skulls with stones. (McClintock 1998, 68)

Sendero shook Peru's countryside during the 1980s and into the 1990s.[5] In the early years of the conflict, the insurgency's support base was located in the departments of Apurímac, Ayacucho, and Huancavelica in Peru's southern highlands. By the mid-1980s, Huánuco and parts of San Martín in the country's central jungle region were added to the list. By the late 1980s, the insurgency had gained control of the central highlands, including the strategically critical department of Junín, through which an important highway passed, connecting the capital city of Lima to most of Peru's highlands and jungle, and thus to Sendero territory. In addition, at the start of the 1990s, the insurgency controlled most of Lima's shantytowns on routes leading from the highlands to the city. The organization controlled approximately 40 percent of Peru's provinces during 1991–92, and by December 1991, 47 percent of all provinces were under a state of emergency. In 1989, Sendero caused state authorities to abandon their posts in at least 28 percent of Peru's electoral districts. That year, its ten thousand full-time combatants inflicted 1,526 deaths.

Small relative to Sendero, the MRTA formed in 1982 from the union of two far-left organizations: the Partido Socialista Revolucionario-Marxista-Leninista (PSR-ML) and a splinter group of the political party the Movimiento de Izquierda Revolucionaria (MIR), the MIR–El Militante (MIR-EM). The MRTA began its armed actions in 1984 (Comisión de la Verdad y Reconciliación [CVR] 2003, 1:64) and claimed approximately one thousand militants at its height (McClintock 1998, 47). The group was based primarily in Lima and in the Huancayo and San Martín departments and was known widely for kidnapping and extortion (CVR 2003, 6:402, 404–21). Unlike Sendero, the MRTA failed to build a coherent organization. Instead, it carried out well-publicized attacks (McClintock 1998, 47), the most famous incident being the 1997 hostage crisis at the Japanese ambassador's home (see below).

Assertive Counterinsurgency

Facing a serious insurgent threat and lacking guidance from the government on how to confront the guerrillas, Peru's army autonomously developed counterinsurgency strategies, starting in the early 1980s, following an initial period in which the government excluded the military from the counterinsurgency effort. President Belaúnde proved slow in responding to the Sendero threat as the insurgency steadily expanded.[6] By May 1981, Sendero attacks totaled 83 in Ayacucho, 81 in Lima, 48 in Cusco, 46 in Junín, and 20 in Ancash (Gorriti 1999, 94–95), and yet the government waited until October 1981 to declare a state of emergency, which gave the police added counterinsurgency authority in five provinces in Ayacucho.[7] Despite steady demands by local politicians, soldiers, and police officials for the central government to send in military assistance (Gorriti 1999, 167–68), the government resisted putting the armed forces in charge of counterinsurgency, because Belaúnde underestimated the extent of the guerrilla threat and also because he was reluctant to grant the military political power in the new democracy (Tapia 1997, 30–31; Gorriti 1999, 44, 46, 52, 110–11, 115, 117, 168; Rospigliosi 2000, 52–53). Belaúnde kept the military out of counterinsurgency even in January 1982, when police forces started removing their posts from towns undergoing guerrilla violence, and when Sendero gained complete control of the city of Ayacucho (the Ayacucho departmental capital, in the province of Huamanga), releasing all prisoners held there (Gorriti 1999, 163–73).

The government finally ordered the armed forces to head up counterinsurgency at the end of the intensely violent year of 1982. During December alone, Sendero used dynamite to destroy the bridge that connected Ayacucho with the department of Cusco and with Andahuaylas province, shot the mayor of Ayacucho and the president of the Departmental Development Corporation, murdered the mayor and a city councilman in the Ayacucho city of Huamanguilla, shot the subprefect (under the interior ministry, which oversees the national police) of Huamanga near police headquarters, and killed the regional director of the National Institute of Culture. Fear of a Christmas attack on the department of Ayacucho was so widespread that emigration from the area overwhelmed airline capacity (Gorriti 1999, 259–60).

When Belaúnde did bring the military into counterinsurgency, he did not give it guidance about how to address the guerrilla threat, leaving the army to develop its own counterinsurgency plan. Army leaders envisioned a strategy that would include both military confrontations with insurgents and socioeconomic development to address the needs of the rural poor, thereby strengthening peasant support for the state and undercutting the insurgency. In terms of combat, in those early years of Peru's internal conflict, the army employed indiscriminate violence, including massacres of the populations of entire towns.[8] More than 45 percent of the 7,260 reported deaths and disappearances that were attributed to state security forces during 1980–2000 occurred in the first five years (figure 3.1). This approach failed to reduce Sendero's power. In many cases, peasants saw Sendero as the lesser evil and sided with the guerrillas (Coronel 1996, 48–49, 58–59; Degregori 1996, 205; Tapia 1997, 32), and the insurgency spread. In December 1982, the army identified Sendero's stronghold as encompassing twenty-six districts in Ayacucho, Huancavelica, and Apurímac; by November 1983, the guerrillas made elections impossible in sixty-four districts (Tapia 1997, 34–35).

To explain the army's choice to use indiscriminate violence against the guerrillas, Carlos Tapia, human rights activist and renowned expert on Peru's internal conflict, points to the military's outdated counterinsurgency doctrine. The doctrine was based on writings from the 1960s that did not analyze the roots or goals of Sendero and overlooked the importance of intelligence.[9] Indeed, the military had conducted counterinsurgency only briefly, in the mid-1960s, against the small

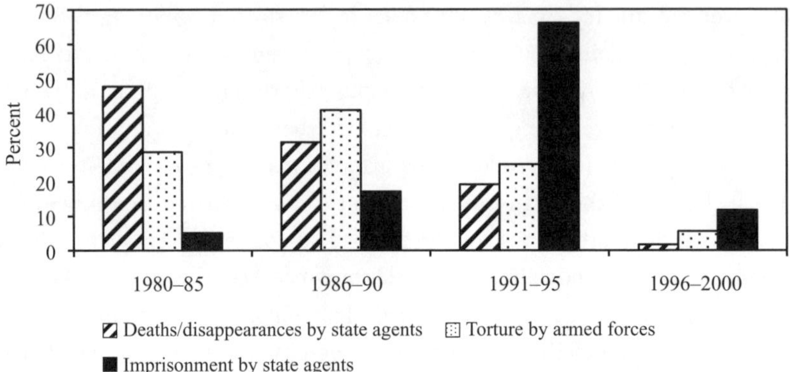

Figure 3.1. Distribution of Peruvian State Counterinsurgency Tactics, 1980–2000
Source: Comisión de la Verdad y Reconciliación 2003, app. 3: 84, 340, 375

Ejército de Liberación Nacional (ELN) and MIR (Tapia 1997, 23–30, 32). When Sendero violence commenced, the armed forces had not amended their outdated strategy; they were oriented toward external warfare, not counterinsurgency.[10]

Complementing this ill-conceived approach to fighting guerrillas, and consistent with the armed forces' historical focus on development, military leaders wanted the state to fund economic development to win over peasants and thus reduce Sendero's popular base (Rospigliosi 2000, 47–69).[11] When, in a grave economic setting, the Belaúnde government refused to implement development projects as proposed by the military, the army went forward with such a policy itself. The military commander in Peru's emergency zone in the southern highlands, "political-military commander" General Adrián Huamán, established economic assistance projects in Ayacucho, including food distribution to poor communities (Tapia 1997, 36). Finally, added to the army's focus on combat and development, from within an important segment of the army leadership there was a desire for the government to grant the army expansive legal economic and political powers in emergency zones, including, for example, control of judges and mayors, as well as funds to perform these roles (Tapia 1997, 32, 36; Rospigliosi 2000, 64–66). Less than two months before leaving power in July 1985, Belaúnde's government took some steps toward meeting the army's demands, expanding military power in guerrilla zones: Law 24150 assigned political-military commanders the capacity to "coordinate, supervise and harmonize" the actions of all public and private entities in their areas of responsibility (Tapia 1997, 38).

The second stage in the army's counterinsurgency effort began in the late 1980s (after a period of army inaction, analyzed below). Like Belaúnde, President García (1985–90) had not provided the army with directives on how to fight insurgents (see also below). Officers were distressed by the continued spread of insurgency, the armed forces' deteriorating image as a feckless military embroiled in an endless struggle, and what they saw as unfair blame of the military by the Peruvian public for human rights violations during the internal conflict.[12] Without guidance from the president, and reacting both to its frustrations with the lack of government initiative and to its failed attempts to contain insurgency, the army created a new strategy (Tapia 1997, 44–45).[13]

The strategy combined a more targeted, intelligence-driven approach to fighting armed guerrillas with the military's interests in gaining political power in insurgency zones and addressing the material conditions of communities there. In August 1989, the head of the army approved the counterinsurgency manual "Non-Conventional Warfare: Counterinsurgency" (*Guerra no convencional: Contrasubversión*). The manual emphasized (1) intelligence, including infiltrating Sendero and building a database on guerrilla leaders and zones controlled by Sendero; (2) gaining the support of the population through inducements (as opposed to coercion); (3) an integral approach to operations, involving centralized direction and decentralized execution; and (4) the military's complete political control of counterinsurgency zones (Tapia 1997, 48–55; see also CVR 2003, 2:194–98).

In conformity with this new strategy, the army began targeting insurgents more effectively, in place of the civilian massacres common in the 1980s (Degregori 1996, 211; CVR 2003, 2:194, 202–7). During Peru's conflict, whereas the majority of deaths and disappearances caused by state agents and the majority of military torture cases occurred in the 1980s, nearly 70 percent of all imprisonments occurred in the first half of the 1990s (figure 3.1). Once identified, insurgents still received harsh treatment: a military directive leaked to the press in July 1991 states that counterinsurgency operations based on intelligence "[are] of a character highly offensive and aggressive, without forgetting that the best subversive is a dead subversive; therefore, prisoners will not be taken" (Tapia 1997, 79).

In part due to the army's new strategy, Peru's insurgent threat dropped during the 1990s.[14] At the national level, Sendero declined precipitously after an elite police force captured Abimael Guzmán in 1992.[15] By the end of the 1990s, only small pockets of the country continued to see Sendero military training, attacks on police antinarcotics operations, and threats and kidnappings in remote towns.

These sites of continued insurgency included the Valley of the Apurímac and Ene Rivers (Valle de los ríos Apurímac y Ene, VRAE), which spans portions of the Apurímac, Ayacucho, Cusco, Huancavelica, and Junín departments in Peru's southern highlands and is where Sendero originated; and the Upper Huallaga Valley (Valle del Alto Huallaga, VAH), which is in the central highland departments of Huánuco and San Martín and has been Peru's major coca-producing zone and a center for the cocaine trade, a key source of Sendero funding.[16] For its part, the MRTA dissolved in the late 1990s following the army's 1997 special forces operation "Chavín de Huántar," in which army commandos rescued the MRTA's hostages that were being held at the Japanese ambassador's residence, killing all of the insurgents at the scene.

Subordination of Police Work

The Peruvian army showed its devotion to counterinsurgency not only by taking the initiative to develop and implement strategy but also by repeatedly putting the mission ahead of its policing duties.

Antinarcotics. Most notably, throughout the 1980s, the army refused to participate in counterdrug operations and even went so far as to protect the cocaine trade on which the VAH's coca-growing peasantry (*cocaleros*) depended, as a means of gaining peasant support for the state, to reduce Sendero's power in the VAH.

To understand the army's approach to counterinsurgency in the VAH, it is first necessary to establish the dynamics through which Sendero exercised power there. Sendero-peasant relations in the VAH were of a highly economic character, contrasting sharply with the insurgency's practice of massacre in villages in the VRAE (Dreyfus 1999, 382; Kay 1999, 104). When Sendero entered the VAH in 1984, it murdered representatives of the (weak) *cocalero* trade unions and eliminated the drug traffickers' illicit security forces, thereby making itself the contact point between traffickers and peasants, as well as the security force for both groups against the police (Dreyfus 1999, 381–82). Sendero's entrenchment made police antinarcotics operations impossible, prompting a July 1984 emergency decree that assigned the military to provide security in the VAH.

Despite this executive order, army leaders refused to fight the drug trade, on the grounds that the work would interfere with the peasant economy, which in turn would drive the *cocaleros* further into the arms of Sendero, interfering with the army's counterinsurgency objectives. For instance, on taking his post as political-military commander in the VAH in July 1984, army general Julio Carbajal actively protected the cocaine trade. He prohibited the police force that provided security for coca-eradication teams from doing this work. Without state protections, the teams were subsequently massacred by Sendero and traffickers, ending state eradication under the Belaúnde government (Dreyfus 1999, 383). Carbajal's actions paid off in terms of counterinsurgency results: by replacing Sendero as security for the drug trade, the army won the favor of the peasants, and within six months the army was carrying out counterinsurgency operations that significantly reduced Sendero's presence in the valley (Obando 1993, 84; Dreyfus 1999, 383).

During the García administration, the army again was ordered to fight drug trafficking in the VAH, and again it, instead, tolerated the cocaine trade. García initially did not assign the military to the VAH, both to try to reduce human rights abuses by the military and because he doubted that the army would be effective in antinarcotics, given its history of refusing the mission (Obando 1993, 85; Dreyfus 1999, 383–84; Soberón Garrido 2005, 200). However, it soon became obvious that the police did not have the capacity to operate alone in the zone. In the army's absence, the MRTA moved into the northern end of the valley by the late 1980s, and Sendero subsequently returned and achieved control of the south (Obando 1993, 85–86; Dreyfus 1999, 384; Soberón Garrido 2005, 201). With the VAH divided between Sendero and the MRTA, in March 1989 the government sent the military back to the valley (Dreyfus 1999, 385).

The army continued prioritizing counterinsurgency to the detriment of antinarcotics. A military joint command directive ordered that operations be conducted against "drug-trafficking subversives, producers, and collaborators, who out of convenience support and/or receive protection from subversion" (CVR 2003, 2:201, quoting Ministerio de Defensa Nacional, Perú 1989, 10). In keeping with this order, army units in the VAH took action against only those drug traffickers connected to Sendero, leaving other traffickers to operate freely and even making pacts with them, with the intent to protect the livelihood of the peasants (Dreyfus 1999, 385–86; CVR 2003, 2:201–2). In conjunction with the army's intelligence operations and civic action, this strategy effectively pushed Sendero out of the VAH (Dreyfus 1999, 385; Kay 1999, 105; Rospigliosi 2000, 32; CVR 2003, 2:201–2).

The army was drawn squarely into antinarcotics in the 1990s, though the transition was not smooth. The armed forces opposed the antinarcotics mission so vehemently that the military leadership successfully pressed the Fujimori government to turn down U.S. economic support that would have required extensive engagement of the armed forces in antinarcotics work (Obando 1993, 88; I.

Rojas 2005, 191). Facing a deep economic crisis and fearing the loss of U.S. financial assistance, however, the government finally withstood military pressures and accepted U.S. security funds earmarked for military antinarcotics work (Obando 1993, 87–93; McClintock 1998, 237, 239–43; I. Rojas 2005, 195). A November 1991 legislative decree (Legislative Decree 749) assigned the armed forces to the mission (Tapia 1997, 74–75; Rospigliosi 2000, 116). As a consequence, the army intensified its presence in the VAH and began assertive drug interdiction (Dreyfus 1999, 388; I. Rojas 2005, 193–94).

It is important to note that when, in the 1990s, the army took on antinarcotics, the work had ceased to compromise the institution's counterinsurgency objectives, for two reasons. First, the VAH had lost some importance to Sendero and therefore also to the army. Sendero's power in the VAH had decreased, because of the 1992 capture of Guzmán and subsequent collapse of the insurgency at the national level, and because reduced coca prices had led *cocaleros* to leave the valley and migrate south (Dreyfus 1999, 386–87). Second, counterinsurgency and antinarcotics were no longer a zero-sum proposition in the 1990s. The government's antinarcotics policy had turned away from coca eradication and toward drug interdiction, which less directly threatened peasants' economic interests (Dreyfus 1999, 386–87). Sendero's strategy in the VAH had also changed, with important implications for counterinsurgency. Once Guzmán was imprisoned, the insurgency abandoned the pursuit of a popular, Maoist struggle in the valley. With this change, instead of aiming to control the population, Sendero sought territorial domination—for example, of coca fields and river mouths (CVR 2003, 2:244). The new strategy, in turn, made obsolete the Peruvian army's earlier focus on protecting the drug trade to earn peasants' trust. For military leaders, the appropriate way to respond to the insurgents' new strategy in the VAH was to employ conventional warfare tactics against guerrillas to achieve control of strategic geographic locations, as opposed to the earlier hearts-and-minds approach (CVR 2003, 2:243–46).[17] In short, we see that the army continued prioritizing counterinsurgency over policing, because it performed the antinarcotics mission (a policing mission) only when this did not interfere with counterinsurgency objectives.

Protest Control. Another indication that the Peruvian army put counterinsurgency ahead of policing during the 1980s and 1990s is that it engaged only minimally in protest control, and generally did the work more aggressively in emergency zones.[18]

When the army worked to manage protests, the police, not the army, tended to confront protesters directly. During national labor strikes in the 1980s, any military involvement was generally limited to helping to plan operations.[19] The armed forces helped the national police provide security amid the 1992 protests against Fujimori's *autogolpe*, but the reported harm to protesters was caused by the police, not by the armed forces (*El Comercio* [Lima] 5/16/92). The army did not participate in containing the (few) 1999–2000 protests during Fujimori's government.[20]

Army aggression against protesters tended to be more evident in insurgency zones. For example, in an August 1989 mining strike, protests were intense near mines in emergency zones in Pasco and Junín and faced army repression (*La República* 8/13/89, 8/17/89, 8/19/89a, 8/19/89b, 8/20/89). The army forcefully controlled a teachers' strike that occurred between May and August 1991 and that allegedly was infiltrated by insurgents. The press reported that two thousand teachers were arrested, twenty were disappeared, and fifteen were killed. Two of the deaths were attributed to the army (CVR 2003, 3:393–95).

Ecuador: Border Defense

Unlike the Peruvian case, Ecuador's army gained little experience in warfare in the decades after the democratic transition. The Ecuadorian police, and not the army, took the lead in countering the small AVC insurgency,[21] and thus the army only truly engaged in combat during the 1981 and 1995 border conflicts. Outside those two episodes, the army was available for police work, which it conducted regularly. In fact, contemporaneous interview data suggest that during the 1980s and 1990s, Ecuadorian army officers valued their police functions. J. Samuel Fitch has analyzed interviews conducted in 1991 with forty-four Ecuadorian military officers, the majority of whom were retired army generals. Ninety percent of the officers named external defense as an appropriate army mission, and 85 percent identified "internal" security work (a category that logically would include policing) as appropriate (Fitch 1998, 64, 120). In spite of the army's apparent orientation toward police missions, it exhibited the same behavior as its Peruvian counterpart, setting aside policing when the work interfered with defending sovereignty.

Assertive Border Defense against Peru

One manifestation of the Ecuadorian army's commitment to sovereignty defense and, specifically, defending the southern border against Peru's armed forces is that in response to the 1981 defeat, the army created new military schools and courses and considerably intensified officers' training in external warfare.[22] The abnormally large number of experienced officers sent to fight in the Cenepa War also makes obvious the army's seriousness about southern border defense. As described in interviews with Ecuadorian army officers who had served in the war, the army ordered many majors and captains to the south during the war, to head patrols. This high concentration of mid-ranking officers broke with army doctrine, according to which low-ranking officers—primarily second lieutenants, the lowest in the army hierarchy—lead such small patrols.

Subordination of Police Work

The Ecuadorian army further proved dedicated to sovereignty work when it subordinated policing to border defense, though the army did participate considerably in police work. One of the army's main policing missions was containing protests, especially mobilizations against oil companies, urban strikes by organized labor in the 1980s, and indigenous uprisings in the 1990s. During Ecuador's general strikes in the 1980s, as in Peru, the police force was the state actor that most commonly clashed physically with protesters. However, unlike the Peruvian case, in which the army was, on the whole, limited to planning, when the Ecuadorian army worked to establish order during strikes, it tended both to coordinate police-military actions and to conduct patrols and clear main highways of protesters and blockades.[23]

The army also directly confronted uprisings by actors opposing the practices of oil companies and/or national oil policies. Especially in Ecuador's oil-rich northeastern lowlands, there has been frequent protest activity by indigenous groups and by "colonists" who settled the region in the context of the burgeoning oil industry and the land reform programs of the 1960s and 1970s.[24] These actors have demanded restitution for use of the communities' land and for adverse environmental impacts of oil exploitation (Kimerling 1991; Gerlach 2003, 55–58; Sawyer 2004, 13; Yashar 2005, 113–15). The army's connection to the oil industry has deep historical roots. It was under military rule (1972–79) that the state, through a contract with a Texaco Gulf consortium, actively developed the oil sector and Ecuador's northeastern provinces. The military's legal responsibility to protect "strategic areas," to include oil infrastructure, is found in legislation passed during the military regime.[25]

The army's heavy involvement in controlling protests surrounding the oil industry is evident when we examine an intense conflict during February and

March 1984 in the provinces of Napo (now Napo and Orellana) and Esmeraldas. Strikes demanding oil rents from the central government paralyzed the provinces, costing the state more than $2 million (*El Comercio* [Quito] 3/14/84). Army personnel protected oil installations from protesters even before a state of emergency was declared in those provinces, clashing with protesters and saboteurs (*El Comercio* [Quito] 3/15/84). Amid the crisis, "The Minister of National Defense warned . . . that any attack against installations of a strategic character such as oil installations will be considered an attack against military installations and, therefore, against national security" (*El Comercio* [Quito] 3/15/84).[26]

Protest control took on new meaning with the national indigenous confederation CONAIE's first mobilization (see chapter 2). President Rodrigo Borja Cevallos (1988–92) used the police and army to contain the mobilization (Zamosc 1994, 37, 39–40). The army also controlled other major indigenous uprisings, such as the April 1992 march for land rights by the Pastaza province's main indigenous organization, the Organización de Pueblos Indígenas de Pastaza (OPIP) (Sawyer 1997, 2004; Fontaine 2003, 397–409), and the successful 1994 mobilization against the government's proposed Agrarian Development Law, which would have halted land reform.[27]

Added to protest control, the Ecuadorian army's other main policing mission during the first decades of democracy was fighting crime. In rural areas, the army conducted patrols and operated checkpoints independent of police forces; in urban areas, it carried out operations both with and without the police. The army's urban anticrime work began under President Febres Cordero.[28] For example, during a period of high crime in the coastal city of Guayaquil—Ecuador's largest city and the country's center for the economic elite—in May 1988, the governor of Guayas (home to Guayaquil) requested military assistance; this request prompted a joint military operation that included the army and involved patrols and arrests (*El Comercio* [Quito] 5/28/88). Amid harsh economic liberalization policies, rising crime, and social discontent about insecurity,[29] President Durán Ballén brought the army squarely into regular anticrime work. Emergency decrees in 1992, 1994, and 1996 assigned the military a permanent role in fighting crime (*El Comercio* [Quito] 3/12/98).[30] In 1994 the national news reported on a "reorganization" of joint military-police operations, such that the armed forces would directly capture criminals in areas of the country—including sectors of Guayaquil and Quito—where police presence was nonexistent, and police and military anticrime actions would "continue indefinitely" (*El Comercio* [Quito] 10/7/94).

Although the army actively fought crime and controlled protests in the 1980s and 1990s, it still prioritized its sovereignty role over policing. It suspended its anticrime operations during the 1995 Cenepa conflict, specifically because army leaders thought the work would distract the army and thereby interfere with its effectiveness in defending the southern border (*El Comercio* [Quito] 3/12/98).[31]

DEVIATIONS: CONTRADICTIONS IN MISSIONS AND SOVEREIGNTY NEGLECT

Despite the Peruvian and Ecuadorian armies' tendency to take seriously their sovereignty missions in the 1980s and 1990s, each case presents an exception. During the second half of the 1980s, Peru's army halted its counterinsurgency work, and Ecuador's army did not defend the northern border in the face of violent attacks by Colombian insurgents. In this analysis, I explain these exceptions by arguing that, above interests in performing legitimate, professional, lucrative missions, the armies have prioritized predictability for their patrols. Within each army's sovereignty mission, a contradiction materialized that significantly reduced predictability for the work of patrol leaders on the ground, leading both armies to neglect the mission.

Peru: Contradiction through Mission Constraint

The Peruvian army disobeyed government orders to conduct counterinsurgency during the García administration, notwithstanding a high insurgent threat. Military personnel in emergency zones remained in their barracks despite guerrilla attacks on self-defense committees (*comités de autodefensa*, CADs) and on government officials carrying out economic development projects (del Pino 1996, 149; McClintock 2005, 71–72). Peruvian security expert Enrique Obando (1998, 391) describes a 1988 case in the central highland province of Tocache, San Martín, as "the most pathetic example" of this military behavior. "The country listened by radio and television" to the Tocache police chief's pleas for help, which continued for eight hours. The guerrillas destroyed the detachment and killed the police personnel, including the chief. Throughout the crisis, all military units within a fifty-kilometer radius refused to help, claiming that they could not act without written orders to do so, that bad weather made travel by helicopter impossible, and that they were afraid of being ambushed by guerrillas.[32] The army's refusal to act allowed Sendero to grow in strength. For instance, insurgent attacks rose from 2,050 in 1985 to 2,489 in 1987 (Tapia 1997, 40).

Decreased Army Autonomy and Paralysis

To explain the Peruvian army's paralysis in Sendero Zones, we can look to the government's human rights policy. The García administration assigned the army to counterinsurgency while also reducing the army's autonomy, holding army personnel accountable for human rights abuses. On taking office, García denounced the human rights abuses perpetrated by state security forces, after mass graves were found in Ayacucho and evidence attributed the massacres to the army. When the military joint command withheld details about the graves, García removed the head of the joint command, the general in charge of the military region based in Lima, and the political-military commander in Ayacucho. This was the first time that a civilian president in Peru purged the military of three top military leaders at one time (McClintock 1998, 143).

Army leaders viewed the orders to fight guerrillas while respecting human rights as contradictory. At the time, the only counterinsurgency method they knew involved harming (many) civilians as well as guerrillas: García had not proposed an alternative strategy that might reduce civilian casualties (Obando 1994, 111; Tapia 1997, 39–40), and the army had yet to develop its intelligence-driven approach to targeting insurgents. A renowned prison massacre illustrates how the government cracked down on army impunity without offering a new strategy, and how this approach created a contradiction in the army's counterinsurgency assignment, from the military's perspective. In June 1986, Sendero prisoners took control of three Lima prisons. García sent in the military and police to establish order, which they did in two of the prisons by killing more than two hundred rioting inmates convicted of terrorism. Subsequently, twenty-four police officers, as well as the army general overseeing the operation, faced legal charges for the acts. García's directive and his later move to punish the leaders of the operation made him a hypocrite in the eyes of military leaders (Tapia 1997, 40–41; McClintock 1998, 143; CVR 2003, 7:161–81). McClintock captures the military's frustration during this period.

> García's human rights initiative infuriated the military . . . The majority of officers believed that—at least in the Peruvian context of ill-paid, ill-equipped, and ill-trained soldiers without an effective intelligence capability against a clandestine, savage, disciplined foe—the war against the Shining Path could not be won without serious human rights violations. (McClintock 1998, 143)

The army's paralysis was in direct response to this "contradiction": "Because military officers were infuriated by [García's] human rights initiative, they refused to send soldiers out of the barracks" (McClintock 2005, 72).

The armed forces resented the García government not only for its new human rights policy but also, as mentioned in chapter 2, for decreasing military spending. Defense budget cuts translated into drastic reductions in officers' salaries, low morale, early retirements by officers, and desertions. Army units in insurgency zones lacked helicopters and were short on gasoline to operate the ones they did have, and they were in need of food, ammunition, and other equipment (Obando 1994, 111–13). The military, experiencing such shortages, certainly could not finance both the combat and economic prongs of the counterinsurgency strategy it had envisioned (Mauceri 1996, 139).

Increased Autonomy and the Resumption of Counterinsurgency

Just as limits to army autonomy created the perceived contradiction, increased autonomy subsequently resolved it, prompting the army to recommence counterinsurgency operations. Toward the end of his term, and facing economic crisis and public and military opposition, García relaxed his human rights policy. For example, when in May 1988 military personnel killed approximately thirty peasants in the Ayacucho village of Cayara, no officer was charged with or removed from the armed forces for committing abuses (McClintock 1998, 144). This renewed autonomy spurred the army to resume aggressive tactics (McClintock 1998, 143–44), and assassinations and disappearances carried out by state security forces rose from 274 in 1987 to 400 in 1988 and 663 in 1989 (figure 3.2).

The army's autonomy increased even further under Fujimori. A 1991 legislative decree expanded the scope of political-military commanders' power with respect to resources in emergency zones: commanders went from merely "coordinating" state funds, goods, services, and personnel to controlling them (Legislative Decree 749; Rospigliosi 2000, 116). Other legislative decrees from that year permitted the military to conduct counterinsurgency operations in universities, prisons, and non-emergency zones, and placed the CADs under military control.[33] Moreover, two 1995 amnesty laws protected state security forces from trial for any abuses committed since 1980 that were related to the internal conflict (Laws 26479 and 26492).

These reforms gave the army the autonomy that officers believed was critical for counterinsurgency operations, as noted by Rospigliosi (2000, 127) and by officers interviewed for this study. Chapter 4 analyzes more fully officers' attitudes

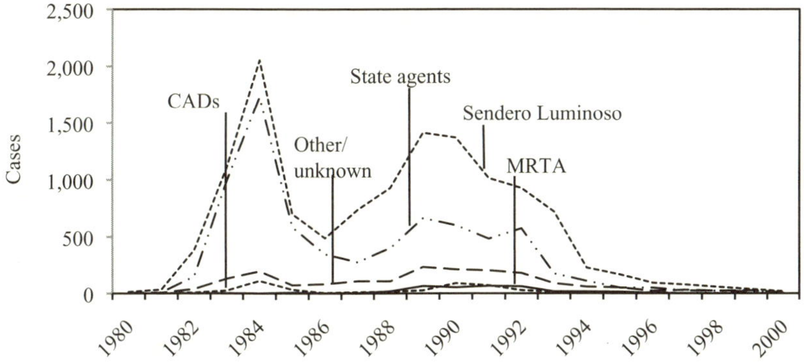

Figure 3.2. Reported Deaths and Disappearances in Peru's Internal Conflict by Responsible Actor, 1980–2000. CADs are self-defense committees (*comités de autodefensa*); MRTA, Movimiento Revolucionario Túpac Amaru. *Source:* Comisión de la Verdad y Reconciliación 2003, app. 3: 84

about the military's authority in Sendero zones under Fujimori; here it suffices to note that a common view among officers interviewed was that the legal protections of the 1990s decentralized the army's counterinsurgency actions and thus made them more effective. Officers of all ranks had a geographic domain for which they were responsible, and they could make decisions quickly, without orders or permission from above. Regarding his work during the late 1990s, a mid-ranking officer said, "I was . . . a political military commander and commander of the base. The way we did things was to act first, deal with the situation, kill who needed to be killed, and then report back to our superiors later."[34]

In addition to granting the army legal and political autonomy, in the positive economic climate, the Fujimori government expanded the military's resource base through several avenues, with the potential for improving the army's counterinsurgency capacity. Overall national defense spending rose from $642 million in 1990 to $783 million in 1992 (McClintock 1998, 133). The government funded the "civic action battalions" that distributed goods and propaganda to politically targeted, poor communities as a means to build and maintain political support for Fujimori. The government financed the army's program to arm CADs, a project that García had initiated toward the end of his administration: by the middle of 1993, the military had provided ten thousand rifles to the roughly three hundred thousand members of the CADs (McClintock 2005, 72).[35] The government also provided the armed forces with substantial monies through decrees (see chapter 2).

A final development pertaining to the army's counterinsurgency capacity in the 1990s was the expansion and complete centralization of Peru's National Intelligence Service (SIN) under the leadership of Vladimir Montesinos, a process analyzed by Rospigliosi (2000, 190–213) and also described by army officers during interviews. Although the expanded SIN spied on and manipulated the army (see chapter 2), Peruvian intelligence was, nevertheless, highly effective for counterinsurgency purposes, according to officers interviewed for this study.

Ecuador: Contradiction through Mission Overload

Ecuador's army also confronted a contradiction in its salient sovereignty mission, causing it to neglect that mission. However, that contradiction arose not through mission constraint but rather through mission overload. The army became overloaded starting in the mid-1980s, when a new external defense mission—northern border defense against Colombian insurgents—was added to the army's duty to defend the southern border. If the army was responsible for defending the northern border, it also had an interest in preventing an escalation of conflict with guerrilla fighters from Colombia, so as to remain effective in the south. The contradiction, then, was that the army was to defend the integrity of the northern border but without fighting those who threatened it. In response to this contradiction, the Ecuadorian army tolerated the insurgents and even engaged in commercial exchanges with them. In the words of a former army helicopter pilot who worked in the north in the mid-1980s, during that period there was "an open border."

The Fuerzas Armadas Revolucionarias de Colombia (FARC), a leftist insurgency, had formed in Colombia during the 1960s. After an initial period of slow expansion, the FARC grew rapidly from the late 1970s into the early 1980s, from ten to more than twenty military "fronts" by the early 1980s. Beginning in 1985, the insurgency grew more and moved into the coca-producing south, including the department of Putumayo, which borders Ecuador's northeastern Sucumbíos province (Echandía 1999; Vélez 2001, 161–62, 164–65).

After establishing a permanent presence in Putumayo, in 1986 and 1987 the FARC carried out a string of armed attacks on Ecuadorian army border posts in Sucumbíos—including the Coembí, El Conejo, and Santa Rosa detachments—and ambushed Ecuadorian army border patrols.[36] For example, FARC guerrillas killed one Ecuadorian army lieutenant while he was interfering with a contraband operation next to the river. These attacks were significant to the army, which honored survivors, such as Second Lieutenant Moreano. Moreano headed the Santa Rosa detachment when the FARC staged a nighttime mortar attack on the border post in early 1987. Because of a tunnel system that he had created, the army personnel under his command escaped the attack. He was decorated as a hero for his bravery and, as of 2009, had risen to the rank of colonel.

Although army leaders took the FARC threat in the north seriously, the army did not defend that border: at three moments during the 1980s and 1990s, the overload in the army's border responsibilities grew, as did the army's attempts to smooth relations with the FARC. The three cases suggest that minimal border defense in the north was the means by which the army protected troops on the ground from having to negotiate the contradictory order of defending the northern border from aggressive, armed incursions by the FARC while avoiding conflict with them. First, in response to the 1986–87 attacks, army leaders removed all army detachments from Sucumbíos's international border, specifically in response to the FARC attacks.[37] Interview subjects who spoke about this decision connected it to an ongoing army concern that conflict in the north would mean fewer resources to defend the southern, Ecuador-Peru border.

In a second incident, the army revealed its inattention to the border during a FARC attack on an Ecuadorian border patrol in 1993. Late that year and with U.S. Drug Enforcement Agency assistance, the Ecuadorian army and police conducted two joint antinarcotics river operations on the border. Between two hundred and three hundred personnel of the FARC's "Front 32" in Putumayo ambushed the second operation, in December, killing eleven members of the Ecuadorian security forces—seven from the police and four from the army—on the Putumayo River, which defines part of the Ecuador-Colombia border (Torres 2009, 179–83). Given that the army had already shied away from northern border defense, it should be no surprise that army contributions to the operation were minimal. In fact, the Ecuadorian patrol was dominated by police. The police sent forty-four police personnel—including several officers (a major, two captains, three lieutenants, and one second lieutenant)—on seven boats, whereas the army contributed only one boat, manned by eight army personnel, the most senior of which was merely a sergeant (Neira 1/6/94).

The army's reaction to the December 1993 "Putumayo Massacre" by the FARC was immediate. When members of Ecuador's national police went to Sucumbíos following the incident, to investigate the killings, they requested protection from an army unit in the north. The army officer speaking on behalf of the unit refused, explaining that the area was FARC territory.[38] The 1993 ambush led to a long period of peace between the FARC and the Ecuadorian army. The army halted assertive river patrols, and there were no further FARC attacks on the army. This peace was maintained by a delicate, mutual understanding that the army would not impede the FARC's free movement in the north, as long as armed FARC guerrillas did not cross into Ecuador.[39]

In spite of the army's limited border work, occasionally patrols did deal directly with the contradiction in the border mission. An officer interviewed described one such case in the late 1990s. His patrol discovered a training camp of the FARC's "Front 48" on the San Miguel River—which runs along part of the border—in Ecuadorian territory. Approximately 150 FARC combatants occupied the camp. The army patrol leader, hiding in the jungle, sought orders by radio from his commanding officer at the battalion base, who in turn contacted the military joint command in Quito. The joint command ordered the unit not to do anything. The officer concluded the story by saying, "You call [the joint command], and they tell you not to do your job. They don't want to get involved in the north."

A third moment in the trajectory of army-FARC ties occurred in the mid-1990s. Peru-Ecuador tensions escalated in 1994, causing the Ecuadorian army to move its forces south.[40] This shift meant that fewer army personnel, especially those experienced in leading patrols, were available to serve in other regions in the country. Tensions in the south lasted until the 1998 Ecuador-Peru peace agreement, including a "war scare" in August of that year (Mares 2001, 168). Therefore, it became even more critical for the army not to engage in armed conflict with the FARC in the north. In this setting, the bond between the two groups strengthened. Army detachments began selling provisions to the FARC, according to army officers and Ecuadorian journalists interviewed. Local commanders first sold food, clothing, and other basic goods,[41] then later sold weapons, drugs, and uniforms. These arrangements continued through the 1990s. FARC-army relations had another dimension, as well: as described by a journalist who specializes in the FARC's presence in northern Ecuador, FARC guerrillas came to serve as a kind of "extension" of the Ecuadorian military by helping to prevent incursions by the Peruvian military into the northeastern corner of Ecuador, where Colombia, Peru, and Ecuador meet.

ALTERNATIVE EXPLANATIONS

In contrast to the predictability framework presented here, hypotheses focused on military interests in resources, professionalism, and legitimacy cannot explain the mission neglect observed in Peru and Ecuador. In terms of resource maximization, the armies potentially could have generated more government funds by reliably and aggressively engaging Sendero (in Peru) and the FARC (in Ecuador).

The professionalism and legitimacy hypotheses would seem to explain army behavior only in Ecuador in the 1980s and 1990s. The Ecuadorian army was inattentive to northern border defense, but still, it did focus on another professional, legitimate mission: defense of the southern border against Peru's armed forces, a mission that presumably gave the army more public legitimacy than focusing on the growing northern border issue would have brought. As chapter 5 will show, however, the professionalism and legitimacy hypotheses cannot explain more recent behavior by the Ecuadorian army.

In Peru, these two perspectives provide even less traction. Neither the army's sudden cessation from counterinsurgency work during the García administration, nor its renewed intensity in counterinsurgency operations under Fujimori, can be explained by changed notions within the army of what constitutes a professional mission. As for legitimacy, if we focus on what was legitimate in the eyes of the Peruvian public, we do see that in the late 1980s, military personnel worried about their reputation within society, and in particular their poor human rights record. However, it is not credible that public opinion changed rapidly enough to explain the army's sudden onset of paralysis under the García administration or the army's renewed aggression toward the guerrillas under Fujimori. Furthermore, to the degree that the army was focused on its human rights record when it developed and implemented its new counterinsurgency strategy in the late 1980s, the army's attention was directed specifically toward local populations in insurgent zones, the ultimate aim being to gain the trust of the population in those zones not for its own sake but rather to achieve the army's counterinsurgency goals. If we treat executive policy as an indicator of what constitutes "legitimate" military behavior, the legitimacy hypothesis still founders: refraining from counterinsurgency altogether was hardly legitimate from the perspective of the government, which consistently ordered the army to perform assertive counterinsurgency (while respecting human rights).

In chapters 4 and 5, the analysis moves on to the period since 2000 and will again show the inadequacies of the resource maximization, legitimacy, and professionalism hypotheses for explaining the mission performance of the Peruvian and Ecuadorian armies. This close-up analysis will demonstrate the power of the alternative framework that focuses on predictability for army patrols—an approach that successfully explains mission neglect by both armies from the 1980s through the 2000s.

CHAPTER 4

Mission Constraint and Neglect of Counterinsurgency

Peru since 2000

Reminiscent of its behavior in the late 1980s, Peru's army underperformed its counterinsurgency mission during 2000–2007 in response to what officers thought was a government-created contradiction in that mission: the army had a mandate to eliminate the guerrillas but lacked the autonomy that army leaders deemed necessary to do the work. In this chapter I analyze the Peruvian army's mission performance in the first decade of the new century, in two parts. The first part describes the army's refusal to carry out counterinsurgency against the remnants of Sendero Luminoso and to conduct available policing duties, and demonstrates that this behavior cannot be explained by frameworks based on military interests in professionalism, legitimacy, and/or resources. The second part explains the army's paralysis, highlighting the importance of mission beliefs and predictability for army patrols.

STAYING IN THE BARRACKS

The Peruvian army refused to perform counterinsurgency in spite of an ongoing guerrilla threat, the highly professional nature of the mission, and the resources and public legitimacy that doing the work would have brought to the army.

Insecurity in Sendero Zones

Since the rapid decline of Sendero Luminoso and the elimination of the MRTA in the 1990s, Peru's remaining guerrilla (i.e., Sendero) zones have been pockets of the VRAE and the VAH. Insecurity in the two regions can be classified into two broad categories. First, armed Sendero guerrillas continue to exercise coercion. Second, in the regions, other types of security threats, including drug trafficking and protests by coca farmers (*cocaleros*), have also been common. Confronting this second category of activities, which have been exacerbated but generally not performed directly by armed insurgents, would be police work.

Coercion Exercised by Armed Guerrillas

Following Abimael Guzmán's capture in 1992, Sendero split into two branches, one armed and one purely political. The focus of this study is on the violent branch.[1] Sendero is much weaker than it was in the 1980s and 1990s in terms of its military prowess and violent tactics, but nevertheless, the group is still active.[2] Because of financing from the drug trade (as analyzed below) and other activities, including the extortion of loggers, Sendero's armed wing is well-off in terms of weapons, communications equipment, uniforms, and other items used in its operations (*El Comercio* [Lima] 8/28/01).[3]

As of 2000, the total annual number of incidents involving insurgents had declined from 1,918 in 1993 to 187 (figure 4.1). Since 2000, Sendero combatants

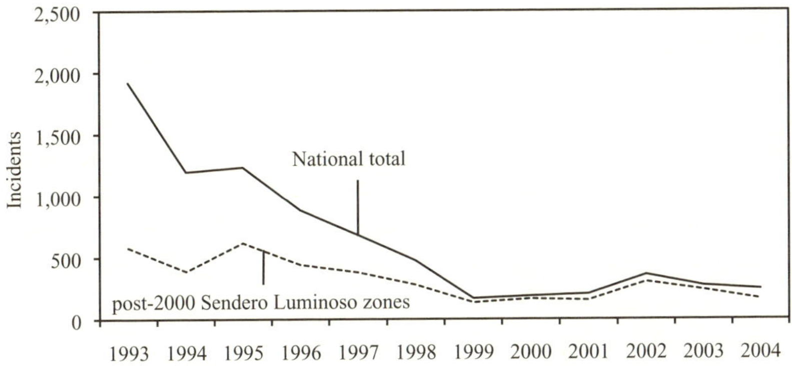

Figure 4.1. Insurgent Activity in Peru by Zone, 1993–2004. Sendero Luminoso zones include the departments of Apurímac, Ayacucho, Cusco, Huancavelica, Huánuco, Junín, and San Martín. *Source:* Instituto Nacional de Estadística e Informática 2005b, drawing on national police data

have numbered between approximately 200 and 450 (*El Comercio* [Lima] 3/3/03, 7/18/03, 12/25/05; McClintock 2005, 79; Balbi 1/2/06), down from 10,000 at the peak of the insurgency (see chapter 3).

We also observe a decline in the guerrilla threat when considering changes in Sendero's tactics. Peru's state security forces divide guerrilla incidents into four categories. A first category is sabotage of infrastructure, extremely common during the 1980s and into the 1990s but almost nonexistent since 2000. A second is intimidation and kidnapping. As an example, in San Juan de Ubiriqui (near Satipo, Junín) in August 2001, hooded, armed Sendero members (*senderistas*) forced the lieutenant governor and twenty other community members to gather on the town's athletic field. The combatants told the political official that they did not want a state authority in the town. The lieutenant governor resigned the next day out of fear (Ramírez 9/2/01). Perhaps the most internationally well-known kidnapping incident occurred in June 2003, in the district of Anco (in La Mar, Ayacucho). Sixty-two *senderistas* kidnapped seventy-one employees of Techint, an Argentine company that was constructing the private Camisea natural-gas line that runs from Peru's eastern jungle to the coastal city of Pisco (*El Comercio* [Lima] 6/10/03; Coordinadora Nacional de Derechos Humanos [CNDDHH] 2004a, 122).

Sendero's third type of insurgent activity is armed attacks, which mainly have been on state security forces. For example, in August 2001, a guerrilla column killed four police personnel in the Junín jungle (*El Comercio* [Lima] 8/9/01). In July 2003, Sendero ambushed an army patrol in El Maizal (in Cusco), killing five army personnel and two CAD guides (*El Comercio* [Lima] 7/18/03). The National Coordinator of Human Rights (CNDDHH) describes the following incident as the "gravest" terrorist act of 2004. On June 3, armed insurgents attacked a mobile police unit near the district of Aguaytía, in the province of Padre Abad (in Huánuco), as well as two vehicles with sixteen navy personnel that happened to be in the area at the time. In the confrontation, one policeman died, and another policeman and two navy officers were wounded (CNDDHH 2004b, 112). One well-publicized case occurred in Lima on March 20, 2002, immediately prior to a planned visit by U.S. President George W. Bush. Sendero guerrillas planted car bombs that exploded two cars in front of the U.S. embassy, killing nine people and injuring thirty others (CNDDHH 2003, 90).

The fourth kind of insurgent activity is "agitation/propaganda"—that is, the distribution of ideological messages and/or materials. For instance, from late October into December 2005, forty heavily armed *senderistas* visited towns in the south of the VRAE, announced that they would not kill the townspeople, asked them to join Sendero's ideological struggle, and encouraged them to grow coca, offering them protection from the police if they did so (*El Comercio* [Lima] 12/4/05b).

Since 2000, Sendero has moved toward a less brutal approach, relative to its tactics in the 1980s and 1990s. The insurgency now prefers the most benign tactic of agitation/propaganda over the other three methods, as shown in figure 4.2 and as observed by experts on Peruvian security themes. According to Sendero specialist Jaime Antezana in 2001, insurgents had begun assuring communities that the group would not kill them and even admitting that it had wrongly exercised violence against civilians in the past (*El Comercio* [Lima] 8/28/01). Similarly, human rights activist and Sendero expert Carlos Tapia said in a 2003 interview that in Ayacucho and Junín, the remaining spaces where Sendero carried out armed incursions, insurgents distributed propaganda, coerced CADs, and threatened to attack police and military personnel, and it did not threaten communities as it had in the 1980s (García Panta 5/17/03). Human rights reports have also observed the trend toward propaganda (e.g., CNDDHH 2003, 90). Given Sendero's changed tactics, it should be unsurprising that the number of fatalities during insurgent incidents dropped from 1,129 in 1993 to 428 in 1995

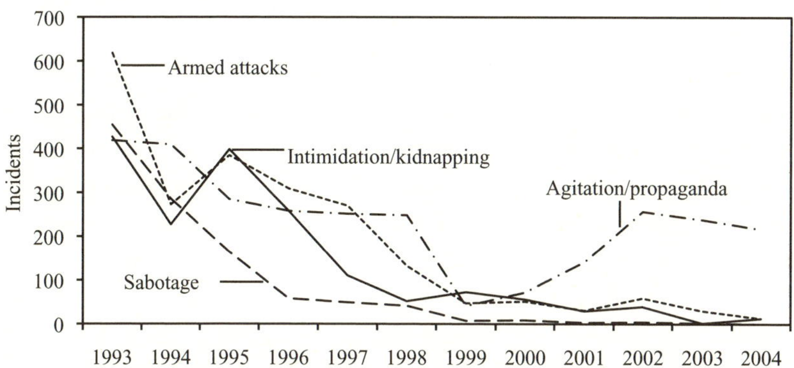

Figure 4.2. Insurgent Activity in Peru by Tactic, 1993–2004. To calculate annual number of insurgent incidents in each category, two data sources were combined: the highly reliable national police data on total annual incidents (not broken down by tactic) and proportions of incidents across the four categories, from military joint command data on incidents in the VRAE and VAH. The joint command proportions are believed to be accurate, based on a snapshot from 2001: for that year, the national police and joint command assigned roughly the same proportions to each type of incident (*El Comercio* [Lima] 5/23/03). *Sources:* Instituto Nacional de Estadística e Informática 2005b, drawing on national police data; Comando Conjunto de las Fuerzas Armadas del Perú 2006

and 54 in 1999. From 2000 through 2004, only 85 people were killed in insurgent incidents (Instituto Nacional de Estadística e Informática [INEI] 2005b, drawing on Peruvian national police data).

The Cocaine Trade

The Sendero threat in the VAH and the VRAE is intermingled with the cocaine trade, in which Peru is central, producing an average of 39 percent of global illicit coca annually between 1990 and 2006 (United Nations Office on Drugs and Crime 2007, 64). Cocaine production and trafficking are also common in Peru.[4] In 2002 alone, coca and cocaine in the country generated between $259 and $318 million, which is equivalent to between 2.5 and 3 percent of the national budget for that year (Cabieses 2005, 35; Ministerio de Economía y Finanzas, Perú, n.d.).

Links between drug production and trafficking, on the one hand, and Sendero, on the other—obvious during the 1980s (see chapter 3)—have persisted. Insurgents have continued to provide security for drug traffickers, as exemplified by the case of the VAH's Monzón Valley, a valley of activist *cocaleros*, organized to defend coca production. Throughout the Monzón, Sendero has ordered peasants to grow coca, guaranteeing them protection from the national police. In November 2004, Sendero's VAH commander "Artemio," along with a column of *senderistas* dressed in military-style clothing and wielding long-range weaponry, entered the town of Tazo Grande in Monzón, called the residents to a meeting, and ordered them to pay Sendero $5 for every twenty-five pounds of coca leaves harvested and $10 for each kilogram of basic cocaine paste produced. The payments amounted to a tax: Artemio said this money would fund Sendero security against police antinarcotics operations (*El Comercio* [Lima] 2/23/05b).

Sendero has worked with *cocaleros* not only by providing security but also by supporting their protests against state eradication measures. For instance, in the VAH in late 2004 and early 2005, the leader of the Confederación Nacional de Productores Agropecuarios de las Cuencas Cocaleras del Perú (CONPACCP)[5] began a campaign to pressure mayors to end their relationships with Programa Pro Descentralización (PRODES), a nongovernmental organization (NGO) focused on scaling back coca production. Sendero's involvement in the campaign included issuing death threats to mayors, who in response terminated their ties to PRODES (*El Comercio* [Lima] 2/23/05b).

During the late 2000s, Sendero went from merely protecting the cocaine trade to participating directly in the drug-production process, most notably in the

VRAE, and especially in Vizcatán, an area deep in the jungles of northern Ayacucho (in the VRAE) under the complete control of Sendero from the 1980s through 2008.[6] In a 2009 interview, an army general said, "We really saw [the shift] starting on August 31, [2008,] when we started the operations in Vizcatán. We saw that Sendero Luminoso had coca, drugs, everything piled in their camps. They weren't just providing security for drug traffickers. They were controlling and running the entire process."[7] Controlling the cocaine trade in the VRAE signifies considerable power on the part of Sendero, given how much cocaine now comes from that region. The VRAE has caught up to the VAH in coca production. In April 2009, the Peruvian magazine *Caretas* reported on a United Nations Office for Drug Control's estimate that there were sixteen thousand hectares of coca in the VRAE, yielding fifty-six thousand tons of coca per year, which is one-half of national production. In 2007, the VRAE produced 152 tons of cocaine, sufficient to satisfy the demands of one-half of all U.S. cocaine users or almost all of Europe's consumers (*Caretas* 4/30/09).

Popular Protest

A final security concern in Peru's remaining areas of insurgent activity has been popular protests, especially in the years that followed Fujimori's removal from office. The number of annual social protests in the country did not reach four hundred between 1994 and 1999, but annual incidents approached seven hundred in 2000 and 2001 and surpassed eight hundred in 2002 (Arce 2008, 42). A significant amount of this conflict has surrounded Peru's mining and hydrocarbon industries. According to the record of "social conflict" kept by the national ombudsman's office (Defensoría del Pueblo, or Defensoría), conflicts over natural resource issues made up 21 percent of the 110 conflicts reported in 2006, and 46 percent of the 57 new social conflicts in 2007 (Defensoría del Pueblo 2007, 243; 2008b, 232). During interviews, a leader in the national mining, oil, and energy association and a private security official said that social protest was by far the greatest security concern for companies operating in the extractive industries.

Though not the epicenter of resource extraction, Sendero zones have seen their share of mobilization against the practices of mining and hydrocarbon companies. Protests against the Camisea conglomerate are noteworthy, given that the gas pipeline passes through the VRAE. As of late 2005, protests had erupted over four pipeline breaks that had occurred since the pipeline's completion, apparently due to construction errors (*La República* 12/3/05). In Cusco in October 2005, thousands of peasants blocked roads and access to the airport and to Camisea's principal encampment (Servindi 10/17/05).

Another type of popular mobilization is *cocalero* actions, which have been powerful, independent of the Sendero coercion described above.[8] For example, in April 2003, thirty-two hundred *cocaleros* traversed the countryside, to the Palace of Justice in downtown Lima. Another major *cocalero* action was in late 2004 and early 2005, following eradication operations by the police counterdrug force Dirección Antidrogas (DIRANDRO) and the U.S. Drug Enforcement Agency in Carabaya province (not a Sendero zone). In protest, about one thousand *cocaleros* seized a hydroelectric center, leaving three people dead and nine wounded, and causing more than $1 million worth of damage to the plant and a mob attack on a local police station. As part of the 2004–5 CONPACCP initiative to cut ties between VAH mayors and PRODES (see above), seven hundred *cocaleros* marched through the city of Tingo María, in the department of Huánuco and in the VAH, demanding that the mayors comply (*El Comercio* [Lima] 2/23/05b). *Cocaleros* have been sufficiently powerful to force Peru's government to recognize their demands, such as through a 2001 supreme decree that created a formal *mesa de diálogo* ("dialogue table") between *cocaleros* and the government. At the subnational level, regional presidents of the major coca-growing departments of Cusco and Huánuco legalized coca cultivation in 2005.

Predictions of the Legitimacy, Professionalism, and Resource Maximization Hypotheses

Using this multifaceted insecurity in Sendero zones as a foundation, we can make some predictions about the Peruvian army's mission performance based on the legitimacy, professionalism, and resource maximization hypotheses. Later in the chapter, I show that these frameworks do not account for what the army has actually done.

Counterinsurgency as Legitimate

A legitimacy framework might predict that the army would vigorously fight Sendero so as to seek public approval. One indicator that counterinsurgency is considered a legitimate army mission is that the constitution and national security and defense laws permit the army to provide internal security. According to Peru's 1993 constitution, the main purpose of the military is "to guarantee the independence, sovereignty, and territorial integrity" of the country (art. 165). The armed forces also can constitutionally "assume control of internal order" during states of emergency (arts. 137, 165). Peru's 1987 Defense System Law assigns the military an ongoing place in internal security: "The State guarantees the Security of the Nation in its internal and external arenas, through National Defense" (Legislative Decree 435, art. 1). The 1987 law's newer versions (see the November 1991 Legislative Decree 743 and the March 2005 National Defense System Law, Law 28478) retained a role for the armed forces in both internal and external security. The 1987 Organic Law of the Defense Ministry (Legislative Decree 434) and the 2002 Ministry of Defense Law (Law 27860; see, in addition, the law's 2003 regulation, Supreme Decree 004-DE/SG) and its 2007 replacement (Law 29075) assign the military to internal security.

Beyond these legal structures, consternation within the country about Sendero also suggests the army could prove its legitimacy through counterinsurgency operations. Security experts, human rights leaders, communities in Sendero zones, and the larger Peruvian public have worried that the guerrillas might resume their violent tactics of the 1980s and 1990s (e.g., Bazán Coquis 8/20/01; Balbi 1/2/06), frequently positing that Sendero has employed its new, less brutal approach simply to gain support and eventually reactivate its armed struggle (e.g., CNDDHH 2004a, 122–23). In January 2006, Fernando Rospigliosi—expert on the Peruvian armed forces, journalist, and former interior minister—complained about what he characterized as state inattention to the insurgency threat in a statement to the press, in which he attributed the death of thirteen policemen in December 2005 to inaction on the part of the state.

> The terrorists of the Apurímac-Ene are in the middle of the jungle, but if nothing is done [to attack their bases] they begin to come out, like now . . . They have increased their radius of action and wounded several police personnel. If you don't act [to contain them], they move. It's obvious! (Balbi 1/2/06)

Another security specialist and former vice-minister of the interior, Carlos Basombrío, echoed this sentiment.

> The year 2005 should remind Peruvians that the horrors of the violence . . . continue to be present in our country, and we have not been capable of eradicating them . . . The problem is that the two armed columns that survive . . . are very active because the State has abandoned all effort to combat them in these zones. (Hidalgo Vega 12/28/05)

In terms of human rights activists, Carlos Tapia has supported military counterinsurgency that respects human rights (e.g., *El Comercio* [Lima] 10/23/05). In its annual reports, the CNDDHH, Peru's main national representative of the human rights community, maintains a section on "terrorist actions," in which it has denounced Sendero for continuing to commit crimes against international human rights law (CNDDHH 2001a, 2001b, 2003, 2004a, 2004b, 2007). The 2001 annual report observed that Sendero continued to enter towns, kill local officials and other individuals suspected of incriminating insurgents, kidnap young people to bring into its ranks, and attack military convoys for their weapons (CNDDHH 2001a, 184–87). The 2007 report criticized the Toledo government for not resolving the "potentially grave" problem of Sendero's "chronic" presence in certain jungle valleys (CNDDHH 2007, 185).

For their part, communities with exposure to Sendero have feared the insurgency and requested more state, including military, protection against it. In the province of Tocache (in San Martín), lieutenant governors of three towns (Alto Limón, Camote, and San Jacinto) abandoned their posts in 2001 because the army had not offered them protection since late 2000, which had made them feel unsafe (CNDDHH 2001b, 118). Following a Sendero attack in July 2003 that killed state security personnel and members of local CADs, the mayor of the Sivia district (in the Huanta province of Ayacucho) said that army presence was needed there (la Rosa 8/6/03). During December 2005—a month of unusually high levels of guerrilla activity—various political leaders in the VRAE demanded more army protection. For example, the mayor of Ccarhuarán, a town in Huanta, went to Ayacucho's departmental capital to request state security assistance (*El Comercio* [Lima] 12/28/05). Even the regional president of Ayacucho, Omar Quezada Martínez, who vocally opposed the idea of completely militarizing the zone, still supported coordinated actions by the army, police, and CADs to eliminate the insurgents (*El Comercio* [Lima] 12/29/05a).

The CADs, too, frequently have asked for more army security. Following a September 2004 incident in which Sendero tried to abduct fifty children for military training,[9] the leader of the Ayacucho CADs communicated the climate of fear in the VRAE and the need for support from the state: "SL [Sendero Luminoso] is a tremendous risk for us. We are afraid. In each town there are three or four terrorists that have been identified, that threaten the townspeople, and therefore no one reports what happens" (Potestá 10/2/04). In December 2005, the long-time leader of the CADs in the Apurimac River Valley made a plea for help.

> One shouldn't wait for another attack so that at the last minute the authorities confront Sendero. Right now I ask for some state guarantee because I am

> threatened . . . As much as [the insurgents] say that now they are peaceful and they are going to defend the coca leaf, the population doesn't believe it. They are the same bloodthirsty actors that continue clandestinely. (Salazar 12/8/05)

Peruvians outside Sendero zones, too, have been anxious about guerrilla violence. This concern is even present in the capital city of Lima, which has never been a Sendero stronghold. In a survey conducted seven times between October 2002 and April 2005 in the greater Lima Metropolitan area, when asked to identify which of three types of violence was of most concern—that caused by crime, Sendero, or popular protest—between 21 and 43 percent of respondents named Sendero (Basombrío Iglesias 2005, 18, using Imasen survey data).

Officers have been aware that counterinsurgency work could earn the army public legitimacy. In statements made to the press, officers often assured the public that the army was taking seriously its counterinsurgency work. When in 2002 it was reported that Sendero insurgents had traveled from the jungle of Satipo (in Junín) to Huancavelica, the army claimed that personnel from two army units stationed in Junín (in Huancayo and Jauja) were ready to provide backup for the three counterinsurgency bases in the areas in question (*El Comercio* [Lima] 5/9/02). In a newspaper interview in February 2005, the army commander of the central military region—the jurisdiction of which extended into Sendero zones—took for granted the army's responsibility to protect citizens from the guerrillas when he said that "the military counterinsurgency bases that we have installed in the jungle and that are operating are . . . able to guarantee the tranquility and security of the population and communities" (Mayo Filio 2/6/05). Similarly, in May 2005, the army general in charge of the infantry brigade in Junín said that the counterinsurgency bases in the central jungle were being provided armaments and that intelligence patrols were constant (*permanentes*). When asked whether the army forces in the area had a counterinsurgency plan there, the general responded, "We are working toward something big. Therefore we are giving equipment and armaments to all of the central jungle military bases" (Mayo Filio 5/10/05).

Despite ample evidence that it is highly legitimate for the army to fight Sendero, there is an important, alternative view. Given the Peruvian army's renowned history of massive human rights abuses during the 1980s and 1990s, it may be that the army would be more likely to gain legitimacy in the post-2000 period by refraining from counterinsurgency, to avoid causing more damage to its reputation. I consider this alternative perspective on public legitimacy in the second part of the chapter, following a more thorough account of the human rights question. For now, it suffices to emphasize that underperforming counterinsurgency was not an obvious avenue to obtain public legitimacy, given that even Peruvian human rights activists, and communities in the heart of insurgency areas that knew firsthand the violence of internal conflict, wanted the army to fight Sendero.

Counterinsurgency as Lucrative

Peru's civilian government consistently has pushed the army toward counterinsurgency more than any other mission, telling us that the mission is not only highly legitimate but also lucrative. The resource maximization hypothesis thus predicts that the army would engage in combat with Sendero so as to obtain more government resources. We might expect the army to be particularly focused on increasing its budget, considering recent defense spending cuts and deficient equipment in the aftermath of the Fujimori government (see chapter 2).

As a caveat to this analysis of Peruvian government policy, I should note that Peru's armed forces have influenced security policy, making it difficult to separate entirely government security policy from military interests. As Rospigliosi said of counterinsurgency, "What is certain is that the Armed Forces do not obey Government orders. There is no civilian control over them. The Armed Forces negotiate with the Government and then do what they want" (Balbi 1/2/06). In fact, the head of the army, rather than the defense minister, has served as the major point person in questions of counterinsurgency. To illustrate this dynamic, we can look to a case described by a retired high-ranking interior ministry official, about former interior minister Gino Costa. When Costa took his post as interior minister, he wanted to develop a more assertive counterinsurgency strategy at the national level. To address the issue, Costa approached the defense minister—Aurelio Loret de Mola, a civilian with no military service background—who, rather than discussing the matter with Costa directly, told him to confer with the head of the army, General Roberto Chiabra.

Keeping in mind the challenge of distinguishing between government security policy and army interests, from what we can observe, Peru's government has wanted the army to focus on its counterinsurgency mission. As codified in Peru's white book, national security policy assigns to the army a responsibility to fight internal threats and, specifically, insurgents (Ministerio de Defensa Nacional, Perú 2005, 101, 107). Moreover, parts of the VRAE have been under a constant state of emergency, with the military in charge of security, for much of the period since 2000. By the end of his administration, Fujimori had lifted all of the emergency decrees, throughout the country, that had been in place for counterinsurgency purposes. This scenario changed in June 2003, when Toledo ended a national state of emergency—called because of countrywide strikes—but left it in place in certain provinces and districts in the VRAE, because of the Sendero threat (Supreme Decree 062-2003-PCM). From that point on, a constant state of emergency has been in place in that region, renewed through decrees that assign the army control of security there. In late 2005, the government also declared a state of emergency in the VAH, placing the national police in control of security there, but assigning the armed forces, as well, a clear counterinsurgency role in the valley (Supreme Decree 098-2005-PCM). That emergency zone, too, has remained in place by successive decrees.

Government support for the army's counterinsurgency mission has been so strong that the congress has encouraged the work outside emergency zones. Under Fujimori, the 1992 Law 25410 granted the armed forces the authority to carry out counterinsurgency operations for up to eight days outside these zones. After Fujimori left office, military leaders claimed that an eight-day interval was insufficient for an effective operation. In response, in May 2004, the national congress passed Law 28222, which extended the period to thirty days to encourage more intensive counterinsurgency.[10]

Peru's government has condoned the military's counterinsurgency mission through less formal channels, as well, such as in public statements. Interior minister Gino Costa signaled the government's support for the mission when he emphasized in a newspaper interview that army counterinsurgency bases in critical areas that had previously been closed ("deactivated") were being reopened (*El Comercio* [Lima] 8/8/02). Similarly, immediately following a Sendero attempt to ambush a patrol of twenty army personnel in Ayacucho in 2003, Vice President Raúl Diez Canseco asserted the importance of military force for combating Sendero: "There is a whole [government] strategy to organize the counterinsurgency bases and increase the presence of the armed forces and the police in that zone in order to eliminate those elements that certainly are considered terrorists" (*El Comercio* [Lima] 7/18/03). In a 2004 interview after a counterinsurgency base was closed and two others were relocated, the defense minister (and retired army general) Roberto Chiabra "assured" the public that counterinsurgency bases would continue to be an important part of the fight against the remaining "terrorism" (Cordero 7/6/04). My interview data reinforce these public statements that attest to ongoing government support for military counterinsurgency efforts:

high-level current and retired officials in the defense and interior ministries and in police leadership said that during meetings with military (including army) leaders in Lima, they had asked the military on several occasions to augment its counterinsurgency work.

As I will show later in this chapter, were the Peruvian army driven mainly by interests in maximizing its budget, it would be required to carry out assertive counterinsurgency and not merely give the mission lip service, because state spending on the army seems to be somewhat elastic in relation to the intensity of army counterinsurgency. The analysis below will show the following: First, politicians have openly debated whether or not to invest in more counterinsurgency, specifically on the basis of whether the military would follow through with patrols. Second, when, during periods of major guerrilla violence, state investments have been made in counterinsurgency in addition to the annual national budget, those monies have gone to both the police and the military. A budget-maximizing army would certainly wish to capture as much of those additional funds as possible. Third, the national police force has expanded its counterinsurgency activities, potentially encroaching on the army's domain and threatening its future budget share.

Counterinsurgency has also been an obvious way for the Peruvian army to obtain resources from beyond the state, and in particular, U.S. monies. The U.S. government channels security support to the Peruvian armed forces through the Southern Command, a U.S. joint military structure that interacts with the armed forces of Central and South America. The two primary foci of the U.S. Southern Command in Peru have been, first, counterterrorism, and second, antinarcotics.[11] Specifically, since 2000, Southern Command representatives in Peru (referred to by Peruvian security experts and U.S. officials in Peru as the "military group") have directed military assistance toward the Peru-Colombia border to prevent Colombian insurgents from crossing into Peru and using the country for logistical and resource support, and has encouraged the Peruvian army to conduct counterinsurgency in Sendero zones, as a means of helping the Peruvian national police's antinarcotics operations.

The connection between counterinsurgency and attracting resources from both the Peruvian government and the United States was not lost on the Peruvian army. The military has requested Peruvian state money to install more counterinsurgency bases (see below). Officers interviewed for this study, who complained frequently and at length that the defense budget was too small, regularly described the military budget as moving in parallel with Peruvian government concerns about insurgency in the country. Concretely, many officers said that the government was not adequately alarmed about the Sendero threat, and therefore government spending on the army for counterinsurgency was insufficient. As for U.S. resources, in its communications with the U.S. military group, Peru's military joint command regularly appealed for U.S. assistance by drawing connections between the Peruvian military's counterinsurgency work and antinarcotics.[12]

Counterinsurgency as Professional

Like the resource maximization and public legitimacy hypotheses, a framework focused on the idea that militaries are drawn to professional missions also predicts that Peru's army would confront Sendero forcefully. It would be difficult to overstate the extent to which interviewed officers valued counterinsurgency as being professional. They thought counterinsurgency was a basic function for which the army was responsible, and they were very proud of the mission.

When officers volunteered explanations for why the army carried out counterinsurgency work (table 4.1), they most frequently gave a "mission belief" explanation—that is, stating matter-of-factly that the size or character of the threat necessitated the work, or that the army did the work to maintain security and peace in Sendero zones, to provide military presence, to gather intelligence, to make communities feel secure, or simply because the work was the army's responsibility. For example, an active-duty senior officer said, "If insurgents are involved, it is the army's role to deal with it." A junior officer said, "The army is prepared for conventional war and nonconventional war. Under the nonconventional [category], if there is an attack on the population, then we need to deal with it." Of the officers who referred to either the size or the character of the threat, or to police shortcomings in responding to that threat, all believed the army should continue the work, and only one expressed anything that could be characterized as bitterness about it.[13] Among the officers who said that government mandates or requests—at the central, regional, or local levels—were a reason for counterinsurgency activities, all complained that the government kept the army from doing *more* counterinsurgency or from doing it more effectively, an attitude described at length in the second part of this chapter. The mission's high salience for officers when research was conducted for this study made counterinsurgency that much more professional as a current mission. Fifty-three officers were asked to identify the biggest security threats for Peru, and officers' first three responses were tallied. Thirty-seven officers mentioned insurgency among their first three

Table 4.1. Officers' Explanations for Peruvian Army's Counterinsurgency Work (in no. of mentions)

Explanation	44 officers
Mission belief*	59 (69%)
Insufficient police capacity	14 (16%)
Government mandate or request	10 (12%)
Other	3 (3%)
Total mentions	86 (100%)

*"Mission belief" explanation: that counterinsurgency was the army's duty; that the size or character of the threat necessitated the work; and/or that the army performed the work to achieve "pacification," collect intelligence, establish army presence, or support CADs.

responses, and 39 of the total of 153 mentions—25 percent—were about the insurgent threat.[14]

A qualitative analysis of interview results makes plain that officers of all ranks were very proud of their past counterinsurgency work. Many said that the army had saved the country from insurgency in the 1980s and 1990s and referred to bravery and deaths among army personnel during combat. A senior officer revealed great pride in his professional work in counterinsurgency when he said that "we killed the terrorists . . . As a professional, as a commando, it was my best moment. I was head of a commando battalion . . . We had commandos from all over help with the operations." A junior cavalry officer who had served in the army during the 1990s described at length how he had participated in counterinsurgency operations in spite of physical discomforts such as patrolling on foot across difficult terrain. He emphasized that, though he was of the cavalry branch of the army—which operates using tanks and specializes in external warfare against other national militaries—he still could patrol effectively: "Cavalry is not just tanks. We have tanks for conventional war. But with nonconventional war, I am a soldier like anyone else." Officers who did not fight Sendero during the height of the insurgency lamented that they had missed out on that "opportunity," including a mid-ranking officer who had been studying abroad in the 1980s. Similarly, a junior officer who had served in the central department of San Martín said that "unfortunately" his unit "did not have the honor" of participating in counterinsurgency operations.

Moving beyond these interview results, we see that army leaders in their actions have recognized the counterinsurgency mission as a professional responsibility. For example, when on March 3, 2001, an army patrol in charge of the Pichari zone in Cusco captured Sendero leader Alipio, it spurred the head of the second infantry division in Ayacucho to travel there to acknowledge the capture (*El Comercio* [Lima] 3/4/01).

IN SUM, HYPOTHESES BASED ON LEGITIMACY, resources, and professionalism predict that the Peruvian army would engage in counterinsurgency: the public wants the army to be more involved in counterinsurgency; the army has wanted resources, which come with the mission; and counterinsurgency is a highly professional mission. With regard to policing, in contrast, a purely professionalism-based perspective would anticipate that the army would resist unprofessional, police work under any circumstances; whereas the legitimacy and resource maximization frameworks lead us to think that, should anything prevent the army from fighting Sendero, then, in place of this counterinsurgency work, the army would focus on its assigned police work to demonstrate its relevance as a security service provider, thereby attracting resources and/or legitimacy.

Army Inaction

Although it might seem overdetermined that the Peruvian army would aggressively fight the guerrillas, in fact we see just the opposite: the army has neglected counterinsurgency. Also somewhat surprising is that in place of that mission, the army has not taken on, in any major way, police work made available to it by the government. Instead, the army has largely remained in the barracks.

Neglect of Counterinsurgency

The most striking facet of the Peruvian army's mission performance since 2000 is its minimal counterinsurgency efforts through 2007. In terms of its equipment, the army passed up the opportunity to improve its decrepit fleet of helicopters, though, according to several officers interviewed, helicopters are vital for counterinsurgency. The army's 2005–8 plan for spending its share of the Camisea defense fund (discussed in chapter 2) prioritized the acquisition of modern antitank systems, the refurbishing of tanks, and the repair of antiaircraft artillery (Páez 1/2/06), investments that would strengthen the army's external warfare capacity but be of little use in counterinsurgency.[15]

Centrally planned operations directed by army leadership in Lima or by regional army commanders—operations that were common in the 1980s and 1990s—were virtually nonexistent from 2000 through 2007.[16] Furthermore, by under-manning the counterinsurgency bases, the army limited their effectiveness. The approximate number of army personnel that worked in and near insurgency zones—including those on counterinsurgency bases and on the bigger brigade and battalion bases—dropped from thirty-one thousand in 1991 to ten thousand in 1996 and between three and four thousand by early 2006.[17] During the 1980s and 1990s, there were typically between sixty and eighty men on any given base.[18] This number facilitated the multi-day patrols that proved most successful in encountering Sendero columns: one group of men patrolled for days at a time so as to cover more terrain, far from the base, where insurgents were more likely to operate, while back at the base another group slept and a third group stood watch, as explained by two junior officers who had worked in emergency zones in the 1990s. After 2000 this system was no longer feasible, because only approximately forty men now manned each base.[19]

In terms of the bases' performance, even taking into account personnel limitations, we still observe inattentiveness to counterinsurgency. The tasks of the patrols generally have been limited to collecting intelligence in communities and leading occasional training sessions with CADs.[20] In areas frequented by Sendero, in 2000–2007 it was not uncommon for CADs to report Sendero activities to the nearby army base. According to two mid-ranking officers, in separate interviews, rather than responding with patrols to find the guerrillas, officers instead routinely directed community members to the police, even when the army base had the capacity to provide the requested security. Bases also denied requests by local units of the national police for help against insurgents.[21] One such case occurred in December 2005 in Ayacucho, shortly before a Sendero column ambushed a police transport operation, as told by a police intelligence official. Weeks earlier, Sendero presence in the area had intensified, and police intelligence had asked the local army brigade in Ayacucho ("Los Cabitos") for help. In response, the brigade commander refused to send out patrols, claiming simply that it was not his problem. The president of the VRAE's CADs and a local leader of the committees had also informed the defense minister and local army commander of Sendero presence in the area (*La República* 12/7/05b, 12/15/05b), but the police, not the armed forces, carried out all significant follow-up operations.[22]

In fact, one measure of the army's idleness in Sendero zones is its poor counterinsurgency performance relative to that of the national police. Given the army's paralysis, the national police increased its participation in counterinsurgency considerably. In the words of an interview subject who had served as a high-level interior ministry official during the period in question, "We decided that we would do counterinsurgency. We would do it alone, since the army wouldn't do its job." Examples of the national police's initiative relative to that of the army abound. From October 2002 through November 2004, it was the national police, independent of the army, that conducted the well-publicized "Tormenta" operations to reestablish state control of an area along the Ene River in the VRAE, where Sendero has held captive members of the Asháninka indigenous group and trained them for guerrilla actions.[23]

The police again demonstrated their commitment to counterinsurgency during the highly violent month of December 2005.[24] Four Sendero attacks that month killed thirteen policemen and wounded other police personnel in the VAH and VRAE. In response to the attacks, hundreds of additional police special forces, antinarcotics, and counterterrorism personnel were deployed to both regions. In contrast to the police's aggressive response to the attacks, the army was timid, described as remaining "at the margin" of response efforts (Arcaya and Navarro 12/25/05). Army assistance involved only patrols by the few units already stationed there, and for one police operation, the loan of a helicopter. Local and regional army commanders waited for orders from their superiors in Lima before taking action[25]—orders that, in fact, were not required in insurgency zones, by either police or military rules, as explained by police and army officers in interviews. The army did not even respond aggressively when insurgents targeted army personnel that month.[26]

When the army and police were given additional resources to finance counterinsurgency operations, the army's use of the funds paled in comparison to police action. The government released the monies to the military and police in January 2006, specifically to support counterinsurgency in the VRAE and VAH, distributed as follows: the defense ministry received 25 million *soles* (more than $8 million) and the interior ministry received 32.3 million *soles* (nearly $9.5 million).[27] These resources were significant, if we consider that setting up a counterinsurgency base cost only approximately 150,000 *soles* (less than $45,000) (Cordero 7/6/04). The police's larger share of the additional funds relative to the armed forces cannot account for the variation across the two institutions in their counterinsurgency performance, in terms of both effort and degree of success. The military's monies went toward reactivating twelve army counterinsurgency bases in the VRAE. Like the army's existing bases, the new ones were manned by few men and did little in terms of patrols, according to high-level army officers and interior ministry officials. Consistent with this observation, for the period after the new bases were added, no major army operations or insurgent captures were reported by the press or by interview subjects. In contrast, the national police used their share of the funds to create a counterinsurgency battalion in the VAH that captured members of the Sendero leadership within weeks of the unit's formation (*El Comercio* [Lima] 1/5/06c, 1/18/06; *La República* 1/19/06; CNDDHH 2007, 187–88).

The army's neglect of counterinsurgency did not go unnoticed. For instance, in January 2006, former interior minister Rospigliosi told the press that he had thought that installing more military bases would facilitate eliminating Sendero, but he had since changed his mind, because the armed forces refused both to assign sufficient men to the bases and to conduct effective operations: "The military asks for 200,000 *soles* [$58,000] to install one base. But if they don't patrol, it's not worth it" (Balbi 1/2/06).[28] Similarly, former interior minister Basombrío highlighted to the press what he saw as misallocation of military funds to external defense equipment, when counterinsurgency should have received priority.

> The argument is always that there is no budget . . . The armed forces have if not the largest state budget, the second largest . . . I ask: wasn't it more important, above [purchasing Italian ships for the navy[29]], to strengthen the counterinsurgency bases and confront adequately these two Sendero columns? Of course the ships are important, but one must choose. If we can't free our territory from the armed action of one band of criminals . . . how can we defend our country from a bigger threat. (Hidalgo Vega 12/28/05)

During my interviews, retired high-level officials in the national police and interior ministry, and active-duty police officers, were also acutely aware of and frustrated by the army's inaction.

Rejection of Police Work

In place of counterinsurgency, the Peruvian army has shied away from policing. This behavior runs counter to the expectation that a military not occupied by sovereignty work would reach out for, or at least accept, police work as a means of demonstrating its relevance for society (i.e., acquiring public legitimacy) and/or justifying defense spending. The professionalism hypothesis does better here, as it predicts that the army would resist police work as being unprofessional. However, this hypothesis does not explain the Peruvian army's prior police work (or the Ecuadorian army's ongoing policing; see chapters 3 and 5).

Minimal Protest Control, Prevention of Land Seizures, and Contraband Interdiction. Peru's army has responded only minimally when called upon to control protests, impede contraband operations, or prevent land seizures. When the army has participated in these missions, which has been infrequently, it has avoided direct contact with civilian perpetrators—which the police, instead, have confronted. Army participation in these missions has not been institutionalized, in that local and regional army commanders have tended to refuse to partake in operations without first receiving specific orders to the contrary. Sometimes officers have required directives from generals in Lima—who themselves, at times, have refused to authorize the work without direct orders from the executive. According to officers I interviewed, army training regimens have not included preparation for these missions, nor do bases have the equipment required for police work. For instance, the brigade assigned to control the protests in Puno in 2003 (discussed below) lacked both teargas and riot-control shields (Defensoría del Pueblo 2003, 42).[30]

Generally speaking, prior to managing protests, army commanders have required an emergency decree, and even then have resisted the work—behavior exhibited during the two main occasions on which the Toledo administration ordered the army to control popular protests. First, during massive demonstrations in June 2002 against the privatization of electricity in the city of Arequipa, Toledo declared a state of emergency that put the army in charge of security in that city.[31] The regional army commander in Arequipa, General Gómez de la Torre, personally toured the battalion bases under his jurisdiction, before soldiers left the barracks, to order all troops not to fire their weapons under any circumstances. An interview subject for this study who served as a high-level interior ministry official during the uprisings said the army was less aggressive toward the protesters than Toledo had ordered. One year later, Gómez de la Torre was retired for his disobedience, according to a former senior officer intimately involved in the Arequipa events, and also as understood by the several senior army officers who discussed the general's retirement.[32]

In a second incident, Toledo commanded the army to control demonstrations throughout the country in May 2003. The army came into direct contact with protesters in the southern city of Puno. Student protesters surrounded a small army patrol, and a soldier in the patrol shot and killed one of the students (*El Comercio* [Lima] 5/28/03; *La República* 5/30/03). Even in that case, the army resisted direct contact with the protesters for longer than we might expect. In an interview, a civilian who had been a high-level defense official at the time of the protests said that, once facing the protesters, the army continued exercising restraint; based on his viewing of a video recording of the Puno incident, he said that the army patrol had followed regulations and directives regarding the army's rules of engagement, in that the soldiers first had fired warning shots in the air before turning their weapons on the protesters.

The army's resistance to protest control has been so strong that, on several occasions, the government did not order the army to control protests, due to preemptive military pushback. For example, in 2004 there was the potential for more protest control by the army in the department of Puno, this time in the town of Ilave. A mob of townspeople had lynched the mayor, because of his corrupt activities. Five individuals were arrested for their roles in the mayor's death, and in response to the arrests, the town exploded in antigovernment protests (Tobar 5/20/04). Army leaders made clear that to do the work of protest control, the army would require a direct, formal order from Toledo, which never materialized.[33] A former interior ministry official gave another example of the army obstructing orders that could bring it into protest control. In that instance, the army demanded an excessive amount of money to control a *cocalero* protest in Huánuco, as a means of avoiding being assigned the task. When the president learned of the amount, he decided against sending in the army. With regard to the army's more general refusal to control protests, the former official said that the military would give the government varying excuses for why it could not control protests, such as its need to focus on a specific part of the country where there was a serious terrorist threat.

This minimal participation during popular mobilizations has been true even in the VAH and VRAE, where the army has had an ongoing mandate to operate. In Tingo María during some of the biggest *cocalero* protests, which occurred between one and three times each year in 2002 and 2003, an army general at the brigade level or an officer higher in the army hierarchy decided whether or not to provide army assistance, and then allowed it only in coordination with the police and local politicians.[34] A senior army officer said that the army's work in those cases consisted of guarding public installations and roads, with the intent to provide security while avoiding contact with demonstrators.[35] These activities were minor relative to the work of the national police and rarely made the national news.[36] An official in the Defensoría del Pueblo's Tingo María office corroborated the army officer's claim that there was no contact between protesters and the army during those operations, explaining that the army's objective was not to control protests but, rather, to protect army base infrastructure when terrorists infiltrated the protests. In fact, as revealed in interviews, army policing during *cocalero* protests has been so minimal that it has gone completely unnoticed by other actors with firsthand knowledge of the protests, including interior ministry officials and representatives of the International Committee of the Red Cross (ICRC).

The army's work during protests in the VRAE has been even less evident than in Tingo María. One vivid example of just how much the army has resisted protest control is a case during a July 2004 protest in the city of Ayacucho. Protestors set fire to municipal and regional government buildings lining the city's main plaza. Police forces proved unable to contain the crowds, and the provincial president and the head of the police unit independently requested army backup from the general in charge of the Los Cabitos brigade located in the city. Insisting that he could not help without a written order from a superior officer, the general telephoned his commanding officer and left a message. As the general did not receive a response, he did nothing to help control the protests.[37]

In a different policing arena, the army has uprooted and prevented the establishment of land-squatter settlements, but again we observe considerable restraint on the part of army personnel. Legal backing for the mission is Law 27308 (2000), which assigns the military to help the agricultural ministry's enforcement agency (Instituto Nacional de Recursos Naturales, INRENA) to protect natural resources in parks, which for a senior officer specializing in laws and directives pertaining to army missions, and to INRENA officials, included removing land squatters from protected land.[38] Those interview subjects also said that army regulations did not permit the army to participate in any operations with INRENA that might lead to direct army conflict with civilians. One example of the army's participation in squatter removal is its actions between February and November 2005 in the protected Pómac forest, in the Lambayeque department, to uproot a settlement that had been there since 2001. The army installed a post that housed between fifty and a hundred troops who carried out patrols. This operation was coordinated with INRENA at the level of the army region.[39] At times, the army has prevented people from creating squatter settlements independent of INRENA. A low-ranking army officer described one such case. In 2003 a brigade general sent him and others to Manchay, a city near Lima, to deal with an anticipated land seizure of a military-owned land parcel. Police units were called to assist, and in the end it was the police, not the army, that directly confronted the would-be squatters.[40]

The army seems to have intervened more aggressively in land squatting in Sendero zones. The Ayacucho office of the Defensoría investigated a July 2005 incident in which army personnel from the Los Cabitos brigade removed a group of peasants that had settled on land near Nobillo, a protected forest eight hours from the city of Ayacucho. According to the Huamanga Defensoría's files, acting on intelligence that there were terrorists among the settlers, the army entered the area at night to clear it of squatters. During the operation, army personnel killed one peasant and badly wounded a second.

More than other policing missions, the army has intercepted contraband in a context in which participants in major contraband operations (*contrabandistas*) have wielded heavy armaments, making police and military assistance necessary for effective interdiction.[41] However, in this arena, too, the army has underperformed the work relative to what is possible, given the mission's legal backing and the financial compensation available for the work. The army's assignment to intercept contraband dates to December 2001, when the national congress created a commission to fight contraband and granted the defense ministry a place on that commission (Law 27595). In 2003 the armed forces were assigned to help with contraband interdiction operations when customs officials and/or police required assistance (Law 28008).[42] The customs agency has been prepared to fund all aspects of operations to intercept contraband, including the army's expenses, according to a customs agent whose job was to oversee and coordinate contraband interdiction operations.

Army officers and a customs official said in interviews that, when the army has participated in interdiction operations, army personnel have not confronted civilians directly, which is one measure of the army's restricted work in this arena. Rather, they have encircled the police, customs officials, and *contrabandistas* so as to deter community members who live off the contraband economy from mobilizing in support of the ongoing contraband operations. As revealed by consultation with the customs agency's main office in Lima in early 2006, army work in contraband interdiction was uncommon.

In the special case of the illegal export of timber, contraband interdiction overlaps with the army's role in protecting natural resources. Along the Peru-Colombia border where there is very little police or customs presence, the army, to a limited degree, has patrolled to prevent the illegal transport of wood, very infrequently in coordination with INRENA.[43]

The army's behavior in southern Peru exemplifies how limited its interdiction work has been. Contraband is common in the south, where the customs office in the city of Puno has requested army assistance on numerous occasions.[44] As of 2007, official army policy was that battalions stationed in contraband-heavy border areas could intercept contraband in conjunction with the police, if customs requested their assistance with specific operations.[45] Nevertheless, in practice, the army's decisions to contribute to Puno operations were actually made higher up, at the brigade level, and then only on a case-by-case basis, resulting in much less army participation than the customs office wanted and requested. In all of 2005, the army worked in only two operations in Puno.[46]

Refusal to Support Police Antinarcotics Operations or Protect the Vicuña. Whereas the army to some extent has intercepted contraband, controlled protests, and removed land squatters, it has rejected altogether two other policing missions: assisting the police during antinarcotics operations and preventing the illegal hunting of the vicuña, an endangered camelid species.

In the late 1990s, the army's direct role in antinarcotics was terminated (see chapter 3), but according to security experts, it can legally perform counterinsurgency operations that support police antinarcotics work, given that Sendero has provided security for drug traffickers. Army officers at all levels of the hierarchy have refused to assist the police. Local and regional army commanders have not authorized counterinsurgency patrols to help police counterdrug operations and have even declined to make army infrastructure—such as bases, runways, and helicopters—available to the police during their counterdrug operations. For example, during the second half of 2005, a police unit asked the commander of an army base in the VAH to give the police access to the base during a coca eradication operation. Local and regional army commanders would not discuss the issue with the police, so all army-police conversations on the matter took place in Lima. Ultimately, army leadership in Lima did not grant the police's request.[47] Even when the defense minister has ordered the army to help with police antinarcotics operations, the army has dug in its heels in resistance. A retired police officer described a police antinarcotics operation that was carried out near Vizcatán when he was serving at the highest echelons of the national police. The head of the police arranged with the defense minister the granting of access to an army air base for the operation. Angry that the police had bypassed him by dealing with the minister, the head of the army gave the police an unusable area of the base for the operation.[48]

The army has also shown its distaste for antinarcotics by turning down opportunities to participate in U.S. combat training programs that, while technically linked to counterdrug goals, focus on skills broadly relevant to army operations—that is, not specific to antinarcotics. A U.S. official stationed in Peru provided an example from 2006. That year, the U.S. embassy planned to train several groups of military and police personnel in antinarcotics. The course was to focus on navigating, first aid, and combat as they might be pertinent along Peru's northern border with Colombia. Army leaders declined the opportunity on the grounds that the army did not do antinarcotics work.

As a final policing mission handed to the army, the army has been responsible for helping to protect the vicuña, a wild camelid that is illegally hunted for its fine wool, in coordination with the national police and the agriculture ministry's National Council of South American Camelids (Consejo Nacional de Camélidos Sudamericanos, CONACS).[49] Despite this mandate, army leaders have not contributed to operations to interfere with hunting. At meetings with CONACS, army officers said that they would only protect the animals against "terrorists" who wielded heavy weaponry. (Between 2000 and 2006, there were no known cases of such hunters.)[50] CONACS officials whom I interviewed said they were in great need of operational support and were constantly disappointed by the army's refusal to help.

The Default: Training for External Defense

Other than counterinsurgency and policing, the army's remaining security mission, external defense, has not been salient during the 2000–2007 period. The Peru-Ecuador border dispute was resolved in 1998. In terms of Peru's southern border, there have been ongoing political tensions between the governments of Peru and Chile, due to Chile's arms purchases and disagreement over water rights off the coast of the two countries (e.g., *El Comercio* [Lima] 11/15/05b, 12/20/05; Páez 12/5/05). Nonetheless, those tensions have not spurred any meaningful discussion in the press or among civilian or military security experts about potential armed confrontations between the two countries. Finally, with regard to the Peru-Colombia border, the spillover of Colombia's internal conflict was not of great concern to military or security experts whom I interviewed, in part because Peru's northern border with Colombia—in contrast to Ecuador's border with Colombia—is sparsely populated, which means that it offers few commercial benefits to Colombian insurgencies (see also Basombrío 2003, 180).

With Peru facing low international threats, the army's external defense work has been mainly training on and near its bases in border areas, including in Tacna, which borders Chile; Tumbes, on the border with Ecuador; and Puno, bordering Bolivia.[51] During the early 2000s, the special military region that focused on the disputed border zone with Ecuador (see chapter 3) was eliminated, as described by officers during interviews and in army publications (e.g., *Actuali-*

dad militar 2002). Peruvian army presence on the border with Colombia has increased somewhat since 2000.

TO SUMMARIZE THIS FIRST PART OF THE CHAPTER, contrary to what we expect of professional, legitimacy-seeking, resource-maximizing militaries, during the 2000–2007 period, Peru's army did little to fight the remnants of Sendero Luminoso, the army's only salient sovereignty mission. Unoccupied by counterinsurgency duties, the army also rejected the opportunity to gain legitimacy and funding through available policing opportunities. Instead, it primarily remained on its bases.

RESTRICTIONS ON ARMY AUTONOMY

The Peruvian army's paralysis following Fujimori's departure from office was due to a combination of its narrow mission beliefs, which have ruled out assertive policing, and senior officers' perception of a contradiction in the army's counterinsurgency mission, which has prevented the army from engaging in aggressive counterinsurgency. As was true in the late 1980s (analyzed in chapter 3), the perceived contradiction can be traced to government restrictions on the army's autonomy.

Contradiction through Mission Constraint

The Peruvian government reduced the army's autonomy vis-à-vis the justice system and, in Sendero zones, the police and political officials. In response, army leaders thought the government was giving them two contradictory signals, thereby challenging predictability for army patrols: the army's main mission was to eliminate the remnants of the insurgency, and yet the officers thought that the government was depriving the army of the autonomy it needed to carry out counterinsurgency operations successfully. Primarily, officers worried that with the accountability measures, patrols in dangerous, guerrilla territory might pause to consider the legal consequences of their actions instead of acting quickly in response to security demands; the hesitation could result in the escape of insurgents and the death of soldiers.

In applying the predictability framework, this analysis devotes special attention to data from interviews conducted with members of the "senior cohort," officers who had worked in the army before and/or during the early 1990s. Because officers of the middle ranks (majors and lieutenant colonels) and upper ranks (colonels and generals) had served in the army when it had significant autonomy to conduct counterinsurgency, in that intensive period of internal conflict, those officers believed such autonomy was necessary to perform the mission, and they therefore saw a contradiction in the assignment.[52]

Reduced Autonomy in Counterinsurgency

A first challenge to the army's autonomy to conduct counterinsurgency was that the government and courts took measures to hold military and police personnel accountable for human rights abuses committed during Peru's internal conflict. Most dramatically, the amnesty granted to state security forces in 1995 (see chapter 3) crumbled. At the domestic level, President Valentín Paniagua (2000–2001) initiated the National Truth and Reconciliation Commission (Comisión de la Verdad y Reconciliación, CVR) to investigate human rights abuses committed between 1980 and 2000 (CVR 2003, 1:35–36). The CVR's 2003 report estimated a total of nearly seventy thousand deaths and disappearances during the twenty-year period, attributing approximately 32 percent to the armed forces and 56 percent to Sendero.[53] Based on its report, the commission presented forty-seven human rights cases to the Peruvian justice system.

International developments surrounding one case were crucial in prompting Peru's courts to take action. "Barrios Altos" concerned a 1991 massacre in a poor neighborhood in the capital city of Lima, carried out by the Colina Group, a death squad linked to the army, Montesinos, and Fujimori. After the Paniagua government reinstated the jurisdiction of the Inter-American Court of Human Rights (IACHR), the CNDDHH submitted to the IACHR a complaint regarding Barrios Altos (González Cueva 2004, 57). In March 2001, the international court found that Peru's 1995 amnesty laws were inconsistent with the American Convention on Human Rights and therefore inapplicable to Barrios Altos and all other human rights cases in Peru (Defensoría del Pueblo 2005, 120).

Following the IACHR decision, Peru's civilian justice system began refusing to employ the amnesty laws, on a case-by-case basis. By September 2001, the alleged perpetrators of the Barrios Altos crimes had been identified and were under investigation (Meza 9/01).[54] Peru's civilian justice system opened all forty-seven of the CVR cases by late 2005 (Defensoría del Pueblo 2005, 49–52). Of the 339 individuals accused in association with the cases, 264 were serving or previously had served in the army (Defensoría del Pueblo 2008a, 139).

While the reversal of the amnesty laws exposed military personnel to formal accusations of human rights abuses, for its part the Peruvian justice system was strengthened in terms of both its jurisdiction over human rights cases involving the armed forces and its investigative effectiveness. Well into Toledo's term, crimes committed by the military and police in emergency zones were considered *delitos de función* (crimes related to the state security forces' assignments) and therefore, constitutionally, within the purview of military courts (per art. 10 of Law 24150 [1985], discussed in chapter 3). This practice was changed beginning in 2004, when the Constitutional Tribunal (Tribunal Constitucional, TC) ruled that *delitos de función* excluded all cases in which civilians are harmed, thus moving those cases to the civilian courts. Following the TC's example, the supreme court also began applying the *delito de función* concept narrowly (Defensoría del Pueblo 2005, 130–35). The civilian justice system's jurisdiction also grew when, that same year, the TC declared disappearances to be ongoing crimes.[55]

In addition to these jurisdictional changes, the justice system took measures to improve its processing of human rights cases. Beginning in 2002, human rights cases were assigned to prosecutors and judges who had specialized training in the subject matter,[56] and a 2003 attorney general resolution created a forensic team to locate victims' bodies. By December 2008, the teams had conducted eighty-four digs, and in 2008 alone, they discovered 236 bodies and identified 134 of them (Defensoría del Pueblo 2008a, 201).[57]

Although the most critical challenges to military autonomy involved these judicial shifts, the army's autonomy in Sendero zones in relation to the national police and politicians has also been diminished in important ways. Intelligence reform can be traced to the dismantling of the national intelligence agency (the SIN, by Law 27351 [2000]) during the "Vladivideo" scandal (see chapter 2). Subsequently, a June 2001 law (Law 27479) created the Consejo Nacional de Inteligencia (CNI) to replace the SIN. Because the CNI had the same structure and human resources as the SIN, the reorganization has been described as merely "a change in name," with the CNI holding onto "the same substance and the same mentality" as the SIN (Chiri Márquez 2004, 120).[58] In late 2003, the Toledo government initiated a new intelligence reform, and in December 2005, the legislature replaced the CNI with the Dirección Nacional de Inteligencia (DINI), representing a true decline in military power in the intelligence sector.[59] In contrast to the status quo under the SIN and CNI, the legislature can now access intelligence information, Peru's national audit office can monitor intelligence funds, and all special operations by intelligence agencies, such as wiretapping, require prior approval by the judiciary (*La República* 6/3/05).

As intelligence was being restructured, judicial and executive decisions also diminished the military's authority in Sendero zones. First, in the VAH, the military was ordered to carry out counterinsurgency, but only in support of the national police, which was placed in charge of security there. Second, in the VRAE, the military was assigned control of security, yet its power stopped there. In 2004, the title of the military security power in these areas was changed from political-military commander to simply military commander (Expedient 0017-2003-AI/TC), and the TC ruled it unconstitutional to grant the armed forces political control of emergency zones, whereas the prior system had granted political-military commanders total control of those areas (see chapter 3).

Military Resentment of the Constraints

Military personnel resent that the army has lost autonomy. For instance, according to a civilian interview subject who was intimately involved in the 2004–5 intelligence reforms and communicated with the military leadership throughout the reform process, the armed forces most disliked the reforms for subjecting the intelligence agency to judicial scrutiny.

In reaction to their increased legal liability, the armed forces, which did not accept institutional responsibility for abuses committed during the 1980s and 1990s, attempted to protect military personnel from conviction. One way that the military has tried to shield individuals from the judiciary has been to process human rights cases in the military court system. Initially, following Fujimori's government, military courts explicitly acknowledged civilian jurisdiction over human rights cases. For instance, the war division of Peru's highest military court (the Consejo Supremo de Justicia Militar, CSJM) ruled that the military justice system was not competent to make judgments about human rights violations in the "Huanta Case," in which six evangelicals were assassinated in Callqui, in the Ayacucho province of Huanta (Defensoría del Pueblo 2005, 138). Nonetheless, under CSJM president Rear Admiral Carlos Enrique Mesa Angosto, from 2003 to 2005, the military courts attempted to reclaim de facto control of the cases.[60] As of August 2005, eleven CVR cases were undergoing investigations in both the military and civilian judicial systems (Defensoría del Pueblo 2005, 145–46).

Once facing charges of abuses, army personnel have received further military institutional support. The head of the army, General Reinoso, was quoted as saying in December 2005 that he gave his "unconditional support to the officers, non-commissioned officers and troops who, in carrying out their institutional duty, risked their lives and fought against terrorism . . . and that today, active-duty or retired, find themselves involved in legal investigations for crimes committed by groups that have risen in arms" (*La República* 12/20/05a). The Sol de Solidaridad, a program instituted by the head of the army in early 2005, transferred one *sol* (approximately 30 cents) from every officer paycheck to help cover the legal fees of army personnel involved in human rights cases.[61] As of late 2008, 650 of the 665 retired and active-duty military personnel who had received legal help from the defense ministry had received it directly from the army's legal assistance office (Defensoría del Pueblo 2008a, 167–68).[62]

Retired officers, too, have protected military personnel from trials. When retired general Marciano Rengifo Ruiz was defense minister (2005–6), he refused to release the identity of military personnel to their would-be accusers. Officers and soldiers stationed in emergency zones in the 1980s and 1990s generally used pseudonyms. Rengifo Ruiz claimed that the military did not have information linking pseudonyms to the true identities of military personnel, thereby sheltering those individuals from being linked to human rights violations. The minister's claim was not credible. Previously, the defense minister Aurelio Loret de Mola (2001–3)—who had not served in the armed forces—had provided such information to the CVR on request (Páez 2/21/06).

The Contradiction

To the senior cohort, these restrictions on the army's autonomy made effective counterinsurgency impossible, by introducing a contradiction into the mission itself. Aggregate data from officer interviews suggest that autonomy restrictions relative to the courts and, in Sendero zones, to political officials and the national police, caused the army to underperform counterinsurgency. Officers pointed to human rights developments more than any other factor when they explained why the army performed little counterinsurgency work, why it was cautious when doing this work, and why the counterinsurgency it did perform was ineffective (table 4.2). Closer scrutiny of officers' responses reveals that, while both the senior and junior cohorts thought that a lack of autonomy had caused the army to underperform counterinsurgency, on the whole it was only the mid-ranking and senior officers who thought the reductions in autonomy created a contradiction in the counterinsurgency mission. In contrast, junior officers observed the army responding to the autonomy restrictions without themselves believing that there was a contradiction in the army's assignment.

In terms of the army's reduced autonomy in relation to the police and local political officials, officers in the senior cohort believed that the restrictions interfered with the coherence of operations, as articulated by a senior officer who complained about the army's reduced authority over the police.

> Communication was one of the best achievements of Fujimori. There was constant sharing of information between the police and the army . . . Intelligence was where the communication happened . . . Before, police-army communication was good because of the political-military [command] structure. Now, [the army and the police] work in separate spheres, and there is no system.

Similarly, commenting on how battalion commanders in the VAH were required to contact the prefect's office prior to conducting operations, another senior officer said, "The [army's] requests are always granted, but this system means there are no secret patrols, which makes the patrols less effective. Battalion commanders choose not to do patrols at all, usually." During a discussion group, a senior officer complained about the general lack of army autonomy in counterinsurgency.

> *How have things changed between the 1980s and 1990s, and now, in terms of how orders are delivered and explained [in the army]?*
>
> Now everything must be in writing, which is different from before. And if you want to do anything in internal security in areas not in an emergency zone, everything must be written out, and a public prosecutor must be with you.

Table 4.2. Officers' Explanations for the Peruvian Army's Limited, Cautious, and/or Ineffective Counterinsurgency Work (in no. of mentions)

Explanation	Senior cohort (22 officers)		Junior cohort (11 officers)		Total (33 officers)	
Lack of army autonomy		45		15		60 (58%)
Possible accusations of human rights abuses	*20*		*14*		*34*	
Low autonomy in relation to politicians/police	*22*		*1*		*23*	
Poor intelligence	*3*		*0*		*3*	
Insufficient army resources		18		10		28 (27%)
Low threat / police are sufficient		3		7		10 (10%)
Other		2		4		6 (6%)
Total mentions		68		36		104 (101%)

> Nothing happens. There is no surprise, there is no effectiveness. It is a disaster . . . Surprise is important, and we don't have this if there has to be so much documentation and planning ahead of time . . . Now, [even] in states of emergency, there is no political-military commander.

In contrast to their superiors, few junior officers discussed this dimension of the army's reduced autonomy.[63]

Members of the senior cohort saw human rights accusations as the most detrimental constraint on the army's autonomy. Overall, this cohort focused heavily on the topic of human rights: thirty-nine of the fifty-one mid- and high-ranking officers interviewed (76%) spontaneously referred to human rights and/or potential harm to civilians during army operations, whereas only nine of the twenty-two junior officers (41%) did so.[64] Officers in the senior cohort who mentioned human rights tended to complain about accusations against military personnel for abuses committed during Peru's 1980–2000 internal conflict and were much more vocal than junior officers in this regard (table 4.3). The more senior officers frequently said that army personnel were being unfairly accused of abuses when those individuals had heroically saved the country from terrorism.[65] A mid-ranking officer said, "This country has a short memory. People don't remember what happened during the 1980s and 1990s, with all of the violence caused by terrorists, and all the good we have done. So what do they do? They punish us for saving the country." Another officer from the middle ranks said, "Politicians are taking revenge by attacking us for doing our job, with all the accusations of human rights abuses. It hurts the image of the army." Officers in the senior cohort often tried to justify abuses by saying that the acts had been unavoidable, given the high insurgency threat, and that there were *always* "excesses" in any major internal conflict. Several of those more senior officers claimed that as "terrorists," *senderistas* should not be subject to legal protections at all, and/or they voiced the (groundless) complaint that the justice system had prosecuted army personnel but not *senderistas* who had committed abuses.[66]

Relative to the senior cohort, junior officers interviewed were less focused on the theme of human rights abuses and, when they broached the topic, they were also less likely to say that accusations of human rights abuses were unfair and more likely to say that abuses were, in fact, committed. All but one of the junior officers who mentioned human rights attributed responsibility for the acts either to the army as a whole or to army personnel, instead of saying the abuses were inevitable (table 4.3). Consistent with these interview data, an internal army

Table 4.3. Officers' Opinions about the Peruvian Army's Responsibility for 1980–2000 Human Rights Abuses (in no. of opinions)

Opinion	Senior cohort (26 officers)	Junior cohort (8 officers)	Total (34 officers)*
Accusations of abuses are unfair	21	4	25
Abuses occurred	12	7	19
Army (army personnel) was (were) responsible for abuses	4	7	11

*The sample includes all officers who mentioned human rights issues related to counterinsurgency during 1980–2000. (It excludes the views of officers who discussed the theme of human rights abuses in general and/or with respect to the post-2000 period, as well as officers who made no mention of human rights issues.) Several officers expressed more than one of the three opinions. All opinions of each officer are presented; for each officer, a given opinion was counted only once.

survey of officers administered in the wake of the CVR report also found cohort differences in attitudes about human rights abuses. A senior army officer who was involved in overseeing the administration and analysis of the survey said the results revealed a "clear rupture" between young officers and officers who had fought Sendero; his summary of the results was that the more junior officers did not sufficiently respect the work of their superiors, were less antagonistic toward the CVR, and tended to condemn the army for past abuses.[67]

Mid- and high-ranking officers thought that human rights developments not only insulted the army but also introduced a contradiction into the army's counterinsurgency work. For these officers, at the same time that the government was ordering the army to perform counterinsurgency work, it was denying the autonomy the army "needed" to perform that mission. Officers asked how an army unit could effectively root out guerrillas, or even protect its men, if it must conduct operations while hesitating at every step, lest a civilian be harmed unintentionally—which could trigger legal investigations and trials. All eleven mid- and high-ranking army officers who complained that human rights developments had reduced the army's participation in counterinsurgency thought the army's current counterinsurgency assignment contained an internal contradiction. For example, during a discussion group of senior officers, the conversation turned to twelve army counterinsurgency bases that were reopened in early 2006 following a recent outbreak of Sendero attacks (see above). A senior officer made the following remark:

These bases are only for presence, not for real patrols—that is, [the troops] don't leave the base to do overnight patrols . . . They just patrol in the daytime and return to the base.

Why?

This is because of international law and the CVR. Individual officers worry that they will be tried for human rights abuses in the future, should they get in some kind of a confrontation, so they avoid it all together.

Similarly, a mid-ranking officer complained in an interview that legal liability interfered with the army's effectiveness.

Do local commanders have the authority under military regulations to plan operations?

Yes. But if I am commanding a unit, and a civilian gets killed, I'll be tried for it . . .

Why do you think that officers don't do more operations against subversion in the country?

The first attack on the morals of the armed forces was the trial for Chavín de Haúntar.[68] We got no thanks for that. And also, we have all these other trials for human rights abuses. With all that, why would we put ourselves on the line?

Several officers in the senior cohort worried that should civilians be harmed, officers up the chain of command, as well as the soldiers directly performing the acts, might be accused of human rights abuses. A senior officer said that NGOs and the CVR were unfairly attributing blame to those involved in commanding—but not carrying out—actions that resulted in human rights abuses.

[The theory] is the idea that if an innocent person is killed, it is not just the fault of the person who did it, but it is also the fault of the person who ordered it . . . It can't apply here because of our situation. If you are on a patrol and the soldier in front kills people, and there is confusion over who was armed, and who was attacking, the officer at the back of the line can't be held accountable. He doesn't know who was armed and who attacked whom! This theory doesn't apply to military personnel, because of the nature of it, because of the hierarchy. The CVR is applying it, that's what is happening. They are accusing everyone.

Even though, like officers in the senior cohort, several junior officers also believed that human rights issues had negatively affected counterinsurgency (table 4.2), only four of them said that the human rights developments were unjust. Of those four officers, only one saw a contradiction in the army's counterinsurgency mission. The other three thought the reduced counterinsurgency was an overreaction on the part of more senior officers or the army as a whole.

The Source of the Senior Cohort's "Need" for Autonomy

The senior cohort's focus on human rights accusations and its perception of the contradiction can be linked to its service in the army at a time when the institution enjoyed exceptionally high levels of autonomy and proved successful in counterinsurgency.[69] Those officers came out of the experience believing that the army required autonomy to perform counterinsurgency work.

In trying to justify the fundamental need for autonomy, officers in the senior cohort talked about the army's reduction of the guerrilla threat in the 1990s and explained that effectiveness by pointing to the army's role in leading the state counterinsurgency effort. Twenty-five of the fifty-one officers in the senior cohort said, without prompt, that the army's autonomy facilitated successful counterinsurgency operations. Several of those officers described counterinsurgency as being seamless during the 1980s and 1990s, when army units collected intelligence without first obtaining approval from any other state actor and when the army had control over the national police. For instance, in remarking on how he thought the military's political powers in emergency zones were critical to fighting Sendero in the 1990s, a mid-ranking officer said, "The military was put in control, not just in the military sphere, but also in politics . . . You didn't know who was a subversive . . . In that period, we had freedom [to act], because the military had political control . . . The only way to do it was to give the military power." A senior officer described how the army and police since 2000 could work together, performing distinct functions during a capture ("we secure the area, and the police go in"), but then remarked wistfully, "Before, we would just do it all."

Members of the senior cohort highlighted both their view that autonomy had facilitated effective operations and the leading role the army had taken in *developing* a successful strategy when it had the autonomy to do so. Officers said that independent of other actors, the army had designed the more effective, intelligence-driven and hearts-and-minds approach at a time when politicians were neither interested in finding a solution to Peru's internal conflict nor capable of guiding or supporting the army. They thought the army had been the only available actor to save the country from "terrorism," and therefore oversight by any other actors would have hindered, not helped, with counterinsurgency. Several officers were bitter that the government had not devoted more resources to counterinsurgency in the 1980s, stating that more resources could have allowed for a broad strategy of which armed combat would have been just one component.[70] Officers emphasized the army's ingenuity in creating strategy, relative to both the Peruvian government and the U.S. military, which they described as not sufficiently thoughtful or knowledgeable about counterinsurgency to provide guidance to Peru's army, as stated by a senior army officer: "Civic action was for fighting subversion. We had great success against Sendero through this work . . . We used our books from the United States, which were used in Vietnam, to attack everyone. But [then] we realized that we had to win over the population, so we did civic action."

A final factor reinforced the senior cohort's belief that autonomy was critical: the idea that it was difficult to distinguish between civilians and insurgents. Of the mid- and high-ranking officers interviewed, sixteen volunteered opinions on whether civilian casualties could reasonably be avoided during counterinsurgency operations. Of these, thirteen thought civilian casualties were unavoidable.[71] With these beliefs about the gray—or, in some cases, nonexistent—line separating guerrillas from civilians, members of the senior cohort thought that it was impracticable to avoid civilian casualties, and thus that the army required autonomy vis-à-vis outside actors, including the justice system, to react quickly to insurgents so that patrols could capture or kill guerrillas while keeping army personnel safe.

A few interview excerpts reveal the reasoning of the senior cohort. According to some of the officers, Sendero's tactics forced the army to harm innocent civilians at times. For instance, a mid-ranking officer described a case in the early 1990s in which an army helicopter flew over a cluster of homes in the countryside. Armed *senderistas* stood in front of one of the huts, along with civilians (among them children) whom the guerrillas were using as human shields. The officer added that "this kind of thing happened all the time during the violence . . . all kinds of scenarios in which civilians were killed while we were hunting terrorists . . . There are always excesses in a war like that—an irregular war."[72]

Irrespective of this example, officers generally spoke not of visible civilians getting caught in the crossfire but, rather, of the difficulty of defining civilians in the counterinsurgency setting. This challenge came through vividly in a senior officer's account of an incident in Ayacucho during the 1980–2000 period. The officer said that many guerrillas had attacked a town. Shortly thereafter, several peasants were seen farming close by, and he concluded that those farmers were the combatants, who would not have had time to flee the area.

> We were told that fifty to sixty *senderistas* had come and attacked the people [in the town], and killed thirty-two people . . . There is no way that so many of them [*senderistas*] could have gotten away. I am sure that the peasants . . . [seen] farming [in the area] were the ones who had come through [the town] and carried out the attack. They were only peasants. But what happened was that Sendero Luminoso leaders would force peasants to fight with them.[73]

Officers in the senior cohort tended to think that unarmed civilians who helped the insurgents constituted a legitimate target for the army during counterinsurgency operations. A senior officer said of the earlier period that "though they might not have been Sendero, peasants helped the subversives openly. So we had to be tough on them." Another officer, of the middle ranks, said that "excesses" or abuses on the part of the army were necessary during the 1980s and 1990s, explaining this opinion as follows: "You might enter a town of one thousand [people]. There may be only two hundred *senderistas*, but the other eight hundred support Sendero, because they have been lied to, convinced, brainwashed. So you go in, and you are confronting one thousand enemies. Of course there are excesses."

Perhaps precisely because of their experiences in the 1980s and 1990s, officers in the senior cohort also tended to think it was hard to differentiate civilians from guerrillas during the years since 2000. For example, the officer who described the incident in which presumed Sendero combatants were farming after attacking the town in Ayacucho stated that the same dynamic had continued in Ayacucho after 2000. Another mid-ranking officer said that ongoing guerrilla activities among communities could spur another major episode of Sendero violence.

> Subversive groups are reorganizing . . . In [1992, Congress] passed the Law of Repentance.[74] The insurgents gave us their weapons at that time, and they also had to name other terrorists, in order to be excused [from charges of terrorism]. At first, [the insurgents] acted fine, and then they moved to other areas, adopting new names. The same people now still have weapons because they didn't turn all of them in . . . Soon they will break onto the scene again.

A senior officer described what he thought to be a threat of a Sendero resurgence by noting how the drug trade often further blurs the lines separating Sendero, communities, and CADs.

> Now that drug trafficking is spreading, peasants are getting involved. Subversives provide security for drug traffickers in return for resources. Self-defense committees and towns don't mind Sendero, and they grow coca. This is a big problem. Now that there aren't Sendero attacks, the people are trusting Sendero.

In contrast to the senior cohort, junior officers interviewed had not served in the army in the late 1980s or early 1990s and did not think the army required autonomy for counterinsurgency operations. Whereas twenty-five of the fifty-one officers in the senior cohort said that army autonomy facilitated effective counterinsurgency, only six of the twenty-two junior officers expressed that opinion. When junior officers raised the issue of autonomy (which was rare), they generally did so by simply referring to the army's reduced autonomy since the 1990s, without claiming that the army required that same kind of autonomy in the more recent period. Some junior officers even criticized the army's earlier practices and implied that autonomy had granted them the freedom to violate human rights. For instance, one junior officer said, "We were prepared for regular conflict when Sendero came onto the scene. But this wasn't the way to fight subversion. The military was put in charge of everything, the war, everything. There were abuses, on our part."

Also in contrast to the senior cohort, junior officers generally described Sendero in the post-2000 period as being distinguishable from the civilian population,[75] as communicated by one junior officer.

> *Do you, as the head of the base, worry ever that you will be accused of human rights abuses should you go out to do an operation, and a civilian gets hurt?*
>
> . . . The [counterinsurgency] bases are far from the townspeople, in virgin jungle, so we are not right in the town . . . When we do operations, we know where the enemy is—he is out in the virgin jungle, not around the town. It is not like the [other military personnel] say, that you don't know who the enemy is. The peasants have shotguns. *Senderistas*, on the other hand, have weapons of war, [purchased with] drug trafficking money, or stolen from the military or the police.

Because members of the junior cohort thought one could discern civilians from guerrillas, it is not surprising that only three junior officers said that civilian casualties could not reasonably be avoided during counterinsurgency operations. (The six other junior officers who mentioned the topic of casualties thought they were avoidable.)

This analysis of the perceived contradiction in the army's counterinsurgency mission has attributed the cohort difference—that the senior cohort identified the contradiction whereas the junior cohort did not—to the fact that mid- and high-ranking officers had served in the army during the high point of Peru's internal conflict, whereas junior officers had not. An alternative explanation is that enhancement in army training in international humanitarian law (IHL) accounts for the cohort difference, as IHL speaks directly to the question of fighting insurgents while respecting human rights. New training in IHL was layered on some general instruction in human rights, which was introduced in the army beginning in the first half of the 1990s, according to officers interviewed and based on a review of course listings for infantry cadets at the Escuela Militar de Chorrillos (1981–2003).[76] Between 2002 and 2004, the ICRC trained 522 Peruvian military instructors throughout the country (United Nations Office of the High Commissioner for Human Rights Committee against Torture 2005, 90). A May 2004 defense ministry resolution approved a military directive to integrate IHL into doctrine and training (Centro del Derecho Internacional Humanitario y Derechos Humanos de las Fuerzas Armadas 2004). As of 2005, the year-long high command course at the army war college (Escuela Superior de Guerra, ESG) consisted of 1,692 class and lecture hours, with 108 hours devoted to international law (Escuela Superior de Guerra 2005), a subset of which presumably consisted of IHL.

Army training in IHL has been inadequate, however, so it is unlikely that recent IHL training explains the junior cohort's propensity to be more accepting of limits to army autonomy. Beginning with the graduating class of 2002, army cadets studied IHL, but that class took only one unit on the topic (of ninety-one total units), and the class of 2003 took only two units on it (of ninety-nine total units). In terms of IHL training content, an official of the ICRC said in an interview that in Peruvian military courses, students received only a few hours of training in IHL and that this instruction was provided by outside instructors, who received less respect and attention from students than would instructors from within Peru's armed forces. The official further said that, as of 2006, the

Peruvian army's tactical training in IHL omitted many important situations, including those involving civilians, schools, or prisoners of war.

Neglect of Counterinsurgency as a Way to Maintain Predictability for Patrols

Turning from the origins of the contradiction to the mechanisms by which it caused the army to refuse counterinsurgency work so as to maintain predictability for patrols, the discussion here emphasizes the actions taken by officers in the senior cohort and by junior officers working within those established structures. Although commanding officers had an interest in preventing patrols from engaging in tentative and therefore dangerous operations, their immediate motivation was generally *not* the well-being of junior officers or soldiers in the field. Rather, by maintaining predictability for patrols, commanders often pursued other ends, including avoiding ordering operations that would result in their being accused of human rights abuses.

Power Play: Army High Command versus the Executive

One mechanism by which the army guarded patrols against the "contradiction" was army leaders' withholding counterinsurgency work as leverage, hoping to regain from the government the army's lost legal autonomy. In meetings with President Toledo about the insurgent threat, successive army commanders-in-chief demanded amnesty for past abuses and immunity from future accusations of abuses, as well as helicopter repairs, new weaponry, and the reinstatement of obligatory military service. The generals promised in exchange to perform more counterinsurgency.

To establish the extent of army leaders' refusal to authorize counterinsurgency operations, a former high-level interior ministry official recalled events at one meeting in early 2002 attended by Defense Minister Aurelio Loret de Mola, Interior Minister Gino Costa, General Chiabra, head of the army, and the director of the national police. At the meeting, Chiabra was "very obnoxious" and "very defiant," saying that "if you want us to get involved, this is what it costs." He wrote a figure on a slip of paper, demanding millions of dollars for each month the army performed counterinsurgency. He then sat back smugly, his arms folded.

In spite of Chiabra's—and other army leaders'—repeated references to the need for more counterinsurgency funding (see also table 4.2), senior army officers used money as an excuse; they placed more importance on attaining amnesty and immunity than on material resources, as told by army officers and interior ministry officials alike—an observation that aligns well with the army's poor use of the resources it did have (see above). A former high-level interior ministry official provided some evidence that the army's inaction was due more to the CVR than to a lack of resources to conduct counterinsurgency.

> [Interior Minister Rospigliosi and Vice Minister Gino Costa had been] in the Interior Ministry for five days . . . and [four] police are killed.[77] And not only that, but the killers had chopped [the police personnel] up into pieces. The police helicopters couldn't go in to deal with it, as they were only unarmed transport helicopters . . . The armed forces [were asked] to help. What was their response? They were angry they had not been called ahead of time, before the operation. They said, "from now on, tell us first." But they say this while they don't do anything themselves, either . . . They feel beaten by the CVR and the proceedings . . . [Military personnel] are not participating in counterinsurgency, because they want to use it as a card to push for amnesty . . . The argument that they don't have resources to do counterinsurgency is ridiculous. The police have a fleet [of helicopters] in good shape. They had the same problems as the army, the same corruption, and they were able to fix up their fleet, also with few resources.

Similarly, another retired interior ministry official described the same stubborn insubordination on the part of the army.

> Toledo had a great opportunity to take control of the armed forces. But he didn't. If he had, he could have given the orders for them to go in and take care of terrorism, and they would have complied. But he never got control, so when he says to go in, they don't go in . . . The armed forces still say no. They have a long list of what they need if they are going to go in: they need a state of emergency; they need mandatory conscription, so they have enough people for the efforts, they say; they need the government to fix all of their helicopters; they need new arms; they need a guarantee that the officers who fought against Sendero get amnesty.
>
> *Where did you get this list from? Or, is this just your sense of what they want, from different conversations?*
>
> No, this is exactly what they would say to Toledo and to us when we were in the interior ministry.

> *I understand that the army doesn't have working helicopters for this work.*
>
> They have helicopters, they have plenty. What do you think, in a country the size of Peru that they don't have helicopters that work? They have them.

A former police officer who had reached the highest levels of the national police prior to retiring also begrudged the army's paralysis and attributed it to the human rights question, not a lack of money.

> The army asks for a lot of resources, and if they don't get everything they want, they won't move. We, the police, we act with what we can, with what we have, even though we lack resources.
>
> *This inaction, this attitude of not doing counterinsurgency, in the army: when did it start?*
>
> It was after Fujimori left government. That was when it all began, this attitude . . . The armed forces . . . want immunity, amnesty, complete amnesty for everything.

At the time I was conducting this research, army leaders had been unsuccessful in achieving amnesty for past abuses, yet their demands for amnesty were not unattainable requests used simply to avoid counterinsurgency. First, and most obviously, the army was not inherently opposed to counterinsurgency, as demonstrated in chapter 3 and in this chapter. Second, politicians had debated granting the amnesty—for instance, in late 2005 and early 2006, amid both Sendero attacks in remote regions of the country and the presidential campaign, when some candidates wanted to grant the amnesty to strengthen the counterinsurgency effort (*La República* 12/31/05a, 12/31/05b, 12/31/05c; Balbi 1/2/06).

Passing the Buck Up

Added to measures taken by army leaders in Lima, members of the senior cohort who worked in the field refused to commence counterinsurgency operations without first receiving specific orders from their superiors (who also would hesitate). The discussion here focuses on majors, lieutenant colonels, colonels, and generals who commanded and served in high-level positions in the army regions (a "region" being the largest unit within the army, comparable to a division), in the brigades belonging to the army regions, and in the battalions belonging to the brigades.

A mid-ranking officer described the practice of "calling up the line" before initiating a counterinsurgency operation.

> *Is there anything in the regulations . . . that [says] that if operations happen [in Sendero zones], they must be approved from the top of the army, as opposed to having civilians or police at the local level ask for help and the army respond to the request at that level?*
>
> No, there are no regulations that say this. It is just army policy, the practice now.
>
> *And if the officer on the ground responded to a local request to help the police, would this be good or bad for his career? For example, if you are working there as a lieutenant colonel and you want to be a general someday, what do you do?*
>
> What do I do? I call up the line for an order. The worst outcome is that I order the operation, a civilian gets hurt, and I am tried for human rights abuses . . . What would I do? I wouldn't give the order to shoot. Because later, I will be tried for human rights abuses. It won't just be that civilians are hurt. It is my future on the line.

Later in the interview, the officer summed up the situation as follows: "If we had a major Sendero flare up now, we would not be prepared to deal with it as an army, because we are so scared to enter, to do operations. We will not act without authority from above. We are paralyzed."

Another mid-ranking officer was frustrated that human rights developments had furthered centralization of the army hierarchy when it came to counterinsurgency, emphasizing how bottom-up pressures had led to the practice of requiring very detailed, written orders for counterinsurgency operations.

> Now the armed forces don't do real patrols in zones where Sendero is active. They only give security to their own bases, doing patrols near the bases . . . Politicians are the biggest problem that we have now . . . The political class talks of human rights and accuses us of all these things. So this affects everyone in the military, all the officers. [Officers] see [other] officers being accused of human rights abuses and being tried . . . [Military personnel] don't lift a finger without asking their superiors. And now everything must be written: political commands, military commands to subordinates, at all levels. Because if something happens, if someone is killed in an operation, a higher-up can al-

ways deny that he gave the order for the operation, after the fact. So everything must be written . . .

What do army regulations, army directives, say about this practice of giving written orders about things?

There is a requirement that orders must be written. So that has always been there. But it used to be that the orders were very general, and brief. Now they are extremely detailed, including all kinds of possible scenarios that might arise, and what the men are to do in case of those scenarios. *Everything* is written down. This is what has changed. It is problematic, because there needs to be a certain level of autonomy at the different levels, so that officers can do their job. That is what it is to be in the army, to have a certain amount of responsibility, and then of course to report all the information up the pyramid. But you need to have autonomy to make some kinds of decisions at any level. Of course you might make a bad decision, so it might be the worst decision, but then you are sanctioned for it. And that is what it means to be in the army: you make decisions and face the consequences. But as it is now, everyone is too scared to do anything, so they don't do anything without having the order written out ahead of time. Civilians are the problem. (his emphasis)

Yet another mid-ranking officer compared the post-2000 reality of the army's centralized hierarchy with how it had been during the early 1990s.

I was in emergency zones in '91 and '92 in [the VRAE] and in '95 on the Huallaga front . . . Now things are very different from before . . . even in emergency zones. Now, you think twice, because of all the human rights accusations against officers these days. Before, you took the initiative and told your superiors what you did, which fit with the regulations, in terms of division of decision-making power. Now, there is no initiative. Army regulations have not changed, but everyone, at every level of the institution, is aware of the human rights trials, so no one wants to take the initiative. In terms of patrolling, everyone does the minimum, for dissuasion only. You do the minimal work . . . for fear of what could happen to your career, for fear of possible [human rights] trials.

This centralized hierarchy, created by the senior cohort in the field, limited how junior officers performed their counterinsurgency responsibilities, which included commanding the small, mobile counterinsurgency bases and leading patrols, both from those bases and directly from the battalion bases. As analyzed above, for the most part these lieutenants and captains did not believe that the human rights developments or other restrictions on army autonomy created a contradiction in their counterinsurgency mission. Nonetheless, junior officers acted within the confines of the centralized hierarchy. A junior officer who recently had served on counterinsurgency bases in the VRAE was matter-of-fact about this reality.

Do you conduct patrols . . . from the bases?

Yes. We do dissuasive patrols. These are about twice a month . . .

Why don't you do more patrols?

Sometimes they are not authorized.

When would that be the case?

If Sendero is around.

On the whole, junior officers accepted without question the requirement for specific orders from above, but some did say that the rules were overly restrictive and said they wanted to perform counterinsurgency more flexibly, aggressively, and therefore more effectively. One junior officer complained that "everything must be on paper. If it is not on paper, we don't do it. Period. Everything is written out in *great* detail" (his emphasis, expressing exasperation).

Return to Assertive Counterinsurgency

Consistent with the predictability framework, Peru's army has returned to aggressive counterinsurgency since late 2008, in direct response to increases in autonomy in relation to the justice system.

The second Alan García (2006–11) government took measures to increase the army's autonomy to intensify counterinsurgency. The government's initial attempt was "Plan VRAE," launched in February 2007 by Supreme Decree 003-2007-DE. The plan was developed during a period of heightened public alarm over Sendero. Edmundo Cruz, a journalist and specialist in security and military themes, found that the number of violent attacks by Sendero rose from only five in 1999, seven in 2003, and five in 2005 to fifteen in both 2006 and 2007, and then thirty in 2008 (J. C. Agüero 2009, 53). The national press reported that between April 2007 and December 2008, Sendero attacks resulted in thirty-five deaths and at least fifty civilians wounded (Gutiérrez R. and Prado 4/12/09). A civilian security expert who had served as an advisor in the defense ministry while Plan VRAE was being conceived said that rising numbers of guerrilla attacks had encouraged the plan's development.[78]

As of 2009, Plan VRAE had three prongs: counterinsurgency (headed by the military), antinarcotics (led by the police), and economic development (under various ministries). The first prong has been described as the most prominent, in part because the defense ministry was charged with coordinating the plan and also because the ministries responsible for contributing to economic development in the VRAE did little in that regard.[79]

With resources from Plan VRAE and a direct order from the defense ministry to fight Sendero, the army added more men and counterinsurgency bases to the VRAE. However, consistent with the pattern in place since 2000, the army was not assertive in conducting operations, because the restrictions on its autonomy were still in place. According to the former defense advisor referred to above, following the release of the CVR report and in a context in which human rights cases against nine hundred military personnel had been opened, "Military personnel would see Sendero Luminoso, and they would go in the other direction on patrol, to avoid confrontations," even after Plan VRAE was implemented.

A second stage in the García administration's endeavor to eliminate Sendero culminated at the end of 2007, when the congress passed Law 29166, which defines military rules of engagement in internal security. The army regained autonomy with this law, which permits military personnel to use their weapons when confronting hostile "intentions" as well as hostile acts (art. 7) and specifies that "all actions that military personnel carry out in exercise of their function and in accordance with the present Law, which are presumed *delitos de función*, are within the jurisdiction and competence of the Military-Police Code of Justice (Fuero Militar Policial)" (art. 13). The law's regulation was approved in July 2008 (Supreme Decree 012-2008-DE/CCFFAA).[80]

The rules of engagement were developed to encourage military counterinsurgency operations, and they succeeded in doing so, resolving the contradiction for members of the senior cohort. When asked whether the law and regulation on rules of engagement were written to increase military counterinsurgency work, the former defense advisor said, "Absolutely, without a doubt. The funny thing is that there are no rules of engagement for external defense in Peru—just for internal security action. The rules of engagement were entirely to get the military to do more in the VRAE." A lawyer in the defense ministry characterized the rules as "a legal umbrella when military personnel enter in combat." "Now, they don't enter [insurgency zones] afraid," he said, a view echoed by the former defense advisor. Similarly, a general working at the highest echelons of the army said, "Well, before there was fear to use arms, due to the CVR. The rules have given more security to young officers and soldiers. I'm talking from the perspective of the army, now, of people in the army. The rules help a little, to provide a legal framework, clear rules. Protections." He emphasized that the rules allowed military personnel to make different choices, depending on the scenarios that arose during operations: "There is flexibility . . . There are different contingencies built into the law." The general later spelled out the resolution of the contradiction even more clearly: "The thing is the rules were very important." Feigning picking up a telephone receiver, as if he were the executive calling a military officer, he said, "Otherwise, 'use your weapons, but don't use your weapons.' It can't be that way!"

For military leaders, it was important that the congress approved the rules of engagement through the standard legislative process, which had not been the case for prior military rules of engagement. When pushed to explain why the rules were so critical, given that the army had operated for many years according to its own rules of engagement,[81] the defense ministry attorney said, "Well, you had a supreme decree that addressed these kinds of issues, but those details were secret . . . And decrees don't have as much power as laws. A law goes through Congress. It has more power." The high-level army general said in response to a general question about his opinion of the new rules, "This is the first time that we have such clear rules *and* with legal backing. This is good. The troops and officers are protected now" (his emphasis).

By giving the army more autonomy in relation to the judicial system, the rules of engagement resolved the perceived contradiction in counterinsurgency, and the army began to perform the mission more assertively. The army worked with the other military branches and with the national police to carry out the military joint command's "Excelencia 777," an operation to start retaking Vizcatán in the VRAE, between August and December 2008. The operation was aggressive, leaving fifteen military personnel dead and thirty-nine wounded (*Caretas* 10/23/08, 4/16/09), and was heralded by security experts as army progress in the VRAE and the first advance in the Sendero-controlled Vizcatán. By the end of 2008, eighteen new bases had been installed in the VRAE, and as of May 2009, four of them were in Vizcatán (J. C. Agüero 2009, 55–56). From the beginning of 2008 through mid-2009, two thousand military personnel—the vast majority from the army—were added to the VRAE, in an "offensive without precedents against the remnants of Sendero Luminoso entrenched in the inhospitable mountains of Vizcatán" (*Caretas* 6/4/09).[82]

The rules of engagement, however, have not prevented the public prosecutor (*fiscal*) from investigating deaths caused by counterinsurgency operations. This is exemplified by the investigations surrounding an incident in which four civilians were killed in September 2008, as a result of "Plan Chupón," part of Excelencia 777.[83] While I was conducting follow-up research in 2009, investigations into the deaths were in progress and were a common topic of discussion within the security community. In spite of these investigations, because officers thought the rules of engagement would protect them against conviction in the civilian justice system, they did not see their counterinsurgency mission as being contradictory.

To conclude this application of the predictability hypothesis to the Peruvian case, it is useful to make a final observation regarding the hypothesis that militaries strive to achieve public legitimacy. I have argued that a legitimate action for the army throughout the period since 2000 has been to carry out assertive counterinsurgency to eliminate the remnants of Sendero while also respecting human rights. To a certain extent, then, the predictability argument can work alongside the legitimacy hypothesis in the Peruvian case, in that it was the passage of one law, on the rules of engagement, that gave officers legitimate legal cover. However, a public legitimacy perspective alone cannot explain the Peruvian army's behavior before passage of the law, when already the legitimate thing for the army to do was to carry out counterinsurgency while respecting human rights. To explain the mission neglect in that period, one must take the next step and identify the contradiction that officers saw in the mission.

Narrow Mission Beliefs and Minimal Police Work

In contrast to the Peruvian army's participation in counterinsurgency, which has ebbed and flowed with changing levels of autonomy, the army consistently has rejected police work, behavior that can be attributed directly to narrow mission beliefs that define policing as inappropriate.

As one indicator of these beliefs, when asked to identify the army's most important activities, officers in both cohorts tended to mention sovereignty work (thirty-four of fifty officers) and economic development (thirty-three of fifty officers). Only two officers came close to mentioning police work, referring to

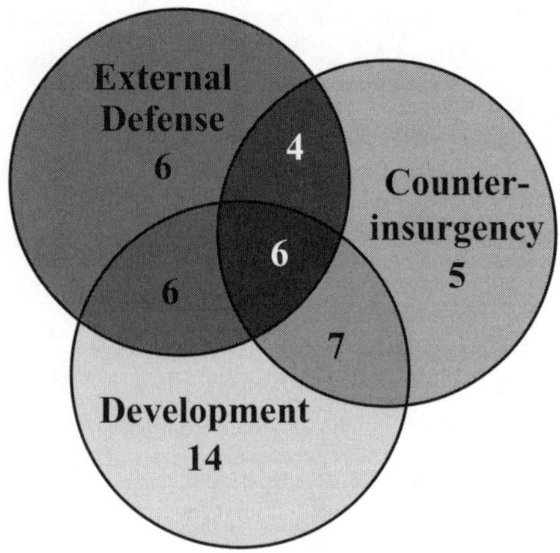

Figure 4.3. Peruvian Army Mission Beliefs by Officer. Fifty officers were asked to name the army's most important activities. The officers are sorted by their first three responses. The *development* category includes civic action, infrastructure projects, and "development" more generally. Other activities mentioned multiple times include training (5 mentions), disaster relief (3 mentions), and internal security (2 mentions). Two officers mentioned only activities that fell outside the external defense, counterinsurgency, and development categories. Responses varied somewhat by cohort: of the 30 officers of the rank major and higher, 16 mentioned external defense; 11, counterinsurgency; and 21, development. Of the 20 officers of the rank captain and below, 6 mentioned external defense; 11, counterinsurgency; and 10, development.

"internal security" (figure 4.3). Further evidence of the army's narrow mission beliefs is that when explaining why the army conducted the little policing that it did perform, officers exhibited a strong dislike for the work. As shown in table 4.4, the most common reason that officers gave for the army's policing actions was that the government—through laws or orders—brought the army into those missions, a situation that officers did not like. For instance, several expressed extreme satisfaction that they could refuse to do the work, barring direct, written orders from the government. Officers also said that the army did policing only if a particular security threat overwhelmed the national police's capacity. Of the five officers who said the army conducted policing because the army was respected more than the national police force, four resented that the army had to do the work.[84] Similarly, when officers explained why the army performed only a very limited amount of policing (table 4.5), they most commonly said that the missions did not belong to the army ("mission beliefs"). In the specific case of

Table 4.4. Officers' Explanations for Peruvian Army's Police Work (in no. of mentions)

Explanation	Protest control (19 officers)	Mining/ hydrocarbon security (6 officers)	Contraband interdiction (5 officers)	Antinarcotics (5 officers)	Total mentions (29 officers)*
Following laws/ government order	19	3	0	0	22 (42%)
Police force is overwhelmed	3	0	3	1	7 (13%)
Army is more respected than police	3	0	2	0	5 (9%)
Insurgents are involved	0	2	0	3	5 (9%)
Other	4	7†	2	1	14 (26%)
Total mentions	29	12	7	5	53 (99%)

*Of the twenty-nine officers, four were of the junior cohort; junior officers' explanations did not differ from those of more senior officers.

†One officer said it was the army's appropriate role to provide security for the companies. This was the only "mission belief" explanation for why the army performed police work.

antinarcotics, officers mentioned corruption as a central reason for not performing the mission.

A final way in which officers exhibited narrow mission beliefs was by saying that the army was an institution that inherently used lethal force and thus should not police civilians. Twenty-four officers voluntarily explained both why they thought the army did not conduct more police work and why the army conducted counterinsurgency. Of those officers, nineteen rejected police work on the grounds that it was inappropriate for the army, while also saying that counterinsurgency was a highly appropriate, natural army mission.

Especially with respect to protest control, officers thought that the army simply was not trained to confront civilians with force and that when the government ordered the army to do policing, the government therefore was to blame for any resulting civilian casualties. For example, when discussing cases in which the army had participated in protest control, a senior officer said, "We are not trained for police work, we are trained to eliminate the enemy . . . It is complicated, because we are thrown in to do the work, but then if things go wrong, the politicians blame us." Officers focused mainly on the 2003 Puno incident, in

Table 4.5. Officers' Explanations for Why the Peruvian Army Conducted Limited Police Work or Should Not Conduct Police Work (in no. of mentions)

Explanation	Protest control (14 officers)	Antinarcotics (13 officers)	Mining/ hydrocarbon security (8 officers)	Crime fighting (5 officers)	Immigration (2 officers)	Contraband interdiction (1 officer)	General policing (8 officers)	Total mentions (32 officers)*
Mission belief†	6	10	7	5	2	1	7	38 (58%)
Avoid accusations of human rights abuses‡	15	0	0	0	0	0	1	16 (24%)
Other	3	7§	1	0	0	0	1	12 (18%)
Total mentions	24	17	8	5	2	1	9	66 (100%)

*Of the thirty-two officers, six were of the junior cohort; junior officers' explanations did not differ from those of more senior officers.

†"Mission belief" explanation: that the mission was not for the army to perform (31 mentions); that the army was not appropriately trained (*preparado*) for protest control; and/or that the insurgent threat was low and therefore the army did not, or should not, do security for the mining or hydrocarbon sectors.

‡In most cases, this indicates that officers referred directly to that goal. Two further explanations in this category were "to avoid civilian casualties"; three others were that the army did not have legal backing for the mission.

§Five of the seven explanations for why the army did not do antinarcotics work were "to avoid corruption in the army."

which an army patrol killed a student protester during a national state of emergency (see above). After the shooting, legal action was taken against army personnel involved in the operation (Defensoría del Pueblo 2003, 51). A mid-ranking officer said of the Puno case, "There were protests that were out of control. The patrol goes out, by order, and is attacked. A student gets killed because the army personnel were working according to army regulations. So now the personnel are facing trial for this." A senior officer said more generally, "police roles are completely different from military roles . . . We are not trained to detain people, but the police are trained for this." Similarly, a mid-ranking officer said of policing, "We get involved in things that aren't our responsibility. Then we get arrested and face court trials if we use our weapons."

As analyzed in chapter 3, in the 1980s and 1990s, the army already separated the two internal security functions—policing and counterinsurgency—prioritizing counterinsurgency. Nonetheless, the army has been driven further from policing, having come out of those decades. The army had undergone the trauma of becoming highly corrupted through antinarcotics work in the 1990s, an experience apparently still important to officers (see table 4.5). Furthermore, intensively fighting Sendero may have led the army to embrace counterinsurgency all the more as a professional combat mission, when compared with other internal security missions. Indeed, as we will see in chapter 5, officers in the Ecuadorian army, which had no history of counterguerrilla warfare, thought policing was appropriate army work.

Passing the Buck Up and Losing Orders in the Bureaucracy

Responding to their narrow mission beliefs, for the most part, Peruvian army officers have refused to perform policing missions. One method, also used during 2000–2007 in Sendero zones (see above), is to "pass the buck up"—that is, refuse to act without orders from a commanding officer.

An excerpt from an interview with a mid-ranking officer captures this dynamic in the policing arena.

> If I am working in Arequipa, like I was [recently], and there is a major uprising and the police withdraws, I can call in my men, but then if anyone gets hurt, it's on my shoulders. So I can call my commanding officer in Arequipa and tell him the situation and ask what I should do. My commander can tell me what to do, then. I can then follow through, or I can demand that I get . . . an order in writing, because I don't want to be blamed should civilians get hurt.

> *And your commander, can he just give you the go-ahead, or is he required to check with the higher-ups?*
>
> He can give the go-ahead, but he might not want to. He, too, might want the order to be written, from higher up.
>
> *Normally, in practice, how is it done? Does the commander wait for it to be in writing before giving the order, or does he make the decision on his own?*
>
> Well, you may know of the case in Arequipa in 2002. The general there was ordered to send in the troops. He said, not unless he got the order in writing . . . Puno in 2004 is another case you must know about, in Ilave. The *pueblo* [community] rose up and killed the mayor. There is a battalion right there in town. They didn't do anything. They shut their doors, and the commander called his boss, who called the higher-ups, who called the President.[85]

Another mechanism by which the army has resisted policing is to use the army bureaucracy to slow down the communication of orders. When asked whether the army ever helped the police to control protests against mining companies in the northern Cajamarca department, where substantial popular mobilization has taken place around the industry, a senior officer responded as follows:

> In Cajamarca, it is . . . the population, not an armed group. Since it is the population . . . it is not the army's problem. The President has pressured the army to enter up there, but the army hasn't done it.
>
> *How is that? If the President says the army should go in, doesn't the army need to go in?*
>
> Well, what happens is that if the President gives the order in Lima, the [army commanders] in Lima say, "yes, of course we'll do it." They then give the order, but in such a way that it will get caught up in the bureaucracy, and the order will never arrive in Cajamarca . . . So that is why the President or his ministers must talk with the regional [army commanders] directly, as was the case in Arequipa in 2002.

Ongoing Resistance to Policing

Despite the new rules of engagement in internal security—which give the army legal cover during both policing and counterinsurgency operations—the army's police work has still been limited, showing us that the army's narrow mission beliefs, not issues of army autonomy, are the primary factor deterring the army from the work.

Executive decrees and resolutions have been necessary to bring the army into protest control, which happened on several occasions between 2007 and 2009. Three such cases were described in early 2009 by the former defense advisor referenced in the above discussion of Plan VRAE, who had worked in the defense ministry on questions of internal security in 2007 and 2008. He said that the army had continued to show antipathy toward policing, as was evident during all three protests. A fourth, highly visible incident occurred in mid-2009, in the northern department of Amazonas. In all four cases, the army avoided direct confrontations with civilians.

The first occurrence was in July 2007, when the armed forces were assigned to assume responsibility for internal security at the national level for thirty days, during a strike by Peru's national labor confederation (Confederación General de Trabajadores del Péru, CGTP). Protesters had taken over the airport in Puno, prevented flights from leaving the Cusco airport, and blocked the Panamerican highway in the south and the highway connecting the cities of Arequipa and Puno. Supreme Decree 060-2007-PCM, referring to Law 28222—which permits the army to conduct internal security operations outside emergency zones for up to thirty days (see above)—assigned the armed forces to guarantee the functioning of public services and to guard "strategic points." In response, the army took a back seat to the national police: the police, not the army, were responsible for the 160 arrests, 18 deaths, and physical harm to 150 others that occurred during the protests, according to the former defense advisor who had followed the case closely. On a second occasion, in February 2008, the army was ordered to control popular uprisings in seven provinces in the departments of Ancash, La Libertad, and Lima, involving opposition to the Peru-U.S. free trade agreement (Supreme Decree 012-2008-PCM, Supreme Resolution 057-2008-DE). Press reports that stated that the national police caused violence, arrests, and four deaths, did not mention military repression (*La República* 2/20/08). In the third incident, in July 2008, the government assigned the military to control another national strike by the CGTP, again employing Law 28222 (Supreme Resolution 242-2008-DE). Once more, the police apparently were the sole state actor that repressed demonstrators: police made 216 arrests, and in the most violent department during the strike (Madre de Dios), sixty-one police personnel were wounded (*La República* 7/10/08).[86]

The fourth case of protest control occurred in response to a major popular mobilization in April through June 2009, when groups in Peru's northern Amazon jungle protested against decrees passed by García that encouraged resource extraction and the breaking up of community lands (Bebbington 2009, 12). As of mid-May, protesters blocked roads and waterways, halting oil transport through the state oil company's (Petroperú) pipeline, which normally pumped approximately forty thousand barrels per day (Ford 5/18/09). On June 5, protests peaked in the town of Bagua in the Amazonas department, where thousands of people gathered. In clashes between communities and the police, at least thirty-three people were killed, and another two hundred were wounded (Bebbington 2009, 12). By decree, the military was placed in control of Amazonas as well as provinces in Cajamarca. The army participated in regaining state control by surrounding Bagua and conducting joint exercises with the police to open roads, in addition to assisting the police with an operation to rescue twenty-three police personnel held hostage by a group of protesters (*El Comercio* [Lima] 6/6/09, 6/7/09; *La República* 6/7/09).

There are signs that under the García government, the army performed a different policing mission, antinarcotics, though to a very limited degree. In a new setting in which Sendero had transitioned from providing security for the drug trade—especially for *cocaleros* and drug traffickers—to also running its own drug-production and trafficking "firm" (see above), army patrols have performed interdictions in the VRAE, specifically through capturing backpackers (*mochileros*) that transport cocaine through the valley (*Caretas* 4/30/09). Nonetheless, this work has been minimal: army officers and other security experts interviewed in 2009 said that in the VRAE, the army fights insurgents and does not participate in antinarcotics.[87]

A final point about the military and counterdrug work is that at least some important sectors of the army have considered coca eradication to be detrimental to counterinsurgency, reminiscent of the army's position in the 1980s and 1990s. This stance was plain when, in 2009, the head of the army proposed a new policy on eradication: state-funded, self-eradication by *cocaleros*, as opposed to forced eradication (*Caretas* 6/4/09). A general serving in a high-level position in the army described the plan thus:

> The problem with eradication is that the poor depend on coca. If you eradicate coca, you leave them poor. This is counterproductive for counterinsurgency, because who do [the poor] turn to? We shouldn't see coca as the en-

> emy . . . Instead . . . the *cocaleros* [should] do [coca eradication] themselves. The government gives them a monthly salary for two years. Six months of that, they eradicate their coca, and for one-and-a-half years, they transition into producing legal crops . . . [and] you win the support of the population. Coca isn't the problem, the drugs are the problem. The United States has spent so much money on eradication down here, but you eradicate in one place, and it just pops up in another. For every fifty hectares that you eradicate, thirty are replanted.

When asked to explain how it was that the head of the army was the individual who proposed a new plan for dealing with coca in Peru, in his response the general referred back to the 1980s, saying that the army had to develop a counterinsurgency strategy: "In the 1980s, everything fell on the army. It's always that way. The army had to figure out how to deal with the problem. It is impossible to think about anything but a multidimensional effort."

SUMMARY

In this chapter I have applied the predictability hypothesis to explain the Peruvian army's minimal counterinsurgency work during 2000–2007 and its return to more assertively confronting Sendero Luminoso guerrillas, starting in 2008. When Peru's government reduced the army's autonomy to plan and carry out operations, counterinsurgency became impossible from the perspective of the senior cohort of officers. These mid- and high-ranking officers thought the reduction in autonomy introduced a contradiction into the army's counterinsurgency mission. The main mission was to eliminate the remnants of Sendero, and yet the army was denied the "necessary" autonomy to conduct that work effectively. For the senior cohort, this contradiction was an important challenge to predictability for troops on the ground. Army commanders in Lima and in the field responded by ordering very few counterinsurgency operations. When rules of engagement granting the army new autonomy were passed under the second García administration, the army returned to its earlier, more forceful, counterinsurgency practices.

In contrast to its renewed aggression against Sendero under García, the army has continued resisting police work—which can be explained by the army's narrow mission beliefs that define policing as inappropriate. This attitude has roots in the 1980s and 1990s, when the army carried out aggressive counterinsurgency that made clear to many officers what "appropriate"—that is, combat-based—internal security missions were, relative to the "inappropriate" work of policing. Furthermore, in the army's antinarcotics work in the 1990s, officers had seen firsthand how that policing mission could corrupt the institution and reduce its capacity to defend sovereignty.

As the next chapter shows, for the Ecuadorian army, very different experiences in the 1990s led to broader mission beliefs that require the army to conduct active police work. This commitment to policing has had implications for the army's performance in both the policing and sovereignty arenas.

CHAPTER 5

Mission Overload and Neglect of Border Defense

Ecuador since 2000

Like the Peruvian army from 2000 through 2007, since 2000, the Ecuadorian army has minimally performed its only salient sovereignty mission: in this case, to defend the country's northern border against incursions by Colombian guerrillas. Chapter 3 analyzed how the army's limited northern border patrols date to the mid-1980s, when Colombian guerrillas first staged attacks on Ecuadorian army border detachments. For the period preceding the 1998 Ecuador-Peru peace treaty, this neglect can be explained by the overload that resulted from the army's preference for and prior commitment to defending the southern border from Peru, combined with the newer threat in the north: that overload resulted in a contradiction in the army's northern border mission. In contrast, the 1998 treaty left Ecuador's army with the sole sovereignty mission of defending the northern border, a mission that grew in significance when a major Colombian counterinsurgency offensive, set loose by the 2000 implementation of Plan Colombia, pushed more Colombian insurgents into Ecuador. Yet the army still has resisted this sovereignty mission. In place of northern border defense, it has enthusiastically conducted policing missions.

The first part of this chapter describes the army's mission performance from 2000 onward and rules out the legitimacy, professionalism, and resource maximization hypotheses as effective explanations for army behavior. The second part applies the predictability framework to the case.[1]

NEGLECTING A POROUS BORDER WHILE POLICING THE INTERIOR

Amid the heightened insecurity that has existed on the northern border and in Ecuador's northern provinces since 2000, the legitimacy, professionalism, and resource maximization hypotheses all predict that the army would actively defend the northern border. As I will show, however, the army has performed little border defense, instead occupying itself with police work.

Insecurity in Northern Ecuador

This analysis of Colombia's internal conflict and its implications for security in Ecuador's north—especially the three northern border provinces of Sucumbíos, Carchi, and Esmeraldas—distinguishes between the Ecuadorian and Colombian sides of the international border, and between Ecuadorians and Colombians. Yet, as a preliminary note, these distinctions are somewhat artificial. In many cases, Ecuadorians living in the north do not perceive the atrocities they have seen in nearby, Colombian towns as harm against the "other," given the renowned close friendship and familial ties among Ecuadorians and Colombians on the border (e.g., P. Andrade 2002, 220–25). In fact, in some Ecuadorian border towns, the majority of the population is Colombian.[2]

Colombia's conflict has involved several insurgencies during the post-2000 period: the Fuerzas Armadas Revolucionarias de Colombia (FARC), the Ejército de Liberación Nacional (ELN), and paramilitaries. In the 1990s, membership in these groups grew by 60 percent (Moser and McIlwaine 2004, 42), and as of the early 2000s, the insurgencies controlled approximately 50 percent of Colombian territory (Rochlin 2003, 3; Sweig and McCarthy 2005, 18). Conflict has continued in spite of the aggressive policy of the Álvaro Uribe government (2002–10) to eliminate the FARC and a 2005 demobilization agreement between the government and the Autodefensas Unidas de Colombia (AUC), which had united many paramilitary groups at the national level. By the early 2000s, there were between seventeen and twenty-two thousand FARC combatants, with the number dropping by between 25 and 50 percent by 2008. The ELN numbered approximately five thousand in the early 2000s and was roughly one-half that size in 2008 (Ramírez

Lemus et al. 2005, 102; Sweig and McCarthy 2005, 17; Gutiérrez Sanín 2008, 12). The trajectory of the paramilitaries is more difficult to determine. Although estimates of the size of the AUC before the demobilization (including estimates by official government sources) ranged between seven and fifteen thousand, the Colombian press reported that up to thirty thousand AUC combatants were demobilized by the program, suggesting that many individuals misrepresented themselves as combatants during the demobilization process (Gutiérrez Sanín 2008, 7). Furthermore, since the demobilization, successor groups have continued their same violent tactics (Human Rights Watch 2009; C. Rojas 2009, 242).

These armed insurgencies have contributed to insecurity in neighboring countries, especially Venezuela and Ecuador, because their shared borders with Colombia are well-populated; border towns serve as attractive sources of assistance for Colombian insurgents.[3] For Ecuador, the FARC's power in southern Colombia is particularly relevant, as the FARC have been the main insurgency in Ecuador's north. In chapter 3 I described the expansion of the FARC into southern Colombia in the 1970s and 1980s. In the 1990s and into the 2000s, the FARC's power in the south was substantial, as demonstrated by the fact that the Andrés Pastrana government (1998–2002) granted the insurgency a liberated zone the size of Switzerland (known as the *despeje*) in that region, from November 1998 until the breakdown of government-FARC peace talks in February 2002 (Crandall 2002, 72–73; Arnson 2007, 136–40).

The ELN and paramilitaries also have carved out pockets of territory in southern Colombia. For instance, in 1997 paramilitaries entered Putumayo, the Colombian department that borders Sucumbíos to the north (Vargas 2004, 117–18). Between June 2000 and May 2002, Ecuadorian military intelligence personnel recorded sixty-three conflict incidents in southern Nariño, the Colombian department bordering Carchi, including Colombian military combat with the ELN (as well as with the FARC) and conflict between paramilitaries and the FARC. In the late 1990s, the ELN maintained a presence along Carchi's stretch of the international border, and the paramilitaries operated in northern Esmeraldas (*El Comercio* [Quito] 5/5/02).

Fighting in southern Colombia among insurgent groups, and between guerrillas and Colombian state security forces, has made northern Ecuador a zone for illegal forces, particularly the FARC, to recuperate, resupply, and carry out military training.[4] Although Colombian insurgents do not stage organized, military attacks on Ecuadorian communities or security forces, their armed presence in Ecuador has challenged the integrity of the international border, a clear threat to

Ecuadorian sovereignty, and has brought various types of insecurity to Ecuador, including targeted assassinations, trafficking in arms and cocaine, extortion, and other criminal activities. The situation heated up after the start, in 2000, of Plan Colombia, a U.S.-Colombian program to reduce drug trafficking and—following terrorist attacks on the United States in September 2001—the "terrorist" FARC (Loveman 2006b). The offensive pushed civilians, as well as guerrillas, into Ecuador: Colombian applications for asylum in Ecuador increased from 362 in 2000 to more than 11,000 in 2003 (Alto Comisionado de las Naciones Unidas para los Refugiados 2006).[5] The U.S.-backed Plan Patriota, a military attack on insurgents in the south of Colombia initiated in April 2004, intensified the spillover of refugees and insecurity from Colombia into northern Ecuador (Bonilla 2006).

This analysis concentrates on security threats related to Colombian insurgents in Ecuador's north. However, another role of insurgents in that region has been economic and largely nonviolent. In 2000, business leaders in the north estimated that as much as 80 percent of commerce in some border towns was brought by the FARC, paramilitaries, and drug traffickers (Faiola 10/1/00). Of Ecuador's northern provinces, Sucumbíos in the northeast perhaps has relied most heavily on FARC business. For example, commerce in Nueva Loja, the capital of Sucumbíos, dropped by 70 percent when, at one point in 2000, the FARC closed roads in Putumayo as a strategy to dissuade the Pastrana government from implementing Plan Colombia (Tamayo 11/18/00). In 2002, it was estimated that each week, the FARC obtained fifteen hundred cylinders of propane—which was subsidized by the government in Ecuador but not in Colombia—from Nueva Loja (Farnam 7/11/02).

Dressed as civilians, insurgents visit Nueva Loja's many restaurants, bars, brothels, and hotels (e.g., *El Comercio* [Quito] 5/17/05a). Those venues charge high prices, presumably due to the substantial amount of drug money flowing through the north, and they are busy seven days a week, according to a high-ranking police officer with recent experience working in that city. The following extract captures vividly one journalist's impression of insurgent presence in Nueva Loja.

> Inside the Panther, a grimy house of prostitution, beefy Colombian men with the trademark flattop haircuts of the FARC and crew cuts of the paramilitaries sit on opposite sides of the room, drinking beer and paying $2 to have sex with Ecuadoran women.

> "You can tell the Colombian jungle fighters from their boots," said one police official in the club. "They are thick, black and more expensive than any Ecuadoran in these parts could afford . . ."
>
> Late at night, when gunshots can be heard around town, the other hot sound is Colombian *corridos prohibidos*—or "forbidden rhythms"—a sort of Latin American country music about narco-guerrilla life. (Faiola 10/1/00)

Nueva Loja's unusually large number of pharmacies and health clinics regularly have treated Colombians suffering from war wounds, according to active and retired military officers and press reports (e.g., *El Comercio* [Quito] 5/17/05a).[6]

The FARC have provided significant economic support to townspeople living directly on the border in the three northern provinces, by purchasing items such as food, cigars, and drinks (e.g., *El Comercio* [Quito] 12/3/04). Residents of Ecuadorian border towns (mainly men and boys) have worked in Colombia's coca fields in FARC territory during the biannual coca harvest.[7] An estimated four thousand peasants from Sucumbíos have crossed each year to farm in these fields (Tamayo 11/18/00). Some Ecuadorians own coca plots in Colombia, as reported in the national press (Tamayo 11/18/00) and by a retired army officer who, in an interview, said that he had spoken with such professionals about these business ventures.[8]

Violation of the International Border by Armed Colombians

The Ecuadorian army's only salient sovereignty mission since the 1998 peace agreement with Peru has been to defend the northern border against incursions by armed Colombian actors. One form of incursion is that insurgents, mainly the FARC, have used Ecuador for military training and to evade their Colombian enemies. Some individual camps have the capacity to accommodate hundreds of FARC combatants at a given time (*Hoy* 8/31/01; Defence Systems Ecuador 2006). In 2003, Ecuadorian military intelligence reported that there were approximately one hundred FARC resting and training posts in Sucumbíos (*El Comercio* [Quito] 8/17/03).[9] In 2008 alone, the military found at least 182 camps in the north (discussed below). On occasion, FARC attacks in Colombia may have been planned and initiated from Ecuadorian soil, as Colombian sources claimed in June 2005, when the FARC killed nineteen Colombian army personnel in a confrontation in Colombia, directly across the border from Carchi.[10] For their part, paramilitaries have entered Ecuadorian territory during escalated conflict in southern Colombia.[11]

Beyond resting and training in Ecuador, Colombian insurgents, like Colombian state security forces, have violated the border by fighting in Ecuador. State security officials and members of the human rights community with experience in the north recounted in interviews that killings of paramilitaries by FARC guerrillas, and vice versa, have been common (see also Tamayo 11/18/00). In what the Ecuadorian minister of external and internal security, Gustavo Larrea, termed "the most serious attempt against Ecuadorian sovereignty committed by Colombia in at least the last century" (Observatorio Político de Defensa, Seguridad y Relaciones Civil-Militares [Observatorio Político] 3/08), on March 1, 2008, the Colombian military conducted a joint operation that decimated a FARC camp located nearly two kilometers within Ecuadorian territory, killing twenty-five individuals (an incident analyzed in more detail in the second part of this chapter). Other examples of Colombian state border violations include a June 2002 armed conflict between insurgents and Colombian armed forces that began in Colombia but then crossed into Carchi, where it continued for approximately forty-five minutes (*El Comercio* [Quito] 6/28/02). Similarly, in July 2005, members of a Sucumbíos community on the edge of the San Miguel River (which delineates a portion of the Ecuador-Colombia border) reported that armed Colombian military helicopters crossed into Ecuador for twenty minutes in pursuit of a FARC column (*El Comercio* [Quito] 7/28/05).[12] Colombian state security forces have most consistently violated the international border with aerial fumigations to eradicate coca crops in southern Colombia. By wind and water, glifosat—a chemical used in these fumigations—has adversely affected Ecuadorians' health and agriculture in the north (e.g., Acción Ecológica et al. 2003; *El Comercio* [Quito] 8/15/05).

Yet another form of border violation is guerrilla hostility against Colombian and Ecuadorian civilians in Ecuador. Armed groups have threatened, kidnapped, and killed subnational public officials (Observatorio Internacional por la Paz [OI-PAZ] 2001, 24–25) and have punished people for collaborating with enemy groups. In August 2000 in Sucumbíos, Colombian paramilitaries unsuccessfully sought to extort money from an individual with ties to the FARC. Soon after the event, the FARC killed two of those paramilitaries' accomplices (Faiola 10/1/00). In 2004, paramilitaries distributed pamphlets in the Sucumbíos border town of Corazón Orense, threatening to attack the town for collaborating with the FARC (*El Comercio* [Quito] 9/7/04, 9/8/04). Insurgents have coerced Ecuadorians—for instance, through kidnappings—to help fund their fight in Colombia. One highly publicized kidnapping occurred in October 2000, when ten oil workers were brought to Colombia for ransom (Associated Press 10/12/00). In April 2001, between forty and fifty armed paramilitaries hijacked six trucks in Ecuador, near the San Miguel River, and drove them to Colombia (Defence Systems Ecuador 2006).

A final way that armed Colombian insurgents have violated Ecuadorian sovereignty is by upholding their own laws, thereby supplanting local Ecuadorian authorities. In various locations along the Sucumbíos border with Colombia, the FARC have successfully enforced curfews and more generally established order.[13] The clearest indication of FARC control along the border may be communities' great fear of the guerrillas, discussed below.

Relative to the FARC, paramilitaries and the ELN have controlled few points along Ecuador's northern border. When the army began patrolling the Esmeraldas border with Colombia in 2000, army personnel learned that the ELN maintained a presence in Ecuadorian towns in that area. The ELN regularly visited communities in Carchi, too, such as the border town of El Chical. As for paramilitaries' influence, the paramilitary influx along the border, beginning in 2001 (*El Comercio* [Quito] 7/26/05), left Ecuadorian communities caught between the paramilitaries and FARC guerrillas, who had already established themselves in the north. Paramilitaries saw some border communities as FARC collaborators and threatened and attacked them because of that presumed relationship. The 2004 Corazón Orense case, described above, exemplifies paramilitary threats against communities presumed to collaborate with the FARC. In July 2005, similarly motivated paramilitaries killed eight peasants in El Azul, an Ecuadorian community on the San Miguel River (*El Comercio* [Quito] 7/26/05).

Not all paramilitary presence was contested by other insurgents, however. Two events in 2002 show how Palma Real, an Ecuadorian border community in Esmeraldas, feared and yet also depended on the paramilitaries.[14] In the first incident, a group of paramilitaries demanded that the town throw them a party. Afraid of the consequences of disobeying, the town obliged. During the party, paramilitaries raped female community members. The one policeman stationed there did not intervene. In the second incident, which occurred that same year along the Mataje River—which runs between Esmeraldas and Colombia—the paramilitaries killed pirates who had interfered with the townspeople's fishing. The townspeople were grateful for this service, especially given that the Ecuadorian state had failed to respond to the community's repeated requests for help.

Spillover of General Violence from Colombia

Added to their armed activities in Ecuador, the insurgencies have been connected less directly to high levels of violence and crime in the north. Civilian and military security experts, human rights representatives, and public officials familiar with the north have viewed the FARC as sufficiently organized and wealthy to hire civilians (both Colombian and Ecuadorian) to carry out criminal activities in Ecuador for them. Therefore, this study treats the fighting of these security threats as police work, not as the defense of sovereignty against organized, armed insurgents.

Violence in northern Ecuador has included targeted killings and gang violence associated with payback by the paramilitaries and/or the FARC for drug and arms deals gone bad, as well as violence caused by Colombian insurgent dissident factions and deserters. Extortion is common, and refusal to pay the amount demanded has led to kidnappings, attacks, and even deaths (OIPAZ 2001, 33). Carchi's wealthy landowners and owners of the large African palm plantations in Esmeraldas have been among the most vulnerable to extortion.[15] In Sucumbíos, the average number of homicides per year from 2000 through 2005 was more than four times that from 1993 through 1999 (Policía Judicial, Ecuador 2006). During the first half of 2002 in Nueva Loja, more than one hundred people were killed by assassins connected to the FARC or paramilitaries, and at that point the FARC maintained a list of three hundred more people to be executed (Farnam 7/11/02). In Esmeraldas, during the first half of 2001, the number of victims of violent acts treated in San Lorenzo hospital was seven times the number for the entire year of 2000 (OIPAZ 2001, 32–33).

Another dimension of insecurity in northern Ecuador that is related to Colombia's conflict is the illegal drug trade, a critical source of funding for insurgent groups and rampant in Ecuador.[16] Although Ecuador is not a coca-producing country, it plays a major role in cocaine production and transport, ranking third in Latin America and fifth in the world for the amount of cocaine intercepted in 2005 (United Nations Office on Drugs and Crime 2007, 78).[17] Of the 11,000 people in the Ecuadorian penal system as of early May 2005, 3,090 (28%) were there for purported criminal activities related to drug trafficking (*El Comercio* [Quito] 5/8/05). Ecuador has contributed considerably to the cocaine trade by producing and moving the chemical precursors used to process cocaine, especially petroleum ether, a by-product of the oil-refining process. Smugglers steal approximately fourteen thousand gallons of petroleum ether daily from the oil refinery in Sucumbíos (International Crisis Group [ICG] 2004, 18).[18] Base and paste made from coca leaves as intermediate stages in the cocaine-production process, as well as the final product of cocaine powder, have also been transported through the north, to be exported via ports along the Pacific coasts of Colombia and Ecuador.[19]

A final dimension of insecurity in northern Ecuador connected to Colombia's conflict is trafficking in weapons, explosives, and ammunition, with their destination being Colombian insurgents. Based on captures between 1998 and August 2000, the Colombian police's central intelligence agency identified Ecuador as the principal provider of munitions to Colombian insurgents, and second to Venezuela as a weapons source (*El Comercio* [Quito] 8/31/00).

The illegal arms and drug markets have corrupted Ecuadorian state actors. Many weapons and munitions confiscated in Colombia have been traced to the Ecuadorian military (*El Comercio* [Quito] 10/19/03). An independent commission headed by retired army colonel Patricio Haro found that, as of April 2009, at least fifty members of the military and police had been "bought" by the FARC and drug trafficking since 2000. According to Haro, a FARC finance official admitted to having paid $15,000 to a military judge and $5,000 to a district attorney so that they would shelve an investigation into a FARC weapons deal (*El Comercio* [Quito] 4/16/09).[20]

Oil Protest

An important dimension of insecurity in northern Ecuador, independent of Colombia's conflict but nonetheless relevant for this analysis, is popular protest against oil company practices and government oil policy. As was true in the 1980s and 1990s, protesters' demands have included restitution from oil companies for use of the communities' land and for the adverse environmental impacts of oil exploitation. Security officials with extensive experience working for oil companies said in interviews that protests are the main security concern for the oil companies.[21] Residents also have sabotaged pipelines to create oil cleanup jobs for community members, according to private security officials interviewed.

At times, uprisings have halted production throughout entire regions. For instance, as of late February 2002, protesters in Sucumbíos and Orellana (the province that borders Sucumbíos to the south), demanding royalties from Oleoducto de Crudos Pesados (OCP) Limited—which at that time was beginning construction of Ecuador's heavy crude pipeline—paralyzed oil extraction and transport, as well as transportation more broadly in the two provinces (*El Comercio* [Quito] 2/26/02). In that case, protesters closed down sixty-two wells and the northeastern refinery, costing oil companies more than $2.2 million (Lucas 3/1/02). As another example, mobilizations in August 2005 throughout Sucumbíos and Orellana disrupted production in 420 of the provinces' 450 wells, leading to approximately $400 million in losses, as well as the cancellation of a major contract with the private oil company Occidental.[22]

Predictions of the Legitimacy, Professionalism, and Resource Maximization Hypotheses

For this period of multifaceted insecurity in the north, the legitimacy, resource maximization, and professionalism hypotheses predict that Ecuador's army would assertively defend the northern border against incursions by armed Colombian actors, a prediction that, as we will see, is incorrect.

Northern Border Defense as Legitimate

Defending the border is a highly legitimate mission for the army. Broad sectors of the Ecuadorian public have been alarmed by the effects of Plan Colombia on security in the north, and the military, especially the army, has been the obvious state institution to guard the border against guerrilla incursions. Subnational public officials in the north have expressed concern about insecurity spreading from Colombia and have asked for military reinforcements there (e.g., *Hoy* 2/9/01; *La Hora* 5/11/04). According to a politician from the Esmeraldas province and a Catholic Church representative with experience working there (in separate interviews), judges in Esmeraldas have commonly kept violent crimes out of the court system, fearing reprisal from the FARC.

Communities all along the northern border have worried about insecurity from Colombia's conflict, as national newspapers have regularly reported, and as found by human rights organizations and Catholic Church groups.[23] During focus groups in Carchi organized by a Catholic Church group, members of border communities tended to avoid mentioning the FARC, which focus group leaders believe was due to residents' fear of being reported to the guerrillas by other participants. Similarly, in interviews for this study, army officers said that residents of Sucumbíos border towns rarely gave the army information about FARC presence and did so only if the particular army officer or soldier had achieved a certain level of trust within the community. In those cases, fearful of explicitly referring to FARC presence, community members instead would say, "strangers are here" (*hay desconocidos* or *hay gente extraña*). In some towns along the San Miguel River, community members scared of facing reprisal by insurgents have refused to identify the bodies of people who were killed (e.g., *El Comercio* [Quito] 7/25/05). Members of Ecuadorian border communities caught between fighting insurgencies may be particularly afraid of insurgents. When paramilitaries threatened to attack Corazón Orense (see above), townspeople feared both the possible attack and the potential onset of war in Ecuador between the paramilitaries and the FARC (*El Comercio* [Quito] 9/7/04, 9/8/04). Following attacks on the Colombian side of the border, northern Ecuadorian communities have emptied out, their members afraid that violence would spread to their towns (e.g., *El Comercio* [Quito] 11/13/04).

Ecuadorians residing outside the northern provinces also have been attuned to insecurity spreading from Colombia. Immediately following the start of Plan Colombia, a poll reported that 35 percent of respondents in Quito and Guayaquil believed that Ecuador would experience problems with guerrillas, as a consequence of Plan Colombia.[24] In late 2004, 83 percent of survey respondents in Quito and 80 percent of respondents in Guayaquil answered affirmatively when asked if they thought Colombian guerrillas were spilling into Ecuador (Informe Confidencial, Oct. 20, 2004).

This widespread concern about the guerrillas has meant that guarding the border would be a highly legitimate state activity. In particular, the army would be the obvious actor responsible for such security, as other agencies lack the capacity to navigate the topographically challenging border zones or fight armed guerrillas.[25] It is important to note that the legitimacy hypothesis predicts that the army would take on police work, as well; as discussed later in the chapter, there has been significant societal support—as well as legal and government backing—for the army to participate in policing.

Northern Border Defense as Lucrative

In contrast to a perspective that emphasizes military interests in attaining public legitimacy, the resource maximization framework would lead us to expect the army mainly to defend the northern border and to leave aside its policing assignments, in the interest of obtaining both Ecuadorian state and U.S. resources.

Ecuadorian government leaders have worried greatly about armed Colombian insurgents' threat to national sovereignty. For example, in a meeting between the defense minister, Hugo Unda, and his Colombian counterpart in August 2000, Unda described the government's concerns about repercussions that Plan Colombia could have for Ecuador.

> The initiation of the Plan could have three consequences for Ecuador: the infiltration of guerrillas into our territory, the spread of coca cultivation . . . to the northern, northeastern, and coastal regions, and possibly the migration of Colombians in a considerable quantity. (*El Comercio* [Quito] 8/4/00)

Official national security policy has revealed further the government's concerns about the armed threat on the border. The Gutiérrez administration's national security plan listed several external "pressures" that the U.S. and Colombian governments created for northern Ecuador: armed groups that carried out kidnappings, assassinations, and arms and drugs trafficking; insurgent camps used for resting in Ecuador; Colombia's violation of Ecuador's air space during fumigations of Colombian coca fields; and Colombian military and paramilitary combat against guerrillas, causing the latter to enter Ecuador (Consejo Nacional de Seguridad de la República del Ecuador [COSENA] 2003).[26] According to COSENA's 2002 plan to provide security in the north, guerrilla border incursions again were a main focus. Security expert Pablo Andrade interprets the policy as follows:

> Ecuadorian security policy seeks to prevent guerrilla groups, paramilitary factions, and groups and individuals linked to drug trafficking and crime with Colombian origins, from taking root in the country by bringing their military or illegal operations to [Ecuadorian] territory. (P. Andrade 2002, 190)

Critically, successive administrations in Ecuador have wanted to protect Ecuadorian sovereignty without being pulled into Colombia's internal conflict (Celi 2004; Bonilla 2006; Moreano 2010, 248), in the face of U.S. and Colombian efforts to bring Colombia's neighbors into a region-wide endeavor to eliminate the FARC. One specific U.S. strategy is to encourage Andean militaries to cooperate with Colombian security forces in their counterinsurgency (or in U.S. government terminology, "counterterrorism") efforts (e.g., *El Comercio* [Quito] 11/17/04, 11/16/05).[27] At international meetings of presidents and defense ministers in the Americas, the U.S. and Colombian governments also have proposed that Latin American governments define Colombia's insurgencies as "terrorist" organizations. The label has been interpreted by Latin American governments as a U.S.-Colombian attempt to make Colombia's insurgents a problem for the region as a whole: whereas an internal "insurgency" signifies to these leaders a state enemy in the insurgents' home country only, "terrorist" connotes a transnational enemy, broadly speaking, that leaders outside Colombia would have to confront. Since the start of Plan Colombia, the governments of the countries bordering Colombia (Brazil, Ecuador, Panama, Peru, and Venezuela) have taken the position that Colombia's internal conflict should not be regionalized (*El Comercio* [Quito] 8/18/00; *Hoy* 9/1/00; Bonilla 2006, 111–12). This stance was evident, for example, at the November 2004 meeting of American defense ministers in Quito, during which Ecuador's defense minister and several other attendees rejected the U.S.-Colombian proposition to define the FARC as a terrorist organization.[28]

In Ecuador, the government has pursued a policy of defending the northern border from armed insurgents and accepting U.S. security assistance, all the while trying to avoid entering a multilateral counterinsurgency effort. This policy was codified, for instance, in Gutiérrez's national security plan; under the "external" category of the Ecuador-Colombia security plan, one "favorable" factor was that Ecuador's government maintained a policy of not entering into the Colombian conflict (COSENA 2003). The delicate balance between defending sovereignty and not regionalizing the conflict is captured nicely by foreign minister Heinz Moeller, who articulated for the national press President Noboa's policy of not interfering in Colombia's conflict, while at the same time affirming the right of all countries to defend themselves "against those who try to infiltrate in order to traffic in drugs or carry out subversive activities" (*El Comercio* [Quito] 3/2/01). Similarly, in July 2005, foreign affairs minister Antonio Parra said that the Ecuadorian state was defending national sovereignty but not getting involved in Colombia's internal conflict, distinguishing between the two by saying, "Defending my sovereignty is not [equivalent to] getting involved . . . Guarding sovereignty does not mean interfering in the Colombian problem" (*Expreso de Guayaquil* 7/6/05).

Amid Plan Colombia, from the Gustavo Noboa (2000–2003) into the Rafael Correa (2007–present) administrations, Ecuador's government has assigned the military—especially the army—to defend the northern border from incursions by Colombian insurgents. This command further substantiates how highly legitimate the mission is for the army and shows that performing the work would seem a logical way for the army to attract additional state resources, considering the government's influence on how those funds are distributed. As is true in Peru, we should expect the army to be especially motivated by resource interests, due to the cuts made to defense spending after the 1995 Cenepa War. Also paralleling the Peruvian case, Ecuador's military influences defense policy considerably. (On these similarities, see chapter 2.) Therefore, in this analysis of government policy regarding the army's work on the border, we should keep in mind the very real challenges to separating government policy from the interests of military leaders themselves.

The government has ordered the army to guard the border against incursions and prevent and interrupt illegal acts committed by the insurgents in northern Ecuador.[29] For example, in October 2000, foreign relations minister Heinz

Moeller said the country needed logistical assistance from the U.S. government to help the Ecuadorian military gain "control of the borders and thereby avoid infiltrations [of Colombian insurgents]" (*Hoy* 10/27/00). In another interview soon after, Moeller specified that enhanced military capacity was necessary to guard the border effectively (*El Comercio* [Quito] 1/29/01). The executive has transmitted this border assignment clearly to the Ecuadorian armed forces. For instance, the Gutiérrez government's national security plan identifies the military's main responsibility in the north as confronting guerrillas, paramilitaries, organized crime, and national and international weapons and chemical precursors networks. In the plan, the "central military objectives" with respect to the north include stopping guerrillas from entering Ecuador (COSENA 2003).[30] Of some importance is that Ecuador's government consistently has refused to authorize coordinated Ecuador-Colombia military operations against Colombian insurgents in the face of U.S. and Colombian pressures to do so (e.g., Celi 2004, 267–73; *El Comercio* [Quito] 6/30/05, 11/16/05).

Consistent with these factors that would seem to drive the army to defend the northern border to justify its budget and potentially attract more future spending on the army, in 2001 the military joint command lobbied the congress for a larger budget, specifically to augment border security (*El Comercio* [Quito] 10/18/01). Similarly, in 2005 military leadership met with President Alfredo Palacio (2005–7) on two occasions to obtain more state funds for northern border defense and, as described by one journalist, referred to the "supposed presence of guerrilla groups apparently linked to Colombian irregulars" to rationalize the request (*Expreso de Guayaquil* 8/10/05).

Within the bounds set by the Ecuadorian government's mandate that the army defend the border but not engage in coordinated operations with Colombian security forces, conducting border defense also would probably attract resources beyond the national budget and, specifically, U.S. security assistance, which has been significant. Whereas annual U.S. security aid to Ecuador totaled between $760,000 and $12.8 million (averaging $5.4 million) during 1996–99, it shot up with Plan Colombia, ranging from $19.1 to $35.7 million (averaging $28.5 million) during 2000–2006 (Isacson, Olson, and Haugaard 2007). Those monies were heavily oriented toward the north, according to U.S. officials stationed in Ecuador (see also Narcotics Affairs Section, U.S. Department of State [NAS] 2005), and the majority went to the military, not the police.[31] U.S. investment in the Ecuadorian armed forces was significant relative to Ecuador's national defense budget; the approved defense budgets for 2001 and 2004 were $345 million and $590 million, respectively (of which approximately 60% went to the army) (Ministerio de Defensa Nacional, Ecuador 2002, 197; Ministerio de Economía y Finanzas, Ecuador, n.d.).

The U.S. "military group" in Ecuador—the U.S. Southern Command unit that coordinates transfers of resources from the U.S. defense and state departments to the Ecuadorian armed forces—has wanted Ecuador's army to defend the northern border. According to a U.S. official stationed in Ecuador, the military group's main priorities for the Ecuadorian army, in order of importance, are as follows:

1. The "war on terrorism"—that is, increasing border security to contain and, ideally, to reduce Colombia's internal conflict ("definitely number one")
2. Counterdrug efforts
3. "Professionalization" of the army
4. Humanitarian assistance

Specifically with regard to border defense and counterdrug efforts, U.S. military group officials have desired that the Ecuadorian army increase its efforts to stop Colombian insurgents from crossing into Ecuador, destroy coca plantations and cocaine laboratories in Ecuador, and interdict illegal drug activities in Ecuador, such as by preventing the theft and trafficking of petroleum ether.[32]

Ecuadorian officers interviewed clearly associated performing border defense with attracting U.S. assistance. Several officers said that it was mainly U.S. monies that funded army operations in the north, and they complained at length that the U.S. government did not give the army more funds. Officers talked about how, by using U.S. support to bring more army presence to the border, the army was demonstrating to the U.S. government its good use of U.S. resources, with the hope of encouraging the international support. For example, a mid-ranking officer said, "By putting our forces on the northern border, we are showing [the U.S. government] how important the threat is there."

Northern Border Defense as Professional

The professionalism perspective also predicts that Ecuador's army would concentrate on guarding the northern border. Officers interviewed displayed a pride in border defense that was qualitatively different from their attitudes toward policing. All officers who discussed the earlier, Ecuador-Peru border conflict took it seriously, demonstrating their high regard for the mission of border defense. For instance, they expressed great appreciation for the army's professionalization following the 1981 defeat (see chapter 3), respect for the army's "Cenepa heroes," and personal fulfillment if they had fought in the 1995 Cenepa War and regret if they had not had the "opportunity" to do so.

Several officers described the course of the Ecuadorian army's focus as a change from southern border defense against Peru to northern border defense against incursions by Colombian insurgents[33]—a narrative that does not include a policing component. For example, a retired army officer said, "We had a main mission, that of Peru. Once that was resolved, with the signing of the peace in 1998, the priority became Colombia, due to the strengthening of the guerrilla." Another officer, of the middle ranks, said, "Since 1995, with the peace with Peru, our attention has shifted to the north, especially with Plan Colombia."

When describing the army's actual work in the north, again officers' attention was on border defense. For example, a retired senior army officer discussed with seriousness and devotion the army's mission to defend the northern border, but he mentioned its work to control crime (*delincuencia*) in the north only after I broached the topic, and then he emphasized that more than crime, the army intervened in arms trafficking, a mission linked to the issue of armed insurgents. Added confirmation that army officers viewed sovereignty work as highly professional is in their voluntary explanations for *why* the army worked in the north. Of these explanations, 62 percent referred specifically to border defense and controlling Colombian insurgent activities in Ecuador, whereas only 17 percent mentioned policing (table 5.1).

If Ecuadorian army officers were, in fact, motivated mainly by an interest in performing their professional mission of sovereignty defense, then defending the northern border would be particularly attractive work, given that officers were heavily concerned by insecurity in the northern provinces. Military statements in the press since 2000 have focused heavily on dynamics in the north relating to Colombia's conflict, including by contributing to national newspaper reports about that topic, frequently featured in the "Judicial" section of *El Comercio* (Quito). Irrespective of where they were stationed, officers interviewed were much more concerned about insecurity in the north than security challenges in any other region of the country, and when they talked about northern insecurity, they primarily worried about threats they associated directly with Colombian insurgents. Specifically, thirty-four of the officers identified explicitly (and without prompt) security threats in Ecuador's north, and thirty of them referred directly to the presence or activities of insurgents. Tallying the thirty-four officers'

Table 5.1. Officers' Explanations for the Ecuadorian Army's Presence in the North (in no. of mentions)

Explanation		23 officers
To conduct sovereignty work		30 (62%)
Control Colombian insurgents	16	
Defend border / national sovereignty	9	
Replace southern border mission	4	
Help Colombia with its problem	1	
U.S. pressures / Plan Colombia		9 (19%)
To conduct policing		8 (17%)
Antinarcotics	4	
Oil security	2	
Other	2	
Lack of army roles		1 (2%)
Total mentions		48 (100%)

threat mentions, we find 69 (or 61%) of the 113 mentions refer to insurgents' presence or activities.

An Army Poised to Defend the Border

In a context in which legitimacy, resource, and professional interests have encouraged Ecuador's army to defend the northern border, the army seems to have been poised to do just that. In 2001, the command center for the fourth division—responsible for security in the northeast, including in Sucumbíos—moved north to Francisco de Orellana (a city otherwise known as "Coca") in the province of Orellana.[34] The number of army personnel in Ecuador's northern provinces has grown significantly since 2000. As of September 2003, the army reported having reinforced the north with seven thousand additional personnel since the buildup began (*El Comercio* [Quito] 9/21/03b). The total number of military personnel in the north in 2004 and 2005 was approximately twelve thousand, most of whom were army personnel, according to a national news source (*La Hora* 1/29/04) and active and retired senior officers. Special forces and jungle battalions have been assigned to the north permanently, in an effort to improve the army's operational capacity there.

Army doctrine has contained clear, specific prescriptions for how to defend the north from armed Colombian insurgents. A high-ranking officer in Quito said,

"There are rules of engagement . . . You take them prisoner if possible, that is, if our numbers are high enough in relation to their numbers . . . But if we are at equal numbers or at smaller numbers, then you have [an armed] confrontation." He further explained that army regulations granted personnel at all levels of the hierarchy the power to initiate combat against insurgents.

> At all levels, there are decisions that can be made . . . What we do and the level of force we use also depends on what the irregulars are doing in our territory.[35] When the situation is clear, then patrols don't need to check with their superiors back at the base. If backup is needed from another battalion, then the head of the battalion asks for backup from the brigade leader, who can send backup units without checking with Quito—that is the brigade commander's job.

In the words of a special forces officer who had recently worked in the north:

> There is always the progressive employment of force. [The insurgents] can't enter [Ecuador] armed. If they enter armed, we capture them, if possible. But if they shoot at us, we shoot back. This information is in *La cartilla de seguridad de las fuerzas armadas* [The Security Handbook of the Armed Forces].

Officers have understood their orders to conduct assertive border operations while not coordinating with the Colombian armed forces. For instance, a senior officer with recent experience commanding a unit in the north discussed at length the issue of Colombian insurgents crossing into Ecuador and valued the Ecuadorian army's efforts to prevent it. At the same time, he supported a policy of not coordinating operations or sharing intelligence with the Colombian military.

> Coordinating with the Colombian armed forces would mean that Ecuador would be getting involved in the conflict. It is best that Colombia deal with its own problems and that Ecuador stay out of it. The Ecuadorian army should stay in Ecuador, and the Colombian army, in Colombia.

In interviews, officers echoed these sentiments when they talked about what it meant for the army to defend national sovereignty in the north. A junior field officer with recent experience in the north said, "We shouldn't get involved in the Colombian conflict. We can only work to block the irregular forces from coming over here, into Ecuador. That's what we do and what we should be doing." When asked what he thought of the amount of military resources devoted to the northern provinces, a senior army officer stationed in Quito responded as follows:

The problem is complicated: it belongs to Colombia, but it is an internal conflict that has outcomes here. We are guarding our border.

What is the military's policy if the irregulars cross [to Ecuador] armed?

You kill them.

Assertive Policing

In spite of the Ecuadorian army's apparent commitment to defend the northern border, it has neglected the mission, instead actively conducting policing throughout the country. This behavior is surprising: policing is less lucrative, less professional, and no more legitimate than northern border defense.

Northern Border Neglect

Army border patrols are infrequent and short in duration and have rarely, only accidentally, resulted in conflict with insurgents. As of 2005, the most operative army unit in the country (special forces unit "Rayo 24," in Nueva Loja) conducted border patrols twice monthly at most, each patrol usually lasting three or four days. The army battalion stationed in the city of Esmeraldas and responsible for border security in the province of Esmeraldas patrolled the border once every four to eight weeks.[36] To supplement patrols by northern army units, army personnel stationed elsewhere have been sent north for the short-term assignment of conducting border patrols, but those rotations have temporarily replaced, rather than reinforced, regular border defense efforts. In particular, units have gone to the north from the "jungle school" (Escuela de Selva) in Coca and from the special forces brigade in the highland city of Latacunga, south of Quito. As of 2005, when a visiting unit patrolled, the permanent northern unit there did not.[37]

Patrol tactics have made violent conflict between army personnel and insurgents unlikely. Based on army officers' descriptions of their recent service in the north, the army's common practice in all three northern border provinces has been to patrol the border during the daytime only, and to steer clear of established FARC strongholds.[38] Indeed, in March 2008 the national news reported on four areas in Sucumbíos that were infiltrated by Colombian insurgents and that received army security only once each year: Angostura, La Bermeja, Nueva Santa Rosa, and Santa Elena (Observatorio Político 3/08).

Another way that army personnel have avoided the FARC is not to pursue guerrillas, even when the trail is hot. Ecuadorian government and police statements indicate that between 2004 and March 2008, 117 FARC bases and camps in Ecuador, the vast majority of which were empty, were destroyed (Observatorio Político 3/08). Officers describing their own experiences with such cases often emphasized how recently the FARC had left the bases; for instance, they recounted finding warm, partially eaten food belonging to guerrillas. Yet on those occasions, the patrols did not search for the insurgents presumed to be nearby. An Ecuadorian investigative journalist who had been on patrol with army personnel described standard army protocol: "You know, you hear about all of these cases where the army finds empty bases. What usually happens is that the army patrol comes, finds the base, destroys it, takes pictures, and leaves, without thinking of where the FARC might go, or how to pursue them." In May 2005, forty armed members of the FARC crossed twenty kilometers inside Ecuadorian territory, in Carchi, fleeing a Colombian army assault. With full knowledge of these developments, the local army battalion commander chose not to respond. He told the press that he had not interfered with the insurgents' return to Colombia (by taking prisoners or fighting them) because the guerrillas were lost and the incursion was "accidental" (*El Comercio* [Quito] 5/19/05).

The army's timid actions on the border have resulted in minimal conflict with guerrillas. The Nueva Loja battalion reportedly engaged in only one armed encounter with the FARC on the border from mid-2003 through mid-2005, resulting in the death of one guerrilla.[39] In all of 2006, two insurgents were detained by Ecuadorian military forces (Fundación Democracia, Seguridad y Defensa 2007a). Between 2004 and March 2008, Ecuadorian state security forces captured between fourteen and twenty-six insurgents (Observatorio Político 3/08, referencing *El Comercio* [Quito] 3/6/08, 3/16/08).[40]

Institutionalized Policing

Instead of defending the northern border, the Ecuadorian army has conducted assertive police work, for which there has been considerable legal, government, and societal support. At a broad level, Ecuador's successive constitutions have permitted the military to participate in internal security (e.g., art. 248 of the 1967 constitution and art. 128 of the 1978 constitution). Relevant to this analysis of post-2000 dynamics are the two most recent charters. The 1998 constitution defined the armed forces' "fundamental mission" as "the preservation of national sovereignty, the defense of the integrity and independence of the state, and the guarantee of its legal order" (art. 183). The 2008 constitution has narrowed the military's role slightly by defining its fundamental (but not sole) mission as being "the defense of sovereignty and territorial integrity" (art. 158). Added to any ongoing military policing efforts, the executive can bring the armed forces into internal security by declaring a state of emergency in all or part of the country "in case of imminent external aggression, international war, grave internal commotion, or natural catastrophes" (1998 constitution, art. 180; similarly, 2008 constitution, arts. 164, 165).

Whereas Ecuador's constitutions have permitted the military to participate in internal security, the Organic Law (Ley Orgánica) of the Armed Forces and the National Security Law have explicitly assigned the armed forces to that work.[41] Ecuador's 2002 white book declares that the military will contribute to "internal defense" during cases of "grave internal commotion," when the military should act to protect "strategic points and areas" (Ministerio de Defensa Nacional, Ecuador 2002, 113–14)—which include oil infrastructure, hydroelectric centers, and airports—thereby reinforcing earlier legislation that committed the military to protect such strategic interests (see chapter 3).

Crime Fighting. The army's anticrime work can be traced to the 1980s and expanded in the 1990s, as discussed in chapter 3. Since 2000, Ecuadorians have continued to be highly concerned about crime, and many have wanted the army to fight it. In two separate surveys that covered Quito and Guayaquil during 2005 and 2006, when asked to identify the principal problem in the area where they lived, respondents named crime more than any other problem,[42] and in January 2003, 92 percent of survey respondents believed the military should fight crime (Informe Confidencial, Jan. 25, 2003), which the government has ordered. For instance, during a 2005 crime wave in the southern coastal province of El Oro, for the first time the government decreed a state of emergency in that province for the purpose of cracking down on crime, mandating that the army (as well as the police) carry out the mission.[43]

With this backing, the army has fought crime assertively, especially in the north. One common example of this work is the army's patrols of the main northern cities and their outskirts.[44] In rural areas in the north, the army's anticrime operations range from running checkpoints ("military controls") throughout the north, to detaining drug and arms traffickers, to patrolling the OCP pipeline, other oil infrastructure, and private landholdings.[45]

Outside the north, too, the army routinely has fought crime. In early 2003, the military distributed approximately two thousand personnel (seven hundred from each branch) across several provinces to carry out a major urban anticrime effort (*El Universo* 2/9/03). In July 2004, 180 military personnel conducted anticrime patrols in Guayaquil, in two shifts that in total spanned a period of twenty-four hours (*El Universo* 7/1/04). As of February 2005, the number of military personnel patrolling the country's main cities as part of an ongoing operation totaled 700 in Guayaquil, 500 in Quito, 250 in Cuenca, and 250 in Machala, a city with exceptionally high crime, located on the southern coast (*La Hora* 2/22/05).[46] In 2005 a high-ranking officer in the army's communications office estimated that approximately 300 to 400 military personnel patrolled Quito every night.

Permanent structures within the armed forces make fighting crime a standard part of army units' responsibilities. When asked to explain the process by which a given army battalion might engage in anticrime work, a high-ranking army officer working for the military joint command explained that the joint command established broad guidelines for the army as a whole. Within this plan, each of the command's four region-level representatives (*fuerza de tarea conjunta*, FTC) was responsible for deciding which roles were "necessary" within his region. Below the FTC, the *grupos de tarea conjunta*—also within the joint command structure—had planning responsibilities, as well. As of 2009, in all three northern border provinces, army personnel conducted anticrime patrols without requests made by the police or subnational governments, and without orders from national politicians or from military command structures above the battalion level.

Weapons Interdiction. As a specific type of crime control, the Ecuadorian military is legally charged to oversee the transport of arms and explosives in the country, by a 1980 decree (Supreme Decree 3757) and subsequent regulations (Executive Decree 2065 [1994], replaced by Executive Decree 169 [1997]).[47] The army has used checkpoints to intercept weapons in the north and elsewhere, such as outside Machala, according to an officer with experience working there.

Contraband Interdiction. The army's work to intercept contraband—yet another anticrime function—is supported by a 1980 decree (Executive Decree 356) that assigns the military to monitor oil derivatives in border zones and ports. President Durán Ballén replaced this decree in 1993 (with Executive Decree 763). According to officers, this newer decree has served as the legal foundation for the army's contraband interdiction efforts, which have been institutionalized, in that army operations have been carried out independent of police operations. That is, the army has performed all aspects of the mission, including directly facing *contrabandistas* and border populations that gather to surround and protect contraband operations.

In the north, the army regularly has intercepted contraband, particularly in Carchi. Some contraband interdiction interferes with insurgent activities. For instance, based on interviews with officers and on news reports (e.g., Farnam

7/11/02), propane illegally transported from Ecuador to Colombia has had a dual use for insurgents: it is used for fuel, and the FARC are known for using propane cylinders as bombs. However, much of the army's contraband interdiction work has been against small-scale transfers of goods across the border. As part of this work, army personnel have confiscated small amounts of food or other goods transported from Ecuador to Colombia by people living on the border and have detained these individuals.[48] Officers with recent experience working in Carchi (in the province's only army battalion, located in the provincial capital of Tulcán) talked more about contraband interdiction when describing the Carchi unit's work than about any other mission, and said that personnel from the battalion's three border detachments intercepted contraband at the twenty-four known illegal crossings between Carchi and Colombia.[49] In addition, the army has intercepted contraband along the southern Ecuador-Peru border, where the illegal transport of Ecuadorian gas to Peru has been rampant (*El Comercio* [Lima] 2/5/06).[50]

Immigration Control. In the north, the army has helped to enforce immigration law as one of its missions. Colombians entering Ecuador legally may use one of the three official border crossings in the north, as opposed to the many other crossings along the border.[51] By law, Colombians must carry with them the standard document required of visiting noncitizens (Tarjeta Andina) and, beginning in 2004, their *pasado judicial*, or documentation of their criminal history.[52]

Support for the army's immigration control work is found in COSENA's 2002 northern border security plan, which proposed posts—Centros de Atención y Control de la Frontera (CENAF)—that would combine the efforts of the immigration agency, the police, and the military. Specifically, the CENAF were to "carry out strict control over the truly displaced and watch for ties that [such individuals] might develop with organizations at the margin of the law" (P. Andrade 2002, 209, quoting from COSENA's 2002 northern border security plan). The CENAF were not operating in any real manner as of 2005, according to retired army officers and a civilian academic with defense policy experience. Nonetheless, independent of the CENAF project, army personnel have actively controlled migration at many clandestine crossings between the two countries, detaining and sometimes deporting Colombians for not having the required documentation.[53]

Protest Control. The army's protest control work—in the north and elsewhere—is considerable. One particularly dramatic case occurred in early 2001, in the face of massive protests against a government privatization program. In the army's work in Napo in that case, soldiers injured twenty-three people and killed at least three (Lucero 2001, 68). Depending on how quickly protests escalate, local commanders have had the authority to decide whether or not to initiate these operations, without explicit approval from their superiors in the military hierarchy. In fact, in December 2005, a local commander was relieved of his position in Machala when he did not order his troops to manage a sudden popular uprising. Officers who spoke of this event provided it as an example of their obligation to intervene at times without first being ordered to do so.

Oil Security. The army's role in controlling protests overlaps with its oil security services, which include guarding oil infrastructure in Ecuador's northeast, mainly from protest against oil company practices. This work has legal backing from the national security law, COSENA's national security plan, and the white book, all of which mandate that the military provide security for strategic areas, as noted above. Other legal structures that assign the army to oil security include a June 2007 decree that obligates the military to provide security for "all installations, equipment, and components of the national hydrocarbon system"; the decree defines oil installations as "strategic objectives vital to the nation" (*El Comercio* [Quito] 12/28/07).

In this context, Ecuador's government has ordered the army to put down protests against oil companies, most emphatically in the form of emergency decrees during times of intense popular unrest. For example, in the February 2002 case of protests in Sucumbíos and Orellana described earlier, an emergency decree ordered the army to control protests. By the end of the month, approximately forty people had been arrested and more than three hundred injured in the clashes (Lucas 3/1/02). In fact, the government fired the defense minister in August 2005 when the army failed to adequately control protesters in Sucumbíos and Orellana, replacing him with Oswaldo Jarrín, in part—as told by a senior army officer interviewed—because Jarrín was known for his experience working in the oil regions and therefore was expected to be more effective at controlling protesters.

The army also has provided oil security outside such crisis moments. An officer working in the joint command estimated that northern battalions devoted roughly 40 percent of their resources to oil security. An army officer with experience providing oil security in the northeast said that throughout Sucumbíos and Orellana, approximately fifteen men were assigned to each oil well. A given army battalion in Sucumbíos or Orellana managed oil protests against oil companies roughly once a month.[54] Army officers said there were between 600 and 920 oil wells in the northeast, all of which received permanent army protection.[55] To supplement the army's work to control and deter protests by guarding infrastructure and wells, brigade and battalion commanders commonly have hosted and participated in negotiations between local communities and oil companies.[56] Beyond the northeast, the army has guarded the OCP pipeline in Esmeraldas and has provided security for Ecuador's La Libertad oil refinery, located on the southern coast near Guayaquil.

A concrete picture of army oil work begins with efforts of the fourth division, which has committed more than two thousand personnel permanently to the mission. Given that the army is made up of approximately thirty-four thousand personnel (according to a journalist with extensive experience reporting on the Ecuadorian military) divided into four divisions, and that the fourth division consists of eighty-four hundred personnel, two thousand is a relatively large proportion of the army, and certainly of the division.[57] Within the fourth division, the nineteenth brigade, housed in Coca and responsible for providing security in much of Orellana and Sucumbíos, has made the oil sector a high priority. As indicated by officers interviewed in 2005, the brigade's battalions have provided continuous security for oil companies, one of the brigade's remaining five combat forces has been assigned solely to oil security, and, at times, the other four units have been sent to perform the work.

Even in the heavily FARC-populated province of Sucumbíos, oil has been a priority. The Shushufindi unit, one of five battalions stationed in the province, generally performs only oil security.[58] Army officers and journalists said that special forces unit Rayo 24 (stationed in Nueva Loja) had two detachments, both of which were assigned wholly to security for nearby oil installations. The remainder of the battalion, working out of its main base, regularly has provided backup in oil matters. Units from the special forces brigade in the highland city of Latacunga have set aside their other assignments to tackle oil "emergencies."[59]

During interviews, officers in the northeast talked about oil security more than other missions, even in reference to army work in Sucumbíos, and suggested that oil security took priority over other missions. For example, when asked how frequently the unit patrolled, a low-ranking officer with experience serving in the Nueva Loja battalion said, "When and for how long we go on patrols depends on information . . . It might be that we are patrolling. Then we get a call that something happened at [some] oil infrastructure, so we all go there."

Antinarcotics. Ecuador's government has backed military counterdrug efforts. For instance, Ecuador's white book specifically assigns the military to antinarcotics:

> Drug trafficking and its related illegal activities being a phenomenon that should be combated from various fronts, the Armed Forces will collaborate decidedly to combat it . . . especially with actions of aerial interception, maritime and river interdiction, border protection, control of arms trafficking, and support of other state institutions. (Ministerio de Defensa Nacional, Ecuador 2002, 114)

The army's antinarcotics effort, funded by the U.S. government, mainly has consisted of interfering with the illegal theft and transport of petroleum ether in the north. Army personnel also have destroyed cocaine laboratories and some of Ecuador's few coca crops in that area.

AS THIS REVIEW OF THE ECUADORIAN ARMY'S MISSION PERFORMANCE since 2000 shows, the army's behavior cannot be explained by hypotheses that emphasize military interests in public legitimacy, resources, or professionalism. To explain why the Ecuadorian army has underperformed its salient sovereignty mission and has carried out extensive police work instead of northern border defense, the following analysis employs the predictability framework.

OVERWHELMING SECURITY RESPONSIBILITIES

The Ecuadorian army has neglected the northern border since 2000 as a means of maintaining predictability for patrols in the face of a contradiction in the border mission. As in the situation on the northern border in the 1980s and 1990s, this contradiction came from the army's overload in security responsibilities. In the post-2000 period, the army's overload in security responsibilities has been due to its commitment to policing, which we would expect to be secondary, because police work has been less professional, less lucrative, and no more legitimate than defending national sovereignty. This commitment to policing developed when the army lost its southern border mission in 1998 and helps to explain both the overload and why, unoccupied by defending the nation's borders, the army has carried out extensive police work.

Policing to Avoid Obsolescence

To explain the mission overload and the resulting contradiction in the army's northern border mission, we begin by examining army mission beliefs. Ecuadorian army officers consistently have considered sovereignty work to be more professional and more worthy of pride than policing (see above). Nonetheless, officers hold broad mission beliefs, in that they think it important that the army conduct police work as well as defend sovereignty and contribute to economic development.

This analysis identifies the historical roots of the army's broad mission beliefs, emphasizing the army's concerns about legitimacy and resources. It was amid challenges to its relevance in society (i.e., legitimacy) and to its budget that the army embraced policing. Subsequently, and even after it was clear that northern border defense, not policing, was a route toward both public legitimacy and maximizing resources, those broad mission beliefs have still influenced army behavior.

Broad Mission Beliefs

Ecuadorian officers said that defending sovereignty, policing, and performing civic action were all important army missions (figure 5.1), in contrast to the attitudes of Peruvian officers, who, as we have seen, have resented being forced into policing. Another indication of Ecuadorian army officers' commitment to policing and sovereignty work is that when explaining why the army conducted police work, they revealed that they accepted the army's police functions as highly appropriate (table 5.2). For instance, common explanations were that the army performed policing to make up for the inadequacy of the national police, because citizens trusted the army, because doing the work was simply the army's responsibility, or because the security situation required it ("mission beliefs"). As shown in table 5.2, explanations for the army's oil security work were particularly likely to involve mission beliefs and the army's legal responsibility—unsurprisingly, if we consider the army's historical participation in oil security (see chapter 3). The one policing mission that officers questioned somewhat was antinarcotics work: ten of the thirty-seven explanations for the army's participation in that mission pointed to U.S. pressures.

Added to these aggregate data, several interview excerpts further reveal the army's enthusiasm for policing. Officers frequently said that the army should be flexible in order to meet whatever security needs might arise. For instance, a senior army officer working on the joint command's plan to restructure the military (a process that was to be completed by 2018) remarked as follows:

> Globalization means that the state, including the military, must restructure. And post-Cold War, we need a different kind of military than before . . . The new context is that of a three-part threat: drug trafficking, subversion, organized crime. These threats are threats that the armed forces must deal with . . . It is hard to decide what is police and what is military, in terms of roles.

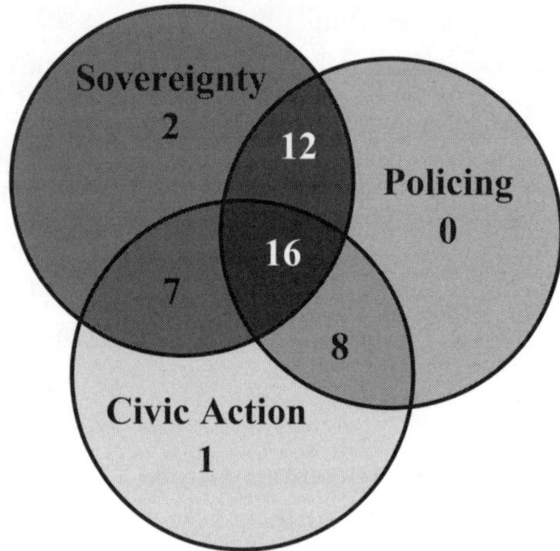

Figure 5.1. Ecuadorian Army Mission Beliefs by Officer. Forty-six officers were asked to name the army's most important activities. The officers are sorted by their first three responses, categorized as sovereignty (border defense, controlling Colombian insurgents, army training), policing (anticrime work, contraband or weapons interdiction, protest control, antinarcotics, oil security, peacekeeping), and civic action (*apoyo al desarrollo*). Other activities mentioned include political oversight (6 mentions), environmental conservation (4 mentions), and being a credible institution (1 mention). Responses do not vary by army rank.

When asked to identify tradeoffs to army anticrime work, a recently retired army officer who had reached the uppermost echelons of the army and joint command said that "like any business," the army needed to adjust to a changing environment, and now that security threats were internal, the army had to address them. A mid-ranking officer said that after the Cenepa War, "the army had the obligation to be prepared and ready for new threats that exist in the world," including drug trafficking. Similarly, with regard to the army's various internal security missions, another officer remarked, "With what the country is facing now, we do internal security work. With the changing threats and needs, we have had to change." Several officers purposefully interpreted security laws broadly to rationalize their police work. Multiple officers said that the arms control law, which assigns the military to monitor weapons, justified policing missions, including one senior officer who referenced the Carchi battalion's work: "We do checkpoints because of the arms control law, but my goal with these checkpoints is really to control crime in general. I use [the law] to justify the anticrime work that we do."[60]

Table 5.2. Officers' Explanations for the Ecuadorian Army's Police Work (in no. of mentions)

Explanation	Crime fighting	Antinarcotics	Oil security	Protest control	Security for landowners	General policing	Total (55 officers)
Mission belief*	17	13	19	6	4	1	60 (40%)
Police are inadequate	7	11	1	4	2	2	27 (18%)
Citizens trust army	6	0	0	4	3	2	15 (10%)
Political pressure	7	0	0	3	0	0	10 (7%)
U.S. pressure	0	10	0	0	0	0	10 (7%)
Legal duty	2	1	3	1	0	0	7 (5%)
Private sector requests	0	0	3	0	2	0	5 (3%)
Other	0	2	6	2	3	1	14 (9%)
Total mentions	39	37	32	20	14	6	148 (99%)

*"Mission belief" explanation: that the mission was the army's duty and/or that the army performed the work to provide security.

Not only were officers highly committed to both policing and defending sovereignty, but they also thought the army should always serve both functions. For example, senior officers in the army's personnel and operations office said the army sought to deploy units such that the institution would be able to fulfill its different security responsibilities throughout the country. The same logic applied, they said, within the northern provinces, where units were supposed to perform antinarcotics, counterinsurgency, border defense, and crime fighting. Beyond the army's central command offices, other officers described a need to manage army responsibilities, as well. Twelve active-duty officers spanning all levels of the hierarchy said that the army should not send more forces north, because doing so would interfere with security efforts elsewhere in the country. For instance, when asked whether the army should place more forces in the north, a senior officer said, "We are guarding our border," but quickly added, "This does not imply that we have abandoned other responsibilities in other parts of the country." Referring to balancing army missions within the north, a senior officer with recent experience commanding a northern battalion held up a glass during an interview and said, "You see this? The rim is the Colombia-Ecuador border. We can't focus on the rim when the border is permeable . . . We have to focus on everything in the glass."

Although officers frequently mentioned civic action when asked to identify the army's most important activities (see figure 5.1), officers who discussed the distribution of army resources between border defense and other tasks emphasized a policing-sovereignty balance, without mentioning economic development or civic action.[61] One explanation for the omission may be that the army's development work generally accompanies the army's more expensive, security efforts; it was clear from interviews with officers that army units were distributed throughout the country based on security plans, not according to economic development projects.[62] Another, complementary explanation is that as of 2005, the army had reduced its civic action efforts and thus had few projects to support. Officers who had worked in and conducted research on the army's civic action (*apoyo al desarrollo*) program that was created at the start of the 1990s (see chapter 2) said it was rolled back during the second half of the 1990s, and one such officer estimated that the program had diminished further, by approximately 60 percent, since 2001.[63] Officers generally attributed the reduction of civic action to defense budget cuts.

Post-Cenepa Role Shift

The army's broad mission beliefs are rooted in past experiences. By the late 1990s, the military confronted pressures to prove itself valuable, as discussed in chapter 2. Coverage by the national newspaper *El Comercio* (Quito) of the Ecuadorian military in 1998—the year the peace accord between Peru and Ecuador was signed—brings to light significant public pressures on the armed forces to reinvent themselves as important to the Ecuadorian state and to society.[64] The press took for granted that the military's role had to be redefined after the southern border conflict was resolved. Journalists asked military leaders and retired officers to describe the future missions of the armed forces (e.g., *El Comercio* [Quito] 11/8/98a). One newspaper article begins as follows: "The visit of the commander in chief of the U.S. Southern Command . . . to Ecuador occurs six weeks after the signing of the peace between Ecuador and Peru and right when the new role for the armed forces . . . is being defined" (*El Comercio* [Quito] 12/8/98a). Editorials assumed that some kind of military role change would take place. A writer who thought that the armed forces were "inevitably forced to redefine their role" opined that "the country now has the possibility of revealing itself . . . as a society disposed . . . to demilitarize the economy and politics" (Arauz Ortega 11/7/98). Another contributor wrote, "It is evident, as the Defense Minister acknowledges, that peace with Peru is a new historical phase that inevitably affects the armed forces . . . There is the possibility of new [military] functions" (*El Comercio* [Quito] 11/2/98). Some writers described the military as having been heroic during the Cenepa conflict, argued that Ecuador's defense budget should keep pace with the defense budgets of other countries in the region, and/or thought that the military should continue and increase its anticrime and economic development work (e.g., for all these views, see Rivadeneira 11/9/98).

In response to these pressures, the military promoted its police work. For instance, in February 1998, in honor of the annual "Army Day," the army published a multipage advertisement about its contributions to security and development. The piece characterizes the armed forces' place in Ecuador's "modern society" as involving "internal action," including "controlling internal order in crisis situations"; participating in dissuasion, coercion, and strategizing for external defense; running the military industrial complex; and "in all arenas of action," fighting "new threats," such as drug trafficking, insurgent groups, and environmental degradation (*El Comercio* [Quito] 2/27/98). A joint command statement in a two-page newspaper advertisement, in May 1998, puts forth many threats to security in Ecuador, including "future social convulsions that could explode and manifest themselves in all levels of violence." The advertisement goes on to say that "the crisis and its multiple faces will oblige, as is obvious, governments to redefine strategies to preserve governability. The Armed Forces will also have to conceive of scenarios according to the new hypothesis and threats that in the future could present themselves." The statement asserts that the armed forces should "act decisively to eliminate" "grave internal threats that endanger the democratic institutionality and internal peace of the state," and it concludes by listing many possible future challenges that, the advertisement claimed, would demand attention from the military—as well as from the government and Ecuadorian society—to "overcome or at least ease the crises that will come." The challenges include insurgents, drug trafficking, land invasions, armed indigenous uprisings, separatist movements, violence from movements opposed to oil and mining companies, popular unrest, and crime (*El Comercio* [Quito] 5/24/98b).

In late 1998, the head of the joint command said that the constitutional missions of the armed forces of "defending territorial integrity, maintaining sovereignty, guaranteeing the legal order and supporting development" were not going to change, yet external defense was now a lower priority than other military responsibilities (*El Comercio* [Quito] 11/19/98).[65] In reference to the military's post-Cenepa roles, the defense minister and retired army general José Gallardo said, "Current events bring the armed forces challenges . . . because it is a new situation that requires us to adjust our thinking and our activities" (*El Comercio* [Quito] 11/1/98). He further specified, in the following month, that the armed forces would participate in economic development efforts and work toward reducing crime, "social dissatisfaction," and "explosions of violence" (*El Comercio* [Quito] 12/8/98a).

Alongside such public statements laying claim to internal security work—as well as other missions, such as contributing to economic development[66]—the armed forces, including the army, actively turned toward police work. In January 1998, the joint command proposed that the national constituent assembly transfer the police from the government ministry to the defense ministry, on the grounds that the armed forces were the appropriate actor to define the country's internal security plans (*El Comercio* [Quito] 2/22/98, 3/28/98).[67] Defense minister Ramiro Ricaurte said the objective of the constitutional revision was to spur military involvement in planning police operations, and the joint command specified that the police would be subordinated to the armed forces for some security plans (*El Comercio* [Quito] 2/18/98). With the constitutional debates in progress, Ricaurte said, "Internal and external defense planning corresponds exclusively to the Joint Command of the Armed Forces, in conformity with the Constitution, the Organic Law of the Armed Forces, and the National Security Law" (*El Comercio* [Quito] 3/28/98). In May 1998, the joint command claimed that the armed forces were in charge of the *Fuerza Pública* ("Public Force," consisting of the military and the police) and therefore of internal security, broadly speaking.

> Often conflicts arise unexpectedly, as motives lie hidden in the unconsciousness of people, waiting only for the sparks that reveal [those motives] and the leaders that channel them. In this sense, the Armed Forces and the National Police, by opting for a great identity like Fuerza Pública, will need to carry out difficult initiatives together . . . The Military Joint Command, in accordance with the National Security Law, as the principal body of the Fuerza Pública, must therefore opt for effective policies and strategies in order to conceive of adequate planning and employment of the Armed Forces and the National Police. (*El Comercio* [Quito] 5/24/98b)

When the constituent assembly rejected their proposal, the armed forces still went ahead with institutionalizing their policing role. Echoing the armed forces' position during the constitutional debates, the military promoted the idea that it would act independently of, and even oversee, the national police. Illustrative are statements about police-military coordination made by General Mendoza, head of the joint command, during a press interview.

> In a normal situation or in a case of disruption of public order, the control plan is the responsibility of the Police and we provide support through complementary operations. But when there is a grave disturbance of public order, the military internal defense plan is activated, and the Police become subordinate to the Armed Forces.
>
> *Does this mean that, in normal conditions, the Armed Forces are subordinate to the Police?*
>
> There is not subordination, but rather support to reduce the stress on the Police in the control of cities. We control basic services, roads, strategic areas, shrimp farmers, etc. (*El Comercio* [Quito] 11/19/98)

The military's intention to expand its internal security functions did not go unopposed by police leaders. When asked what he wished of the armed forces within the new structure, the head of the national police said, "A support [from the military] with respect, with joint planning . . . A recognition of the historical presence of the National Police just as we recognize the historical presence of the Armed Forces, which do not need to disappear" (*El Comercio* [Quito] 11/9/98).

This comment highlights both the military's interest in policing and the question within the security community of what the military's role should be.[68]

Meetings among the head of the joint command, chief of the national police, minister of government, and minister of defense in late 1998 (*El Comercio* [Quito] 11/21/98, 12/1/98) precipitated the implementation of army crime-fighting plans throughout the country. Provincial military and police commanders were ordered to institute plans for permanent coordination.[69] In response, the army increased its anticrime work in urban and rural settings, through added coordination and joint patrols with the police and through patrols independent of the police (*El Comercio* [Quito] 11/27/98, 12/19/98, 12/21/98).[70]

The new plan involving the first and second divisions exemplifies the army's intensified crime-fighting efforts.[71] The divisions' brigades and battalions were to coordinate operations with the provincial police commanders. The police were in charge of urban zones, and the army, rural areas (such as highways, including entrances to and exits from cities). Overall, four thousand army personnel of the first division participated in such operations (*El Comercio* [Quito] 12/1/98). The security plan allowed the armed forces to work in the cities by police request, in which case, the military joint task force (the FTC) would take charge of fighting urban crime (*El Comercio* [Quito] 11/27/98).[72] In accordance with the plan, the first and second divisions conducted operations for two days in Quito and in Guayaquil, respectively, resulting in the detention of 276 suspected criminals by joint army-police operations (*El Comercio* [Quito] 12/19/98, 12/21/98).

My analysis of the military's expanded anticrime role in the late 1990s has centered on military initiatives and meetings involving politicians, the police, and the armed forces. Nonetheless, other important social actors, and particularly business elites in Guayaquil, also contributed to the army's expanded policing role. For instance, shortly after the system of police-military coordination had begun at the provincial level, amid business pressures for the government to decree a state of emergency in the province of Guayas, military and police officers planned to meet with the chambers of production and banking in Guayas to inform them of the new strategy (*El Comercio* [Quito] 12/23/98). Ultimately, the declaration of a state of emergency throughout Guayas, lasting from early January into July 1999, was a result of direct pressures by industry actors in Guayaquil on President Mahuad, the police, and the military (*El Comercio* [Quito] 12/19/98, 1/18/99).[73]

Other than the creation of new provincial structures for fighting crime, another way that Ecuador's armed forces institutionalized their policing role was by incorporating the police into military training programs, beginning in 1995. After Cenepa, according to army officers interviewed, police personnel began participating in exercises, such as antinarcotics scenarios, with army lieutenant colonels studying at the army's war academy; and the national police sent officers to the joint command's National War Institute (Instituto Nacional de Guerra, INAGUE), where military colonels seeking promotion to the rank of general are required to study.

The army's experience of suddenly losing its legitimate mission of southern border defense has continued to affect officers. In interviews, officers were insecure about the army's appearing valuable to society and complained at length that civilians had not appreciated the armed forces since Cenepa and/or since the 1998 peace agreement—frequently referring to budgetary concerns. For example, a retired army officer said that the defense budget had faced reductions since 1998, and continued as follows:

> What happens if tomorrow the [Colombian] conflict ends? . . . The biggest threat for the army is the northern border . . . But the problem is to deal with threats against which the army and the armed forces could participate . . . terrorism, drug trafficking, organized crime.
>
> *Throughout the entire country?*
>
> Throughout the country, in everything that remains for the armed forces to do.

Officers also expressed concern about the army's relevance when they complained that private security companies were encroaching on the army's policing duties. For example, a senior officer said that the private security companies hired by the oil sector could ultimately become a "security force" that would displace the army. More than their concern about private security companies, however, officers were intensely competitive with the police. Several officers thought the police's internal security work was encroaching on the army's domain. One retired officer stated his concerns as follows:

> [The police] want to seem like the army . . . They have greatly widened their spectrum of activities, not only in internal security. It's . . . immigration, antinarcotics . . . They have . . . environmental protection . . . security on the beaches, on the riverbanks . . . so, they are always looking . . . to widen this spectrum so much.

Another retired officer begrudged the national police's "protagonism" and said that the police's "role identity problem" was clear when the police special forces were formed (in the 1980s under President Febres Cordero), mimicking the military.

Some officers complained that the police wrongfully received recognition for army accomplishments during joint operations. For instance, a junior officer bitterly said that a joint patrol might consist of sixty army personnel and only two police personnel, and yet the police would claim credit for any successful captures made during the operation.

Although officers competed with the police, they still tried to make the painstaking distinction between the army's policing efforts and the work of the national police, to present the army as an institution with its own valuable functions. Officers commonly differentiated between army and police security missions, even while describing similar activities. Some such explanations were entirely semantic, as was the case with the terms "check points" (*retenes*), which officers classified as police work, and "military controls," military work.

As a final note on the army's shift toward police work, the legitimacy, resource maximization, and professionalism hypotheses seem to explain quite well the Ecuadorian army's behavior in the late 1990s. That is, only after losing its professional role of southern border defense, and facing a challenge to its budget and its worth to the country, did the army fully embrace policing. Yet what we observe in Ecuador that is not anticipated by the resource maximization or professionalism approaches is that the army's experience in the late 1990s has had lasting effects on its priorities. The army's mission beliefs require that it operate in *both* sovereignty and policing arenas, even though the most professional, lucrative mission of northern border defense has now become highly salient. Even the legitimacy hypothesis falls short. Although the army may have sought to maintain legitimacy through policing, northern border defense is highly legitimate, too.

Contradiction through Mission Overload

The predictability framework can explain the Ecuadorian army's mission performance. The army's overload of security responsibilities introduced a contradiction into its northern border mission. Officers thought that aggressively defending the border would mean combat and possibly war with the insurgents, leaving insufficient resources for policing. Thus, to continue both border defense and police missions, the army has sought to prevent war by avoiding clashes with the FARC. This mandate creates a contradiction: the army is supposed to defend the border from FARC incursions, and yet it also has tried not to confront the guerrillas.

Lack of Constraints on Army Autonomy

Before analyzing the overload and the resulting contradiction, it is essential to establish that Ecuador's army could not have followed the same path as that of Peru—that is, contradiction through mission constraint. We observed that when the Peruvian government took measures to hold the armed forces accountable for their past human rights abuses in the late 1980s, and then again after 2000, it restricted the army's behavior during operations. In contrast, the Ecuadorian army has faced no such restrictions, consistent with the Ecuadorian military's more general autonomy in the current democracy (see chapter 2).

Because Ecuador has not experienced major internal insurgency, human rights abuses committed by army personnel have been relatively limited,[74] and the army has not faced widespread societal demands that it be held accountable for abuses. In this setting, Ecuador's military courts have operated independently of the civilian judiciary and have exercised jurisdiction over all types of acts committed by on-duty military personnel, leading to impunity for military personnel (Duque 2005).[75] For example, in 1994 the national human rights organization Comisión Ecuménica de Derechos Humanos (CEDHU) submitted a case to the Inter-American Court of Human Rights (IACHR) involving three individuals who were killed the year before in a joint military-police anticrime operation in Guayaquil. Fourteen years after the events, in 2007, the IACHR's decision on the case admonished the Ecuadorian state for failing to initiate criminal proceedings in the civilian justice system (IACHR 2007, 34).

Civilian courts have even voluntarily bowed out of cases involving military personnel, thereby narrowing their own jurisdiction, as exemplified by a 2008 case that CEDHU filed with the IACHR on behalf of two youths.[76] Military personnel in the northeast had shot the two individuals, killing one, for purportedly stealing petroleum ether. After a case was filed against the military personnel in the civilian justice system, the Nueva Loja supreme court sent the case to the military courts for their action, on the grounds that the defendants were military personnel. This case exemplifies the army's extreme autonomy near the northern border, where the army often serves as the only state presence.[77]

Plan Colombia and the Army's Overload in Security Responsibilities

If the contradiction in the Ecuadorian army's northern border mission arose through overload, what was the source of that overload? The army's commitment to police work, combined with the mission to guard the northern border against the FARC, overloaded the army with security responsibilities. Specifically, for Ecuadorian officers interviewed, war with the FARC (which no officer wanted) was a real possibility, could be triggered by frequent clashes with the guerrillas, and would be intense, given the FARC's high level of military skills, experience, and resources, including strong relations with Ecuadorian border communities.

Many army officers thought that war with the FARC was possible. For example, a retired senior officer said, "The guerrillas cross and suddenly are in our territory. This conflict needs to be taken very delicately . . . This will undoubtedly be an irregular war, a counterinsurgency . . . So [our army does] everything to be prepared for this." Officers widely believed that frequent combat against FARC columns could trigger a war, as described by a mid-ranking officer: "[At the moment] it's not an open war with the guerrillas. As soon as we get into a confrontation with them, we start a war." A statement by a junior officer also connects armed skirmishes to potential war with the FARC.

> With Plan Colombia . . . without realizing it, little by little, Ecuador is getting more involved in Colombia's problems. Of a hundred people that cross over from Colombia, maybe fifty are guerrillas. The guerrillas see that the Ecuadorian army is destroying [their] bases in Ecuador. They see their camps getting ruined. They might retaliate if enough of this happens. After a while, the guerrillas might see the Ecuadorian army as their enemy.

A mid-ranking officer said, "We shouldn't have more people here, because that might look like a threat, and it might lead to conflict between the Ecuadorian military and the guerrillas . . . [Should the Ecuadorian army put] more force [along the border]? No. We don't want guerrillas here."

War with the FARC could overload the army because, according to officers, the insurgency was militarily effective, in part due to considerable economic resources acquired through illicit activities, especially drug trafficking. Several officers said that the FARC had sufficient resources to hire civilians to do their "dirty work," such as assassinations, kidnappings, and drug trafficking. Yet, officers spoke less of the insurgents' material resources than of their discipline, commitment to a cause, and experience, which for officers further substantiated that the FARC would have an advantage over the army if the two groups went to war. For instance, a junior officer said army intelligence had found that the FARC trained between twelve and fifteen hours each day, which, he said, was more than Ecuadorian army units in the north trained. A mid-ranking officer commented that the main challenge to working in the north was to know that, at some point, the army would have to fight guerrillas—a challenge because the army had no counterinsurgency experience. A senior officer also expressed his admiration for the FARC's guerrilla warfare experience.

> We knew the south and [the border with] Peru very well. The enemy in the north knows the border and knows to use different weaponry—for instance they use gas cylinders as cannons. We don't know how to use such weapons, nor do we know the northern border like the irregulars do. Also, the tactics are different. It's new to us.

Officers were so concentrated on the FARC's military power that many complained during interviews about the lack of Colombian state security forces on Colombia's side of the international border,[78] because, for officers, the lack of a buffer meant that if war broke out with the FARC, the Ecuadorian army would be exposed to the insurgency's full force. The concern about the absence of the Colombian military from the border came through during interviews in many ways. For instance, a retired officer raised the issue in response to a basic, factual question.

> *Do you have experience working in the northern border provinces?*
>
> Yes. The regular forces in Colombia are absent. This I saw very personally in Putumayo [in Colombia] . . . The FARC had absolute control over that sector. The Colombian state was not at all in the sector . . . So, there in that sector, the border with Ecuador, the FARC controlled all of the authorities, the mayors, the courts. The Colombian state wasn't there.

When asked whether the Ecuadorian army communicated with Colombians on the northern border, a mid-ranking officer said, "I have never seen Colombian military personnel on the border."

Finally, officers thought that the support the FARC received from Ecuadorian border communities, especially in the form of intelligence, contributed to the insurgency's power in the north. Of the forty-one officers who spoke of the relationship between Ecuadorian border residents and Colombian insurgents, twenty-seven said that border communities collaborated with the FARC out of fear of retribution and/or because the FARC met residents' material needs in ways the Ecuadorian state did not.[79] Illustrating this view, a special forces officer made the following observation:

> When you go to patrol on the border, and you enter towns, [the population is] really reserved . . . They appreciate our gifts . . . but when it comes to

> information, they don't give it. And we don't have resources. For instance our doctor only attends two or three kids when we go through a town, or we bring notebooks with the national anthem [on them] . . . It is not enough to win their trust . . . Guerrillas, on the other hand, have helped them build houses . . . They do big projects, because they are right there, across the border.

Officers worried that support from border communities gave the FARC greater power relative to the army in the north: thirty-five officers described community support for the guerrillas and for the army as a zero-sum situation.

From Overload to Contradiction

Ecuador's army has sought to prevent war with the FARC in order to manage its mission overload. As I show here, army leaders' *means* of preventing war introduced a contradiction into the northern border mission: leaders maintained the goal of defending the border against guerrillas, while also demanding—though often not explicitly—that army units not fight the insurgents.

> If the battalion commander calls headquarters, no one answers . . . The commanders in Quito don't want to hear about the FARC in the north, so they don't pick up the phone. So, the battalion commander has to make the decision. If he arrests the . . . FARC, it could ruin his career.[80]

During interviews, army officers did not worry that their superior officers might sanction them for not capturing or killing Colombian insurgents. Indeed, following a 2005 incident in which forty members of the FARC were found in Carchi (see above), the local commander did not face negative consequences for not pursuing the guerrillas. When questioned about that incident, officers either viewed the commander's decision favorably or denied the events entirely.[81]

A few examples from interviews reveal the resulting contradiction in the army's border mission. A senior officer with experience commanding a northern unit said both that it was crucial that the army defend the integrity of Ecuador's international borders, including in the north, and that more army presence on the northern border could provoke the guerrillas, which he characterized as a negative outcome. Another senior officer said that if troops encountered armed insurgents in the north, army policy was as follows: "If the guerrillas are armed, we assume that they are attacking us, and we fight them." Yet when asked to discuss a recent case in which a northern battalion commander did not pursue armed FARC combatants in Ecuador, the same officer justified the choice as follows: "There could be reprisal . . . against the army. It was a delicate decision . . . If the commanding officer had ordered an attack on the FARC, the war [in Colombia] could regionalize [to Ecuador]." A mid-ranking officer said that the army's most important mission in the north was to keep Colombian insurgents from crossing into Ecuador, but he also said that increasing army presence would be a bad idea, because it could lead to conflict with the guerrillas. Similarly, a junior officer said both that the army's border responsibility was to protect Ecuadorian territory by blocking insurgents from crossing into the country and that more military presence on the border would have the adverse consequence of provoking the guerrillas.

This contradiction in the army's border mission suggests anything but predictability for border patrols. After all, what is a patrol leader to do when his patrol encounters a FARC column in the north, and how can he respond quickly enough to the situation so as to keep his men safe?

Managing the Contradiction

It has fallen chiefly on battalion commanders in the north to provide an army presence on the border without inciting armed conflict with the FARC, as those colonels and lieutenant colonels have had considerable discretion to decide which missions their units prioritize over others. According to a senior officer who had recently held a high-level position in the army's operations office, local commanders—particularly in the north—required such discretion so that they could perform multiple missions and respond to the ebb and flow of different security threats.

Northern commanders have ordered few, cautious patrols, thereby lowering the chance of contact with the FARC and helping to maintain predictability for patrols, so that the patrols do not have to negotiate the competing goals of (1) defending the border and capturing or killing insurgents and (2) avoiding combat with the FARC. Besides the norm of patrolling only during the daytime and along familiar parts of the border not controlled by the FARC (see above), another practice has been to order patrols that begin inland and run northward until they reach the border. A junior officer explained that this approach, as opposed to patrols along the borderline, reduced the chance of FARC encounters.

In spite of northern commanders' efforts, army patrols sometimes have come across armed guerrillas and thus have had to face the contradiction directly. In those instances, junior officers heading patrols, like their commanding officers, have taken measures to minimize the possibility of combat. An officer with recent experience working at the army's jungle school in Coca said that when classes conducting border patrols saw FARC river operations (in which the FARC were armed and in uniform), the patrols would call out to the guerrillas, telling them to return to Colombia. On several occasions, junior officers commanding border detachments have met with FARC leaders in the river separating the two countries.[82] During these brief encounters, FARC leaders have reassured army officers that they want no conflict with the Ecuadorian state, including the army. The meetings have been tense but nonviolent. For example, a junior officer described his experience as head of a border detachment in Carchi. While he and the FARC commander from across the border were speaking together in the river, members of both the FARC and the army units were lined up along their respective riverbanks, their weapons in firing position—yet neither side fired.

In a March 2007 meeting, an Ecuadorian army patrol of eighty men discovered an abandoned FARC base near Sucumbíos's northern border. During the operation, the patrol came face to face with FARC insurgents. According to the army report written up immediately after the encounter, the lieutenant colonel heading the patrol, José Hidalgo, interacted with both the FARC column commander, "Martha," and the second in command, "Marleney," as follows:

> [MARLENEY] Don't be afraid, the problem isn't with the Ecuadorian army, nothing is going to happen (*no pasa nada*).
>
> [HIDALGO] You crossed to the Ecuadorian side.
>
> [MARLENEY] We crossed, yes, but only to rest. We don't want problems with you. Our direct enemy is the Colombian army.
>
> [MARTHA] We know we are entering your territory, but only to rest after combat. We're revolutionaries and intend to destroy the Colombian oligarchy through armed means. We dream of a just country . . . Señores, with pleasure we are going to share with you half of a cow, so that you can have a good meal.
>
> [HIDALGO] It isn't possible to accept your offer. I only want to remind you that our work is to keep insurgent elements from crossing to the Ecuadorian side.[83]

Hidalgo then permitted the guerrillas to leave the camp peacefully. His patrol remained at the camp, where they proceeded to collect items including a notebook belonging to a key FARC leader, Raúl Reyes.[84]

Besides their patrol practices, Ecuadorian army personnel in the north also have smoothed relations with the FARC through weapons and drug deals. The Ecuadorian military's role in arms and munitions transfers to the FARC is dis-

Table 5.3. Officers' Explanations for the Ecuadorian Army's Lack of or Infrequent Combat with the Fuerzas Armadas Revolucionarias de Colombia (FARC) (in no. of mentions)

Explanation		18 officers
Intentional: to avoid conflict with the FARC		20 (61%)
They are Colombia's enemy, not ours	6	
Combat would harm army personnel	5	
We do not want conflict with them	5	
Other	4	
Beyond army control: difficulty of guarding border		13 (40%)
FARC are indistinguishable from civilians	6	
Ecuadorian communities help insurgents	4	
Other	3	
Total mentions		33 (101%)

cussed above. A senior army officer explained in an interview that it was relatively easy for army personnel stationed in the north to sell ammunition to the FARC, as doing so simply involved reporting that the stolen materials had been expended during army training exercises. As described in interviews, army personnel sometimes participate in the cocaine and arms trades out of fear for their safety. One senior army officer recounted a case in which FARC guerillas told an Ecuadorian soldier that if he did not sell them weapons, they would harm his family. Irrespective of the reasons for the deals, they are another facet of nonviolent contact between the FARC and Ecuador's army.

Revealing the great extent to which army personnel have sought to prevent armed conflict with the FARC, when officers explained why confrontations with the guerrillas did not occur more often (or, according to some, at all), they primarily mentioned the army's intentional actions to stave off conflict (table 5.3).

Minimal border defense directly explains the other main outcome that is of interest in the Ecuadorian case: the army's substantial policing. As shown earlier, Ecuador's army has been strongly committed to maintaining some degree of participation in both sovereignty defense and policing. Given that the contradiction in the army's border mission has interfered with border defense, the army has been available to police, which it has done vigorously.

The Contradiction Escalates

Eight years after Plan Colombia was initiated, another shock intensified the Ecuadorian army's overload in security responsibilities: the highly publicized revelation of a guerrilla camp in the north that housed Raúl Reyes. The army's reaction was to step up security work in the north while aiming not to fight the FARC, as this study would have predicted. Army personnel assigned to the north have continued managing the contradiction.

On March 1, 2008, a Colombian military joint operation entered Ecuador and destroyed a FARC camp located 1.8 kilometers inside Ecuadorian territory, in the zone of Angostura, Sucumbíos, without Ecuadorian government approval. The operation killed twenty-five individuals on the base, many of them insurgents, including Reyes (*Hoy* 3/2/08; Bachelet 3/28/08). In the camp, the Colombian military discovered a laptop computer belonging to Reyes, and in the computer's files Colombian intelligence agents purportedly found evidence of contact between Ecuadorian President Correa's left-leaning government and the FARC.[85]

Amid strained international relations following the Colombian military's border violation, Correa denounced as "slander" the Colombian government's accusations that he supported the FARC (*Hoy* 5/17/08) and claimed that any communication between his administration and the FARC was related to ongoing efforts—also pursued by the French and Venezuelan governments—to release FARC-held hostages (Robles 3/4/08).[86] Correa further said that the U.S. government sought to connect his administration to the FARC in order to remove him from power and guarantee the continuation of U.S. presence on the Manta air force base (see below), the contract for which was set to expire the following year (*Hoy* 3/16/08). Although Correa vehemently rejected assertions that he had ties to the FARC, his government was still compelled to prove that it was not in bed with the guerrillas. Later that year (2008), the Correa government invested in more military border presence in the north—for instance, funding an "emergency plan" that assigned $388 million to the military for northern border defense.[87]

Along with government pressures, a public skeptical of the military's effectiveness on the border drove the army to do more. An excerpt from a March 2009 press interview with Fabián Varela, head of the joint command, makes plain the open criticism of the military, as well as military leaders' own acknowledgment that they had poorly defended the border.

> *March 1 [2008] demonstrated the weakness of the armed forces. What are the main changes made since then?*
>
> . . . starting with the Angostura attack there was justification to pay much attention to this issue. A new defense plan . . . is going to allow us to [become more effective] . . .

> *But [these changes] started in December. What were the immediate reforms that were made in 2008?*
>
> We increased operations significantly. We have done 176 operations and our effectiveness has been higher than in 2007, with pleasing results, and in that way we fulfill our constitutional duty and satisfy the demands of Ecuadorian society. (*El Comercio* [Quito] 3/1/09b)

General Fabián Narváez, head of the army's fourth division, acknowledged military shortcomings when he said in February 2009, "When the Angostura [attack] happened, in reality we had many limitations of an operational nature" (*El Comercio* [Quito] 2/8/09).

Obligated to defend the border, the Ecuadorian army has intensified its work in the north, as it did following the implementation of Plan Colombia.[88] Additional personnel were sent to the border provinces, and more border posts were installed.[89] In early 2009, the army restructured such that responsibility for northern security was centralized under "Task Force 1" (Fuerza de Tarea No. 1), in part to defend the border more effectively.[90] Of the $388 million emergency fund, approximately $194 million went to weaponry, $35 million to other equipment purchases, and $160 million to maintenance.[91] Between March 2008 and February 2009, 1,211 officers and troops were trained or retrained in the jungle school in Coca.[92] General Narváez stated that the army's operational capacity improved by 50 percent during 2008.

The military has been vocal about taking northern border defense seriously since the Angostura attack, as suggested by Varela's and Narváez's comments to the press quoted above. Furthermore, in early 2009, the military joint command announced that Colombian insurgents—which it now referred to as the GIAC (*grupos irregulares armados de Colombia*, or "irregular armed Colombian groups")—were the military's primary enemy, and that GIAC presence in Ecuador would not be tolerated. In public statements, military intelligence blamed the GIAC for causing drug and arms trafficking, contraband, and other crimes in the north. Army general Celso Andrade, head of the fourth division and of the new Task Force 1, also defined the military's primary mission as combat against the GIAC (followed by, in order of importance, protecting the oil industry and antinarcotics work).

The military's attention to the border has had some results. The added investments supported patrolling: in 2008 alone, military (mainly army) operations destroyed 182 guerrilla bases and posts, whereas during the prior three years combined they had eliminated a total of only 106. Furthermore, there are signs that the Ecuadorian military has instituted some adverse consequences for military personnel whose jungle conversations with FARC members have been exposed. Publicity surrounding the 2007 Hidalgo-FARC river meeting described above obliged the military justice system to penalize Hidalgo for speaking to the FARC.[93] Shortly after Hidalgo reported the encounter to his superiors, the military justice system opened investigations into the case, but according to military sources in their communications with the press in late 2008, those investigations were a formality, and the military courts were going to absolve Hidalgo.[94] Only after the press publicized the case on March 29, 2009, did the military come down harder on the colonel: on March 30, the defense minister denounced Hidalgo's behavior as "grave" and said that the lieutenant colonel would face trial for it, and the military joint command issued a statement saying that the army did not tolerate Colombian insurgents in Ecuador. In late April 2009, Hidalgo's case was brought before the national congress as part of an investigation into possible links between government officials and the FARC.

Since the Angostura attack, the army has continued trying to defend the border but not fight the FARC. In 2008, the military registered only thirteen confrontations with guerrillas (*El Comercio* [Quito] 3/15/09), and skirmishes have been unintentional. For example, in late July 2008 in the canton of Lago Agrio (in Sucumbíos), an army patrol surprised ten guerrillas, who then opened fire so as not to be captured. No one was killed or wounded in the conflict. Similar incidents occurred in Sucumbíos in July 2008 (one case) and in late February 2009 (two cases).[95] A journalist knowledgeable about army patrol tactics said that patrols have maintained the practice of not pursuing FARC columns after locating empty insurgent bases.[96]

The contradiction in the army's border mission played out powerfully in a near confrontation between an army patrol and FARC insurgents in July 2008, in a zone known as El Ají, in Sucumbíos.[97] The case can be thought of as being highly likely to lead to armed conflict between Ecuador's army and the FARC, for three reasons. First, the patrol leader, Colonel René Paredes, was reputed to be very knowledgeable about the FARC's activities in Ecuador and committed to uprooting them from the north.[98] Second, prior to the patrol, Paredes had collected considerable intelligence about the zone and about the FARC column in question. He knew there was a FARC base in the area, close to a (civilian) house that was believed to be a source of supplies and intelligence for the column. Paredes expected that the base, like other FARC bases, would be near a hill, which would serve as a security lookout point. Third, Paredes's patrol came across an influential FARC leader, a valuable target for an army patrol seeking to reduce FARC presence in the north.

Initially, the army patrol seemed to be in true pursuit of the guerrillas. The fifteen army personnel reached the house, which was in the expected location and was filled with excessive amounts of provisions, suggesting that it was a FARC storage facility. The patrol followed a river from the house to the FARC base, which appeared to have been constructed recently and housed a large stockpile of explosives and fuses. Paredes ordered his men to climb a nearby hill to locate the guerrillas, with the idea that if the hill served as a lookout, FARC combatants might be there.

Even in this case of likely army-FARC combat, the army patrol managed, with great effort, to avoid armed conflict with the guerrillas it encountered on the hilltop. On arriving at the summit, the three army personnel at the front of the patrol saw five insurgents—two women and three men—eating. The guerrillas immediately grabbed their guns and pointed them at the army patrol leaders, who also had their weapons ready. The rest of the men in the army patrol immediately dropped to the ground. Paredes did not order the patrol to attack the FARC, nor did he direct any of his men to circle around the crest of the hill to surprise the insurgents from behind, both of which were available options.

Instead, the army personnel at the rear of the patrol, who wielded heavy-duty weaponry, retreated, and at the top of the hill, communication and negotiations between the FARC and army personnel began. The five insurgents were joined by seven other, armed guerrillas. The three army personnel shouted, "What are you doing here? You shouldn't be here!" At that point, Paredes arrived at the scene and began firing his weapon into the air. He still gave no order to shoot at the insurgents, even after he recognized Edgar Tobar, commander of the FARC's "Front 48" (the FARC organization in Putumayo), standing behind the other insurgents. A member of the FARC responded to the yelling and to Paredes's shots by saying, "Don't worry, we're going. There is no problem. Nothing is wrong here. We'll go." A member of the Ecuadorian patrol demanded that, before departing, the insurgents leave their weapons, but the guerrillas' response was, "We won't leave our weapons. We'd die before doing that."[99] The army personnel did not insist and instead remained in place while the insurgents, including Tobar, backed down the hill in the opposite direction and disappeared into the jungle, weapons in hand.

Alternative Explanations: Revisiting Legitimacy

At this point, it is invaluable to rule out more thoroughly explanations for the Ecuadorian army's mission performance that rest on legitimacy. The analysis thus far has shown that the army's concerns about legitimacy drove it to police work, but the legitimacy hypothesis would (erroneously) predict that the army would perform intensively both policing and northern border defense, as both missions are highly legitimate and viewed as such by officers.

Another legitimacy argument focuses on an interest within Ecuadorian society and/or within government not to be drawn into a regional conflict. However, also as discussed, that argument, too, founders. The goal of defending national sovereignty without engaging in a multilateral effort to contain Colombia's conflict provides context for, without explaining, the army's border neglect.

A final scenario would be that, as part of its effort to avoid becoming enmeshed in Colombia's internal conflict, Ecuador's government has sent the military north with the order to permit FARC combatants to operate in Ecuador. The facts suggest that no such government order has existed, and even if it had, its issuance would merely reinforce this study's basic finding that the army has faced an overload in responsibilities that has created a contradiction in its northern border assignment.

Any leniency toward the FARC in the north, in fact, feasibly would originate from within the armed forces, not the executive. The military tolerated nonviolent FARC activities in the north long before Plan Colombia (see chapter 3). In interviews, officers distinguished between the insecurity caused by armed guerrillas in northern Ecuador and the unarmed dimension of the FARC presence there, which they viewed as relatively benign. On the latter—for example, nonuniformed guerrillas' frequent visits to northern Ecuador's bars and hotels—officers often referred to the arrangement between the army and the FARC as a "modus operandi." A retired officer described what he referred to as a "tacit agreement"—"that the guerrillas don't cause problems for the Ecuadorian army, for the Ecuadorian people, and pass by very friendly, right? To have fun, to shop, but not to cause problems here."

Relative to the military's allowance of this type of guerrilla presence in Ecuador, the government's position toward the FARC has been uncompromising. In a February 2007 session of COSENA that included a conversation between the head of the military joint command, Hector Camacho, and President Correa, Camacho said that the guerrillas entered Ecuador on Fridays to amuse themselves, rest, and get medical attention. Correa's response was, "That the guerrillas come to amuse themselves and to resupply, I can't permit it" (*El Comercio* [Quito] 5/15/08). In another COSENA session, held two days after the March 2008 Colombian armed forces' attack on a FARC base in Sucumbíos, Correa scolded the armed forces for not having detected the FARC base: "How can it be that armed personnel enter our territory, and we don't have the capacity to take care of it?" (*El Comercio* [Quito] 5/15/08).[100]

Furthermore, if we consider the government's goal to defend sovereignty while not entering into Colombia's conflict, the government has erred on the side of entangling Ecuador in the neighboring war. Most notable is the 1999 U.S.-Ecuador agreement that granted the U.S. government ten years of access to Ecuador's Manta air force base. As a U.S. "Forward Operating Location," Manta was to serve as a take-off and landing point for U.S. drug-surveillance flights in the north. Security analyst Adrián Bonilla (2006, 117) characterizes the agreement as "probably the most controversial piece of [Plan Colombia] that [was] intended to bring [Ecuador] into line with the U.S.-backed antidrug policy."[101] Ecuadorian security experts worried that U.S. flights from the base gathered intelligence, both on the drug trade and on insurgency activities in Colombia; and that information on the guerrillas was shared with Colombian state security forces, which could pull Ecuador into a regional counterinsurgency effort.[102]

Although I found no evidence that Ecuador's government has ordered the army to allow armed guerrillas to operate in the north, if such an order did exist, it would only reinforce the dynamics identified here. Within the framing of this analysis, such a policy would add to the contradiction in the army's border mission. One mechanism is direct: by ordering the army to patrol the north without fighting armed insurgents there, the government would be handing the army contradictory commands.

Less directly, the policy would exacerbate anxiety within the army leadership over the institution's overload in security responsibilities. First, one president's policy to allow armed guerrillas into the north would set the stage for more overload under subsequent administrations, which might choose to adopt a stronger stance against the FARC. Second, an overtly friendly policy toward the guerrillas could spur a sufficiently heavy FARC presence in northern Ecuador such that, eventually, the army might well have no choice but to respond aggressively, due to pressures from outside the administration to deal with the problem—analogous to the post-Angostura dynamic. Third, if Ecuadorian society believed that the policy existed, the government could be pushed to take a hard line against the FARC as a way to disprove or compensate for the government's supposed pro-FARC orientation, again, like the situation faced by Correa after the March 2008 attack. Fourth and finally, those rumors in society could destabilize the government, due to a nationalist reaction in society and/or within the armed forces themselves. Ecuadorian history tells us that when the government is destabilized, it is the military, above all other institutions, that serves as arbiter and is expected to reestablish some level of political stability—as was true during the premature removal of presidents in 1997, 2000, and 2005 (see chapter 2). In all four scenarios, the army's mission overload is exacerbated, and my argument concerning tensions over military missions becomes even more salient.

SUMMARY

As in the Peruvian case, the army in Ecuador has underperformed its most salient sovereignty mission as a means of maintaining predictability for troops on the ground, in the face of a contradiction in the mission. However, the cases differ in terms of how that contradiction arose. Whereas the contradiction in Peru emerged through mission constraint, in Ecuador, where the military has not faced significant restrictions on its autonomy, the contradiction in the army's sovereignty mission was caused by mission overload. In Peru, then, factors external to the army proved significant: the army's senior cohort thought that government restrictions created a contradiction in the army's counterinsurgency mission. In contrast, in Ecuador, army leaders created the contradiction by responding as they did to those parameters. That is, it was the generals, not the politicians, who initiated the policy not to fight the FARC.

Another factor that helps to explain both the distinct paths to the contradiction and the armies' different roles in police work is mission beliefs, shaped by experiences during the 1980s and 1990s. Facing major internal insurgency, Peru's army was heavily involved in sovereignty work—namely, counterinsurgency—throughout most of those decades. In contrast, the Ecuadorian army engaged in combat on only two discrete occasions and, instead, was brought into policing assignments. These different experiences contributed to the divergent directions taken by the armies' mission beliefs. In Ecuador, the combination of ongoing police work and the sudden loss of the southern border mission led the army to reach out to police work to prove its worth. Those broad mission beliefs help to explain both the army's overload in security responsibilities—and therefore its neglect of the northern border—and its substantial police work. Having experienced no such sudden loss of a sovereignty mission and having been thoroughly corrupted by one specific police mission, antinarcotics, Peru's army instead developed narrow mission beliefs that essentially have prevented the army from policing.

CHAPTER 6

Battalions for Hire

Private Army Contracts in Peru and Ecuador

In this chapter, the discussion shifts from explaining how much sovereignty and police work the armies of Peru and Ecuador have carried out to the question of who benefits from those missions, with a focus on the post-2000 period. In each country, actors other than the national government—especially private companies in the extractive industries—have hired the army for security work, arrangements that have occurred predominantly at the local level. That is, local army commanders make their decisions based, not on technical evaluations of security needs, but rather on how much clients will pay for security. The analysis in this chapter thus identifies a major way in which resources have affected the armies' behavior.

Nevertheless, and as also shown in this chapter, at the local level, as at the national level, a resource maximization approach to explaining military behavior breaks down. Army units perform work for the highest bidder, but only subject to firm constraints: clients' influence on army units is checked by the army's mission beliefs and its drive to maintain predictability for patrols on the ground.[1]

RESOURCE-HUNGRY ARMY UNITS

Army units face pressures from army leadership to finance themselves, in a setting of increased government oversight of military financial practices at the national level. The Peruvian army can legally contract its equipment, infrastructure, and services to other state or private actors in return for "resources directly collected" (*recursos directamente recaudados*, or RDR); these resources are reported as part of the defense budget and, from 2003 through 2005, made up roughly 8 to 11 percent of defense spending (Robles Montoya 2003, 159–61; 2005, 145).[2] In interviews, Peruvian army officers said that the military has been more diligent about reporting this income since Fujimori's departure from office, amid the greater oversight and accountability in state financial practices (reviewed in chapter 2).

In Ecuador, in the broader climate of increased oversight of military finances (see chapter 2), national-level deals between the military and clients have been thwarted. Efforts to end military security work done for private sector resources were invigorated in late 2005, immediately after the national press printed an article describing a 2001 contract between the armed forces and private oil companies (discussed below), including details about material benefits the army received in return for its oil security services (*El Comercio* [Quito] 12/19/05a). As part of a new effort to achieve civilian control of the armed forces, the 2007 defense sector law (see chapter 2) outlawed direct resource exchanges between the military and the private sector. National contracting between Ecuador's military and private oil companies ended in response to this law. (As of early 2009, however, local deals between army units and private oil companies continued, according to a journalist interviewed who was experienced in reporting on the army and its operations in the north.)

Army leaders confronting these pressures at the national level have pushed local commanders to subsidize funds received from the central army budget with outside income. My analysis of these pressures is based on information provided by local army commanders and other officers with direct knowledge about the named units' finances, gained through their work on those bases. These officers had experienced, firsthand, the mounting demands from army leadership to self-finance base activities.

In Peru, an army officer described local army poverty as follows: "The army has its priorities, which include rations for the troops, ammunition, and fuel. But what is not prioritized by the army is electricity, water . . . paper for the office . . . So the units have to come up with this, to make up the difference." Local commanders throughout Peru have relied on various activities to support their units. Active and retired army officers said that unit commanders have leased their base infrastructure.[3] Across the country—for example, in the southern departments of Puno and Tacna, the northern department of Tumbes, and the northeastern city of Iquitos—army units run large plantations that provide subsistence for the unit personnel and generate revenue through sales to surrounding communities. Army engineer battalions are paid for their construction services, particularly roadwork. Units report only some of the income to the generals in Lima in the form of RDR, as explained by a retired officer from the army corps of engineers: "We need resources to fix the equipment, for maintenance . . . So the units might work for twelve hours, rent the equipment and men out for that period of time, but then report to Lima that they worked for only three hours."

The proportion of base operating expenses obtained through these arrangements varies—for example, from 15–20 percent in Tumbes to 20–30 percent for one particular battalion in Arequipa and 50 percent in Tacna. Some units that do not have access to clients have relied on subsistence work, further demonstrating their poverty. In detachments near the Peru-Colombia border, soldiers fish and hunt, and other remote units operate small ranches and gardens to help feed their personnel. Peruvian army leaders have pushed local commanders to bring in more money each year, as described, for example, by a mid-ranking officer reflecting on his own experience.

> Information [regarding a unit's self-financing] goes to Lima. Based on this information, the next year's budget is calculated. For instance, I tell the general that we raised 80,000 *soles* last year, and I say that to run the [unit] I need 300,000 *soles* for . . . this year. He gives me 200,000 and tells me to work harder this year to come up with the extra 100,000 *soles*.

In Ecuador, too, the army's national spending policies have starved army units, encouraging their commanders to be entrepreneurial. An officer reported that the Nueva Loja battalion received only $200 from the army each year to pay for maintenance of its thirty vehicles. A different officer, who had managed finances for that battalion, commented that the job was stressful, because the unit was perpetually unable to pay vendors on time. Yet another officer said that the brigade in Machala received from the army approximately one-tenth of the diesel and one-sixth of the gasoline that the unit used. Finally, there is the case of the Latacunga brigade. As the training center of the army's special forces that have rotated through the north to supplement the work of units permanently stationed there (see chapter 5), the brigade is critical to the army's northern efforts. An officer familiar with the brigade's accounting said that, not including salaries and food, the army covered only about 20 percent of the brigade's operating expenses. According to this officer, when a general in Quito ordered the unit to perform security tasks, the colonel in charge of the brigade could not refuse; he had to find a way to pay for the work. The same officer, who had worked in finances on more than ten bases throughout the country, said that other units fared similarly and that since the mid-1990s, pressures on local commanders to be entrepreneurial had risen.

Although Ecuadorian army units have generated the most outside revenue through selling their security services (as discussed below), micro-enterprises also support base functions, illustrating the units' financial desperation. At the time I conducted this research, the Nueva Loja battalion's sales from its fish and chicken farms yielded a precious $6,000 to $7,000 each year, which was spent on fuel. The Latacunga brigade sold its dairy and other farm products to military and civilian families to earn income that matched the amount of money provided by the central army budget, covering nearly 20 percent of the brigade's operating expenses (omitting salaries and food).

LOCAL CLIENT INFLUENCE

Army commanders, facing resource scarcity, have decided when and where to provide security in response to client payments. Clients generally have reimbursed army units in kind, thereby ensuring that the army's services directly benefit them and diverting army units from providing security for the general public. High-paying private hydrocarbon and mining companies have been particularly influential, winning out over other clients for the Ecuadorian army's substantial policing services in northern Ecuador and successfully hiring Peru's army to perform counterinsurgency to protect their own private interests.

The analysis here focuses mainly on the influence of private companies operating in the extractive industries, and thus it is critical to recognize the overlap between these private client interests and (public) national security interests in the two countries. Security for the hydrocarbon and, in Peru, mining sectors is in the national interest, according to political and military leaders. However, this overlap in national security interests does not explain the great extent to which local army units have provided security for the private sectors.

In both countries, and certainly in northern Ecuador and in Peru's Sendero zones, national security policy has prioritized security goals other than protecting the extractive industries, in which the private sector has been central. Private investment in the Peruvian mining and hydrocarbon sectors was encouraged and greatly expanded during Fujimori's radical neoliberal reform efforts (Kay 1996, 62, 64; Bury 2005, 222–27). In terms of national security interests, Peru's national constitutions have assigned the armed forces to "participate in the country's social and economic development" (1979 constitution, art. 280; 1993 constitution, art. 171). In interviews, both army officers and lawyers in the national mining, oil, and energy association (Sociedad Nacional de Minería, Petróleo y Energía, SNMPE) pointed to this legal backing to justify the army's security work for hydrocarbon companies. Lawyers working for the SNMPE said that a 1992 decree law that assigned the military to provide security for the storage and transport of explosives used by civilians (Decree Law 25707, especially art. 10) provided the foundation for the army's security work in the mining sector throughout the 1990s. More recently, in a 2000 agreement between Camisea and the Peruvian state, the armed forces were assigned to provide "the necessary security measures" when possible.[4] Nevertheless, security for the extractive industries has not been identified—in law or in interviews—as the *main* reason for the army's presence in Sendero zones, where the army is instead supposed to focus on eliminating the insurgency. Of the fifty Peruvian army officers who were asked to identify the army's most important missions, twenty-two mentioned counterinsurgency as one of their first three responses, whereas none mentioned security for natural resources (see figure 4.3).

Similar to the Peruvian case, private actors gained a more influential role in Ecuador's oil sector beginning in the early 1990s, during the country's most extreme period of neoliberal reform (Conaghan 1988, 85; Sawyer 2004, 94–97; Benton 2008). As we have seen, historically, oil also has been considered a national security interest, and the armed forces' legal responsibility to protect the sector was institutionalized under military rule and subsequently reinforced (see chapters 3 and 5). The military itself has sought to justify its oil work on the basis of national security interests. For instance, national contracts between the military and oil companies (discussed below) consistently referred to Ecuador's 1979 National Security Law when stating that oil was a national security interest and therefore within the military's realm of responsibility.[5] Furthermore, as shown in chapter 5, officers interviewed for this study expressed a strong commitment to security for the hydrocarbon sector.

Yet, again as in the Peruvian case, there is a general understanding within the Ecuadorian army that oil security should not be the army's main priority. During interviews, officers consistently emphasized that the army's central mission in the north was border defense, as described in chapter 5, not oil security. A 2001 directive issued by the commander of the army's fourth division indicates that the division would provide security to oil companies "without neglecting its fundamental missions and assignments" (Jarrín Roman 2001, sect. D).

Following the Money: Army Counterinsurgency Patrols in Peru

Private hydrocarbon and mining companies have hired Peruvian army units to conduct counterinsurgency patrols as defense against potential insurgent attacks on the companies and their infrastructure. Because of those payments, the army's limited counterinsurgency work has benefited private interests disproportionately, relative to more public security needs. In highly unusual cases, the army also has conducted police work for companies outside Sendero zones in exchange for company resources.

The influence of private hydrocarbon and mining companies on Peru's army was particularly strong in the 1980s and 1990s. During those years of intense conflict, Sendero's main weapon was dynamite stolen from mines (McClintock 2005, 63), used, for instance, in sabotage of infrastructure—a common guerrilla tactic at the time (see figure 4.2). In interviews, officers said that in the face of widespread dynamite theft, army units were assigned to all the main mines.[6] Officers and private sector representatives said that as reimbursement for army security, private companies commonly built and fully equipped bases to house these groups of approximately thirty to forty-five men each. A former private security official noted that companies contracted with the local army commander, who usually ranked no higher than a colonel. Another retired private security official provided the following example:

> When we put Mobil [in the Upper Huallaga Valley in 1991] we asked the commander in [the nearby city of] Tarapoto to put a base there. We set up the base, communications, and food . . . That was a platoon, thirty to forty men . . . We did one thing where [the troops] would have to patrol up to the site where Mobil was . . . on a hill. To pick up their meals, they had to patrol up a certain way we wanted them to patrol. The food would be strategically placed so that they would patrol where we wanted them to. We had nice

places for them to sleep. They were very well fed. Oil companies do that, by the way—they have incredible food.

During retrospective interviews with Peruvian officers about the security provided by the military for mining companies in the 1980s—before the neoliberal reforms and therefore when few private companies had stakes in the country's extractive industries—officers named only the U.S. Southern Peru Copper Corporation as a company (public or private) that received army protections, suggesting that *private* mining companies have proved exceptionally influential in terms of affecting army behavior. For example, a mid-ranking officer mentioned Southern to illustrate the more general phenomenon of army security contracts in the 1980s and 1990s.

During the worst conflicts with Sendero, we had much of the country under a state of emergency. If a mining company was in an emergency zone, then the military was responsible for protecting it, mining being a national security interest and a possible target for terrorist attacks. So for Southern, a small army unit was sent to provide security for the copper company.

What did the army unit get in return for this work?

It got housing, food, transportation, to carry out this work, from the company.

Even when private contracts did not determine army base locations, they could still influence patrol routes, a dynamic illustrated by a case in Huanta, in Ayacucho. An anonymous source observed the following events involving the army's Huanta battalion in the late 1990s. One of the battalion's counterinsurgency bases was located near the town of Ocros. Initially, troops from the base maintained regular patrol routes in and around the community. At one point, an official of a private mining company asked that the battalion commander move the base closer to the mine and order the troops to patrol in the company's vicinity. In response to the request, the base itself was not moved, but all patrols leaving from it began patrolling the company's installations and mine, neglecting Ocros entirely. Five days after the mining official asked for the help, new items appeared on the battalion base, including several televisions. The interviewee explained that the counterinsurgency base had not been relocated because decisions about base placements had to be reported back to the Huanta commander's superior, the brigade commander. However, the Huanta commander on his own had authority to change patrol routes, reaping the material benefits of the arrangement for his unit.

As we have seen, during 2000–2007 the Peruvian army's counterinsurgency efforts were highly limited. Yet still the private sector has influenced who benefited from those minimal counterinsurgency services. Private security officials and army officers interviewed said that after Peru's guerrilla threat was reduced, companies generally no longer fully funded army units.[7] One private security official summed up the current dynamic as follows:

> Now there are relations, though more informal, more friendly than anything. A company will . . . say, "Can you pass through the nearby town . . . ?" So the army, which can be doing its patrols anyway, walks the route that the company wants. The company will say, "Then, stop in at my encampment for food, for medicine, in return for these . . . patrols" . . . But none of this is official. Officially, the army doesn't do patrols and security in this way for the companies.

Although the main purpose of the army–private company deals has continued to be counterinsurgency, a private security official explained that companies also have enjoyed an important added benefit from the patrols: a deterrent against civilian criminal activity.

The case of the private natural gas consortium Camisea illustrates the ongoing influence of private clients in the VRAE. An official in the energy and mining ministry said that as of 2005, the army had a small unit near each of Camisea's fourteen installations along the pipeline. In separate interviews, an army officer and a private security official said that all counterinsurgency bases belonging to the Ayacucho brigade (Los Cabitos)—numbering more than ten—were lined up along the pipeline. Additionally, counterinsurgency bases in the department of Cusco provided security for Camisea installations, according to a security expert knowledgeable about the army's base placements. Considering that counterinsurgency bases in the VRAE at the time numbered between twenty-seven and thirty-five,[8] this amount of focus on Camisea represented a large proportion of the army's overall counterinsurgency efforts.

The army has conducted its Camisea work in accordance with agreements between local army units and the natural gas consortium. A private security official said of the army's security services for Camisea, "Officially Los Cabitos in Ayacucho has its strategic plans that determine where its bases are and what patrols it does, but somehow, *coincidentally*, its bases end up by Camisea and its patrols are there, as well" (his emphasis, expressing sarcasm). Specifically, the head of the Ayacucho brigade has negotiated directly with Transportadora de Gas del Perú (TGP), the Camisea consortium that operates the pipeline. Army officers knowledgeable about the case said that TGP had built and equipped the bases along the pipeline and covered all patrol costs. Conditions on the TGP bases were much more comfortable for army personnel than army-funded bases, as described by a mid-ranking officer.

> There is rotation [through the Camisea bases] so that the troops have the chance to be on the bases, as it is a better situation on these bases than on other bases of the brigade not located at Camisea . . . In these kinds of bases, there is better treatment of soldiers . . . The situation is better where these companies are, as they have more resources. They have [civilian] engineers living there, professionals, so the food is good there.

Peru's army has contracted directly with Techint, a leading member of the TGP consortium that handles Camisea construction. According to a retired military officer working for Techint in a security capacity, the army's security work was ongoing, as of early 2009, for Techint's Block 57 construction project in Chiquintirca in the Ayacucho province of La Mar. The army's two nearby bases conducted regular patrols in the project's vicinity, and in return, Techint supplied the bases with provisions. The army planned to add another base in La Mar, and Techint was also seeking security services from that base through direct negotiations.

At times, army-client relations in Peru have existed above the local level. For instance, there has been involvement by the joint command and/or head of the army in agreements about the use of major army equipment, particularly helicopters, as explained by a senior army officer, a retired interior ministry official, and a former private security official who had participated in several such deals. Army officers recounted that helicopter rentals were common and highly lucrative during the 1980s and 1990s. One retired general said of that period that "with the money that oil companies have and give us for using the helicopters, you can buy two helicopters . . . We did well."

The army has continued renting out its helicopters. As of 2006, TGP leased army helicopters continuously, even when those helicopters were needed for strictly public services.[9] A former official in the interior ministry recalled a time in the early years of Toledo's government when the executive needed army helicopters to provide backup for the police, but the helicopters were unavailable because they were being rented out to Camisea.

> We needed . . . high-altitude helicopters because there was a cold snap in [the department of] Puno, and we needed to reach the people with supplies. We had two or three [helicopters] but needed another one. The army said that theirs were in poor condition. One month later . . . [I learn that the army] *had* a working helicopter, but it was being rented out to Camisea, for these famous *recursos directamente recaudados*. (His emphasis of *had*)

The majority of the Peruvian army's work for private companies has been counterinsurgency in Sendero zones, but on rare occasions the army has performed strictly policing work in return for private resources. My research uncovered two such cases. The first, occurring in 2005, involved army patrols to preempt (but not repress) protests against Xstrata, a Swiss mining company. The company had been in the process of setting up a major exploration operation in the department of Apurímac, near the border of Cusco (and not in a Sendero zone). According to information provided by the Defensoría del Pueblo in Apurímac, the Provincial Federation of Communities of Cotabambas organized a protest to demand more resources from the company as compensation for land use (see also Peruinforma.com 10/12/05). The Defensoría contact said that army units from Cusco conducted "dissuasive patrols" in the area for approximately two weeks to preempt protests.

A second case of army policing for a private company is that of the army unit stationed in Andoas, near the Peru-Ecuador border. That unit has provided security for the Argentine oil company Pluspetrol, in addition to the work that was supposed to be its main assignment—border patrols—as explained by a mid-ranking army officer: "Right next to the company [Pluspetrol] is a military unit. It is there to care for the border zone, but it also works to provide security for the oil company." Officers who described the arrangement talked at length about the generosity of Pluspetrol toward the army unit. In the words of a mid-ranking officer:

> The men in the unit work twenty days and have ten days off each month. In return for the security that they provide for the company, the company provides [airplane tickets] so that people can go to Lima and Iquitos to see their families on their ten days off. And these people are very lucky who work there, because others working on the northern border with Colombia don't have anything or anyone around, and they can go months without seeing their families, because of the expense of traveling.

Similarly, an active-duty senior officer described the relationship between the army unit and the oil company as follows:

> There is reciprocity between the company and the army unit. Pluspetrol has . . . an airport to serve the oil workers. They have helped our army unit, too . . . The unit provides security . . . People working in the army unit there get to fly home from there, get discounts or free plane flights . . . This is due to a local agreement between the army and the oil company.

Outside the private sector, public sector clients have had variable success at procuring the Peruvian army's (highly limited) policing services. In 2005, the municipal government in Lambayeque contributed $20,000 to help cover the cost of the army's effort to remove land squatters (*El Comercio* [Lima] 2/10/05, 2/23/05a), an operation analyzed in chapter 4. In contrast, the army turned down resources from the customs agency and from CONACS (under the agriculture ministry) that were offered in exchange for army support for contraband interdiction efforts and operations to intervene in illegal hunting, respectively; and the army has also passed up U.S.-funded antinarcotics training opportunities (see chapter 4).

The Ecuadorian Army as Rent-A-Cop

Similar to the Peruvian case, in Ecuador, clients have hired army units for security—though client influence in Ecuador is more evident than in Peru, given the vast amount of policing that the Ecuadorian army takes on. Brigade and battalion commanders stationed in northern Ecuador have contracted their security services to four types of clients: the U.S. military, private landowners, local and provincial political officials, and private oil companies. These local agreements have affected how intensively army units perform different policing missions, as well as who benefits from that work (i.e., the paying clients). Private oil company payments have been particularly handsome, and in return, companies have received the most army security.

From 2000 through 2008, the U.S. military group increasingly supplemented its contact with the Ecuadorian army in Quito with relations with Ecuadorian army commanders in the north. According to U.S. officials in Ecuador, after Plan Colombia was initiated, military group officials grew frustrated that U.S. logistical support, such as Humvees, backpacks, and radios, often did not reach northern military units to support antinarcotics or border defense. The U.S. military group therefore implemented a system of direct engagement with local Ecuadorian army commanders, and as of early 2005, that structure was institutionalized: two military group officials were permanently assigned to the north—one in Esmeraldas to interact with Ecuadorian military commanders there, and a second in Coca to liaise with commanders in Sucumbíos and Orellana. A third official, stationed in Quito, communicated directly with the Ecuadorian army battalion commander in Tulcán, Carchi.[10]

The U.S. military group's local influence was palpable in 2005 and 2006. Northern army commanders employed their forces for antinarcotics work in direct response to U.S. pressures and regularly sought more resources from military group officials. In one interaction, an Ecuadorian army base commander told a U.S. official that the poor condition of his unit's equipment kept the unit from conducting more patrols. The U.S. official responded that he would see whether he could channel more resources to the unit and later confided to me that he did not know what he would do for that unit, because he did not like to continue giving resources to Ecuadorian army units if those resources were not going to be used effectively.

Wealthy landowners make up another client group of the Ecuadorian army in the north. As discussed in chapter 5, the army has provided considerable security for landowners facing threats of crop and livestock theft, extortion, kidnapping, and even death. Landowners have given army personnel food, lodging, fuel, and tires in return. These resources have been so vital to the Carchi battalion that officers focused on them during interviews. Of the nine officers who described the unit's security work, six voluntarily broached the fact that landowners reimbursed the unit for its security services. When I raised the topic during an interview with a seventh officer, he expanded at length on the arrangement and then complained that the resources provided by landowners were not sufficient. Two of the nine officers immediately responded that resources provided by elites were critical, when they were asked to discuss the importance of "local support" for the army in Carchi—with no mention of *material* support. In the words of a mid-ranking officer, "For us to move, we need gasoline. But if we don't have the people's support, we can't do the job. We need to get fuel from the landowners." Army services for Carchi's wealthy landowners were not public security; as a noncommissioned officer explained, the patrols protected wealthy landowners, not the impoverished people who lived within the same cantons.

A third type of client of northern battalions is subnational political officials: municipal mayors and, at the provincial level, prefects. These officials have used subnational government resources to subsidize army units' security services, particularly urban patrols. An officer with recent experience commanding a unit in the north said, "The prefect and the municipality ask for night patrols. I am happy to do this, but I need resources for it. [If I have] better relations with the mayor and prefect, I get resources." Public officials reimbursed battalions not only with fuel subsidies but also by helping with base improvement projects, providing items such as tractors on loan, building materials, and labor. The Nueva Loja battalion commander periodically requested assistance from the local or provincial governments, each of which usually responded to the request by giving the army unit five hundred gallons of fuel. Positive relations between the Tulcán battalion commander and local and provincial authorities yielded approximately the same amount of fuel. At least for a period, the provincial government in Esmeraldas gave the battalion in the city of Esmeraldas $1,500 per month, money that one army officer said was "necessary" for the unit to be able to patrol the province.[11]

As for local interactions between private oil companies and the army, brigade and battalion commanders have negotiated directly with oil companies to determine the amount and type of security to be provided and the payments for those services. A senior army officer and an oil company representative said, in separate interviews, that the Nueva Loja, Santa Cecilia, and Shushufindi battalions in Sucumbíos all maintained separate agreements with each of their clients. Army officers and oil company employees explained that in return for security, oil companies often gave army units the food, housing, vehicles, communications equipment, and fuel used for the patrols. For example, as of 2005, OCP Ecuador S.A. provided the Esmeraldas battalion with gas, supplies, and vehicles for patrols along the heavy crude pipeline. In Sucumbios, oil companies gave battalions vehicles, fuel, and food in return for patrols. In addition to resources used during actual oil security operations, companies have provided the army with added benefits. For example, the oil company Texaco Petroleum financed a potable water system and visitors' quarters for the Nueva Loja base. Texaco paid for both projects in accordance with an agreement between the oil company and the army's fourth division (*El Comercio* [Quito] 12/19/05a).[12]

Noteworthy is the power that *private* oil companies wielded. Interview conversations regarding the army's oil security work in Sucumbíos revealed that even where the state oil company (Petroecuador) operated, army units drew up agreements with the company's private contractors. Furthermore, prior to the liberal economic reforms in the oil sector in the 1990s, the army worked for at least some of the (few) private oil companies that operated in Ecuador at the time. For example, in an interview, a retired army helicopter pilot recounted his work for oil companies, beginning in the mid-1980s. He and other pilots had helped perform seismic evaluations from the air, in the northeast and on the coast. The officer also had transported exploratory materials to mining encampments for companies. Contracts for these projects were signed by the companies and either the army aviation commander or the head of the army.

Two caveats should be made about the local nature of army-oil relations in the north. First, though local agreements have influenced how much security oil companies receive from the army in calm periods and for small and moderate protests, the national government has declared states of emergency during periods of massive popular unrest over oil company practices. In these latter cases, the intensified army attention to oil has been the result of a direct executive order, as in the case of the emergency decrees to manage the 2005 oil protests in Sucumbíos and Orellana (see chapter 5).

Second, leaders drew up contracts at the national level before this practice was outlawed in 2007 (see above). (The defense minister would sign the contracts, but private oil company officials whom I interviewed explained that the real center of gravity in the state in those cases was the military joint command and army high command.) The largest known agreement was a 2001 five-year contract, which was signed by the defense minister, the head of Petroecuador, and sixteen private oil companies.[13] Nonetheless, the broad nature of national contracts left much to be negotiated at the local level, as described by a private oil company executive, referring to contracts between the army and OCP Ecuador S.A.

> The agreement is made at the highest levels here in Quito, and then the army delegates power down to the level of the battalion head. That battalion head and the local manager of the oil company in question work out the distance that the battalion will patrol along the pipeline and how much fuel, food, and housing will be offered to the soldiers and officers working the pipeline.

An executive in a private security company who had worked with several oil companies described the same dynamic more generally: "Usually there is a macro agreement, for instance between OXY [Occidental Petroleum] and the military here in Quito. There are also micro deals at the battalion levels, so that the military gets infrastructure for [its] bases." In some cases, resource exchanges happened at the national level. For example, through an agreement with the military joint command, OCP Ecuador S.A. provided the army with communications towers, according to a private sector representative knowledgeable about that case.

Private oil companies have been the Ecuadorian army's most influential client in the north, as illustrated, first and foremost, by the substantial amount of security work that the army has performed for these companies (see chapter 5). Furthermore, private oil companies have won out over other clients in competition for army services. For instance, during protests in Dayuma, Orellana, in late 2007, the U.S. military group gave supplies to a local school. The military group's goal was to help satisfy local needs so as to quell protests, and thereby enable the Ecuadorian army to conclude its oil security work and turn to U.S. priorities: antinarcotics and border defense efforts farther north.[14] When describing a 2005 plan by Ecuador's defense minister, Oswaldo Jarrín, to create a special oil security command structure within the military, a U.S. official stationed in Ecuador thought it was necessary to accept that the Ecuadorian armed forces prioritized oil security. He said that the military group had been "pushing a gringo strategy" in the north, which, he said, focused on having the Ecuadorian military guarding the border against incursions by Colombian guerrillas. He found that strategy erroneous, saying that the military group should "go with Jarrín's plan, because he is strong, supported, respected [within Ecuador's military]."

Landowners have also lost out to oil companies. In Carchi, where there is no oil or associated infrastructure, landowners have been the army's most important client. In contrast, that mission constituted a relatively small part of the work of the unit located in the city of Esmeraldas, which *did* have an oil client, OCP, and which devoted more attention to the OCP pipeline than to security for landowners. This practice of favoring oil security can be explained by the sheer wealth of oil companies. In one interview, a mid-ranking officer compared the amount of third-party resources received by the army unit in Carchi with those from oil companies in Nueva Loja (also known as "Lago Agrio"): "In Lago Agrio . . . there is more money . . . and more compensation for the military's security work for the oil companies . . . When I was [there,] . . . oil companies gave us food, housing, fuel . . . The oil company would give us dorms, good food, a good life."

In varied security settings outside the north, commanders have been highly entrepreneurial by selling their units' many policing services to local political officials and private actors. As analyzed in prior chapters, the Ecuadorian army has fought crime in Guayaquil. When asked about local financing of these anticrime efforts, a mid-ranking officer knowledgeable about the army's work in that city said that the municipal government provided "means." At least for a period during 1998, the provincial government of Guayas gave the Guayaquil army unit money for fuel to conduct urban anticrime patrols.[15]

The army brigade based in Machala also has relied on client financing. According to mid-ranking officers who had recently served in the unit, to support anticrime efforts in the city, political officials in Machala provided the brigade with fuel, trucks, and money, as well as materials and labor for base renovation projects. For example, the prefect's and mayor's offices donated materials for the construction of an on-base swimming pool. The Machala arrangements involved considerable entrepreneurship on the part of the unit commander; officers said that the brigade commander initiated the agreements, approaching the public officials for resources.

This case is noteworthy not only because Machala has high crime levels but also because the city is located on Ecuador's southern coast, the center of the country's important banana and shrimp industries and the location of one of Ecuador's three oil refineries. Officers with work experience in Machala said that the brigade engaged in agreements with Petrocomercial, the state's oil transport company (under Petroecuador), which gave the brigade money for fuel, to use for patrols. The brigade also contracted with private businesses in the banana sector and with the port captain, who provided the army unit with fuel for port security. The brigade's greatest commitment, however, seems to have been security for the shrimp industry, prominent in the Arenillas Ecological Reserve (Reserva Ecológica Arenillas), south of Machala.[16] Officers said that the Machala brigade received nearly $75,000 each year from the shrimp industry. These monies paid for army security services against theft, as well as rent to the brigade for use of the army's land and industry-specific equipment.[17] The army began this work at least as early as 2002; at that time, the army brigade devoted six trucks to patrols to provide ongoing security for shrimp producers (*El Comercio* [Quito] 11/19/02).

Latacunga is another example of local army entrepreneurship beyond the north. Unlike Machala and Guayaquil, Latacunga is a relatively nonviolent and low-crime city. Furthermore, in contrast to the two coastal cities, Latacunga is located in the heavily indigenous, highland province of Cotopaxi, where, starting in the early 1990s, the army carried out civic action (*apoyo al desarrollo*) projects to gain support among indigenous communities (see chapter 2). Yet, even in this relatively tranquil area, the army's central outside revenue source has been security work, as opposed to support generated from farming—the unit's other main business operation (see above). According to army officers interviewed who had recently worked in Latacunga, approximately twenty men from the unit rotated to provide constant security to the nearby hydroelectric project, run by the Brazilian company Odebrecht. An officer familiar with the brigade's finances said that the unit earned more than one-third of its operating resources—excluding food and salaries—through that contract.

LIMITS TO CLIENT INFLUENCE

In spite of their influence on who has benefited from army missions, clients have not overcome the constraints established by mission beliefs and the drive to maintain predictability for troops. For instance, Camisea has not caused Peruvian army units to perform more aggressive counterinsurgency work. In fact, security along the Camisea pipeline diverted the Los Cabitos brigade from what might have been more effective counterinsurgency operations, because Camisea work did not bring army personnel to specific zones where Sendero trained or otherwise openly operated. An officer with recent experience serving in the brigade said that in case of an emergency, men stationed near the pipeline or other Camisea infrastructure could leave those posts to address the problem, suggesting that emergencies were unlikely to occur near the infrastructure. Furthermore, unlike patrols from Camisea infrastructure, some patrols that left directly from the brigade's larger battalion bases spent a night away from the base and thus covered more remote areas where Sendero might operate.

Client influence in Sendero zones is also limited in that army-client contracts have not overcome the army's narrow mission beliefs that deter the army from policing. A former private security company executive who had worked with the army throughout the 1990s and into the early 2000s said that at least up until 2002, written agreements between army units and companies included language specifying that the army would not control protests as part of its work. Despite the army's ongoing relations with Camisea, it was the police that controlled popular uprisings over the environmental and social effects of recent pipeline breaks in 2005 (*La República* 12/3/05). Outside Sendero zones, the army resisted being drawn into controlling mining protests in the northern department of Cajamarca (see chapter 4). In spite of the army's ongoing security work for Pluspetrol, the army did not participate in controlling protests in Andoas against the oil company during major popular unrest in October 2006 and May 2007; reports stated that the national police, not the army, worked to establish order in those cases (*La República* 10/11/06; *El Comercio* [Lima] 10/21/06, 5/10/07).

In contrast to the Peruvian case, the Ecuadorian army's mission beliefs, being broad, have not limited client influence. However, as in Peru, clients' influence on the army has been circumscribed by the army's efforts to maintain predictability for patrols. That is, payments from clients have not caused the army to more assertively defend the northern border from Colombian guerrilla incursions. U.S. officials expressed frustration in interviews that despite their material support for Ecuadorian army units, the army patrolled the border only minimally. One such official discussed how the military group had come to realize that the Ecuadorian army would continue, at least at present, to avoid border defense.[18]

Even oil companies have been unable to induce the army to confront Colombian guerrillas. When the army's work for oil companies has entailed possible combat with Colombian insurgents, the army has been lax in conducting operations. Two examples illustrate this behavior.[19] First, there is the case of the EnCana Corporation's oil block. In February 2005, EnCana oil workers identified approximately thirty heavily armed men in one of the company's oil blocks. The men wore military fatigues but were not Ecuadorian military personnel. The oil workers thought the armed men were FARC guerrillas (who have been known to wear uniforms during their military training and operations). A contracted employee in a private security company office in the zone telephoned the local Ecuadorian army unit and asked that it pursue the insurgents. The unit responded by sending one patrol, which employed the "snaking" tactic, in which soldiers follow one another in single file. The private security official recounting the case—who had a military background (outside Latin America)—criticized this tactic, explaining that it was highly ineffective, given that the supposed goal at hand was to sweep a vast area to locate guerrillas. The troops made a single loop over the course of one hour in this formation, encountered no insurgents, and returned to their base.

Second, a 2002 case involving army security for the Bellwether oil block also demonstrates how oil monies did not encourage the Ecuadorian army to pursue Colombian insurgents. The oil block was located due north of Nueva Loja, on the Ecuador-Colombia border. An official from the oil company, Rio Alto, called the local army unit to report that Colombians presumed to be members of the FARC were using stolen pipeline materials from the company to build a bridge across the San Miguel River (on the international borderline). Rio Alto asked the army to resolve the problem. Members of the army unit then consulted with the Colombians working on the bridge and arrived at the following solution: the Colombians could continue taking materials and building the bridge as long as the materials were not currently being used by the oil company.

IN SUM, THIS CHAPTER HAS DEMONSTRATED how local clients, especially private companies in extractive industries, have used resources outside the national defense budget to buy army security services in the two countries, thereby influencing army mission performance. Yet, also as shown here, there have been important limits to clients' influence on army units' behavior. Although third-party financing has affected who benefits from army services, in neither country have clients caused army units to perform more sovereignty work—in Peru, counterinsurgency, and in Ecuador, northern border defense. Furthermore, the Peruvian army's narrow mission beliefs have preempted units from carrying out more intensive policing, even when doing so could attract much-needed client resources for the army unit. That is, more powerful than local client influence—and thus a resource-centered view of military behavior—are this study's two central independent variables: mission beliefs and the idea that armies prioritize maintaining predictability for patrols on the ground.

CHAPTER 7

Comparative Perspectives on Military Mission Performance

The research presented in this book on the Peruvian and Ecuadorian armies challenges three expectations about military behavior in Latin American countries: that militaries act so as to maximize their budgets, that they perform missions thought to bring more public legitimacy for the institution, and that they focus more intensely on the professional missions of external defense and counterinsurgency than on policing. In fact, at different times since democratization, the two armies have neglected lucrative, legitimate, sovereignty missions.

Through a close-up analysis of the armies, I have explained this surprising behavior by using a two-stage argument. The first stage explains how a military forms its mission beliefs, which can vary in the degree to which they commit the armed forces to policing. The analysis emphasizes how a military's sudden loss of a sovereignty mission can cause the military to do police work as a way to obtain legitimacy and financing, and how those broad mission beliefs can then last even after a different sovereignty mission becomes salient—as in Ecuador. In contrast, in the absence of such a mission loss, trauma to a military organization resulting from the performance of police work can lead the organization to reject policing—as was true in Peru, in response to corruption resulting from the army's antinarcotics work in the 1990s.

The second stage of the argument explains how the military can be deterred from performing even those missions to which it is committed. A contradiction introduced into each army's salient sovereignty mission challenged predictability for troops on the ground. In response to the contradiction, the army underperformed the mission as a means of maintaining predictability for patrols. Army resource interests ultimately did affect the army's behavior at this point, but only insofar as the resources in question (1) financed security missions that officers deemed "appropriate" and (2) did not increase patrols' exposure to the contradictions. That is, resources from beyond the national defense budget greatly influenced *who benefited from* the armies' security services.

As noted in chapter 1, there is high, multifaceted insecurity in the Andes, and the region's armed forces commonly have been assigned a wide range of security missions. In this final chapter, I set out to understand better Andean military missions by applying the framework of this study to the region's other armed forces. This comparative analysis of the Colombian, Venezuelan, and Bolivian armed forces lends support to the study's framework. In the three countries, there is no evidence of mission constraint or mission overload that would lead to a contradiction in any missions, and mission performance is thus predicted by whether or not a military underwent sudden loss of a salient sovereignty mission and/or organizational trauma resulting from police work (table 7.1). With regard to trauma, the chapter specifically focuses on intense internal divisions within the military, in Bolivia and Venezuela.[1] I should note that the analysis is based mainly on secondary sources and therefore necessarily faces limitations; as shown by the analysis of the Ecuadorian and Peruvian cases, in-depth fieldwork is crucial for identifying contradictions in military missions, as well as the understudied phenomenon of mission neglect.

COLOMBIA: TOLERANCE OF POLICING AMID ONGOING INSURGENCY

Colombia's military has focused on counterinsurgency and has prioritized that sovereignty mission above police work, akin to the behavior of the Ecuadorian and Peruvian armies during the 1980s and 1990s. The Colombian armed forces, like Peru's military, have faced criticism for their human rights record. However, unlike the Peruvian case, we observe a lack of initiative on the part of Colombia's executive and legislature to hold military personnel accountable for

Table 7.1. Military Mission Performance in the Andes under Democracy

Salience of sovereignty mission	Organizational trauma due to police work? Yes	No
Sudden loss of salience	Priority: defending sovereignty; rejection of policing Venezuela (1989–present)	Priorities: defending sovereignty, and policing Venezuela (1973–89) Ecuador (late 1990s–present)*
Salient	Priority: defending sovereignty; rejection of policing Peru (1995–present)*	Priority: defending sovereignty; acceptance of policing Venezuela (1958–73) Colombia (1958–present) Peru (1980s–1995)* Ecuador (1980s–late 1990s)*
Not salient	Priorities: defending sovereignty, and policing Bolivia (2003–present)	Priorities: defending sovereignty, and policing Bolivia (1982–2003)

*Contradiction in a sovereignty mission led the army to neglect the mission (in Ecuador, northern border defense, 1980s–present; in Peru, counterinsurgency, late 1980s and 2000–2007).

past abuses and ongoing military impunity vis-à-vis the Colombian courts. The Colombian military therefore has faced no contradiction in its counterinsurgency mission and has continuously performed the work. With regard to policing, the military has accepted the antinarcotics mission, but mainly as a means of obtaining U.S. resources for counterinsurgency purposes. The analysis focuses on the dynamic period since the 1980s, when the internal threat became highly salient for policymakers and the military.[2]

Prioritization of Counterinsurgency

In the 1990s, the FARC achieved major military victories in central and southern Colombia (Borrero Mansilla 2006, 131). Borrero Mansilla (2006, 130) writes that 1996–98 was a "nightmare" for the military, which faced accusations of human rights abuses and major resource and equipment shortages. Nonetheless, in the 1990s, like the Peruvian army in the 1980s, which fought Sendero Luminoso despite an economic crisis, Colombia's impoverished military, too, threw itself into counterinsurgency.

For instance, the armed forces modernized so as to fight guerrillas more effectively. Partly because of the guerrillas' effectiveness as professional war fighters, in the 1980s the Colombian military began to transition away from relying on short-term conscript soldiers—who had little familiarity with or skills for combat—to a more professional model, whereby soldiers worked as long-term, fully compensated state employees. Starting under the César Gaviria Trujillo administration (1990–94), the army restructured such that army units became modular to combat mobile guerrillas: units could now be moved across command structures, to respond to orders from, for example, an army division, the army commander, or the head of the armed forces. Also to improve the military's counterinsurgency performance, as of 1994, the armed forces were pursuing the manufacture of small arms and of ships for maneuvering in rivers (common in FARC territory), and the conversion of transport helicopters to attack helicopters (Borrero Mansilla 2006, 117–19, 126–31).

The Colombian military also demonstrated its dedication to counterinsurgency by maintaining a hard line against the guerrillas. Whereas at different moments the government negotiated with guerrillas, culminating in the Pastrana government's (1998–2002) failed strategy toward the FARC (see chapter 5), the armed forces consistently pushed for a policy centered on destroying the insurgents militarily (Isacson 2009, 186–92). From 1990 through 1997, annual state-led combat incidents were (slightly) more common than combat incidents led by the FARC or by other groups in the conflict (Center for International Policy Colombia Program 2008).

Colombia's military grew substantially in size and capacity, starting in the late 1990s, due to increases both in Colombian national defense spending and in U.S. security assistance. The Colombian government's absolute spending on defense nearly doubled between 1994 and 2005, and the military's budget increased from 3 to 5.1 percent of GDP across those same years, and then to 6.3 percent of GDP by 2007 (Borrero Mansilla 2006, 142; Isacson 2009, 204). Beginning in 2000 with Plan Colombia, U.S. security assistance for Colombian counterdrug efforts—which ranged from $243 million to $765 million annually during 2000–2004 (Haugaard, Isacson, and Olson 2005, 18)—went mainly to the armed forces, in contrast to the prior focus on the police (Ramírez Lemus et al. 2005, 101, 108).[3] With more resources, Colombia's military, especially the army and naval infantry, expanded greatly in numbers, starting under Pastrana (Borrero Mansilla 2006, 119). The army went from having approximately 120,000 units in 1998 to 160,000 in 2002, and almost doubled in size in terms of personnel between 1998 and 2004 (Borrero Mansilla 2006, 119, 134). Between 2000 and 2009, the army expanded from five to seven divisions (Isacson 2009, 204).

The new investments and military expansion, as well as initiative on the part of some military leaders, led the armed forces to adopt an "offensive" counterinsurgency strategy to achieve territorial control, an effort that involved entering guerrilla strongholds and closing off corridors through which guerrillas traveled (Borrero Mansilla 2006, 124). From 1997 through 2007, the annual number of state-led combat incidents remained almost as high as FARC-led incidents (Center for International Policy Colombia Program 2008), and in those years, the FARC—as well as the ELN—shrank considerably in size (see chapter 5).

The Colombian military has put counterinsurgency ahead of its major policing assignment, antinarcotics. A main reason that U.S. security aid favored the police during the 1990s was that the funds were earmarked for antinarcotics, a mission the Colombian armed forces resisted on the grounds that it might distract them from counterinsurgency (Tickner 2007, 327). When the military finally accepted the antinarcotics mission, it was for the purpose of obtaining U.S. assistance to use, in addition, for counterinsurgency. As of 2009, the military's focus on counterinsurgency rather than antinarcotics was still evident: Colombian military personnel complained that U.S. representatives "too frequently" vetoed the use of U.S. helicopters for anything other than antinarcotics (Isacson 2009, 200).

Human Rights Abuses

Since the expansion of Colombia's guerrilla threat, the military has been continuously implicated in human rights abuses. Initially, abuses by military personnel were rampant. Analyzing data processed by the Colombian Commission of Jurists,[4] human rights expert Gustavo Gallón (2007, 360, 362) notes that in 1993, state agents performed more than 50 percent of all acts of political violence that took place outside combat. Subsequently, military personnel scaled back their abuses, instead allowing for and supporting paramilitary violence (Chernick 2003, 200). In 1996, paramilitary acts accounted for more than 50 percent of political killings, whereas state agents carried out 20 percent. In 2000, the paramilitaries were responsible for nearly 80 percent of political killings, and state agents, less than 5 percent (Gallón 2007, 362).[5]

Investment in the Colombian military through Plan Colombia may have led the armed forces to return to committing human rights abuses. Between mid-2001 and mid-2005, the responsibility (as percentage) of state agents for total annual illegal killings, political homicides, and forced disappearances in Colombia rose from 3 percent to 9 percent. This number then jumped to between 17 and 22 percent during the period from mid-2005 to mid-2008.[6] Moreover, the armed forces also have been responsible for higher *numbers* of killings, disappearances, and, more broadly, violations of international humanitarian law (IHL). Average annual illegal deaths and disappearances caused by the state rose from 131 between mid-1996 and mid-2001 to 232 between mid-2001 and mid-2008 (Comisión Colombiana de Juristas 2009). Whereas IHL violations by state agents averaged 140 cases (ranging from 63 to 193) annually during 1990–99, from 2000 through 2006 the annual average was 500 cases (ranging from 270 to 686) (Center for International Policy Colombia Program 2008).

Some might argue that more combat on the battlefield would inherently lead to more human rights abuses, thereby explaining the increase in military abuses. However, contrary to this hypothesis, as the number of FARC- and state-initiated combat incidents declined between 2002 and 2006, there were annual increases in the numbers of state-caused IHL violations and illegal deaths and disappearances (Center for International Policy Colombia Program 2008; Comisión Colombiana de Juristas 2009).[7]

Military Autonomy in Relation to the Justice System

Domestic and international actors have tried to hold Colombia's armed forces accountable for abusing human rights, but these attempts have been feeble compared with the Peruvian case, making it unlikely that Colombian officers have perceived a contradiction in their counterinsurgency mission that could deter the military from performing the mission. I review here the measures taken to improve the Colombian military's respect for human rights and underscore the weakness of those actions.

Beginning in the 1980s, pressures grew in Colombia to address the human rights question (Isacson 2009, 192). For instance, in 1987 the supreme court ruled that the military justice system could not try civilians, a position confirmed by the constitutional court in 1993 (Ramírez Lemus et al. 2005, 127). The 1991 constitution, shaped in part by the human rights movement, guaranteed "the full range of human rights" and established institutions to protect those rights, including the constitutional court and a public ombudsman (Ramírez Lemus et al. 2005, 124). Human rights activists took advantage of the new constitutional protections, such as by putting pressure on the judiciary with regard to certain cases of human rights violations. Domestic human rights groups brought cases to the Inter-American Court of Human Rights (IACHR) and helped bring about the 1996 opening of the United Nations Office of the High Commissioner for Human Rights (UNOHCHR) in Colombia (Ramírez Lemus et al. 2005, 127–28). In 1997, the supreme court ruled that cases involving human rights violations were outside military judicial jurisdiction, a step toward trying military personnel in civilian courts (Ramírez Lemus et al. 2005, 127; Gallón 2007, 378). Shortly after Pastrana took office in 1998, a revision to the military code, introduced during the administration of Ernesto Samper Pizano (1994–98), became law. The revised code, which defined torture, genocide, and forced disappearances as human rights crimes that could not be tried in military courts, challenged military autonomy—according to the armed forces themselves: "General Manuel Bonnet, commander of the armed forces at the time, characterized the new penal code as seeking to 'criminalize' the army and complained that 'society should not send [troops] to combat unarmed, because the *fuero* [i.e., the prior military code of justice] is our shield'" (Ramírez Lemus et al. 2005, 127).

In terms of international pressures, the Colombian military's reputation for abuse and the failure of the Colombian government to take a consistent, public stance against this behavior were important reasons for the U.S. government's limited investment in the Colombian armed forces in the 1990s (in conjunction with the Colombian military's resistance to antinarcotics, described above) (Tickner 2007, 326–27). Until 1997, the Colombian military "had repeatedly refused U.S. military assistance on the grounds that such unilateral impositions [from the U.S. regarding human rights] 'violated the dignity of the army'" (Tickner 2007, 327). Attached to annual Plan Colombia appropriations was the requirement that a percentage of military assistance be withheld until the U.S. secretary of state certified the following actions: that the Colombian military was suspending officers believed to have abused human rights and/or to have relations with paramilitaries; that the Colombian government was cooperating with investigations into human rights abuses; and that actions were being taken to end the military-paramilitary connection (Ramírez Lemus et al. 2005, 128–29).

Another important U.S. constraint on Colombia's military is the 1997 Leahy Amendment, according to which no foreign military unit implicated in human rights violations can receive U.S. military assistance, unless the foreign government acts to bring the implicated military personnel to justice. In 2002, the Leahy Amendment froze U.S. assistance to a Colombian air force unit that had bombed and then fired on the village of Santo Domingo in December 1998, killing seventeen civilians. U.S. pressures led to the forced retirement of the air force commander, for delaying the investigation into the case (Ramírez Lemus et al. 2005, 129). Also as a response to U.S. pressures, four generals were dismissed in 1998, and 388 other military personnel in 2000 (Gallón 2007, 382–83; Tickner 2007, 328).

The limitations to U.S. human rights policy with regard to Colombia are well known. The U.S. government has defined narrowly its expectations for human rights protections. In spite of the annual presentation of facts by human rights groups to the U.S. government that demonstrate Colombian noncompliance with U.S. requirements, only in the case of the first certification, in 2000, did the U.S. government find Colombia noncompliant. Even in that year, funding was dispersed when President Bill Clinton invoked a built-in waiver (Ramírez Lemus et al. 2005, 128–29; Tickner 2007, 328).[8] Further revealing its lack of interest in bringing about genuine change to the Colombian armed forces' human rights practices, the U.S. government has invested "considerable funds" in public relations companies assigned to improve the Colombian military's human rights image (Isacson 2009, 193).

Accompanying this weak pressure on the part of the U.S. government, neither Colombia's executive nor its legislature has taken serious actions to hold military personnel accountable for human rights abuses (Isacson 2009, 192–95). In fact, the executive has defended the armed forces' actions in the internal conflict. For example, in 1995, Samper "publicly criticized" an IACHR decision on a military-paramilitary case of forced disappearance for not placing sufficient responsibility on guerrillas (Gallón 2007, 375). When U.S. human rights pressures led to the dismissal of several officers in 1998 and 2000 (see above), officially the government did not link the dismissals to human rights violations, to demonstrate its loyalty to the armed forces (Gallón 2007, 382–83; Tickner 2007, 328). In 2003, in front of an audience of Colombian military personnel (with high-ranking U.S. officials also present), President Uribe (2002–10) called a lawyers' NGO that brought the Santo Domingo case to the IACHR "politickers at the service of terrorism" and asked that the new air force commander avoid letting "traffickers in human rights" interfere with his work (Ramírez Lemus et al. 2005, 130).

These inadequacies in progress in human rights policy have meant that the Colombian armed forces have enjoyed sweeping impunity. In the 1990s, impunity rates for human rights crimes in the country were almost 100 percent (Ramírez Lemus et al. 2005, 128). For instance, none of the 388 officers dismissed in 2000 were brought to justice. The military courts, renowned for their bias, have retained jurisdiction over the vast majority of cases against military personnel accused of violating human rights (Gallón 2007, 367, 383), in spite of the above-mentioned actions taken to move those cases to civilian courts. In the 1990s, specialized units in the civilian justice system that were created to investigate state abuses, including human rights abuses carried out by the military, were "woefully underfunded" and lacked support from other government branches (Chernick 2003, 202–4; Gallón 2007, 372–73). In 1999 the national congress approved a bill that weakened civilian courts' jurisdiction over military human rights abuses, considering, case by case, the issue of whether the military personnel in question committed the act while on duty (Gallón 2007, 380–81). The military justice system's jurisdiction expanded again with the creation of emergency zones (Chernick 2003, 202–4).

An exception to the Colombian military's impunity relates to the "false positives" phenomenon, whereby military personnel murdered civilians, mainly from the lower social classes, and then made the victims look like insurgents killed in combat.[9] This practice enabled military units and officers to appear effective in the eyes of army and government leaders (Isacson 2009, 209; McDermott 5/7/09). The false positives scandal erupted in late 2008. It led to investigations by the human rights community, the courts, and the Colombian defense ministry, and attracted the attention of the U.S. state department (U.S. State Department Bureau of Democracy, Human Rights, and Labor 2009). The Centro de Investigación y Educación Popular reported a total of 465 false positives cases as of 2009, involving 940 victims. CINEP dated the phenomenon to at least as early as 2001 and identified 2007 as its peak (CINEP 2009, 3, 5).

Some military personnel have been brought to justice for their participation in false positives cases. CINEP attributes the drastic reduction in the number of false positives victims since 2007 (declining from 337 in that year to 195 in 2008 and 4 in 2009) to the following factors: measures adopted in late 2008 by the defense ministry, pressure from the UNOHCHR in Colombia, and investigations by the Colombian Office of the Inspector General (Fiscalía General de la Nación y la Procuraduría), which has initiated legal proceedings against implicated military personnel (CINEP 2009, 3, 5). As of mid-2009, for their connections to false positives, 67 soldiers had been found guilty, more than 400 others had been arrested, and 1,177 members of Colombia's security forces were under investigation (McDermott 5/7/09).

Training in International Humanitarian Law

As a final note on the Colombian case, the armed forces have expanded greatly their training in IHL. Colombian military personnel are receiving concrete instructions on how exactly to carry out counterinsurgency operations while respecting human rights. IHL was introduced into Colombian military education in 1992, in response to recommendations of the International Committee of the Red Cross (ICRC). Beginning in 1999, the army created its first "human rights and international humanitarian law training platform" to coach personnel in the field on how to respect IHL and human rights during simulations. As of 2008, there were more than thirty-five such platforms throughout the country, used by all branches of the military, and by 2010 the number had climbed to forty-nine (Permanent Mission of Colombia to the United Nations 2008; Ministerio de Defensa, Colombia 2010, 11).[10] Military Directive No. 800-04, issued in 2003, triggered the gradual integration of IHL lessons into the military's curricula. Between 2003 and 2010, 358,217 military and civilian personnel working for the armed forces were trained in "situational issues" (Ministerio de Defensa, Colombia 2010, 11). This instruction reached more than four times the number of military personnel in 2009 than it had in 2006 (Ministerio de Defensa, Colombia 2010, 11). The military's rules of engagement approved in 2007 (by Directive No. 012) outline clear guidelines for conducting operations that respect human rights and IHL (Permanent Mission of Colombia to the United Nations 2008).

The international human rights community has acknowledged the Colombian military's progress in IHL. The UNOHCHR Committee against Torture (2008, 71–73) has praised the armed forces' ongoing efforts to "ensure their members' full respect for human rights and IHL." As reported by the ICRC (2007, 281), the Colombian military has taken measures to make "IHL an integral and permanent part of their doctrine, training and operating procedures." An interview in 2006 with an ICRC official who recently had worked in both Peru and Colombia demonstrates clear differences between the two cases. When asked to compare IHL training across the two countries, the ICRC official said that IHL training in Colombia was much more extensive than in Peru, and, unlike in Peru, Colombian military personnel themselves, who had more legitimacy within the armed forces than outsiders, led the training. Finally, in Colombia, again unlike the Peruvian case, IHL training included scenarios that involved civilians.[11]

VENEZUELA: MISSION LOSS, ORGANIZATIONAL TRAUMA, AND REJECTION OF POLICE WORK

The Venezuelan military's mission performance since the democratic transition exhibits three patterns. From democratization in 1958 until 1973, the armed forces endured neither sudden loss of a sovereignty mission nor organizational trauma from policing. In those years, they prioritized sovereignty work while not refusing to take on policing, much like in Ecuador and Peru in the 1980s and 1990s and in Colombia. In 1973 the dynamic changed. That year, a Venezuelan military operation eliminated the country's ongoing insurgent threat, marking an abrupt end to the armed forces' salient sovereignty mission of counterinsurgency. As in Ecuador in the late 1990s, facing a role crisis, the armed forces of Venezuela took measures to redefine their purpose. Yet in contrast to the Ecuadorian case, the existence of the Venezuelan national guard meant that policing was generally not available to the military as an alternative mission. Not until the late 1980s was the military given the opportunity to take on police work—specifically in the form of controlling popular protests—which military leaders welcomed. However, just as the armed forces were moving into serving a policing function, the work proved extremely traumatic, deepening divisions between factions and contributing to two military coup attempts in 1992. As in Peru in the 1990s, the trauma of policing drove Venezuela's armed forces away from the policing arena.

Prioritization of Sovereignty Missions

Venezuela's military has defended national sovereignty when that work has been salient, except during the Chávez government (1999–present), as discussed at the end of this chapter.

In the new democracy, eager to overcome its reputation for corruption and repression established under the military dictatorship of Marcos Pérez Jiménez (1952–58), the military performed security missions in place of its prior political responsibilities. In the 1960s, it successfully combated leftist rural and urban insurgents and enjoyed prestige: successive governments "went out of their way" to give the military more resources, including in the form of salaries and benefits, improved professional training, and public praise (Burggraff and Millett 1995, 56). In terms of police work, from the late 1950s into the 1970s, the national guard performed more internal security functions than the armed forces, which helped to establish order only on rare occasions, during crisis situations of civil unrest and riots (Trinkunas 2005, 133–34, 161).

The military's most traditional sovereignty mission has been defense against the country's traditional regional rival, Colombia, in a border conflict that dates to the breakup of Gran Colombia (into Colombia, Ecuador, and Venezuela) in 1830 (George 1988–89, 143). Venezuela's armed forces have defended the border assertively whenever the international conflict has escalated. For instance, major militarized interstate disputes—defined as military combat resulting in battlefield-related deaths that number fewer than one thousand—occurred between the two countries in 1982, 1987, 1988, 1995, and 1997 (Mares 2001, 42–43). The 1987 dispute constituted a serious war scare, leading Colombia and Venezuela to engage in military buildups that continued through 1991 (Mares 2001, 90; Trinkunas 2005, 177). The Venezuelan military prepared for external warfare even in the early 1970s, when war with Colombia was unlikely (Trinkunas 2005, 165).

As final evidence of their commitment to sovereignty work, the Venezuelan armed forces have guarded the Venezuela Colombia border against Colombian guerrillas. In a region where tensions were already elevated over the demarcation of the international border, Colombian guerrillas carried out multiple attacks on Venezuelan military detachments between 1994 and 1998, marking heightened FARC aggression in Venezuela and causing "significant" casualties (Trinkunas 2005, 200). This security situation paralleled that in Ecuador in the mid-1980s (see chapter 3). However, different from the Ecuadorian case, Venezuela's armed forces were not overloaded by security responsibilities and therefore were able to defend the border from FARC incursions, which they did forcefully (Trinkunas 2005, 200).

That the Venezuelan armed forces have consistently defended sovereignty is expected, based on this study's framework, as the armed forces have not faced contradictions in their sovereignty missions that would deter them from carrying out the work. Not only has the military not been overloaded by missions, but research on Venezuelan civil-military relations points to no move to alter the military's human rights practices that would have created a contradiction in the military's sovereignty missions.

In Search of Relevance

Between 1973 and 1989, Venezuela resembled Ecuador in the late 1990s, in that the military suddenly lost its most salient sovereignty mission and, in response, tried to demonstrate its relevance by expanding into non-sovereignty arenas. In Ecuador, the key events were the 1995 Cenepa War and the 1998 signing of the peace with Peru; in Venezuela, the critical moment was 1973, when a military counterinsurgency operation eliminated the remnants of the country's leftist Partido Comunista de Venezuela Movimiento de la Izquierda Revolucionaria (PCV/MIR) guerrilla movement (Trinkunas 2005, 160–61).

As noted above, policing generally was not a possible mission for the Venezuelan military at the time, due to the presence of the national guard.[12] Therefore, instead of reaching out to policing, in the 1970s the armed forces took on an economic development role, creating a "soft version" of national security doctrine (Trinkunas 2002, 46). For instance, officers' training emphasized egalitarianism and economic development, and a 1976 security and defense law linked security with development (Burggraff and Millett 1995, 57; Trinkunas 2005, 162–63). These changes caused new generations of officers to adopt "a state-led vision of development, concern for social equity, and a broad definition of security" (Trinkunas 2005, 163).

Nonetheless—and analogous to the Ecuadorian case—when policing did become available to the Venezuelan armed forces, military leaders took on the mission. Beginning in the 1980s and continuing into the 1990s, civil unrest in Venezuela reached exceptionally high levels, and both the army and the national guard "were repeatedly called on to quell civil protests and disturbances" (Burggraff and Millett 1995, 57). The most renowned such occasion that involved the army occurred in February 1989, during an uprising in Caracas (the Caracazo) against the higher fuel and transportation costs caused by President Carlos Andrés Pérez's (1989–1993) liberal economic shock program. Protests intensified over two days, during which demonstrators burned buses and engaged in widespread looting (Trinkunas 2005, 174). When the police could not establish order, the armed forces were sent in; almost ten thousand soldiers patrolled the city's streets (Burggraff and Millett 1995, 59). Poorly equipped for policing, the military personnel used live ammunition and killed between three hundred and three thousand civilians (Trinkunas 2005, 174; Pion-Berlin and Trinkunas 2010, 407). In spite of this repression, in the months following the protests the armed forces received popular approval, apparently due to the efficiency with which the military reestablished order (Burggraff and Millett 1995, 60).[13]

The Pérez administration's unpopular policies and outrage over corruption within the government meant that protests continued into the 1990s, as did the military's work to control them (Burggraff and Millett 1995, 61; Trinkunas 2005, 175). In fact, Venezuelan military leaders took measures to institutionalize the armed forces' police work. In mid-1989, an army general was placed in charge of the metropolitan police (despite strong police objections). The armed forces testified before the congress, taking the stance that military work to control protests was important (Burggraff and Millett 1995, 60–61). The military also carried out publicized joint exercises to train personnel in protest control (Trinkunas 2005, 174–75).

Deepening Factionalism

Whereas military leadership approved of policing, mid- and low-ranking officers did not. This tension over police work—which, as described below, ultimately has had important implications for the military's overall mission performance—has roots in preexisting rifts within the officer corps. As analyzed by Harold Trinkunas (2002, 2005), in the early years of democracy, the Venezuelan government maintained civilian control of the military by granting the armed forces resources and combat missions (Trinkunas 2002, 44–45) and through a strategy of "divide and conquer," according to which politicians exercised direct control over the military branches through appointments and promotions. Contact between politicians and senior officers politicized the officer corps, as officers aligned themselves with one of the two main political parties (either Acción Democrática, AD, or Comité de Organización Política Electoral Independiente, COPEI) to help get themselves promoted—in a setting in which high-level promotions were based heavily on political connections (F. Agüero 1995a, 150; Trinkunas 2005, 167). Junior officers, "who were held to strict ethical and professional standards during their careers," resented the politicization of their leaders (Trinkunas 2002, 48).

Beginning in the 1970s, minimal civilian oversight of the military, along with the soaring defense spending that came with the oil boom, contributed to corruption within the senior officer corps, furthering bitterness among junior officers toward their superiors. At the same time, the military raised educational standards for cadets and increased the emphasis in the academies on nationalistic patriotism, creating a generational divide in which, as of the 1990s, the mid and lower ranks viewed themselves as more professional and patriotic than the generals (Trinkunas 2002, 45–47, 53–54).

Given the military's factionalism, in the late 1980s mid- and low-ranking officers resisted protest control as a mission, which for them was a means of protecting the standing of corrupt politicians who were closely connected to the generals (Burggraff and Millett 1995, 61). Junior officers' antipathy toward controlling protests was only exacerbated by the younger generation's experience in conducting civic action work as part of the military's focus on economic development: having had contact with the poorer social classes, that generation of military personnel resented being asked to shoot on the masses (Norden 2003, 96).

Trauma Resulting from Controlling Protests

Controlling the Caracazo traumatized Venezuela's armed forces. After the Caracazo, junior officers' aversion to policing contributed to the 1992 military coup attempts, the first of which was led by then army lieutenant colonel Hugo Chávez Frías and the Movimiento Bolivariano Revolucionario 200 (MBR-200) movement, which had formed within the army's junior officer corps (Trinkunas 2002, 52).[14] "President Chávez himself justified his 1992 coup attempts using the 1989 Caracazo, blaming the civilian and military leadership for a massacre" (Pion-Berlin and Trinkunas 2010, 407). In the aftermath of the coup attempts, and facing civil-society groups that wanted military personnel to be held accountable for the violence during the Caracazo (Pion-Berlin and Trinkunas 2010, 407), Venezuela's armed forces rejected policing and instead turned to sovereignty work—for instance, protecting the Venezuelan border from Colombia (see above). In part responding to the 1989 trauma, the military refused to obey (now) President Hugo Chávez Frías's command to take control of Caracas in April 2002, when protesters numbering in the hundreds of thousands mobilized in the city center in the lead-up to the coup that removed Chávez for two days before he was reinstated as president (Pion-Berlin and Trinkunas 2010, 406–7).[15]

BOLIVIA: POLICING DESPITE ORGANIZATIONAL TRAUMA

Unlike the other Andean militaries, the Bolivian armed forces have not had a salient sovereignty mission under democracy (1982–present), as Bolivia's last major international conflict was the Chaco War (1932–35). Insurgency in the country has also been minimal: though weak in comparison to other armies in Latin America, the Bolivian army still easily eliminated the country's small guerrilla movement in 1967 (Wickham-Crowley 1992, 62, 84). In this context, the Bolivian armed forces were encouraged to conduct policing missions by an incapable police force, the hard-line tendencies of elected President (and former military dictator) Hugo Banzer Suárez (1997–2001), and U.S. material assistance. The military's lack of a salient sovereignty mission in recent history and into the foreseeable future has made the armed forces so committed to policing that, even after police work traumatized them by bringing discredit to the institution and reinforcing internal factionalism, they have continued performing police missions.

Police Work

Since the mid-1990s, Bolivia's armed forces have engaged in widespread policing, including fighting crime in cities, conducting antinarcotics operations, and controlling protests. Despite the trauma of exercising large-scale repression against protesters in 2003, they have continued police work.

Perhaps the military's best-known policing mission is antinarcotics, as U.S. drug control policy has devoted longstanding attention to Bolivian coca production. Bolivian counterdrug policy, supported actively by military (and police) operations, has vacillated between coca eradication and drug interdiction since the late 1980s. The armed forces took on an important antinarcotics role in spite of their concerns about the corruption that it can bring, especially following democratization, when the military bore the reputation of having participated in drug trafficking during the military government of García Meza (1981–82). Nonetheless, "within the military, participation in drug control efforts was widely viewed as an opportunity to regain legitimacy and to restore lost funding by making use of U.S. antidrug aid," and the armed forces' existing police work and ongoing military-police competition made antinarcotics palatable (Ledebur 2005, 156).[16]

The first major U.S. counterdrug initiative in Bolivia was the 1980 creation of the Unidad Móvil Policial para Áreas Rurales (UMOPAR), a rural drug police unit. The Bolivian military became involved in antinarcotics starting in 1988, when the U.S. government helped create Bolivian air force and naval interdiction units. In 1990, a U.S.-Bolivian executive agreement formalized U.S.-funded military antinarcotics work, especially by the Bolivian army (Ledebur 2005, 149–51).

Following the change in U.S. policy from interdiction to eradication in the mid-1990s, the Bolivian military engaged in antinarcotics in earnest. A police-military joint task force conducted campaigns between 1998 and 2003 as part of Operation Dignity, intended to eliminate all illegal coca in Bolivia.[17] By 2001, Operation Dignity had brought 4,500 police and military personnel to the Chapare region, a major center of coca cultivation. The operation was brutal: between 1997 and August 2003, 33 coca growers and 27 police and military personnel were killed, and 567 coca growers and 135 police and military personnel were injured (Ledebur 2005, 154, 164).

Bolivian antinarcotics policy swung back to interdiction beginning under President Carlos Mesa (2003–5), and continuing under President Evo Morales (2006–present), who rose to the national political scene through his work as a *cocalero* union leader. A repressive, hard-line drug eradication policy had become highly risky, both because of the violence in the Chapare coca zone during Operation Dignity and because of recent state repression of protests, in February and October 2003 (see below). The government returned to an interdiction-centered policy following a 2004 incident in which a joint military-police unit had killed two *cocaleros*. After the killings, "Mesa faced down vocal U.S. opposition," allowing for growers in established coca zones to cultivate up to one *cato*—produced on between sixteen hundred and two thousand square feet of land (depending on the coca zone)—of the crop. With the policy in place, protest in the Chapare halted immediately, and by 2008, 17,500 acres of coca were legalized (Farthing and Kohl 2010, 204).

Security forces, including the military, have reoriented toward drug interdiction (Ledebur and Youngers 2006, 2008). In mid-2010, Morales convened military leaders to create a national antinarcotics policy, during an event to honor the 181st anniversary of the head of the armed forces (*El Deber* 6/1/2010). In response, the army expressed its dedication to the mission.[18] To the extent that coca eradication has taken place since 2004, the military has participated in that work, too. For example, the armed forces have carried out some forced eradication in the Yungas coca zone, which, in contrast to the Chapare region, has not been receptive to the one-*cato* policy (Ledebur and Youngers 2008; Farthing and Kohl 2010, 204). In September 2006, a military-police joint task force that had been in the Yungas region since February of that year killed two coca growers in a confrontation (Ledebur and Youngers 2006).

Another policing mission of the Bolivian armed forces is crime fighting. The government assigned the military to contribute to "citizen security" beginning in 1995, when there was strong societal pressure to reduce crime and the police had little capacity to do so (Quintana 2004, 152). The armed forces seem to have welcomed the work, establishing a presence in major and medium-sized cities in all nine of Bolivia's departments (mainly in the departments of Beni, Cochabamba, La Paz, and Santa Cruz). Many military personnel were involved in the "Citizen Security Plan"; for instance, in 2001 the plan included 9,153 military personnel, numbering nearly two-thirds of the 15,538 police personnel participating in the initiative (Quintana 2004, 152–53).

The Bolivian armed forces also have controlled protests. This work has been traced to the Banzer government, which used the military in place of the "impotent" police to contain mounting mobilization against neoliberal economic policies (Mayorga 2009, 120). The military first performed this mission during the April 2000 "water war" in the city of Cochabamba, a conflict surrounding the privatization of water (Mayorga 2009, 112). The best-known military action to control protests was in the 2003 "gas war," in which groups mobilized in favor of nationalizing Bolivia's natural gas reserves. The government had planned to export Bolivian gas through the landlocked country to the coast, via a port belonging to Bolivia's long-time rival, Chile. Indigenous peasants, miners, neighborhood associations, factory workers, students, and intellectuals mobilized to demand renationalization of the country's gas reserves and the resignation of President Gonzalo Sánchez de Lozada (Postero 2007, 206–10; Perreault 2008, 14–15). Sánchez de Lozada did resign and was replaced by Vice President Carlos Mesa, but not before calling on the armed forces to control the demonstrators. The military was a central actor in state repression that killed sixty people and wounded hundreds of others (Ledebur 2005, 162). In one incident alone, on October 8, 2003, the military killed thirty-eight people who were trying to prevent gas tankers from entering La Paz (Postero 2007, 207–8).

The gas war was traumatic for Bolivia's military. At the time, Bolivian military expert Juan Ramón Quintana said, "The Armed Forces are reaching the limit of their tolerance for a situation in which they are being blamed for these deaths" (Rohter 10/14/03; also cited by Pion-Berlin and Trinkunas 2010, 405). As was true of the Venezuelan Caracazo, in Bolivia the repression proved very divisive because of preexisting schisms between mid-ranking and senior officers. "Field grade officers resented the senior command for its unswerving alliance to an illegitimate government, which was using the military as a way out for not being able to solve problems politically" (Pion-Berlin and Trinkunas 2010, 405).

In spite of this trauma, the armed forces have continued their counterdrug work and have controlled protests since the 2003 repression. During the second gas war (in 2005, in the western highland cities of El Alto, Cochabamba, and La Paz)—which triggered Mesa's resignation—the military called the troops to the barracks, and some cities were "militarized" (Mayorga 2009, 122). Another case occurred in late 2008, when the military worked, at least in some capacity, to control antigovernment protests led by "civic committees" that formed part of Bolivia's conservative autonomy movement in the east.[19] During a state of siege in the eastern department of Pando, in September 2008, military personnel participated in an operation that involved violent, forced entry into peoples' homes and the arrest of between twenty-five and thirty-eight citizens, who were taken to a military base located near La Paz (Inter-American Commission on Human Rights 2009, 10).

The armed forces have been entrenched in policing to the point where they have competed with the police over missions, including, as mentioned above, antinarcotics. In addition, the two institutions have vied with each other over anticrime work and the responsibility for controlling weapons, ammunition, and explosives in the country, and the two institutions' intelligence services have been known to spy on each other (Quintana 2004, 153–54). The military-police rivalry has escalated to the point of armed conflict.[20]

Military Impunity

Presumably, the Bolivian military could be deterred from performing police work should a contradiction develop in one or more of its policing missions. However, as shown above, Bolivia's security reality is not one that would overload the military with responsibilities. A contradiction through constraint is also unlikely. The military is renowned for enjoying impunity in the area of human rights violations. As of 2002, the United Nations Development Programme characterized the Bolivian judicial system as "subordinated to political powers, immersed in a world of corruption, inefficiency and professional mediocrity" (Ledebur 2005, 168; see also Pion-Berlin and Trinkunas 2010, 405). High-profile human rights cases have been transferred from the civilian justice system to the military courts, which have "refused to cooperate" with attorney general investigations. As of 2005, of the cases opened against members of state security forces for the fifty-seven deaths resulting from antinarcotics efforts between 1987 and 2002, only four had actually come to trial (Ledebur 2005, 168–71).[21] At least until late 2007, the armed forces had blocked the civilian justice system from processing cases against military personnel accused of repressing individuals during the 2003 gas war (Mayorga 2009, 121). For their part, the military courts have acquitted even the most blatant cases of human rights abuses (Ledebur 2005, 170).

EXTREME EXECUTIVE CONTROL: TRENDS IN VENEZUELA AND BOLIVIA

This study has focused on armed forces that have had high levels of autonomy to carry out their security work, and thus dynamics internal to military branches have influenced the military's behavior in important ways. As we have seen, even in Peru in the years following Fujimori's departure from office, when the country was undergoing a political transition that involved conscious government attempts to regain control of the military, the army was able to withstand government pressures to root out the remnants of Sendero Luminoso. Going against this trend of military autonomy in the Andes, in Venezuela and Bolivia the current presidents have increased their direct power over the armed forces, which the executive has used to shape military missions.

Venezuelan President Chávez has been able to influence military missions in important ways due to personnel decisions. On being elected president, he reinstated thirty-seven soldiers who had been removed from the military for participating in the 1992 coup attempt that he had led (McCoy 1999, 74). As president, Chávez has faced episodes of military dissent, including the 2002 coup, the 2003 occupation of the Plaza Altamira in Caracas by several officers protesting his policies, and in the 2004, the signing of petitions by officers to effect a referendum to remove him from office (Trinkunas 2009, 92). Chávez used those moments to force out of the armed forces those suspected of opposing him and his policies. Other measures that Chávez took to control the military included creating a reserve force that answers to the president, bypassing the defense ministry and serving as a counterweight to potential military antagonism to his presidency. As of 2008, thousands of civilian Chávez supporters had received military training through the program. Chávez also raised military salaries and invested heavily in military equipment, thus appeasing the armed forces (Trinkunas 2009, 91–93). Shortly after taking office, Chávez appointed former military colleagues to posts that included minister of transportation, governor of the federal district, chief of the Federal Bureau of Taxation, director of the secret police, and viceministers and directors within ministries (McCoy 1999). Even some active-duty officers were given political appointments, especially in the state oil company, Petróleos de Venezuela, S.A. (PDVSA) (Norden 2003, 102).[22]

In terms of shaping military missions, one of Chávez's earliest and most noteworthy military policies was Plan Bolívar 2000, a civic action program that brought military units to impoverished areas, primarily to provide dental and medical services (Trinkunas 2009, 88).[23] Venezuela's 1999 constitution—a project of Chávez and his followers[24]—emphasizes military participation in economic development and internal security, including possible policing, functions formally institutionalized through a 2005 military organic law. Since 2007 Chávez has ordered the armed forces to modify training and education to prepare for possible war against the United States, and he has increased joint exercises between the military and reservists to resist U.S. invaders (Trinkunas 2009, 89, 93, 96).

Chávez's anti-U.S. stance has been evident in another area of security policy, regarding Colombia's internal conflict. Political dynamics connected with Venezuela's shared border with Colombia exhibit many commonalities with the

Ecuador-Colombia border case—including, for example, the transfer of weapons from Venezuela to the FARC through illegal weapons trafficking, Colombian and U.S. claims that the Venezuelan government has provided a sanctuary for the guerrillas, and Colombian accusations that the Venezuelan government has allowed the FARC to initiate attacks in Colombia from Venezuelan territory (Pérez 2006, 96). Even more so than successive Ecuadorian governments, Chávez has taken on neutral roles with regard to Colombia's conflict—for instance, serving as an international observer in Colombia's peace talks with the FARC (Pérez 2006, 96). In addition, and unlike the Ecuadorian case, Chávez has refused to allow U.S. planes to monitor drug trafficking along the Venezuela-Colombia border (Ellner 2008, 197).

Any Venezuelan military leniency toward the FARC on the border, however, is unlikely to have been the outcome of a contradiction in the mission resulting from mission overload, as in Ecuador, or from constraint, as in Peru. As noted above, both mission overload and mission constraint would be unlikely in Venezuela. Instead, Chávez may be personally responsible for any military permissiveness toward the FARC, considering his direct, personal influence on military missions and given "growing discontent" within the Venezuelan armed forces over the Chávez government's non-aggressive policies toward the FARC (Pérez 2006, 96).

Evo Morales has exercised personal power over the Bolivian military in several ways similar to those in the Venezuelan case, a resemblance perhaps partly due to the Venezuelan government's influence on Bolivia's armed forces, such as through Venezuelan investment in Bolivian military units (Mayorga 2009, 131–36). Shortly after taking office, Morales passed over twenty-eight generals for promotion, forcing them to retire. Those generals were believed to have been involved in an illegal operation in which missiles were transported to the United States to be deactivated, and they also had served in important leadership positions in the army when it repressed the 2003 protesters, many of whom were coca growers and Morales supporters (Pion-Berlin and Trinkunas 2010, 405–6).

With friends in the armed forces, Morales has expanded the military's functions. He increased its participation in state bureaucracies, including in the critical hydrocarbons sector, bringing officers into the Ministry of Hydrocarbons and the national oil company (Yacimientos Petrolíferos Fiscales Bolivianos, YPFB), as well as onto the boards of foreign oil companies as state representatives. When he read out the May 1, 2006, "Heroes of the Chaco" decree that nationalized hydrocarbons, in one of the largest gas camps, Morales was surrounded by ministers as well as military and police leaders. Troops were sent to dozens of other camps for the event (Mayorga 2009, 124–25). Under Morales, the armed forces have engaged in new civic action projects.[25] For instance, the military headed the distribution of transfers to families of children who attended school (in January 2007 and January 2008) and monthly assistance to the elderly (beginning in February 2009), and it participated in a literacy campaign (supported by the Cuban and Venezuelan governments) (Mayorga 2009, 125). As of 2010, there were reports that Morales was training a reserve force for the stated purpose of defending Bolivia against a U.S. invasion (Reuters 8/6/2010).

Morales's personal influence on the military seems to have encompassed political ideology, as well. In late 2010, at a ceremony celebrating the Bolivian army's two-hundredth anniversary, the army's commander characterized the army as "'socialist,' 'anti-capitalist,' and 'anti-imperialist,' positions that were immediately echoed by President Evo Morales" (*Los Angeles Times* 11/18/10).

REFLECTIONS ON ASSIGNING MILITARIES TO CONDUCT POLICE WORK

This comparative analysis of the Colombian, Venezuelan, and Bolivian armed forces suggests the generalizability of the findings of this study, which explains militaries' mission performance by focusing on mission beliefs that are shaped by organizational traumas; predictability for the everyday work of the military; and, in the armed forces' missions, contradictions that may threaten such predictability. In this final note, I reflect on lessons that the research teaches us about the challenges faced by political leaders when bringing the armed forces into police work, to meet societal demands for public security, ensure stability, and/or maintain those leaders' place in government. Police institutions throughout Latin America have tended to be less efficacious than the military, which has generated pressure for the armed forces to take on policing. Yet, as this study has demonstrated, there are four main challenges that governments may face when choosing to use the military to fulfill police functions.

First, assigning the armed forces to police work may lead to competition between the military and the police, and to the militarization of internal security and the police forces themselves. In Ecuador, the army has instructed police personnel in military academies, commanded the police during joint operations, and even attempted to subsume the police under the defense ministry. In Venezuela in the 1980s, the military successfully gained control of some police forces. In Bolivia, rivalry between the military and police resulted in armed conflict between the two institutions.

Second, by bringing the armed forces into policing, politicians ultimately may compromise the military's performance of sovereignty missions. Antinarcotics work and the resulting corruption adversely affected the Peruvian army's performance during the 1995 conflict with Ecuador. Even more directly, assigning Peru's army to antinarcotics meant asking the army to upset peasants' livelihood, which interfered with the army's goal of winning over the peasants in the counterinsurgency effort. Ecuador's army became so committed to policing that it would not let go of those responsibilities to defend the northern border against incursions by armed non-state actors.

Third, particularly when policing involves massive repression of civilians, the work can prime existing internal divisions within the armed forces, damaging military cohesion, as occurred in Venezuela and Bolivia. The Venezuelan case showed us how such military disunity ultimately can contribute to coup attempts against the sitting government.

Finally, if a government orders the armed forces to carry out police work, they simply may reject such assignments, as has been true in Peru with respect to protest control. In Venezuela, too, the military refused to control protests at a time when doing so allowed a coup coalition to remove the president from office, in 2002. Military refusal to perform policing could signal to the general public that the government is weak in relation to the armed forces and might thereby challenge the government's very legitimacy.

Appendix

Field Research Methodology

This study finds that army behavior in democratic Peru and Ecuador is best understood by considering two aspects of the organizations: mission beliefs and a drive to maintain predictability for patrols on the ground. That finding was made possible through in-depth interviews with army officers in the two countries. This appendix therefore focuses mainly on the sample of army officers, the procedures used to interview them, and the resulting data.

INTERVIEWS

Table A.1 summarizes information on my interview subjects for research conducted during 2005 and 2006 in Ecuador and Peru, according to basic professional categories.[1] I returned to both countries in 2009 to conduct follow-up interviews with existing contacts and with new interview subjects.[2]

Officers were selected according to a combination of referrals that began with academics, journalists, and retired officers; self-introductions at conferences about security topics; and access granted by superior officers to their army subordinates. Other interview subjects were identified through referrals, self-introductions, and formal requests submitted to ministries.

Army Officer Sample

In Ecuador, I interviewed officers in Quito and on seven army bases within the army's four regional commands, which cover the full expanse of Ecuador's mainland. For four bases, interviews were conducted with most or all officers assigned to the base at the time of the visit, generally excluding only officers occupied with off-base work. On three other bases, due to time constraints, I interviewed a small proportion of all officers assigned to the units—between three and seven officers on each base—and those officers were chosen by the officer overseeing my visit. On each base visited, the officers interviewed varied in rank and type of assignment, such that I interviewed, for example, instructors, finance officers, officers charged with civic action responsibilities, intelligence officers, and patrol leaders. Anonymous data were collected based on casual conversations with officers in group settings during mealtimes on all seven bases and on an eighth base.

In Peru, army officer subjects included (but were not limited to) instructors and students from the war college (Escuela Superior de Guerra, ESG) and at several branch (e.g., infantry, cavalry, artillery, engineering) schools in Lima. Study at these schools was required of all officers who wished to be considered for promotion at different stages of their careers, and therefore this sampling method allowed for access to officers who had recently served in dif-

Table A.1. Interview Subjects in Peru and Ecuador, 2005–6

Group	Peru	Ecuador	Total
Army officers, active and retired	75	77	152
Academics, journalists, researchers, and analysts	23	24	47
Appointed civilian public officials, active and retired*	27	14	41
Human rights and Catholic Church officials†	15	12	27
U.S. officials, military and civilian	6	8	14
Police officers, active and retired	7	6	13
NGO representatives and political activists	4	6	10
Private sector representatives	5	5	10
Non-army military officers, active and retired	5	4	9
Elected officials	1	4	5
Total	168	160	328

*The majority of defense and interior ministry officials were active or retired ministers.
†Employees of Peru's national ombudsman's office (Defensoría del Pueblo) are categorized as human rights officials.

ferent capacities, on bases throughout the country. To supplement these interviews, I conducted interviews on a key army base located in an insurgency zone.

Table A.2 summarizes the 2005–6 sample of army officers, sorting officers by rank, interview location, and "rank group," a category that I created and that merits further explanation. The two countries differ in terms of which ranks are sorted into the high, middle and low groups (see table A.2). Because very few Ecuadorian officers were promoted to general, colonels took on significant leadership responsibilities, as did lieutenant colonels, who, for instance, often commanded battalions. In contrast, Peruvian officers were more likely to reach the rank of general, and therefore lieutenant colonels were not given such leadership roles. Due to their different track in the army hierarchy, the noncommissioned officers (NCOs) in the sample are distinguished from the high, low, and middle rank groups, but most NCOs interviewed had served in the army for many years and, uninhibited, offered valuable perspectives and information.

Officers in the high, middle, and low ranks tended to provide different kinds of information. Active-duty high-ranking officers often displayed a higher level of inhibition than other officers, perhaps due to their lengthy indoctrination into the status quo and their loyalty to a system that had enabled them to reach prominent positions in the hierarchy (Huntington 1957, 75). Furthermore, we might expect senior officers—especially generals—to be more guarded, because they tend to play a more political role, as they are called upon at times to speak on behalf of the institution. These officers were generally the most helpful in providing information about high-level issues such as (1) the overall mission trajectory of the army and interactions between military leadership and external actors such as politicians, U.S. government officials, and business sectors; (2) institutional rules and structures, including discretion across levels of hierarchy and task areas and the professional training trajectory of officers and troops; and (3) changes over time in these arenas.

Table A.2. Interview Subjects from the Peruvian and Ecuadorian Armies, 2005–6

Rank	Ecuador*			Peru[†]			Total
	Number of officers	% Field officers	Rank group	Number of officers	% Field/school officers	Rank group	
General	4	0	High: 32	9	11	High: 26	High: 58
Colonel	24	17		17	59		
Lieutenant colonel	4	75		9	100	Middle: 25	Middle: 44
Major	7	100	Middle: 19	16	100		
Captain	12	100		14	93	Low: 23	Low: 41
Lieutenant	10	100	Low: 18	9	100		
Second lieutenant	8	100		0	0		
Noncommissioned officer (NCO)	8	88	NCOs: 8	1	100	NCOs: 1	NCOs: 9
Total			77			75	152

*Ecuadorian interviewees were active-duty officers, with the exception of three retired generals and eleven retired colonels.
[†]Peruvian interviewees were active-duty officers, with the exception of five retired generals and one retired low-ranking officer.

Retired senior officers often provided the same type of information as active-duty senior officers, due to their lengthy work experience in the army and the fact that in both countries, officers maintained relations with the military institution long after retiring—both through unstructured ties and through organizations such as lobbies and health clubs. One difference between the two groups was that retired officers, whose careers often would not be affected by speaking openly about army missions, were generally less inhibited than senior officers still serving in the army.[3]

Overall, officers from the middle and low ranks were pleased to offer opinions and recount their professional experiences, possibly because they were unaccustomed to being approached for interviews. They were particularly helpful in providing concrete information about operations and tactics (as opposed to strategy), given their direct involvement at these levels. Like senior officers, mid-ranking officers had a great deal of knowledge about how the institution worked, yet relative to their superior officers, they were less wedded to the status quo or to protecting the institution and thus were more likely to criticize the workings of the army and the military, divulging information about tensions internal to the armed forces and the army.[4]

The sample of army officers was ideal for this study, for several reasons. Because the analysis focuses on the duties, actions, and views of officers at all levels of the army hierarchy in each case, it was important that I interview officers of different ranks. Furthermore, by interviewing officers assigned to bases and attending courses required for promotion, I ensured that I was not interviewing officers from particular professional, ideological, or friendship circles within the armies—a common risk in research that relies entirely on referral chains. For the case of Ecuador, because the study focuses centrally on army action (and inaction) in the north near the border with Colombia, it is noteworthy that I visited mainly northern bases and that the officer sample consisted heavily of infantry officers, who, given their expertise in conducting patrols, tend to be assigned to the north and northeast more than members of the other branches. In Peru, I interviewed slightly more infantry officers than officers of other branches. (Because mid- and high-ranking Peruvian officers of all specialties tended to have experience overseeing or leading patrols in Sendero zones during the 1980s and 1990s, focusing on infantrymen was less critical in Peru than in Ecuador.)[5]

Interviewing the Officers

Prior to conducting interviews, I vetted my questions with retired officers and other experts on security and military themes, who helped me to clarify appropriate in-country terminology and phrasing. In the interest of protecting the validity of the interview data and subjects' comfort during interview sessions, I did not audio-record interviews, nor did I broach topics that tended to be sensitive among officers, including human rights, defiance of government orders, and the underperformance of missions. When such themes arose during interviews, it was because the officers themselves raised them.

Officers' interviews were conducted primarily in offices. Interviews ranged from brief conversations to three-hour interviews, most lasting between forty-five and ninety minutes. Some officers were interviewed on more than one occasion. In Peru, I led two discussion groups for senior officers, one group consisting of four army officers, and the other, three army officers and one navy officer. All officers in each group were of the same rank, to facilitate more comfortable, honest responses from all subjects present.

Data Analysis

I analyzed the interview data for officers' attitudes and beliefs, using two main methods. First, from officers' answers to standard, open-ended questions, I created response categories and tallied answers. Second, I analyzed each interview—or, if I interviewed an officer more than once, that cluster of interviews—to identify explanations that officers voluntarily provided for why the army did or did not conduct specific missions, their attitudes toward missions, the relative importance they placed on different issues or missions, and any inconsistencies that arose during a given interview (and across different interviews with the same officer).[6] According to this second approach, a given explanation or viewpoint was marked as having been mentioned more than once only if the officer raised it at different points during the interview. In cases where analysis involved grouping officers and/or their responses by cohort group, I coded interview content before classifying it based on cohort. Views of one Peruvian officer are omitted from the study's analysis of officers' attitudes (in chapter 4): one low-ranking officer who left the army prior to 2000 for ideological reasons. (Factual information provided by that officer about army practices was not omitted from the study.)

ADDITIONAL DATA SOURCES

The interview data are supplemented and triangulated with data gathered through my review of newspaper and government archives, army doctrinal materials, and other documents. I base my analysis of the 1980s and 1990s mainly on these additional sources.

Army Doctrinal Materials

I reviewed army doctrinal materials, including army and military journals, training manuals, class schedules, and syllabi, to supplement interview data in the areas of police work, training in human rights, and attitudes toward different missions, and for factual information. This portion of the research served largely as a validity check.

I reviewed issues of the military journals most read by army officers in each country, published from 1985 through 2005: in Peru, *Desarrollo y defensa nacional* (of Centro de Altos Estudios Militares [CAEM], renamed Centro de Altos Estudios Nacionales [CAEN] in 1997), *Actualidad militar, Expresión militar: Ejército del Perú*, and *Revista de la Escuela Superior de Guerra del ejército del Perú*;[7] and in Ecuador, *Revista de las fuerzas armadas del Ecuador.*[8]

I obtained course listings, syllabi, and instructional manuals from civilians and officers whom I interviewed, and in Peru, from the Centro de Información de la Defensoría del Pueblo. In Peru, cadet course listings and various instructional manuals were available for 1981–2005. In Ecuador, the only manuals made available for this research were those on internal defense for the War Academy's advanced course and the general staff course, current as of 2005. I was also provided with a summary of the lessons on internal defense in the Ecuadorian general staff course for the years 2001–6.

Newspaper Archives

Newspaper articles were particularly helpful for characterizing each army's participation in different security missions, relations between the army and outside actors, government security policy, and the military's official stance on different issues. I obtained articles from the newspaper archives discussed here, from newspapers I monitored while in the field, and, in a very few cases, from interview subjects.

In Peru, I ran numerous keyword searches of the electronic archives of the national newspaper *El Comercio* for the years 1990 through early 2006, and I obtained from the research institute Centro de Estudios y Promoción del Desarrollo (DESCO) the results of an "armed forces" search of the DESCO electronic news archives for 2000–2005, for *El Comercio* and a second national newspaper, *La República*. For key events involving emergency decrees and other cases in which the armed forces were employed in internal security during the post-2000 period, I used the news archives of the human rights organization Asociación Pro Derechos Humanos (APRODEH). Finally, I searched the Catholic University's archives of *La República* for articles on specific events during the 1980s.

In Ecuador, I was granted access to the newspaper archives on the armed forces maintained by the Catholic University's Fundación Democracia, Seguridad y Defensa. The archives consist of articles from multiple national newspapers on all topics related to the armed forces, beginning in 2000.[9] I also used the Catholic University's general newspaper archives to conduct a thorough review of *El Comercio* throughout 1998 and 1999, as well as news on selected events from the 1980s through 1997. To fill gaps that existed in the Catholic University's archives, I visited the newspaper archives of the Casa de la Cultura Ecuatoriana and Central Bank libraries.

Legal Materials

I identified relevant laws and decrees through interviews with civilian and military experts and searches of electronic and paper records. In Peru, I benefited from the extensive knowledge and analyses of the defense and military reform group of the Instituto de Defensa Legal. I also used APRODEH's electronic archives on emergency decrees declared since 2000. For full text of other laws and decrees, I used the legislature's online archive, and *El Peruano* (online for issues published beginning in 1996 and as hardcopy in the Catholic University's newspaper archive for prior years). I located defense ministry resolutions and military directives at the Defensoría del Pueblo's Information Center. For the text of Ecuadorian laws and decrees I relied on Lexis Nexis, as well as the *Registro oficial* (on the Internet and in hardcopy at the congressional archives). I benefited from the Fundación Regional de Asesoría en Derechos Humanos' (INREDH) compilation of emergency decrees. Records of legislative debates surrounding laws were available in Ecuador's national congressional archive and by request at Peru's national congress.

Event, Survey, and Statistical Data Sources

The Peruvian office of APOYO Opinión Mercado S.A. shared with me survey data, and in Ecuador I obtained data from the Alto Comisionado de las Naciones Unidas para los Refugiados (ACNUR), the Central Bank, the Comisión Ecuménica de Derechos Humanos (CEDHU),

Defence Systems Ecuador, and Informe Confidencial. Military and civilian government officials in both countries provided me with government statistics not available online.

Secondary Sources

In Peru, I visited the libraries of the Catholic University, DESCO, and the Instituto de Estudios Peruanos (IEP). In Ecuador, I used the libraries of the Andean University, the Catholic University, the Central Bank, Facultad Latinoamericana de Ciencias Sociales (FLACSO) Ecuador, and the San Francisco University. Researchers in both countries generously shared with me their personal libraries.

Notes

CHAPTER 1. Military Mission Performance in Latin America

1. This treatment of security is, admittedly, narrow in relation to some research in the field of security studies. For limitations to defining the concept of security more broadly, see Paris 2001.

2. In this book, some of the Peruvian army's work in emergency zones in the 1980s resembles policing, including patrols in towns, home searches, and arrests. This research classifies these tasks as counterinsurgency when they are conducted in emergency zones in the name of fighting the guerrilla threat.

3. For example, see Stepan 1988; Isaacs 1993; F. Agüero 1995b; Norden 1996a; Hunter 1997; Pion-Berlin 1997; Fitch 1998; Loveman 1999; Arceneaux 2001; Weeks 2003; and Trinkunas 2005.

4. Unlike scholarship on Latin American military missions, work on the U.S. military has analyzed military shirking more generally (e.g., Feaver 1998). Given the fundamental differences between the U.S. and Latin American contexts, applying this work to Latin American cases is problematic (Jaskoski 2012a, 72–73).

5. This framing of mission neglect as push-back against challenges to the military's autonomy, along with select, related details for the Peruvian case in the post-2000 period (in chapters 2 and 4), is described in Jaskoski 2012a.

6. The vast majority of Latin American countries have been a part of one or more border disputes. Yet, unlike the dynamic in other regions, negotiation or authoritative third-party rulings rather than war have been the main form of dispute settlement in Latin America (Simmons 1999, 5–9). Military clashes that have occurred have mostly been a nineteenth-century phenomenon (Centeno 1997, 1570–73; 2002, 37, 44–47).

7. Ernesto "Che" Guevara, a key player in the Cuban Revolution, "believed that the revolution could only be achieved by destroying the prevailing repressive military-bureaucratic apparatus of Latin America's capitalist states" (Loveman 1999, 161). See Stepan (1971, 155–58) on concern within Latin American militaries that, as in Cuba, the armed forces would be the first state institution to be sacrificed should communist insurgencies take over government.

8. "Countersubversion" went beyond fighting armed combatants. For instance, the Argentine armed forces—under the civilian government of Isabel Perón (1974–76)

and during the brutal military regime of 1976–83—are known for repressing nonviolent individuals purported to support or sympathize with ideologically armed insurgents (Pion-Berlin 1989).

9. On the linkage between Venezuelan officers' "equity-oriented vision of development" and this disgruntlement, see also Trinkunas 2002, 46, 51–53. In chapter 7, I discuss in more detail internal factionalism within Venezuela's armed forces and its ties to the Caracazo repression.

10. I am grateful to J. Samuel Fitch for pointing out this argument.

11. Drawing on role theory, O'Donnell (1973, 79–89) argues that "technocrats" in the private sector and in civilian and military sectors of the state learned "role models" while studying at schools abroad or at domestic schools shaped by international influences. The clash between these foreign-born, technocratic role conceptions and the social realities of Latin America promoted the formation of coup coalitions between civilian and military technocrats and, ultimately, military authoritarian rule (see also Collier 1979, 27–28).

12. Stepan (1971, 172–87) argued that the military's changed beliefs about its role were a key cause of the Brazilian military's 1964 transition from serving as intermittent political moderator to directly ruling government. Dissemination within the Superior War College (Escola Superior de Guerra) of new conceptions of national security, development, and the military's role in politics strengthened officers' confidence in their capacity to govern, causing them to view military rule as a legitimate form of government.

13. Lawrence and Lorsch (1967) coined the name *contingency theory* (Scott 2003, 96). Since its inception, traditional contingency theory has undergone critiques but has been the main approach to studying organizations (Scott 2003, 97). For a discussion of how contingency theory holds up to challenges from other approaches, see Donaldson 2001, 161–79.

14. Thompson (1967, 10–13), borrowing from Parsons (1960), constructs his conceptualization of organizations as consisting of the technical, managerial, and institutional levels.

15. Thompson's observation that organizations protect their technical cores from environmental uncertainty has been applied to a wide range of organizations (e.g., Posen 1984, 2004; Fennell and Alexander 1987; Koberg 1988; Demchack 1991; Meznar and Nigh 1995; Brechin 1997; Kamps and Polos 1999; Simon 1999; Sorenson 2003).

16. For instance, research has resulted in valuable insights into internal and external impetuses for military learning and change (e.g., Rosen 1991; Avant 1993; Zisk 1993; Goldman 1999; Farrell and Terriff 2002).

17. This supposition is consistent with Posen (1984), who finds that organizational interests in maintaining predictability in battlefield scenarios influenced military doctrine in interwar France, Germany, and Britain, but only during periods in which civilian policymakers were not actively involved in security matters.

18. The budget percentages do not take into account general funds, including those spent on the defense ministry, joint command, or military pensions. The refer-

enced source does not provide branch-level budget information for Bolivia, Ecuador, or Peru.

19. Pion-Berlin (1988), Leal Buitrago (1994, 23–56), and Fitch (1998, 106–12) analyze different variants of National Security Doctrine in the region. Loveman (1999, 160–62, 165–94) discusses U.S. influence on Latin America's militaries, including as it pertained to National Security Doctrine following the Cuban Revolution.

20. In Peru, General Juan Velasco Alvarado's "revolutionary" government (1968–75) nationalized much of both industries (Stepan 1978, 263–70; Guasti 1983, 187–92). The Ecuadorian oil sector was gradually nationalized under military rule (1972–79), when the state oil corporation, Corporación Estatal Petrolera Ecuatoriana (CEPE, now Petroecuador), renegotiated oil concessions, causing most companies to withdraw rather than accept the relatively unfavorable terms (Conaghan 1988, 85; Isaacs 1993, 41–46).

21. In Peru, the military regime's progressive character was linked to the armed forces' prior counterinsurgency effort. Velasco's government pursued economic redistribution to discourage a revival of the small insurgencies that the military had eliminated in 1965 (Cotler 1978, 194–95; Stepan 1978, chap. 4). Similarly, the Ecuadorian military's major economic development efforts date to the late 1950s, when the military looked to development as a way to eliminate the structural conditions that could spur insurgency (Fitch 1977, 140–43).

22. Mention of a specific location or army unit does not imply that I was there. During interviews, officers often spoke about prior assignments.

23. The appendix includes greater detail on the processes employed for gathering and analyzing data for the study.

CHAPTER 2. Civil-Military Relations in Democratic Peru and Ecuador

1. Peru's growth rate as a percentage of gross domestic product (GDP) dropped from 2.8 percent in 1980 and 1981 to −2.3 percent in 1982 and −15.2 percent in 1983, and remained negative through the end of Belaúnde's administration (Rospigliosi 1994, 57).

2. With the transition, officials in the interior ministry—which oversees Peru's national police—found that the prior, militarized interior ministry's intelligence files were missing. Nervous about spurring a civil-military conflict and a potential backslide to authoritarianism, the new government did not demand the files from the armed forces (Gorriti 1999, 44).

3. The coup plan initially outlined the installation of military rule, but during 1989 and 1990 the coalition changed to a strategy to control government from behind the scenes (Rospigliosi 2000, 85–86).

4. Peru's GDP grew approximately 7 percent annually between 1993 and 1997, more than any other country in Latin America at the time, with the exception of Chile. Inflation in Peru during that same period never rose above 15 percent (McClintock 2003, 100–101).

5. On Fujimori's authoritarian practices, see also Levitsky and Way 2002; Carrión 2006.

6. The penalty for disloyalty to Montesinos or Fujimori was expulsion from the armed forces or worse, as demonstrated by the case of General Rodolfo Robles Espinoza. When, in 1993, Robles publicly denounced the SIN and the head of the army for their ties to massacres at La Cantuta University, he was forcibly retired from the army and received death threats. Fearing for his life, he fled the country (Inter-American Commission on Human Rights 1999).

7. Several officers interviewed described the specialized civic action battalions that operated during the 1990s. As noted in chapter 1, the Peruvian armed forces were not new to economic development efforts. Their participation in civic action, in particular, has been traced to the 1950s, when some officers promoted the work (Masterson 1991, 159), and to the early 1960s, when, under Belaúnde's first government (1963–68), the military's three branches created civic action initiatives (in 1963) that constituted "the largest non-military role that the Peruvian armed forces had ever assumed and the first organized civic action effort in their history" (Rozman 1970, 560).

8. Military corruption was also reinforced by practices of Peru's intelligence forces; Montesinos and the SIN were deeply involved in the cocaine trade (CVR 2003, 2:242–43; I. Rojas 2005, 208–9).

9. For instance, by January 1992, each counterinsurgency base in the area of Uchiza (a city in San Martín, in the VAH) received $2,000 for each flight with drug cargo that departed from the base's runway. Some of these monies were reserved for food, fuel, and improvements to the base, while the rest were divided among officers and troops proportionally, based on rank. Sendero, the Santa Lucía police base, and the local governor, mayor, and *cocalero* organization also received regular payoffs from drug trafficking in Uchiza (CVR 2003, 2:242).

10. On the fall of Fujimori's government, see Cameron 2006.

11. Based on estimates made by Peruvian judicial authorities, Ángel Páez—Peruvian investigative journalist and the main expert on arms purchases during the Fujimori government—has reported that, from the arms deals, Montesinos skimmed $140 million, which he kept in Swiss bank accounts. This money came from bribes for the purchases of MiG-29 and Su-25 fighter planes, Mi-17 and Mi-6T helicopters, and other equipment, such as that used for telephone espionage (Páez 11/14/05). Montesinos also sold ten thousand AK-47 assault rifles to the Fuerzas Armadas Revolucionarias de Colombia (FARC) insurgency (I. Rojas 2005, 204–5, 209).

12. Several officers who participated in the failed November 1992 coup attempt also formed part of this later rebellion (*El Comercio* [Lima] 10/30/00b).

13. Journalists investigating the case put forth the idea that the revolt was, in fact, "a smokescreen for Montesinos's escape from Peru" (McClintock 2006b, 101).

14. Because of Montesinos's power over the armed forces, Paniagua's government had great difficulty locating officers who had *not* been loyal to Montesinos to appoint to leadership posts. Three months after taking office, Paniagua's govern-

ment learned that the heads of the army, navy, and air force, and the head of the police force, all of whom the government had promoted, had signed a document during Fujimori's government attesting to their allegiance to Montesinos. As replacements, the transitional government appointed generals who had been "separated" from the state security forces by Fujimori during the 1990s for their lack of loyalty and "reincorporated" under Paniagua. In an interview, a high-ranking officer with intimate knowledge of the appointment process commented, "I am sure [those new appointees] would have signed the document had they still been in the armed forces at the time [the document was circulated]!"

15. In December 2002, in an effort to achieve a pyramid structure within the armed forces, the defense minister retired 420 officers (*Economist* 1/11/03).

16. This change in cadet education was described during interviews with a civilian security expert and a mid-ranking officer, both of whom had participated in the army's education reform process. See also Hurtado 2005, 69.

17. Prior to 1997, CAEN was CAEM (Centro de Altos Estudios Militares), which originated as an army institution and was known widely for its role in indoctrinating the leaders of General Velasco's progressive military government (1968–75) on themes of underdevelopment and poverty in Peru (Cotler 1978, 192–95; Stepan 1978, 117–57). According to an officer with experience in the CAEN administration, in 2005 the student population was approximately 60 percent military and 40 percent civilian. With CAEN no longer strictly a military institution, the army sidestepped the school in 2003 by creating its "high command" course within the war college (Escuela Superior de Guerra, ESG), to replace CAEN's defense and development class as the most prestigious course for colonels seeking promotion to the rank of general.

18. These transfers lacked oversight—for example, urgency decrees were not approved by the Council of Ministers as they should have been (Hernández Breña 2003, 85). Between 1990 and 2002, the armed forces spent nearly $992 million from the privatization process, and nearly $141 million from the external debt, on weapons purchases (Hernández Breña 2003, 86).

19. At the allocation stage, for instance, by law, the army, navy, air force, and police each automatically receives 25 percent of the defense fund.

20. This assessment is based on statements made by the following interview subjects: active-duty senior army officers, a journalist highly experienced in engaging with the military, and U.S. officials stationed in Ecuador who worked directly with the Ecuadorian defense sector.

21. On the events surrounding Vargas Pazzos and his insurrection, see also Arboleda et al. 1986, 27–33; Borja 1987, 45–79; Bustamante 1989, 31; Peñaherrera 1989; and Isaacs 1993, 138–39.

22. Defense spending dropped from 10.9 percent of national spending in 1995 to 8.8 percent in 1997, then to 7.3 percent in 2006 (Ministerio de Economía y Finanzas, Ecuador, n.d.).

23. For another analysis of the 1997–2005 cases of premature executive removal, see Conaghan 2011, 262–64.

24. Ecuador's most radical reforms were enacted under President Sixto Durán Ballén (1992–96) and included an end to traditional protections and subsidies to domestic firms and strategic sectors, withdrawal from the Organization of Petroleum Exporting Countries (OPEC), passage of a hydrocarbons law that opened petroleum investment to private investors, and measures that invited foreign investment into virtually all sectors open to domestic investors (Hey and Klak 1999, 78–79). On the uneven nature of neoliberal reform in Ecuador from the 1980s through the 1990s, see Hey and Klak 1999.

25. Bustamante (1999) and Lucero (2001, 65) also highlight the military's role in the 1997 removal of Bucaram.

26. North (2004, 201–3) describes in more detail the economic crisis under Mahuad.

27. Military personnel stationed at the congressional building for security purposes stepped aside and even helped indigenous protesters clear the barbed wire constructed around the government buildings (Lucero 2001, 63).

28. For these programs, the army used its own resources as well as material and human resources provided by communities, the private sector, and local offices of non-defense ministries such as the education and health ministries. A senior officer who had played a leading role in *apoyo al desarrollo* programs in the sierra during the early 1990s estimated that approximately 40 percent of the resources needed for the projects were provided by the army, about 30 percent by private actors, and 30 percent by non-defense ministries. Ortiz (2006) provides a historical analysis of the relationship between the Ecuadorian indigenous population and the armed forces that covers decades prior to the 1990s.

29. High-level active and retired finance ministry officials interviewed in 2005 and 2006 described this lack of oversight.

30. Of particular focus was equipment for northern border defense, discussed in chapter 5.

CHAPTER 3. Army Mission Performance in Post-Transition Peru and Ecuador, 1980s–1990s

1. Between 1884 and the final, 1995 war, the two militaries engaged in thirty-four episodes of armed conflict (Simmons 1999, 10; Mares 2001, 161). Many of these cases resulted from disagreement over the meaning of the 1942 Rio Protocol, which, due to questions about the accuracy of its geographic references, proved unsatisfactory for the Ecuadorian government. U.S. military mapping flights between 1943 and 1946 found that the length of the Cenepa River, running in the zone of the Rio Protocol line, was longer than Ecuadorian cartographers had previously recorded. From the Ecuadorian perspective, this finding made the provisions of the protocol invalid, and beginning in 1960, successive Ecuadorian presidents demanded that it be reversed (García Gallegos 1999, 197–98; Marcella and Downes 1999, 6; Mares 2001, 161–66).

2. Combat occurred on January 9 and January 11, 1995, and then again starting later that month (Marcella and Downes 1999, 2). During the war, the two countries mobilized a total of approximately 150,000 troops, and between one hundred and five hundred military personnel died (Palmer 1997, 119; Marcella and Downes 1999, 1–3; Herz and Pontes Nogueira 2002, 47).

3. This restructuring of the army was described by a mid-ranking army officer who had served in an army unit that relocated from the jungle, where it had been conducting counterinsurgency, to the north, to join the new, sixth region.

4. On the organizational roots of Sendero Luminoso, see Degregori 1987, 190–201.

5. Data in this paragraph are from McClintock 1998, 73, 80–81.

6. For another summary of Belaúnde's failure in the counterinsurgency effort, see McClintock 1998, 140–42.

7. The provinces consisted of Cangallo, Huamanga, Huanta, La Mar, and Víctor Fajardo. In October 1981, Sendero took control of a police station in La Mar, prompting the decree (Gorriti 1999, 132–35).

8. One example of a massacre carried out by the army occurred in the district of Santillana, in Huanta, Ayacucho, where army personnel killed at least 123 people from several communities in December 1984. The victims were buried in a mass grave in the community of Putis, which they were forced to dig themselves (CVR 2003, 7:95).

9. Many of those sources had been developed by the U.S. army, which had used them to teach Peruvian officers at the School of the Americas in Panama (Tapia 1997, 27–30).

10. This focus on external defense was described by retired and active-duty army officers during interviews and was also made clear by troop placements: in 1980, military forces were concentrated on and near the northern and southern borders, while the interior military regions were understaffed (Obando 1994, 106–7; Tapia 1997, 27–30; McClintock 1998, 133; Palomino Milla 2004, 127).

11. In 1984, war minister General Luis Cisneros said publicly, "In the modern war there are four domains . . . the political, the economic, the social, and the military" (Rospigliosi 2000, 60). There was consensus within the armed forces that these four dimensions were crucial (Rospigliosi 2000, 64–65).

12. Cynthia McClintock's 1988 survey of thirty-three military officers of different services and ranks found that approximately one-half of these officers resented being blamed by Peruvian citizens for abuses and for the economic downturn between 1978 and 1980, under military rule (McClintock 1989, 136).

13. U.S. foreign policy also helped to move Peru's state security forces away from the use of indiscriminate violence. For instance, in the early 1990s, one condition of U.S. economic assistance was that the International Committee of the Red Cross (ICRC) be granted access to detention centers. As a result of this pressure, a registry of prisoners was updated daily and supervised by the ICRC and Peruvian public prosecutors. This system of oversight meant that registered detained Sendero leaders

were no longer disappeared, tortured, or killed (CVR 2003, 2:227–30). (According to a personal communication with a scholar who conducted research on the army's role in the conflict, for Peru's national truth and reconciliation commission, army personnel continued disappearing, torturing, and killing many individuals; they simply did so off-base, thus sidestepping the new rules that pertained to registered detainees.)

14. Self-defense committees (CADs) were also critical in reducing Sendero's power in the countryside (e.g., Degregori 1996). CADs began organizing on their own in Ayacucho as early as 1982, in response to Sendero attacks (Yrigoyen Fajardo 2002, 33–36), and later they received government support (as discussed later in this chapter).

15. The Grupo Especial de Inteligencia (GEIN), a special intelligence group within Peru's police antiterrorist unit, Dirección Nacional Contra el Terrorismo (DINCOTE), captured Guzmán. Although Guzmán was arrested during the Fujimori government, García's government is more appropriately credited for the arrest; the GEIN was created by García, and its leadership and strategy remained unchanged under Fujimori (McClintock 1998, 144–45, 147–48).

16. Peruvian peasants have grown coca for traditional uses, and yet the cocaine trade has become the main driver behind coca production in the country. In the vast majority of Peru's current coca zones, coca cultivation began in the 1980s for cocaine production, and as of the early 2000s, between 68 and 80 percent of all Peruvian coca was for cocaine (Cabieses 2005, 29). Added to the VAH's production, parts of the VRAE, too, have produced significant quantities of coca, going back to the 1980s. Although, historically, those quantities have been small relative to the VAH's production (Durand Guevara 2009, 277), more recently, the VRAE has contributed substantially to Peru's overall coca production (see chapter 4).

17. As an illustration of the army's new approach, army efforts in the VAH during 1993 and 1994 culminated in "Operation Aries" in the province of Leoncio Prado, Huánuco, from April to July 1994. In that operation, the army attacked insurgent bases with force that included firing rockets from helicopters (CVR 2003, 2:243).

18. Peru saw high levels of labor mobilization, involving many national strikes, in the 1980s. In contrast, during the 1990s there was little popular protest or strike activity (Instituto Nacional de Estadística e Informática [INEI] 2005a; Arce 2008, 42). This low level of mobilization has been attributed to growth in the informal sector that came with neoliberal economic reforms (Roberts 1998, 241–43; 2006).

19. This level of military participation occurred during national strikes in March 1983, November 1984, and July 1988. On these three cases, see, respectively, *La República* 3/11/83a, 3/11/83b; *La República* 11/29/84, 11/30/84a, 11/30/84b, 11/30/84c, 11/30/84d, 12/1/84a, 12/1/84b; and *La República* 7/19/88, 7/20/88a, 7/20/88b, 7/20/88c, 7/20/88d.

20. For reports on protests in 1999 and 2000, I conducted a search of the *El Comercio* (Lima) electronic archives. Social movement experts and activists confirmed in interviews the lack of military action in protest control during those years. There

were exceptions to the army's low level of involvement, such as during the May 1987 national strike that overlapped with a police strike, when the police were unavailable to control demonstrations (*La República* 5/16/87, 5/17/87, 5/20/87, 5/21/87).

21. Between 1985 and 1989, of all cases reported to the human rights organization Comisión Ecuménica de Derechos Humanos (CEDHU), 62 percent were committed by the police and only 17 percent by the armed forces (X. Andrade 1994, 140). Most military counterinsurgency actions against the AVC were executed by the navy infantry, not by the army, according to the human rights leader and documented by human rights organizations and security analysts (CEDHU 1991, 123; García Gallegos 2006, 14).

22. Army professionalization in this period was described by several army officers during interviews, including three retired senior officers, three active-duty senior officers, and one active-duty mid-ranking officer. The army's actions were part of an impetus within the military toward greater professionalism after the 1981 conflict. On the Ecuadorian military's post-1981 professionalization efforts, see Bustamante 1989, 29–30; Isaacs 1993, 109–11; Fitch 1998, 80; Mares 1999, 183–84; 2001, 171; and García Gallegos 2000, 170.

23. For example, this heavy military involvement occurred in 1982, when a drastic drop in international oil prices brought economic crisis to Ecuador and helped to spur a national strike opposing President Osvaldo Hurtado's economic austerity measures (*El Comercio* [Quito] 10/19/82, 10/21/82, 10/22/82a, 10/22/82b, 10/22/82c; Oviedo 1991, 250; Conaghan and Malloy 1994, 112). In mere anticipation of labor mobilization, the Febres Cordero government assigned the army to protest control when it decreed a national state of emergency prior to a planned strike in early June 1988 (*El Comercio* [Quito] 6/1/88).

24. On the development of and migration to Ecuador's oil regions, see Kimerling 1991, 43–45; Espinosa 2003; Fontaine 2003, 99–102; García Gallegos 2003; Sawyer 2004, 13, 110–12; and Yashar 2005, 112–16.

25. Key legislation has been Ecuador's 1978 Organic Law (Ley Orgánica) of the Armed Forces and 1979 National Security Law (in effect at the time research for this study was conducted, and undergoing reform as of mid-2009). According to army officers interviewed, examples of "strategic areas" include oil infrastructure, hydroelectric centers, and airports.

26. On this case, see also *El Comercio* (Quito) 3/13/84, 3/16/84, 3/17/84, 3/23/84, 3/28/84.

27. Sawyer (2004, 149–81), Van Cott (2005, 112), and Yashar (2005, 147–49) analyze the 1994 mobilization. The army's security work during and following the mobilization was characterized in the press as restrained, but it was sufficient to cause CONAIE president Luis Macas to demand publicly that the government halt military operations (*El Comercio* [Quito] 6/23/94a, 6/23/94b, 6/24/94, 6/25/94).

28. This description of the army's urban anticrime work under Presidents Febres Cordero and Durán Ballén is based on interviews with a human rights leader who

had been active in the human rights community for many decades and with other security experts, in addition to other referenced sources.

29. Complaints of crime against property (low-level theft, theft and assault, and commercial assault) jumped by nearly 50 percent between 1995 and 1999 at the national level, by 43 percent in Guayas, and by 71 percent in the province of Pichincha, where the capital city of Quito—Ecuador's second largest city—is located (Arcos et al. 2003, 91).

30. Durán Ballén's Executive Decrees No. 86 (1992) and No. 2128 (1994) and President Bucaram's Executive Decree No. 30 (1996) assigned the armed forces to fight crime at the national level, without specifying any end dates. The two decrees under Durán Ballén remained on the books at the time this research was conducted. Bucaram's decree, however, was treated as a (temporary) declaration of a state of emergency and was abolished in 2002, along with a string of emergency decrees (Executive Decree 3156).

31. The army was brought back into anticrime work after the conflict, with decrees passed during the Bucaram administration (1996–97) (*El Comercio* [Quito] 3/12/98).

32. In a very similar, well-known incident, which also took place in Tochache but in March 1989, guerrillas killed ten police personnel and wounded fourteen others. During the attack, which lasted for several hours, local army commanders did not assist the police, claiming that they did not have access to helicopters for night-time operations and that they required a signed order from García himself (CVR 2003, 7:226–38).

33. See Legislative Decrees 726, 734, 738, and 741 (Tapia 1997, 62–77; Rospigliosi 2000, 113–20).

34. A civilian academic specializing in Peru's internal conflict in the 1980s and 1990s also described, in an interview, the decentralized nature of the army's approach to counterinsurgency during those years.

35. Until the 1990s, officers generally resisted giving the CADs weapons. A research team that surveyed state security force personnel in 1990 found that only 37 percent of respondents favored arming the CADs, whereas 52 percent opposed doing so (McClintock 1998, 145n244). Among these opponents were officers in key leadership positions, including, for instance, the head of the political-military command in Ayacucho (General Rodríguez) in mid-1989. There were some exceptions to this trend in the 1980s, including efforts by General Huamán—political-military commander under Belaúnde—and a case in which an army patrol leader helped expand CADs in La Mar, Ayacucho, in 1984 (del Pino 1996, 138–39). For analysis of army-CAD relations, see also Coronel 1996, 51; Mauceri 1996, 143–45; Tapia 1997, 56; McClintock 1998, 145, 148–49; and Yrigoyen Fajardo 2002, 38–39.

36. The analysis of FARC and Ecuadorian army behavior during the 1980s in this discussion of mission overload is based on an interview with a former Ecuadorian army helicopter pilot who worked in the north during this round of attacks, supplemented by other, referenced sources.

37. The reasoning behind the decision was divulged by the former helicopter pilot mentioned above, an Ecuadorian journalist highly knowledgeable about dynamics in the north, and Neira (1/6/94).

38. This anecdote was shared by a security specialist in Ecuador, who learned of the case from a police officer who had participated directly in the police investigation in the north.

39. During interviews, army officers generally described this modus operandi as unofficial, but there are indications that it was formalized through explicit agreements between the FARC and military intelligence after the Putumayo attack. These agreements are documented in military intelligence reports accessed by an Ecuadorian journalist who was interviewed for this study and who has extensive knowledge of army activities in northern Ecuador.

40. A retired army officer said that beginning in mid-1994, Ecuadorian army personnel observed growing numbers of Peruvian patrols in Ecuadorian territory. There were also purported cases in which Peruvian soldiers killed Ecuadorian mine workers in southern Ecuador. Such incidents prompted the Ecuadorian army to send more personnel south. The 1994 Peruvian patrols, in fact, were brought on by activities of the Ecuadorian military, which, starting in 1991, deployed personnel to the disputed territory along the Cenepa River (Mares and Palmer 2012, 38).

41. One officer gave the example of a cow and salt.

CHAPTER 4. Mission Constraint and Neglect of Counterinsurgency

1. The violent branch has also undergone internal divisions. After Guzmán was captured, leader "Feliciano" headed the armed faction of Sendero until his arrest in 1999, at which point the insurgency split once more, with one group controlling the organization in the VRAE, the other in the VAH. "Alipio" took control of the organization in the VRAE, while "Artemio" was in charge in the VAH (*El Comercio* [Lima] 5/4/02; Hidalgo Vega 12/28/05). By 2005, Artemio shared power with "Clay." Clay was arrested by state security agents and released multiple times across the years. In early 2006, he was killed in a national police operation (*El Comercio* [Lima] 12/22/05, 2/20/06).

2. To supplement this overview of Sendero's power and activities since 2000, see McClintock 2005, 77–83.

3. On Sendero's ties to logging, see *New York Times* 9/28/03.

4. From 1983 through 1994, annual police captures of cocaine ranged from 12 to 595 kilograms, averaging 214 kilograms per year. Captures subsequently soared: from 1995 through 2004, annual captures ranged from 1,006 to 7,659 kilograms, averaging 3,974 kilograms per year (Policía Nacional, Perú 2006 [no data for 1998]).

5. The one *cocalero* organization that has not joined the national CONPACCP is the Monzón Valley Association of Agricultural Producers (Asociación de Productores Agropecuarios del Valle de Monzón, APAVM) (Obando 2006, 188–89).

6. This total control was described by several interview subjects, including a leading expert on the CADs in the VRAE; a retired police officer who, while serving

at the highest levels of the national police, planned operations in Vizcatán; a police officer who had worked in Ayacucho during episodes of guerrilla violence against police personnel in Vizcatán in the post-2000 period; and an appointed government official at the regional level in Ayacucho. Press reports about Vizcatán also frequently refer to the insurgency's historical and continued power there (e.g., *El Comercio* [Lima] 12/11/05; *La República* 2/10/06, 1/13/09; *Caretas* 10/23/08). The second part of this chapter analyzes the Peruvian army's efforts since late 2008 to gain control of Vizcatán.

7. On Sendero's contemporary role in the drug trade in the VRAE, see also *La República* 1/13/09; Romero 3/18/09; and *Caretas* 4/30/09.

8. This paragraph is based on Obando 2006, 188–92, and other referenced sources.

9. At least thirty guerrillas attempted to kidnap the children from a school in Percos, a Huanta community, with the intent of transporting them to a Sendero military camp in the Ayacucho jungle where the insurgency trained and indoctrinated children ages five to fifteen. On learning of a nearby Peruvian army patrol, the guerrillas canceled the kidnapping operation (Potestá 10/2/04).

10. This discussion of the trajectory of Laws 25410 and 28222 is based on an interview with a former high-level interior ministry official who worked in the ministry under Toledo. In congressional debates over whether to lengthen the time period, retired general and congressman Marciano Rengifo Ruiz (2001) also supported extending it, on the basis that counterinsurgency operations required more than eight days.

11. Information on U.S. goals in Peru presented in this paragraph was provided in 2005 by a U.S. official stationed in Peru.

12. A U.S. official stationed in Peru described this behavior on the part of the joint command.

13. That mid-ranking officer said the police should do "counterterrorism," because it is internal security, but that "unfortunately, because the police are not prepared for this work, they ask for the army's help."

14. Officers commonly used either *subversion* or *terrorism* to refer to the Sendero insurgency. Five of the mentions of Sendero combined the threat with drug trafficking, employing the term *narcoterrorism*. Those five mentions are classified as "insurgency," since they are referring to an aspect of Sendero operations. Second to insurgency were mentions pertaining to economic development (thirty-one, or 20% of total mentions), including reference to poverty, economic globalization, or poor education. The third most common threat category mentioned was illegal drug-related activities, with twenty-three mentions, or 15 percent of the total.

15. The army's portion of the defense fund was $11 million in 2005, the first year that the relevant law was in effect (Páez 1/2/06). The $11 million was significant, considering that capital expenditures for the entire defense sector totaled only about $14.4 million in 2004 (Hernández Breña 2003, 72).

16. One example of these rare operations was an October 2005 operation planned from Lima and consisting of two simultaneous special forces patrols by

members of the brigades in Cusco and Ayacucho. The case was described by an army officer involved in the operation and was also discussed by the press (*La República* 10/18/05, 10/19/05).

17. These estimates were provided by a retired senior officer who had handled personnel matters in the 1990s, including in emergency zones. According to security experts interviewed, decreases in manpower in Sendero zones cannot be fully explained by the reduced size of the overall army (in terms of personnel) that occurred across the same time period.

18. The information on the number of personnel assigned to counterinsurgency bases in the 1980s and 1990s was provided during an interview with a retired general who, in the 1990s, had worked in a leadership capacity on operations and personnel assignments to emergency zones, and during a discussion group consisting of two senior army officers and one senior navy officer.

19. The description of post-2000 personnel assignments to counterinsurgency bases was provided during interviews with a mid-ranking army officer and a civilian researcher who specializes in Peru's internal conflict, and during an army-navy discussion group. Similarly, the CNDDHH (2001b, 118) reported that in the VAH as of 2001, several counterinsurgency bases had been dismantled and the remaining bases lacked personnel and logistical support, which explained "the limitation of regular patrols through Upper Huallaga communities."

20. These tasks were described during a discussion group with four senior army officers and during one-on-one interviews with four active-duty senior army officers, a retired senior officer, and a mid-ranking officer.

21. A mid-ranking army officer and a police officer, both of whom had worked in Sendero zones since 2000, described this practice in interviews.

22. For instance, a hundred police special forces officials were sent to the zone—fifty on the day of the attack and fifty the following day (Castillo 12/6/05; Castillo, Navarro, and Tóvar 12/7/05). A police operation using three helicopters searched for the insurgents involved in the attack (Castillo 12/9/05). The army's response was limited to participation in joint patrols with the police, two days after the attack (*La República* 12/7/05a). On the guerrilla attack, see also Ascue Sarmiento 12/25/05; and *El Comercio* (Lima) 12/4/05a, 12/21/05b.

23. One Sendero base used for these purposes, discovered by a November 2002 police operation in the extreme south of Junín in the Ene River Valley, had fifty-five cabins, an indoctrination school, and a farm. The base's supplies included shotguns, grenades, and ammunition for automatic weapons, as well as medicine and "terrorist literature" (*El Comercio* [Lima] 11/7/02). A police operation in late 2003 rescued an indigenous community of Asháninkas that had been enslaved for five years by Sendero in Mapotoa, Junín (Ascue Sarmiento 12/15/03). The success of this police effort to provide security for the Asháninkas was partial: in May 2004, an Asháninka leader of eighty native communities estimated that approximately seven hundred members of his group were still enslaved along the Ene River (specifically, between the Tambo, Ene, and Perené rivers, in Junín) (*El Comercio* [Lima] 5/11/04).

24. Details on the December 2005 violence and the police and army responses in this paragraph were gathered from the following news articles: *El Comercio* (Lima) 12/4/05a, 12/21/05a, 12/21/05b, 12/23/05, 12/29/05b; Castillo 12/6/05, 12/9/05; Castillo, Navarro, and Tóvar 12/7/05; *La República* 12/19/05, 12/20/05b, 12/21/05, 12/28/05; Ascue Sarmiento 12/24/05, 12/25/05; Navarro and Arcaya 12/24/05; Arcaya and Navarro 12/25/05.

25. The press reported that army personnel on the five counterinsurgency bases in the zone remained on base, awaiting orders (Arcaya and Navarro 12/25/05). After meetings between local police and army commanders, the latter requested instructions from the army high command on what to do, rather than providing immediate support. This last sequence of events was described by the following subjects knowledgeable about the incident: a high-level interior ministry official and a police major who had been involved directly in the December 2005 events, officers in an army-navy discussion group, a retired senior army officer, an active-duty senior army officer, and a retired high-ranking police officer.

26. About twenty Sendero insurgents attacked an army counterinsurgency base, as well as a patrol from that base, in Satipo, Junín, in December 2005. Three army personnel were wounded. In response, local military patrols left from Satipo to search for the insurgents (*La República* 12/19/05, 12/20/05b).

27. On the resource allocations, see *El Comercio* (Lima) 1/5/06a, 1/5/06b, 1/6/06, 1/21/06; *La República* 1/5/06a, 1/5/06b; and CNDDHH 2007, 187.

28. The article quotes Rospigliosi as saying that the army requested 200 million (*millón*) *soles* per base, not 200 thousand (*mil*) *soles*. However, I believe *millón* was meant to be *mil* in the text of the article, considering that in 2004, military sources indicated that installing one counterinsurgency base cost 150,000 *soles* (see above).

29. Basombrío was here referring to the purchase during Toledo's government of four used Italian ships for Peru's navy (Páez 11/14/05).

30. From information provided in an interview with one junior army officer, it seems that some army personnel did receive ad hoc training in protest control. The officer recounted his assignment during the 2004 Ilave protests, described later in the chapter. In preparation for a possible order to manage the uprising, he was sent as part of a small group of army personnel to the town, where the group remained on base and trained with clubs, shields, and other riot-control equipment.

31. On the 2002 "Arequipazo," see Eaton 2010.

32. In contrast to the army's restraint in Arequipa, the national police were harsh, as told by an official in the Defensoría del Pueblo's Arequipa office. For instance, two protesters were struck and killed by police teargas canisters.

33. This executive-army interaction during the Ilave incident was recounted by a mid-ranking army officer who had been stationed in an army unit that was on call, in case Toledo did give the order. After the protests, the army and police jointly patrolled the city for two or three days to help clear the roads of obstructions left over from the protests (*El Comercio* [Lima] 5/25/04, 5/27/04, 5/30/04). Toledo's council of ministers monitored this work closely (*El Comercio* [Lima] 4/29/04, 5/27/04).

34. This information was provided in interviews by a mid-ranking officer and a senior officer.

35. A handful of officers said that the army employed this approach during some protests in the city of Iquitos, in Peru's northeastern jungle, approximately three times each year between 2002 and 2004, and then only with the approval of the regional army general.

36. There were exceptions to this lack of news coverage of army work during *cocalero* mobilizations. For instance, the press reported on the army's participation in late May 2004, when two hundred soldiers opened highways for transit in a coordinated police-army effort (*El Comercio* [Lima] 5/24/04, 5/30/04).

37. This description of communications involving the provincial government, army, and police in Ayacucho is based on interviews with two officers who had been involved in the communications—one senior and the other mid-ranking.

38. Earlier legal support for military involvement in protecting Peru's forests is an August 1996 decree (Supreme Decree 013-96-AG), referred to in Ministerio de Defensa Nacional, Perú 2005, 101.

39. An interview subject who had worked in the interior ministry and in the Defensoría del Pueblo on themes of popular protest explained that large, organized mafias involved in illegal logging were responsible for the settlement. On the army's operation and INRENA participation in the case, see *El Comercio* (Lima) 2/10/05, 11/15/05a. On the ongoing case of squatters in the Pómac forest and opposition to the settlements by local community members, see *El Comercio* (Lima) 11/17/09.

40. One of the army unit's routine patrols saw buses pull up that were transporting five thousand squatters. Army personnel were ordered to do no more than shoot into the air, which they did. This tactic helped "control the situation" until the morning, when eighteen more army patrols and two hundred police personnel arrived. At that point, the police confronted the population directly, using teargas. The soldiers walked forward, "advancing in parallel" with the police line, which served as a buffer between the soldiers and the squatters.

41. A customs official described these contraband operations on the basis of his experience working in Puno. For cases in which the Peruvian army has intercepted contraband, see *El Comercio* (Lima) 5/15/01, 6/19/01, 7/13/01, 8/14/01, 11/27/01, 8/27/02, 11/22/04, 8/20/05.

42. Peru's defense "white book" refers to this law in identifying contraband interdiction as one arena in which the military participates (Ministerio de Defensa Nacional, Perú 2005, 101).

43. The information about army interdiction in the illegal exportation of timber is based on a compilation of data collected through interviews with a junior army officer and an INRENA official, and on newspaper articles (*El Comercio* [Lima] 10/20/00, 5/8/04).

44. The information on dynamics in southern Peru was provided by the above-referenced customs official with experience working in Puno.

45. This policy was relayed by a senior army officer who had specialized knowledge of laws and army regulations relating to the army's policing assignments.

46. The second operation involved a battalion that participated without receiving prior approval from the brigade general. In response, that general prohibited the battalion's involvement in future operations.

47. This case was recounted by a U.S. official stationed in Peru.

48. As of late 2005, the U.S. state department had funded the installation of a police base in that zone (in Palmapampa, Junín), so that the police would no longer need to rely on the army's help there. Details on this case were provided by the retired police officer mentioned in the text and by a U.S. official stationed in Peru.

49. See Law 26496 (1995) and article 3 of its 1996 regulation, Supreme Decree 007-96-AG, referred to by officers knowledgeable about laws and regulations pertaining to army missions, and in Ministerio de Defensa Nacional, Perú 2005, 101–2. Other common camelids in Peru include llamas and alpacas.

50. According to CONACS officials, there was one case of suspected Sendero involvement in vicuña hunting during that period that spurred the army to plan an operation to confront the hunters, but when army intelligence revealed that Sendero, in fact, was not involved, the army canceled its plans.

51. Several mid-ranking and senior army officers described such training in these locations.

52. Many of the officers in the senior cohort who were interviewed had been stationed in emergency zones, irrespective of whether their specialty prepared them specifically for that work (e.g., army infantry) or whether they were more obviously trained for external defense (e.g., cavalry). As recounted by one retired general who had played a leading role in the army's operations department during the 1990s, "there were two armies: one doing external defense, one counterinsurgency, and every six months they flipped." An active-duty senior army officer made a similar statement about army practices in the 1980s.

53. Of the reported deaths and disappearances, about 2 percent were caused by CADs, 1.5 percent by the MRTA, and 8 percent by unknown perpetrators (CVR 2003, app. 3: 86).

54. In April 2009, Peru's supreme court found Fujimori guilty for his involvement in Barrios Altos and in the 1992 La Cantuta University massacres, which were also carried out by the Colina Group. Fujimori was sentenced to twenty-five years in prison. At that time, trials of members of the Colina Group were still in progress.

55. The national congress created a registry for disappearances (by Law 28413), maintained by the Defensoría del Pueblo (2005, 223). Between 2004 and the end of 2008, the Defensoría received 2,888 requests to add names to the registry and approved 1,044 of them (Defensoría del Pueblo 2008a, 268–69).

56. These positions were created in direct response to IACHR recommendations (Defensoría del Pueblo 2005, 23–48).

57. At that time, the Defensoría tracked fifty-nine cases—the forty-seven original CVR cases and an additional twelve cases opened by the Defensoría itself (De-

fensoría del Pueblo 2008a, 149–52). Successful prosecutions of military personnel accountable for past abuses continued to prove difficult. Of the fifty-nine cases, the courts had decided on only nineteen and had found only nineteen army personnel guilty of human rights abuses (for their roles in four of the nineteen cases) as of November 2008 (Defensoría del Pueblo 2008a, 149–52).

58. Unlike the SIN, the CNI saw great instability in its leadership and lacked a clear mission, both of which help to explain its ineffectiveness (Alegría Varona 2004; Chiri Márquez 2004, 120–22; Piscoya 2004, 359–60; Robles Montoya 3/19/04).

59. On creation of the DINI, see *La República* 4/14/04, 12/15/05a; and Law 28664.

60. In late 2008, President García appointed Mesa Angosto to serve again as CSJM president (*La República* 12/29/08).

61. By the end of the program's first year, the contribution had shifted from a voluntary donation to an obligatory withholding, according to a mid-ranking army officer, the source of information about the program.

62. In October 2008, the government decreed that defense ministry funds would cover all legal fees of retired and active-duty military personnel being investigated by the justice system (*La República* 10/29/08).

63. One junior officer said that the main disadvantage of army counterinsurgency work was that the police did not want to be subordinated to the army. Another junior officer said, "Before, we were sent to destroy the enemy . . . Now . . . politicians must approve everything. The army has no autonomy to do its job. This is not good."

64. There was no relationship within the sample between valuing counterinsurgency as an appropriate army mission and raising the topic of human rights. That is, it seems that concerns about human rights did not cause officers to reject counterinsurgency altogether, and that officers did not complain about human rights as a way to justify their existing distaste for counterinsurgency.

65. Two members of the junior cohort also expressed this opinion.

66. In addition to several members of the senior cohort, one junior officer also expressed this view. This complaint was not based in fact: according to the antiterrorism laws of the 1990s, individuals found responsible for the crime of terrorism by anonymous ("faceless") judges were to serve between twenty years and life in prison (Decree Law No. 25475; Inter-American Commission on Human Rights 2000, chap. 2). Records kept by the Defensoría del Pueblo indicate that the highest number of prisoners held for terrorist acts at one time was 3,878, in 1997. As of the end of 2005, approximately one thousand individuals in Peru's prisons were there for terrorism (*La República* 12/26/05). In contrast, as mentioned earlier in the chapter, very few army personnel have been found guilty of human rights abuses since 2000.

67. Beyond this description, details on the survey were not made available for this study.

68. In this special forces operation (also mentioned in chapter 3), army commandos killed fourteen MRTA insurgents. Following Fujimori's departure from office, approximately forty commandos along with their commanding officers faced prosecution

for the deaths. Forensic evidence showed that before they were killed, the insurgents had already been badly wounded or had surrendered. The supreme court sent the troops and a few leaders to military courts, and sent some of the other commanding officers and members of intelligence units that had been linked to Montesinos to be tried in civilian courts (CNDDHH 2001b, 119; González Cueva 2004, 65–66).

69. In this study, *effectiveness* and *success* with regard to the Peruvian army's counterinsurgency efforts refer to reducing the insurgent threat, which often did not mean also respecting the rights of civilians.

70. Only one junior officer expressed this attitude.

71. Here, officers' statements about whether army personnel could reasonably (1) distinguish between civilians and insurgents, (2) target insurgents, and/or (3) avoid civilian casualties are all considered to be references to avoiding civilian casualties.

72. The officer did not say whether or not the helicopter fired on the individuals in this case.

73. This excerpt is drawn from an interview conducted in English, as preferred by the officer.

74. The officer actually misspoke and stated that the "Law of Repentance" (Decree Law 25499) was passed in 1994, when in fact it was passed in 1992.

75. An exception was one junior officer who thought that the former insurgents who had "repented" in accordance with the Law of Repentance still posed a threat in terms of propagating support for insurgents within communities.

76. Beginning with the graduating class of 1994, infantry cadets took between two and four units of human rights instruction over the course of their studies at the Escuela Militar, with the exception of the graduating class of 1997, which took no units in human rights, and the class of 1998, which took one unit in the subject. The number of human rights units that cadets took increased across time: cadets graduating through 2000 took two units (with the exceptions of the classes of 1997 and 1998), the class of 2001 took three units, and the classes of 2002 and 2003 took four units. Cadets took between eight and twenty-four units total each year, in a curriculum that lasted five years beginning with the graduating class of 1997 and four years for prior cohorts.

77. I believe the interviewee misspoke when he said that five police personnel died in the attack. At that time, four police personnel on patrol, in search of a meeting of Sendero's key leaders in the province of Satipo, in the VRAE, were reportedly killed (*El Comercio* [Lima] 8/8/01; Costa and Basombrío 2005, 249).

78. As evidence, he provided me with army data about Sendero incidents, according to which incidents increased from an annual average of 248 in 2000–2004 to 426 in 2005 and 605 in 2006.

79. Plan VRAE has been widely understood as mainly a military effort and has been criticized for failing to bring development programs to the region (e.g., J. C. Agüero 2009, 55–56). In a 2009 interview, a civilian who had worked in a high-level capacity in the defense ministry during the first year of the García administration said that, in terms of economic development, Plan VRAE was simply a list of pre-

existing project plans compiled by ministries involved in infrastructure, production, and social programs.

80. The legal interpretations in this paragraph are based on my reading of Law 29166 and on a personal communication with Gerardo Arce of the Área de Defensa y Reforma Militar, Instituto de Defensa Legal, January 27, 2009.

81. For instance, the army maintained a very clear rule that if it was called on to control protests and its personnel found it necessary to fire their weapons, then they must first shoot into the air before using their weapons against people. On this practice, see the discussion of protest control in the city of Puno in the first part of this chapter.

82. As of early 2009, the former defense advisor referred to above estimated that about 90 percent of military personnel in the VRAE were from the army and about 10 percent from the navy infantry, based on his knowledge of the military's ongoing efforts in the valley. Once the rules of engagement brought the army back into the counterinsurgency effort, certain organizational and resource-related developments further facilitated army operations. For instance, within the broader Plan VRAE, in early 2009 a new army region was created for security in the zone (Supreme Decree 001-2009-DE/EP). Helicopter repairs have also helped the army's operations.

83. Information on these events was obtained during interviews and from *Caretas* 10/23/08; Castillo 11/20/08; *24 horas libre* 3/6/09; and Aguirre 5/17/09.

84. The fifth officer, who discussed contraband interdiction, did not express a positive or negative attitude about that mission.

85. See the first part of this chapter for further information about the Arequipa and Puno cases.

86. Although the armed forces did not come into contact with protesters, when about one hundred protesters took over the central hydroelectric plant in Huancavelica, a group of military personnel shot warning bullets into the air (*La República* 7/10/08).

87. For example, a journalist with decades of experience reporting on Peru's internal conflict and involvement in the cocaine trade, who has reported on army counterinsurgency efforts on the basis of firsthand field experience since the start of Plan VRAE, confirmed that army patrols and operations have been focused on counterinsurgency, not on antinarcotics.

CHAPTER 5. Mission Overload and Neglect of Border Defense

1. Portions of this chapter are adapted from Jaskoski 2012b.

2. For example, the community of General Farfán in the province of Sucumbíos is 60 percent Colombian (*El Comercio* [Quito] 12/3/04).

3. Montúfar and Whitfield (2003), International Crisis Group (2004), and Loveman (2006a) analyze the implications of Colombia's conflict for its neighbors.

4. This dynamic can be traced at least as far back as the late 1980s (Stanski 2007, 66–69). On the FARC's reliance on Ecuadorian army detachments in the north for basic goods as well as weapons in the 1980s and 1990s, see chapter 3.

5. These numbers omit the many displaced people in Ecuador who did not formally request asylum. As of 2002, there were approximately seventeen hundred people in the north in this situation: five hundred in Carchi, six hundred in Sucumbíos, and six hundred in San Lorenzo, Esmeraldas (P. Andrade 2002, 205–6).

6. Colombian insurgents also have established their own medical facilities in the north, as reported by the national press and noted by a retired army officer in an interview. With the availability of these facilities, from 2003 through 2005 the majority of patients with bullet wounds in Ecuador no longer received treatment at Nueva Loja's main hospital (*El Comercio* [Quito] 5/17/05b).

7. The general dynamic of Ecuadorian residents crossing into Colombia to work in coca fields was described, during interviews, by a Catholic Church representative who had worked in border communities and by an army officer who had patrolled Ecuadorian border towns emptied of young boys during the week.

8. According to a Catholic Church representative with several years of experience working on the border, some families have both legal farms on the Ecuadorian side of the border and coca plantations on the Colombian side. They work in the Colombian coca fields but return to work their fields in Ecuador when the Colombian state carries out fumigation operations to eradicate coca.

9. During interviews, army officers with experience working in Sucumbíos said that periodically their units had identified FARC camps there while on patrol.

10. In that incident, a local Colombian mayor and a Colombian soldier who had witnessed the confrontation reported that the FARC column had come from Ecuador and had retreated there afterward. The Colombian government also stated that the FARC had led the attack from Ecuador (*Hoy* 6/28/05).

11. In one such case, in 2001, twenty-five Colombian paramilitaries crossed to Carchi (OIPAZ 2001, 31).

12. Colombian security forces have not clashed with paramilitaries in northern Ecuador. Historically, the Colombian state has not taken a strong stance against the right-wing paramilitaries and, in fact, has provided them with support as they have sought to eliminate the ELN and the FARC (see chapter 7).

13. At least for a period, the FARC prohibited transit after 6:00 p.m. in the towns of General Farfán, Pacayacu, Santa Elena, and Santa Rosa (*El Comercio* [Quito] 5/17/05a). The FARC's role in providing order was described by border community members, Catholic Church representatives, military officers, and the press (e.g., Faiola 10/1/00; *El Comercio* [Quito] 5/17/05a).

14. The first case was described by a Catholic Church representative and the second by an Ecuadorian academic. Both accounts were based on the individuals' communications with residents of Palma Pampa.

15. Between January 2003 and May 2005, Ecuador's national police reported sixty-seven cases of kidnapping in Carchi, Esmeraldas, and Sucumbíos combined (*El Comercio* [Quito] 5/17/05a).

16. In the early 2000s it was estimated that the FARC obtained between 40 and 70 percent of their annual budget—which is approximately $500 million—from

the cocaine trade, and that the AUC raised approximately 80 percent of its more than $100 million annual budget through that industry (Peceny and Durnan 2006, 107, 111).

17. Unlike Bolivia and Peru, Ecuador has not produced coca for traditional uses (Bonilla 1991), and unlike Colombia, the country has not moved into coca production in a major way to feed the cocaine industry (Secretaria Ejecutiva CONSEP, Observatorio Ecuatoriano de Drogas 2004).

18. Thieves tap the pipeline surrounding the refinery and drain the gas into barrels or into empty swimming pools on the property of nearby residents, as explained by numerous civilian and military security experts during interviews. Another common substance used to process cocaine is cement. Multiple interview subjects familiar with Nueva Loja commented on the city's unusually high number of cement stores and explained the phenomenon by noting the relevance of cement for cocaine production.

19. Approximately 20 percent of Colombia's illegal drugs pass through Ecuador (ICG 2004, 11). Ecuadorian antinarcotics officials have reported that northern Ecuador is attractive for transporting these substances because, by circumventing much of Colombian territory, drug traffickers avoid having to pay the obligatory tax to the FARC at many of the group's checkpoints in southern Colombia (*El Comercio* [Quito] 5/8/05).

20. On weapons and munitions scandals involving the Ecuadorian armed forces, see also *El Comercio* (Quito) 7/11/00, 7/15/00, 2/19/02, 11/29/03; ICG 2004, 13.

21. There have been only a few cases of kidnappings of oil workers following the widely publicized October 2000 kidnapping incident mentioned earlier in this chapter.

22. The 2005 mobilization opposed oil company practices as well as Ecuador-U.S. negotiations over the Free Trade Area of the Americas treaty (Benton 2008; Valdivia 2008, 465).

23. On fear among border communities, see, for example, *El Comercio* (Quito) 10/14/01, 3/18/05, 7/26/05, 8/1/05; OIPAZ 2001, 30–33; and Observatorio Político 11/08.

24. The other potential consequences most frequently named by respondents included crime and violence (20%), migration (20%), and drug trafficking (8%) (*Hoy* 8/18/00). In Ecuador, the term *guerrillas* refers primarily to the FARC, but sometimes also to the ELN.

25. The perception that the army has been the sole state actor in any major effort in the northern jungles was shared by security experts whom I interviewed, including, for example, a U.S. official who had worked with the Ecuadorian military and national police, a private sector official who described the importance of army work in the north and northeastern jungle zones for providing security for private oil infrastructure, and a high-level police officer who had worked in Sucumbíos. Perhaps most relevant, army officers themselves communicated this viewpoint often and vehemently during interviews. Additional evidence that the army has been the only

security institution in Ecuador equipped to carry out jungle operations is that following the 1993 "Putumayo massacre" (see chapter 3), the national police halted their own border patrols.

26. Each president makes a national security plan, which is released to the public after ten years. A retired military officer made the Gutiérrez administration's 2003 plan available to me.

27. As a U.S. official stationed in Peru explained in an interview, "Our idea . . . is to get the Latin American militaries to work together. We don't want to put more money into [U.S. government agencies]. It is better if they do it on their own down here. The ultimate goal is to keep drugs out of the U.S. We are working at the source, the supply side."

28. A retired army officer who was involved in the meeting described the proposal and its rejection. On the Conference, see also VI Conferencia de Ministros de Defensa de las Américas 2004; and *El Comercio* (Quito) 11/22/04.

29. This mandate has been handed to the military as a whole. Yet, as mentioned earlier, the army has been the main state ground force equipped to operate along the border. The Ecuadorian government has ordered the army to combat criminal activities by civilians in northern Ecuador, as well as confront insurgents there.

30. The other central military objective with respect to the north was military power in strategic areas (COSENA 2003), which include, for example, oil zones.

31. I did not obtain a precise breakdown of the proportion of U.S. resources directed to the military. However, based on interviews with U.S. officials, for the years 2001–4, between one-third and one-half of NAS monies went toward the military (NAS 2005). All U.S. defense spending in Ecuador from 2001 through 2009 went toward the Ecuadorian military, not the police (U.S. Military Group, Ecuador 2009).

32. U.S. state department funds for the Ecuadorian armed forces provided through NAS are earmarked specifically for antinarcotics work. However, in addition to serving that function, they can also be used for other missions, according to a U.S. official in Ecuador.

33. This trajectory was often described by officers who reflected on broad questions about the army's roles and its across-time institutional experiences, and who tended to be stationed in Quito. In contrast, officers on bases generally talked about the tactical and operational levels. Of the twenty-seven officers interviewed in Quito, fifteen spoke of a north-to-south shift on the part of the army. Nine other officers in that subsample did not talk about such a shift but were clearly proud of the Ecuadorian army's earlier border defense responsibilities against Peru.

34. This relocation was described by a senior army officer who had helped to plan and implement it and by a journalist who regularly reported on military operations in the north.

35. The term *irregulars* was used commonly by Ecuadorian officers to refer to Colombian insurgents, including the FARC, ELN, and paramilitaries.

36. This information about the patrol practices of the Nueva Loja and Esmeraldas battalions was provided by army officers, based on their recent experience in the unit in question.

37. A journalist with experience reporting on Ecuadorian army work in the north, as well as a mid-ranking officer with recent experience working in Latacunga, described this system.

38. The daytime rule was maintained both by patrols sent from battalion bases and by battalions' smaller detachments.

39. The battalion's single armed conflict was mentioned by officers familiar with the battalion's recent record, based on their work in the north.

40. There is some evidence that increased army presence in the north in the form of patrols has reduced the insurgent presence in one small zone. Several officers explained that when the army first began patrolling the northern border of Esmeraldas in 2000, patrols found houses with "ELN" painted on the sides of structures. As of 2005, officers proudly said, there were no longer indications of ELN presence there.

41. Article 2 of the 1990 organic law added "collaborating and intervening in the remaining aspects concerning national security" to the constitutional responsibilities to protect national sovereignty, defend the integrity and independence of the state, and guarantee the legal order of the state. (The 1990 law replaced the 1978 organic law, which was passed under military rule.) In 1997, the 1990 law underwent minor revisions, none of which affected military missions, and this broad mandate remained in the text of the new organic law passed in 2007 (art. 2). Article 38 of Ecuador's main national security legislation, the 1979 National Security Law, similarly states that the armed forces "will lend their collaboration to the country's social and economic development and in the remaining areas concerning National Security." Article 39 of the law explicitly assigns the military to maintain public order.

42. In the Informe Confidencial surveys of December 10, 2005, and January 21, 2006, crime was named by 21 and 16 percent of respondents, respectively.

43. Several months of pressure by the El Oro citizen security and civil defense council triggered the decree, which assigned $1.2 million to fund police and army anticrime efforts in El Oro (*El Comercio* [Quito] 1/27/05). President Lucio Gutiérrez's Executive Decree No. 1056 (November 2003) for the province of Azuay, home to the city of Cuenca, is another example of an emergency decree issued to bring the army into crime fighting. In addition to the executive actions taken after 2000 to assign the army the anticrime mission, some decrees from the prior decade that supported such work remained in place (see chapter 3).

44. When I was carrying out research for this study, the army patrolled Nueva Loja and Esmeraldas nightly, and more intensively during periods of high criminal activity. The battalion in Esmeraldas meticulously tracked the numbers and exact locations of illegal gold sales, juvenile gangs, and drug and weapons deals in the city. In Carchi's capital city of Tulcán, urban patrols were more sporadic than in Nueva

Loja or Esmeraldas, occurring approximately once a month, and the patrols tended to be called in more for crowd and protest control than for urban crime.

45. Regarding security for landowners, according to officers with recent experience serving in the Carchi battalion, in five of Carchi's six cantons, a group of approximately ten men patrolled in a Humvee at any given time, rotating weekly, to provide security against kidnappings and livestock theft. The sixth canton is located along the border with Colombia, and the army's presence in that canton consisted of three border detachments used mainly for intercepting contraband (as discussed later). The army battalion in the city of Esmeraldas provided security for owners of African palm plantations, according to officers who had worked there.

46. Machala was sufficiently close to Guayaquil that it served as an "escape valve" for criminals during particularly intensive military anticrime operations in Guayaquil, in the late 1990s, according to an academic with expertise in security matters.

47. The national police also have a legal responsibility to monitor weapons purchases and transport.

48. A Catholic Church representative with experience working with border communities said that this practice has made daily life difficult and frightening for border communities that depend on Ecuadorian suppliers to survive.

49. The army also intercepted contraband at the legal Rumichaca crossing, outside Tulcán, Carchi.

50. An Ecuadorian army officer with recent experience serving in the south described the army's contraband interdiction work there.

51. In practice, as of 2006, there was only one feasible legal crossing for many people, Rumichaca, in Carchi. As two retired army officers explained during interviews, there was no paved street at the legal crossing in Esmeraldas, and the crossing in Sucumbíos, at La Punta, was manned on the Colombian side by the FARC, not by Colombian state agents.

52. These requirements were explained by a representative of the Catholic Church who worked on legal issues regarding Colombians' rights in northern Ecuador.

53. These practices were described by army and police officers, as well as by representatives of the Catholic Church who had experience working with northern border communities.

54. The estimate is based on information provided during interviews with a senior Ecuadorian army officer and a U.S. official with experience working on security matters in the northeast.

55. According to Arteaga (2003, 56), as of 2003 there were 438 wells in Sucumbíos and 363 in Orellana.

56. For example, a senior army officer recounted how, in June 2005, a unit from the country's special forces brigade in Latacunga traveled to Coca in anticipation of a planned mobilization in Sucumbíos and Orellana, where indigenous groups and colonists were demanding from companies a highway, electricity, and other com-

pensatory public works projects and payments. In the end, the issue was resolved in a meeting convened at the nineteenth brigade base in Coca. Visiting army personnel from Latacunga moderated and provided security during the meeting.

57. On the size of the fourth division and the commitment of two thousand personnel to oil security, see *El Comercio* (Quito) 12/28/07.

58. The Shushufindi battalion's focus on oil was common knowledge among Ecuadorian army officers, U.S. officials, journalists, and other security experts interviewed for this study. In 2005–6, the other four battalions in Sucumbíos included the unit in Nueva Loja and units in Puerto El Carmen, Santa Cecilia, and Tiputini.

59. This description of the oil security work conducted by the Nueva Loja and Latacunga units was provided by army officers, based on their direct experience in the unit in question.

60. By referring to army "checkpoints" (*retenes*), the senior officer quoted in the text deviated from the more common term used by officers, "military controls" (discussed later in the chapter).

61. The exception to this trend was the officer who, using the glass as a metaphor for the north, referred to the army's security and development responsibilities.

62. Once in position, most units discussed in interviews did perform some civic action, ranging from constructing low-cost housing to cleaning local town squares.

63. One exception to the downward trend in civic action in the late 1990s was the *apoyo al desarrollo* project Compañías de Acción Cívica y Forestación (CACYF), its purpose being to strengthen "allegiance to the nation" near the Peruvian border. That project expanded in the second half of the 1990s (Selmeski 2002, 5).

64. Discussion about the Ecuadorian military's appropriate function following the Cenepa conflict by no means began in 1998. For example, in 1996 and 1997, a debate between civilians and officers over civil-military relations and future roles of the armed forces was covered by the press and culminated in a book (Programa de Estudios Interamericanos, Pontificia Universidad Católica del Ecuador, and Democracy Project, American University 1997; *El Comercio* [Quito] 11/8/98b).

65. In a debate organized by *El Comercio* regarding the new roles of the military, retired army general Paco Moncayo also emphasized police work (as well as sovereignty missions), saying that certain threats could require military attention, including *narcoguerrillas* and *narcodelincuencia* (drug-related crimes) (*El Comercio* [Quito] 11/8/98b).

66. Military advertisements in early 1998 devoted attention not only to the military's police work but also to the armed forces' contributions to economic development. For instance, in May, the joint command published a two-page spread praising the military for its work in national development through disaster relief during the recent El Niño climate disturbance (*El Comercio* [Quito] 5/24/98a, 5/24/98c).

67. Military leaders, including the head of the joint command, Paco Moncayo, also claimed that the police force was unduly politicized in its current place in the government ministry (*El Comercio* [Quito] 2/22/98).

68. As further evidence of the national police's opposition to the military's engaging in policing, the joint command's proposal to the constituent assembly to place the police under the defense ministry's control triggered strong opposition from national police leaders, who argued that internal security work was for the police alone and that the military should focus solely on external defense (*El Comercio* [Quito] 2/16/98, 2/17/98, 2/18/98, 2/22/98). The issue was so charged that in March 1998, approximately five hundred members of the police-run neighborhood watch program (*brigadas barriales*) and police personnel (not in uniform) protested the military's proposal. Brawls exploded between protesters and the military guards outside the assembly, which was held at the army war college (*El Comercio* [Quito] 3/21/98).

69. Before the meetings in late 1998, some provincial military-police collaboration had already taken place. For instance, coordination in Guayas brought the military into internal security there in January 1998, and then again in July of that year, when arrangements for military anticrime efforts were also made through agreements between the army's third division, the police, and the chamber of production in Azuay, for security in that province (*El Comercio* [Quito] 1/14/98, 7/5/98, 7/29/98).

70. An overall augmentation in the army's anticrime efforts in the late 1990s was observed by army officers interviewed who had joined the military before the 1995 Cenepa conflict and in newspaper reports at the time (e.g., *El Comercio* [Quito] 3/12/98, 11/8/98c).

71. For defense matters, Ecuador's mainland has been divided into four military regions, and security in each region is provided by one of the army's four divisions.

72. In other areas of the country, the armed forces were to be involved in rural and urban crime-fighting operations, without the need for police requests—for instance, in the northeast and in the coastal province of Manabí (*El Comercio* [Quito] 11/28/98, 12/16/98).

73. In January 1999, President Mahuad placed Guayas under a state of emergency due to the "crime wave that [was putting] in danger the lives and property of citizens." Mahuad ordered the armed forces to participate in anticrime measures there, in conjunction with the police (Executive Decree 483, arts. 3, 4, 7). The state of emergency was extended through several subsequent emergency decrees (Executive Decrees 679, 852, and 1051).

74. For a discussion of the army's minor role in counterinsurgency against the AVC in the 1980s, see chapter 3. More recently, between 1999 and 2003, the total number of military abuses reported to the national human rights organization Comisión Ecuménica de Derechos Humanos (CEDHU) was 2,172, which was 14 percent of the reported abuses committed by the police (CEDHU 1999–2004).

75. According to both the 1998 and 2008 constitutions and the January 2007 national defense organic law—and as explained in an interview with an Ecuadorian human rights lawyer—the military justice system should be subordinate to the civilian judiciary (1998 constitution, transition order 26; 2008 constitution, art. 160, transitional disposition 8; see also Fundación Democracia, Seguridad y Defensa

2007a). As of early 2009, however, this structure had yet to be created, leaving the military courts to function separately from the regular justice system.

76. An Ecuadorian human rights attorney provided this example during an interview.

77. This perception of exceptional army autonomy in the north was communicated by many interview subjects, including foreign ministry officials, Catholic Church representatives, human rights activists, journalists, academics, U.S. officials, and Ecuadorian army officers themselves.

78. As of the time this research was conducted, the Colombian military's strategy in the south was to attack the FARC in border zones from bases located farther inland; the military did not have established posts or bases along the international border (*El Comercio* [Quito] 9/21/03a; Celi 2004, 269; ICG 2004, 5).

79. Forty of the officers voluntarily broached the subject of relations between Ecuadorian border communities and the FARC. When they explained why they thought communities collaborated with the guerrillas, eleven officers mentioned economic interests; six, community fear; and ten, both factors.

80. This scenario was provided by a U.S. official with experience working in the north.

81. The high command's inaction in no way reflected a practice of condoning poor behavior on the ground or a limited capacity to reprimand officers for performing poorly. Rather, the army leadership has acted swiftly to rotate officers deemed to have fulfilled their duties inadequately. For instance, this type of rotation occurred in late 2005 when a commander stationed in the city of Machala did not effectively control protests, a case mentioned in the first part of this chapter.

82. Officers said that the FARC have initiated these meetings by way of civilian messengers.

83. The conversation was printed in *El Comercio* (Quito) 3/29/09 and in Torres 2009, 27–28.

84. This case was of particular interest in Ecuador when the national press reported on it in 2009, because it involved Reyes, who was killed during the highly publicized Colombian military operation in Ecuador in 2008, analyzed later in the chapter.

85. Correa is not the first Ecuadorian president to be suspected of communicating with the FARC. It was rumored that during their respective terms, Noboa's administration planned such contact, and Gutiérrez met with a FARC leader (*El Comercio* [Quito] 7/17/01, 1/14/05). Independent of the laptop scandal, evidence collected in Ecuador as of early 2009 suggested that high-level officials in Correa's government (but not Correa himself) had ties with drug traffickers and the FARC (*El Comercio* [Quito] 2/22/09b).

86. The March 1, 2008, attack was one of a series of violations of the border by Colombian military forces that had caused tensions between the two governments. For instance, the crossing by Colombian military helicopters of the international border in mid-2005 (discussed above) triggered discussions in Ecuador's government

about implementing a visa requirement for Colombians (*Expreso de Guayaquil* 7/6/05). The adverse effects in Ecuador of aerial fumigation efforts in southern Colombia also have caused ongoing tensions between the Colombian and Ecuadorian governments (e.g., Montúfar 2003, 213–216; *Expreso de Guayaquil* 6/23/05) and led Ecuador's government to file a complaint against the Colombian government with the International Court of Justice at The Hague in 2008 (Observatorio Político 6/08).

87. In addition, the military's 2008 armament and equipment budget was approximately $463 million, up from $167 million in 2007 (*El Comercio* [Quito] 3/1/09a).

88. This and the following two paragraphs are based on articles from *El Comercio* (Quito, 2/8/09, 3/1/09a, 3/1/09b), as well as other referenced sources.

89. In February 2009, the army created a detachment in El Palmar, a town on the Colombia-Ecuador border on the Putumayo River (*El Comercio* [Quito] 2/22/09a). In May 2009, Ecuador's defense minister, Javier Ponce, announced that later that year, four additional detachments would be constructed on the border with Colombia (*El Comercio* [Quito] 5/11/09).

90. Headed by an army general, the joint task force included army, navy, and air force units and was to be responsible for security in the provinces of Carchi, Esmeraldas, Imbabura, Napo, Orellana, Pastaza, and Sucumbíos. According to officers and journalists interviewed in early 2009 who spoke about the new structure, the task force was created to facilitate more efficient border defense and oil security. Army security efforts in the north previously had been under the jurisdiction of three different army divisions.

91. For the army, the breakdown was $21 million for weaponry, $26 million for other equipment, and $31 million for maintenance. Examples of purchases for the north included backpacks, combat jackets, armament, GPS devices, night goggles, munitions, trucks, and helicopters.

92. The trainees were all from the army, with the exception of 198 personnel from the air force and navy. The school also created a new course involving simulated FARC bases.

93. Information on the Hidalgo case in this paragraph was obtained during a 2009 interview with a journalist and from *El Comercio* (Quito) 3/29/09, 3/31/09, 4/29/09.

94. Indeed, according to Hidalgo, the case had been declared null in September 2008.

95. On the four cases, see *El Comercio* (Quito) 7/25/08, 3/1/09a; *Correo* 2/26/09.

96. ICG (2011, 11) mentions more recent evidence of inefficiencies of Ecuadorian military operations in the north.

97. Information about this case was provided in 2009 by an anonymous source who had witnessed the events.

98. Paredes's exceptionally strong interest in pushing the FARC out of the north explains why he, and not a much lower-ranking officer, led the small patrol. Further confirming this commitment, on learning of the FARC's Angostura camp in July 2007, Paredes recommended to the head of the army that the army send patrols to find the exact location of the base.

99. On FARC combatants' attachments to their weapons, see Gutiérrez Sanín 2008, 21–23.

100. In May 2008 the government distributed to the press previously secret transcripts from these two sessions of COSENA in an effort to demonstrate that Correa did not support the FARC, in response to allegations made by Uribe and the U.S. government that Correa had ties to the insurgency (*El Comercio* [Quito] 5/15/08).

101. The bilateral agreement was highly controversial from the start, as Ecuador's government signed it without first obtaining congressional approval—a legal requirement for Ecuador's international treaties (Cox 2005; Rivera Vélez 2005, 244).

102. These concerns were expressed, during interviews, by a senior air force officer, a high-ranking foreign affairs ministry official, and retired and active-duty army officers.

CHAPTER 6. Battalions for Hire

1. This chapter draws on portions of Jaskoski 2012c.

2. The armed forces earned more than half of those resources by charging for services such as air and sea transportation and medical assistance (Palomino Milla 2004, 144–45).

3. For example, a battalion in the department of Arequipa rented out its facilities for religious retreats so that it could pay for on-base repairs.

4. See Comité Especial del Proyecto Camisea, República del Perú 2000, clause 17.4.

5. I am grateful to the individual who gave me access (on April 1, 2009, in Quito) to copies of several contracts.

6. A senior officer estimated that in the departments of Junín and Huancavelica alone, there were thirty or thirty-five such units.

7. The biggest mining and oil installations, however, still had army bases nearby, be they permanent battalion bases or the small, more mobile bases, which, when located in Sendero zones, are counterinsurgency bases (Soberón Garrido 2006).

8. This estimate is based on interviews with army officers and private sector officials and on research conducted by security expert Ricardo Soberón Garrido (2006).

9. An official in the energy and mining ministry said that at least one of TGP's fourteen installations along the pipeline regularly leased one or two army helicopters.

10. In 2009, a U.S. official stationed in Ecuador said that local ties between the military group and the Ecuadorian military had weakened since late 2008. Tense relations between Correa's administration and the U.S. government led the Ecuadorian defense minister to eliminate the military group's Coca position. In early 2009, the military group began requiring specific, written requests from the Ecuadorian military joint command before transferring items to Ecuadorian army units.

11. The information about the Tulcán, Nueva Loja, and Esmeraldas cases was provided by officers who had experience working in, and specific knowledge about the finances of, the unit in question.

12. Army officers who knew about the two projects explained that Texaco financed the construction of the modern, on-base housing. In exchange, Texaco employees were allowed to live in the guest quarters during investigations for an ongoing lawsuit about the company's environmental practices. (On the lawsuit, see Kimerling 2006.) Texaco paid the fourth division $3,000 monthly in rent for the accommodations (*El Comercio* [Quito] 12/19/05a).

13. The private companies included Agip Oil Ecuador B.V., Bellwether International Inc., Petrobell S.A., Ecuador TLC S.A., City Investing, City Oriente Limited, Cía. General de Combustibles, Energy Development Corporation, Kerr McGee Ecuador Energy Corporation, Lumbaqui Oil, Occidental, Petróleos Sudamericanos, Pérez Companc, Repsol YPF, Tecpetrol, and Vintage Oil Ecuador. I obtained a copy of this contract (Ministerio de Defensa Nacional, Ecuador 2001), which is also referred to by *El Comercio* (Quito) (12/19/05a, 12/19/05b) and Beltrán and Oldham (2005).

14. This example was provided in 2009 by a U.S. official stationed in Ecuador.

15. In addition, gasoline distributors provided credit to the Guayaquil military unit to support patrols (*El Comercio* [Quito] 7/5/98).

16. Shrimp theft in Ecuador was an ongoing concern in the Arenillas Military Reserve and in the province of El Oro, more broadly. By October 1998, shrimp companies had lost approximately 350,000 pounds of shrimp for exportation due to theft in that year alone, with a total loss of more than $1 million (*El Comercio* [Quito] 10/25/98).

17. As mentioned in chapter 2, the Ecuadorian army has invested in the shrimp industry.

18. He said that, by maintaining ongoing local contact with Ecuadorian battalion commanders, the U.S. military group could not guarantee that the equipment would lead to increased border patrols, but at least it was able to ensure that materials reached the north.

19. The examples are drawn from an interview with a private security executive who had worked with oil companies and with Ecuador's army.

CHAPTER 7. Comparative Perspectives on Military Mission Performance

1. In their analysis of one dimension of military mission performance—military obedience or shirking in the face of an order to control antigovernment protests during government crises—Pion-Berlin and Trinkunas (2010) also take seriously internal military unity when explaining whether or not militaries repress such protests. The following analysis draws on the authors' descriptions of the Bolivian and Venezuelan cases.

2. This analysis examines military mission performance during one period of Colombia's democracy. The origin of Colombia's modern democracy is generally dated to 1958, when a popularly elected government took office following the 1957 elite Pact of Sitges between Colombia's two traditional political parties, the Liberals and the Conservatives. However, there were significant limitations to democratic

competition until the mid-1980s (Hartlyn 1988), and the quality of Colombian democracy has also been called into question since the 1980s, due to the country's internal violence and the lack of protections granted to citizens (Gutiérrez Sanín and Ramírez Rueda 2004; Bejarano and Pizarro 2005).

3. The U.S. government had begun to increase its counterdrug assistance to Colombia's security forces in the late 1980s, but until 2000 that support was oriented toward the Colombian police, not the armed forces (Ramírez Lemus et al. 2005, 101; Tickner 2007, 326). Until the late 1990s, the Colombian national police received almost 90 percent of U.S. military spending on Colombia. In contrast, between 2000 and 2001, the United States invested $512 million in the Colombian army and only $123 million in the police (Tickner 2007, 327).

4. The commission's data draw on cases brought directly to the organization as well as on data collected by other organizations—including, for example, the Popular Research and Education Center (Centro de Investigación y Educación Popular, CINEP) and the Consulting Agency for Human Rights and Displacement (Consultoría para los Derechos Humanos y el Desplazamiento, CODHES) (Gallón 2007, 403).

5. The Colombian military's ties to the paramilitaries are longstanding. Between 1965 and 1989, the armed forces legally could arm civilian self-defense groups—the antecedents to the paramilitaries—and since 1989, the military-paramilitary relationship has been strong. In 2000, Human Rights Watch reported that one-half of Colombia's eighteen army brigades had "clear and documented links to paramilitary activity" (Chernick 2003, 200). As of 1999, "there [had] been no reports of any paramilitary group that [did] not have the support or at least the tolerance of the armed forces" (Gallón 2007, 363). In 2004, the U.S. state department and the UNOHCHR reported new cases of military-paramilitary cooperation (Ramírez Lemus et al. 2005, 130). Dube and Naidu's (2010) quantitative, subnational analysis of the Colombian conflict from 1989 through 2005 finds that U.S. military funding in that period was associated with greater paramilitary violence—but not guerrilla violence—in municipalities near Colombian military bases, implying that this additional funding went to strengthen the paramilitaries by way of the Colombian armed forces.

6. Gallón (2007, 362–63) argues that negotiations between the Colombian government and paramilitaries caused drops in paramilitary violence as of 2003.

7. There were exceptions to these trends. Between 2002 and 2003, the number of IHL violations by the state dropped by ninety-one, and in the twelve-month period from July 2004 to July 2005 compared with the previous twelve months, state-caused deaths and disappearances were reduced by thirteen (Center for International Policy Colombia Program 2008; Comisión Colombiana de Juristas 2009).

8. According to the legislation, the human rights condition could be waived for vital U.S. national interests (Tickner 2007, 328).

9. The Colombian army has been responsible for the vast majority of reported cases (CINEP 2009, 3, 5).

10. By 2010, the army alone had created twenty-five battalions throughout the country that focus on human rights and IHL training, including applications of

appropriate rules of engagement at the tactical level (Ministerio de Defensa, Colombia 2010, 10).

11. Chapter 4 also discusses IHL instruction in the Peruvian military.

12. The Venezuelan national guard performed policing duties that mainly consisted of providing security in border zones, protecting state property, and leading some major metropolitan police forces (Trinkunas 2005, 160–61).

13. In an August 1990 poll, respondents approved of the military more than of any other national institution (Burggraff and Millett 1995, 60).

14. The second attempt was organized by senior officers who were in contact with the MBR-200 and other military personnel and civilians. Chávez was in prison at the time (Trinkunas 2002, 56–57).

15. The coup took place following a successful general strike in late 2001 and amid mounting criticism of various policies of the Chávez government, particularly with regard to the oil sector (Trinkunas 2005, 217–19).

16. There has been some discord within the military about the appropriateness of antinarcotics as a mission after the transition years. In a 1998 survey of military personnel (during the repressive Operation Dignity, described later), more than one-third of respondents thought that antinarcotics "forced the military to neglect its traditional duties," and 66 percent thought that external defense should be the most important military mission (Ledebur 2005, 156–57).

17. Law 1008, passed in 1988 amid strong U.S. pressure to do so, made coca production illegal outside traditional growing zones (Ledebur 2005, 151).

18. The army's eighth division publicly declared its cooperation, referring to the military's longstanding support for interdiction (*El Deber* 6/2/10). For a discussion of Morales's antinarcotics policy within his broader foreign policy toward the United States, see Madrid 2011, 246–47.

19. On the autonomy movement, see Eaton 2007.

20. In February 2003, in the lead-up to the first gas war, there were major protests against a new income tax. When the La Paz police force joined the mobilization, the president ordered the military to control the protests. In the confrontation, thirty-two people, including police and military personnel, were killed (Quintana 2004, 143–44; Ledebur 2005, 161).

21. For just one of those four cases a decision had been reached: a police official accused of shooting and killing an individual was to serve no jail time for the act (Ledebur 2005, 168–71).

22. The militarization of Venezuelan politics leading up to and following Chávez's victory went beyond appointments, as "increasing numbers of military officers—and especially former coup participants—threw their hats into the electoral ring" (Norden 2003, 101).

23. This project was controversial within the armed forces and contributed to military opposition to Chávez prior to the April 2002 coup (Norden 2003, 108).

24. On the power of Chávez's supporters in the constituent assembly that produced Venezuela's 1999 constitution, see Coppedge 2003, 178–79.

25. The Bolivian armed forces increased their civic action work starting well before Morales took office (Quintana 2001, 57–58).

Appendix. Field Research Methodology

1. Subjects who fell into more than one group were placed in only one category, based on the main type of expertise that I sought from them.

2. In Peru, I conducted follow-up interviews with a journalist and two civilians who had been working as academics during my prior fieldwork but had since moved into positions in the national defense sector. I also interviewed six new subjects: a retired military officer working in the private security sector, two retired senior army officers, an active-duty senior army officer, a journalist, and an anonymous individual with direct knowledge of the army's work in Ayacucho in the late 1990s. In Ecuador, I conducted follow-up interviews with two academics, a journalist, a human rights attorney, and an active-duty senior army officer. I also interviewed for the first time an indigenous rights activist, a retired mid-ranking army officer, and an anonymous informant knowledgeable about details of recent army operations in the north.

3. Such lack of inhibition among retired officers is why Fitch (2001, 68) recommends that scholars interview them.

4. These findings about the openness of the middle ranks in Peru and Ecuador are consistent with those of Huntington (1957, 75–76) and Avant and Lebovic (2000, 40).

5. The sample of Peruvian army officers underrepresents officers who, under the Fujimori government, were most devoted to Fujimori and his intelligence advisor, Vladmiro Montesinos. Following Fujimori's departure from office in late 2000, many officers loyal to Fujimori and Montesinos were removed from the armed forces. The officers linked to Fujimori and Montesinos were most heavily involved in corruption and therefore were distinct from the officers interviewed. (Indeed, whereas both active-duty and retired officers in the sample tended to hold highly positive attitudes about Fujimori's national security policies, several officers complained that his government had politicized the army.)

6. I followed Fitch (1998, 65–70; 2001, 68–71), who also allows for such contradictions.

7. In Peru, I reviewed issues of the journals in the libraries of the ESG, CAEN, and Centro de Estudios Históricos Militares. I reviewed the annual publication of *Desarrollo y defensa nacional* for 1984–2004, with the exception of the unavailable 1985 issue. Two issues were published in 1986, both of which I examined. The only issues of *Revista de la Escuela Superior de Guerra del ejército del Perú* from 1985 through 2006 were published annually in 1991, 1997, 1998, and 1999, all of which I analyzed. I reviewed the thirteen available issues of *Expresión militar* (2000–2005), of the twenty-three published. I reviewed ninety-seven issues of *Actualidad militar*, spanning 1985 through 2004.

8. I reviewed all available fifty-three issues of *Revista de las fuerzas armadas del Ecuador*, published from February 1985 through May 2005, from the collections of the Biblioteca Aurelio Espinosa Politécnica and libraries of the Catholic University, Colegio Militar Eloy Alfaro, Escuela Politécnica del Ejército, and Instituto de Altos Estudios Nacionales. The collections may have been missing one issue from 1993 and issues dated prior to 1992, when issues were not numbered. (For each year from 1985 through 1991, the collection included two or three issues per year, with the exception of 1988, for which I located only one issue.)

9. Given the strong regionalism in Ecuador, it is noteworthy that the archive of the Fundación Democracia, Seguridad y Defensa includes articles from newspapers published in the country's two main cities, coastal Guayaquil and the highland, capital city of Quito.

References

Articles, Books, and Other Published and Unpublished Documents

Acción Ecológica, Acción Creativa, CAS, CDES, CEDHU, CONAIE Entrepueblos, HIVOS, INREDH, OIPAZ, and Plan País Clínica de Derechos Humanos de la PUCE. 2003. *Impactos en Ecuador de las fumigaciones a cultivos ilícitos en Colombia.* Amicus curiae brief in relation to Expediente No. 01-0022. Dec. Quito: Acción Ecológica et al.

Actualidad militar. 2002. "Reestructuración del ejército en marcha." Vol. 182, no. 418. Lima: Ejército del Perú.

Agüero, Felipe. 1995a. "Debilitating Democracy: Political Elites and Military Rebels." In Louis W. Goodman, Johanna Mendelson Forman, Moisés Naím, Joseph S. Tulchin, and Gary Bland, eds., *Lessons of the Venezuelan Experience*, 136–162. Washington, DC: Woodrow Wilson Center Press.

———. 1995b. *Soldiers, Civilians, and Democracy: Post-Franco Spain in Comparative Perspective.* Baltimore: Johns Hopkins University Press.

———. 2005. "Educación militar y democratización." In Felipe Agüero, Lourdes Hurtado, and José Miguel Florez, *Educación militar en democracia: Aproximaciones al proceso educativo militar*, 11–45. Ser. Democracia y Fuerza Armada. Lima: Instituto de Defensa Legal.

Agüero, José Carlos. 2009. "Situación de derechos humanos en la zona del VRAE-Vizcatán." In Coordinadora Nacional de Derechos Humanos, *Informe anual 2008: El difícil camino hacia la ciudadanía*, 51–61. Lima: CNDDHH.

Alegría Varona, Ciro. 2004. "Inteligencia: El 'ni contigo ni sin ti' de la democracia peruana." *Quehacer* 148 (May–June): 12–20. Lima: DESCO.

Alto Comisionado de las Naciones Unidas para los Refugiados (ACNUR). 2006. Statistics. Quito: ACNUR.

Andrade, Pablo. 2002. "Diagnóstico de la frontera Ecuador-Colombia." *Comentario internacional* (Quito) 4 (Semester II): 189–240.

Andrade, Xavier. 1994. "Violencia y vida cotidiana en el Ecuador." In Julio Echeverría and Amparo Menéndez-Carrión, eds., *Violencia en la región andina: El caso de Ecuador*, 131–163. Quito: FLACSO.

Arboleda, María, Raúl Borja, Walter Spurrier, Diego Borja, and Manuel Chiriboga. 1986. *Los placeres del poder: El segundo año del gobierno de León Febres Cordero, 1985–1986.* Quito: Editorial El Conejo.

Arce, Moisés. 2008. "The Repoliticization of Collective Action after Neoliberalism in Peru." *Latin American Politics and Society* 50 (3): 37–62.

Arceneaux, Craig L. 2001. *Bounded Missions: Military Regimes and Democratization in the Southern Cone and Brazil.* University Park: Pennsylvania State University Press.

Arcos, Carlos, Fernando Carrión, and Édison Palomeque. 2003. *Ecuador: Informe de seguridad ciudadana y violencia 1990–1999.* Quito: FLACSO.

Arízaga González, Alfredo, and Bertha García Gallegos. 2006. Ecuador: Análisis del control de transparencia del presupuesto de defensa. Unpublished manuscript. Quito.

Arnson, Cynthia J. 2007. "The Peace Process in Colombia and U.S. Policy." In Christopher Welna and Gustavo Gallón, eds., *Peace, Democracy, and Human Rights in Colombia,* 132–164. Notre Dame, IN: University of Notre Dame Press.

Arteaga, Aída M. 2003. "Indicadores de gestión e impactos de la actividad petrolera en la región amazónica ecuatoriana." In Guillaume Fontaine, ed., *Petróleo y desarrollo sostenible en Ecuador: Las reglas de juego,* 51–77. Sept. Quito: FLACSO and Gerencia de Protección Ambiental, Petroecuador.

Avant, Deborah D. 1993. "The Institutional Sources of Military Doctrine: Hegemons in Peripheral Wars." *International Studies Quarterly* 37 (4): 409–430.

Avant, Deborah, and James Lebovic. 2000. "U.S. Military Attitudes toward Post–Cold War Missions." *Armed Forces and Society* 27 (1): 37–56.

Basombrío, Carlos. 2003. "El Plan Colombia y el Perú: Una primera aproximación a sus efectos en la política, el narcotráfico y la seguridad." In César Montúfar and Teresa Whitfield, eds., *Turbulencia en los Andes y Plan Colombia,* 179–204. Quito: Centro Andino de Estudios Internacionales, Universidad Andina Simón Bolívar Ecuador.

Basombrío Iglesias, Carlos. 2005. *Percepciones, victimización, respuesta de la sociedad y actuación del estado: Evolución de las tendencias de opinión pública en Lima Metropolitana 2001–2005.* Lima: Instituto de Defensa Legal.

Bebbington, Anthony. 2009. "The New Extraction: Rewriting the Political Ecology of the Andes?" *NACLA Report on the Americas,* Sept.–Oct., 12–20.

Bejarano, Ana María, and Eduardo Pizarro. 2005. "From 'Restricted' to 'Besieged': The Changing Nature of the Limits to Democracy in Colombia." In Frances Hagopian and Scott P. Mainwaring, eds., *The Third Wave of Democratization in Latin America: Advances and Setbacks,* 235–260. New York: Cambridge University Press.

Beltrán, Bolívar, and Jim Oldham. 2005. "Oil Multinationals Privatize the Military in Ecuador." *Synthesis/Regeneration.* Vol. 38. Gateway Green Education Foundation. St. Louis, MO: WD Press.

Benton, Allyson. 2008. "Political Institutions, Hydrocarbons Resources, and Economic Policy Divergence in Latin America." Paper presented at the annual meeting of the American Political Science Association, Boston, Aug. 28–31.

Bonilla, Adrián. 1991. "Ecuador: Actor internacional en la guerra de las drogas." In Bruce Bagley, Adrián Bonilla, and Alexei Páez, eds., *La economía política del nar-*

cotráfico: El caso ecuatoriano, 9–45. Quito: FLACSO and North-South Center, University of Miami.

———. 2006. "U.S. Andean Policy, the Colombian Conflict, and Security in Ecuador." In Brian Loveman, ed., *Addicted to Failure: U.S. Security Policy in Latin America and the Andean Region*, 103–129. Lanham, MD: Rowman and Littlefield.

Borja, Raúl. 1987. "La cita del jaguar." In Fernando Aritada, Raúl Borja, José Steinsleger, and Alfredo Pareja Diezcanseco, *El secuestro del poder*, 45–80. Quito: Editorial El Conejo.

Borrero Mansilla, Armando. 2006. "Los militares: Los dolores del crecimiento." In Francisco Leal Buitrago, ed., *En la encrucijada: Colombia en el siglo XXI*, 113–146. Bogotá: Grupo Editorial Norma.

Brechin, Steven R. 1997. *Planting Trees in the Developing World: A Sociology of International Organizations*. Baltimore: Johns Hopkins University Press.

Burggraff, Winfield J., and Richard L. Millett. 1995. "More Than Failed Coups: The Crisis in Venezuelan Civil-Military Relations." In Louis W. Goodman, Johanna Mendelson Forman, Moisés Naím, Joseph S. Tulchin, and Gary Bland, eds., *Lessons of the Venezuelan Experience*, 54–78. Washington, DC: Woodrow Wilson Center Press.

Bury, Jeffrey. 2005. "Mining Mountains: Neoliberalism, Land Tenure, Livelihoods, and the New Peruvian Mining Industry in Cajamarca." *Environment and Planning* 37 (2): 221–239.

Bustamante, Fernando. 1989. "The Armed Forces of Colombia and Ecuador in Comparative Perspective." In Augusto Varas, ed., *Democracy under Siege: New Military Power in Latin America*, 17–34. Westport, CT: Greenwood Press.

———. 1999. "Las FF.AA. ecuatorianas y la coyuntura político-social de fin de siglo." In Rut Diamint, ed., *Control civil y fuerzas armadas en las nuevas democracias latinoamericanas*, 339–362. Buenos Aires: Nuevohacer Grupo Editor Latinoamericano.

Cabieses, Hugo. 2005. "Coca compleja, drogas y cocaleros en los Andes." In Hugo Cabieses, Baldomero Cáceres, Róger Rumrril, and Ricardo Soberón, *Hablan los diablos: Amazonía, coca y narcotráfico en el Perú; escritos urgentes*, 15–103. Quito: Ediciones Abya-Yala.

Cameron, Maxwell A. 2006. "Endogenous Regime Breakdown: The Vladivideo and the Fall of Peru's Fujimori." In Julio Carrión, ed., *The Fujimori Legacy: The Rise of Electoral Authoritarianism in Peru*, 268–293. University Park: Pennsylvania State University Press.

Carrión, Julio F., ed. 2006. *The Fujimori Legacy: The Rise of Electoral Authoritarianism in Peru*. University Park: Pennsylvania State University Press.

Celi, Pablo. 2004. "La vulnerabilidad estructural de la agenda de seguridad ecuatoriana frente al deterioro regional andino." In Marco Cepik and Socorro Ramírez, eds., *Agenda de seguridad andino-brasileña: Primeras aproximaciones*, 243–292. Bogotá: Friedrich-Ebert-Stiftung en Colombia (Fescol).

Centeno, Miguel Angel. 1997. "Blood and Debt: War and Taxation in Nineteenth-Century Latin America." *American Journal of Sociology* 102 (6): 1565–1605.

——. 2002. *Blood and Debt: War and Nation-State in Latin America*. University Park: Pennsylvania State University Press.

Center for International Policy Colombia Program. 2008. "CINEP: Colombia's Conflict Is Far from Over." Apr. 10. Washington, DC: Center for International Policy. www.cipcol.org/?p=580.

Centro de Investigación y Educación Popular (CINEP). 2009. *Primer semestre de 2009: De los "falsos positivos" a la intolerancia social y las amenazas colectivas*. Informe Especial. Bogotá: CINEP. www.cinep.org.co/index.php?option=com_docman&Itemid=117&lang=en.

Centro del Derecho Internacional Humanitario y Derechos Humanos de las Fuerzas Armadas. 2004. *Manual para las fuerzas armadas: El derecho internacional humanitario*. Lima: Comando Conjunto de las Fuerzas Armadas, Ministerio de Defensa.

Chernick, Marc W. 2003. "Colombia: Does Injustice Cause Violence?" In Susan Eva Eckstein and Timothy P. Wickham-Crowley, eds., *What Justice? Whose Justice? Fighting for Fairness in Latin America*, 185–214. Berkeley: University of California Press.

Chiri Márquez, Renzo. 2004. "Fuerzas armadas, inteligencia y control democrático en el Perú." In Rolando Ames Cobián, Alfredo Arízaga, Fernando Bustamante, Renzo Chiri Márquez, Tomás E. Concha Sanz, Nelson Daniels, Francisco Gutiérrez, et al., *El control democrático de la defensa en la región andina: Escenarios para una integración civil-militar*, 113–122. Ser. Democracia 9. Lima: Comisión Andina de Juristas.

Collier, David. 1979. "Overview of the Bureaucratic-Authoritarian Model." In David Collier, ed., *The New Authoritarianism in Latin America*, 19–32. Princeton, NJ: Princeton University Press.

Collier, David, and James Mahoney. 1996. "Insights and Pitfalls: Selection Bias in Qualitative Research." *World Politics* 49 (1): 56–91.

Comando Conjunto de las Fuerzas Armadas del Perú. 2006. Intelligence office statistics. Lima: Comando Conjunto de las Fuerzas Armadas del Perú.

Comisión Colombiana de Juristas. 2009. "Violaciones de derechos humanos y violencia sociopolítica en Colombia—Derecho a la vida: Ejecuciones extrajudiciales, homicidios sociopolíticos y desapariciones forzadas." June 9. www.coljuristas.org/Portals/0/vida_96_08.pdf (accessed 2009).

Comisión de la Verdad y Reconciliación (CVR). 2003. *Informe final*. Lima: CVR.

Comisión Ecuménica de Derechos Humanos (CEDHU). 1991. *A mí también me torturaron*. Quito: Editorial El Conejo.

——. 1999–2004. Banco de datos. CEDHU, Área de Documentación. Quito: CEDHU.

Comité Especial del Proyecto Camisea, República del Perú. 2000. *Contrato de licencia para la explotación de hidrocarburos en el Lote 88*. Nov. 28. Lima: Comisión de Promoción de la Inversión Privada (COPRI). www.minem.gob.pe/minem/archivos/contratogas.pdf.

Conaghan, Catherine M. 1988. *Restructuring Domination: Industrialists and the State in Ecuador*. Pittsburgh, PA: University of Pittsburgh Press.

———. 2005. *Fujimori's Peru: Deception in the Public Sphere*. Pittsburgh, PA: University of Pittsburgh Press.

———. 2011. "Ecuador: Rafael Correa and the Citizens' Revolution." In Steven Levitsky and Kenneth M. Roberts, eds., *The Resurgence of the Latin American Left*, 260–282. Baltimore: Johns Hopkins University Press.

Conaghan, Catherine M., and James M. Malloy. 1994. *Unsettling Statecraft: Democracy and Neoliberalism in the Central Andes*. Pittsburgh, PA: University of Pittsburgh Press.

Consejo Nacional de Seguridad de la República del Ecuador (COSENA). 2003. *El plan nacional de seguridad*. Quito: COSENA.

Coordinadora Nacional de Derechos Humanos (CNDDHH). 2001a. *Informe anual 2000*. Lima: CNDDHH.

———. 2001b. *Informe anual 2001*. Lima: CNDDHH.

———. 2003. *Informe anual 2002*. Lima: CNDDHH.

———. 2004a. *Informe anual 2003: Año de avances y retrocesos en la vigencia de los derechos humanos*. Lima: CNDDHH.

———. 2004b. *Informe anual 2004: Situación de los derechos humanos en el Perú*. Lima: CNDDHH.

———. 2007. *Informe anual 2006*. Lima: CNDDHH.

Coppedge, Michael. 2003. "Venezuela: Popular Sovereignty versus Liberal Democracy." In Jorge I. Domínguez and Micheal Shifter, eds., *Constructing Democratic Governance in Latin America*. 2nd ed., 165–192. Baltimore: Johns Hopkins University Press.

Coronel, José. 1996. "Violencia política y respuestas campesinas en Huanta." In Carlos Iván Degregori, José Coronel, Ponciano del Pino, and Orin Starn, *Las rondas campesinas y la derrota de Sendero Luminoso*, 29–116. Lima: Instituto de Estudios Peruanos.

Costa, Gino, and Carlos Basombrío. 2005. *Liderazgo civil en el Ministerio del Interior: Testimonio de una experiencia de reforma policial y gestión democrática de la seguridad en el Perú*. Lima: Instituto de Estudios Peruanos.

Cotler, Julio. 1978. "A Structural-Historical Approach to the Breakdown of Democratic Institutions: Peru." In Juan J. Linz and Alfred Stepan, eds., *The Breakdown of Democratic Regimes: Latin America*, 178–206. Baltimore: Johns Hopkins University Press.

Cox, Lee Ann. 2005. "El uso del acuerdo ejecutivo en el establecimiento del puesto de avanzada estadounidense en la base de Manta, Ecuador." Master's thesis, Universidad Andina Simón Bolívar Ecuador.

Crandall, Russell. 2002. *Driven by Drugs: U.S. Policy toward Colombia*. Boulder, CO: Lynne Rienner.

Cruz, Consuelo, and Rut Diamint. 1998. "The New Military Autonomy in Latin America." *Journal of Democracy* 9 (4): 115–127.

Defence Systems Ecuador. 2006. Incidentes petróleos 1995–2005. Quito: Defence Systems Ecuador.

Defensoría del Pueblo. 2003. *Restricción de derechos en democracia: Supervisando el estado de emergencia*. Informe Defensorial 76. July. Lima: Defensoría del Pueblo.

———. 2005. *A dos años de la Comisión de la Verdad y Reconciliación*. Ser. Informes Defensoriales, Informe Defensorial 97. Lima: Defensoría del Pueblo.

———. 2007. *Décimo informe anual de la Defensoría del Pueblo: Enero-diciembre 2006*. Lima: Defensoría del Pueblo.

———. 2008a. *A cinco años de los procesos de reparación y justicia en el Perú: Balance y desafíos de una tarea pendiente*. Informe Defensorial 139. Dec. Lima: Defensoría del Pueblo.

———. 2008b. *Undécimo informe anual de la Defensoría del Pueblo: Enero-diciembre 2007*. Lima: Defensoría del Pueblo.

Degregori, Carlos Iván. 1987. "Sendero Luminoso: Los hondos y mortales desencuentros—Lucha armada y utopía autoritaria." In Norberto Ceresole, ed., *Peru: Sendero Luminoso, ejército y democracia*, 163–215. Madrid: Prensa y Ediciones Iberoamericanas, S.A.; Buenos Aires: Instituto Latinoamericano de Cooperación Tecnológica y Relaciones Internacionales.

———. 1996. "Cosechando tempestades: Las rondas campesinas y la derrota de Sendero Luminoso en Ayacucho." In Carlos Iván Degregori, José Coronel, Ponciano del Pino, and Orin Starn, *Las rondas campesinas y la derrota de Sendero Luminoso*, 189–225. Lima: Instituto de Estudios Peruanos.

del Pino, Ponciano. 1996. "Tiempos de guerra y de dioses: Ronderos, evangélicos y senderistas en el valle del río Apurímac." In Carlos Iván Degregori, José Coronel, Ponciano del Pino, and Orin Starn, *Las rondas campesinas y la derrota de Sendero Luminoso*, 117–188. Lima: IEP Ediciones.

Demchak, Chris C. 1991. *Military Organizations, Complex Machines: Modernization in the U.S. Armed Services*. Ithaca, NY: Cornell University Press.

Diamint, Rut. 2003. "The Military." In Jorge I. Domínguez and Michael Shifter, eds., *Constructing Democratic Governance in Latin America*. 2nd ed., 43–73. Baltimore: Johns Hopkins University Press.

Dieterich, Heinz. 2000. *La cuarta vía al poder: El 21 de enero desde una perspectiva latinoamericana*. Quito: Ediciones Abya-Yala.

Donaldson, Lex. 2001. *The Contingency Theory of Organizations*. Thousand Oaks, CA: Sage.

Dreyfus, Pablo G. 1999. "When All the Evils Come Together: Cocaine, Corruption, and Shining Path in Peru's Upper Huallaga Valley, 1980 to 1995." *Journal of Contemporary Criminal Justice* 15 (4): 370–396.

Dube, Oeindrila, and Suresh Naidu. 2010. "Bases, Bullets, and Ballots: The Effect of U.S. Military Aid on Political Conflict in Colombia." Working Paper 197. Jan. Washington, DC: Center for Global Development.

Duque, César. 2005. "Solicitud audiencia sobre situación general derechos humanos en Ecuador." Letter to the Interamerican Commission on Human Rights. Oficio No. 607-CEDHU/05. July 29. Quito.

Durand Guevara, Anahí. 2009. "'Aquí están los cocaleros.' Un acercamiento a las protestas cocaleras en el valle del río Apurímac." In Romeo Grompone and Martín Tanaka, eds., *Entre el crecimiento económico y la insatisfacción social: Las protestas sociales en el Perú actual*, 263–319. Lima: Instituto de Estudios Peruanos.

Eaton, Kent. 2007. "Backlash in Bolivia: Regional Autonomy as a Reaction against Indigenous Mobilization." *Politics and Society* 35 (1): 71–102.

———. 2010. "Subnational Economic Nationalism? The Contradictory Effects of Decentralization in Peru." *Third World Quarterly* 31 (7): 1205–1222.

Echandía, Camilo. 1999. "Expansión territorial de las guerrillas colombianas: Geografía, economía y violencia." In María Victoria Llorente and Malcolm Deas, eds., *Reconocer la guerra para construir la paz*, 99–150. Bogotá: Cerec.

Eckstein, Harry. 1975. "Case Study and Theory in Political Science." In Fred I. Greenstein and Nelson W. Polsby, eds., *Handbook of Political Science*. Vol. 7, 79–137. Reading, MA: Addison-Wesley.

Ellner, Steve. 2008. *Rethinking Venezuelan Politics: Class, Conflict, and the Chávez Phenomenon*. Boulder, CO: Lynne Rienner.

Escuela Militar de Chorrillos. 1981–2003. Course lists for infantry cadets. Lima: Escuela Militar de Chorrillos.

Escuela Superior de Guerra. 2005. "Exposición a la Delegación de la Escuela Nacional de Guerra de la Universidad Nacional de la Defensa de los Estados Unidos de América." Power Point presentation. Nov. Lima: Escuela Superior de Guerra.

Espinosa, Carlos 2003. "La Frontera Norte en perspectiva histórica: Entre la simbiosis transfronteriza, el abandono y la militarización." Unpublished manuscript. Oct. Quito.

Falconí Ramos, Fidel. 1991. "La visión de los militares sobre la respuesta indígena a la crisis." Master's thesis, Facultad Latinoamericana de Ciencias Sociales Ecuador.

Farrell, Theo, and Terry Terriff, eds. 2002. *The Sources of Military Change: Culture, Politics, Technology*. Boulder, CO: Lynne Rienner.

Farthing, Linda, and Benjamin Kohl. 2010. "Social Control: Bolivia's New Approach to Coca Reduction." *Latin American Perspectives* 37 (4): 197–213.

Feaver, Peter D. 1998. "Crisis as Shirking: An Agency Theory Explanation of the Souring of American Civil-Military Relations." *Armed Forces and Society* 24 (3): 407–434.

Fennell, Mary L., and Jeffrey A. Alexander. 1987. "Organizational Boundary Spanning in Institutionalized Environments." *Academy of Management Journal* 30 (3): 456–476.

Ferreyra, Aleida, and Renata Segura. 2000. "Examining the Military in the Local Sphere: Colombia and Mexico." *Latin American Perspectives* 27 (2): 18–35.

Fitch, John Samuel. 1977. *The Military Coup d'Etat as a Political Process: Ecuador, 1948–1966*. Baltimore: Johns Hopkins University Press.

———. 1998. *The Armed Forces and Democracy in Latin America*. Baltimore: Johns Hopkins University Press.

———. 2001. "Military Attitudes toward Democracy in Latin America: How Do We Know If Anything Has Changed?" In David Pion-Berlin, ed., *Civil-Military Relations in Latin America: New Analytical Perspectives*, 59–87. Chapel Hill: University of North Carolina Press.

Fontaine, Guillaume. 2003. *El precio del petróleo: Conflictos socio-ambientales y gobernabilidad en la región amazónica*. Quito: FLACSO-Ecuador.

Fundación Democracia, Seguridad y Defensa. 2007a. *Democracia, seguridad y defensa: Boletín bimestral.* Vol. 3, no. 21. Quito: Pontificia Universidad Católica del Ecuador.

———. 2007b. *Democracia, seguridad y defensa: Boletín bimestral.* Vol. 3, no. 23. Quito: Pontificia Universidad Católica del Ecuador.

Gallón, Gustavo. 2007. "Human Rights: A Path to Democracy and Peace in Colombia." In Christopher Welna and Gustavo Gallón, eds., *Peace, Democracy, and Human Rights in Colombia*, 353–411. Notre Dame, IN: University of Notre Dame Press.

García Calderón, Ernesto. 2001. "High Anxiety in the Andes: Peru's Decade of Living Dangerously." *Journal of Democracy* 12 (2): 46–58.

García Gallegos, Bertha. 1999. "New Perspectives on Using Diplomacy for the Resolution of the Ecuador-Peru Conflict." In Gabriel Marcella and Richard Downes, eds., *Security Cooperation in the Western Hemisphere: Resolving the Ecuador-Peru Conflict*, 195–209. Coral Gables, FL: North-South Center Press, University of Miami.

———. 2000. "La redefinición del rol de los militares." In María Fernando Cañete, ed., *La crisis ecuatoriana: Sus bloqueos económicos, políticos y sociales. Memoria del seminario, realizado el 19 y 20 de enero del 2000*, 159–173. Quito: Ediciones CEDIME.

———. 2003. "Petróleo, estado y proyecto militar." *Ecuador debate* 58 (Apr.): 111–133.

———. 2006. "Seguridad interna: El desarrollo como estrategia de negociación de conflictos." Unpublished manuscript. Quito: Pontificia Universidad Católica del Ecuador.

George, Larry N. 1988–89. "Realism and Internationalism in the Gulf of Venezuela." *Journal of Interamerican Studies and World Affairs* 30 (4): 139–170.

Gerlach, Allen. 2003. *Indians, Oil, and Politics: A Recent History of Ecuador.* Wilmington, DE: Scholarly Resources.

Goldman, Emily O. 1999. "Mission Possible: Organizational Learning in Peacetime." In Peter Trubowitz, Emily O. Goldman, and Edward Rhodes, eds., *The Politics of Strategic Adjustment: Ideas, Institutions, and Interests*, 233–266. New York: Columbia University Press.

González Cueva, Eduardo. 2004. "The Contribution of the Peruvian Truth and Reconciliation Commission to Prosecutions." *Criminal Law Forum* 15 (1–2): 55–66.

Goodman, Louis W. 1996. "Military Roles Past and Present." In Larry Diamond and Marc F. Plattner, eds., *Civil-Military Relations and Democracy*, 30–43. Baltimore: Johns Hopkins University Press.

Gorriti, Gustavo. 1999. *The Shining Path: A History of the Millenarian War in Peru.* Translated by Robin Kirk. Chapel Hill: University of North Carolina Press.

Guasti, Laura. 1983. "The Peruvian Military Government and the International Corporations." In Cynthia McClintock and Abraham F. Lowenthal, eds., *The Peruvian Experiment Reconsidered*, 181–205. Princeton, NJ: Princeton University Press.

Gutiérrez Sanín, Francisco. 2008. "Telling the Difference: Guerrillas and Paramilitaries in the Colombian War." *Politics and Society* 36 (1): 3–34.

Gutiérrez Sanín, Francisco, and Luisa Ramírez Rueda. 2004. "The Tense Relationship between Democracy and Violence in Colombia, 1974–2001." In Jo-Marie Burt and Philip Mauceri, eds., *Politics in the Andes: Identity, Conflict, Reform*, 228–246. Pittsburgh, PA: Pittsburgh University Press.

Hartlyn, Jonathan. 1988. *The Politics of Coalition Rule in Colombia*. Cambridge: Cambridge University Press.

Haugaard, Lisa, Adam Isacson, and Joy Olson. 2005. *Erasing the Lines: Trends in U.S. Military Programs with Latin America*. Dec. Washington, DC: Latin America Working Group Education Fund, Center for International Policy, and Washington Office on Latin America.

Hernández Breña, Wilson. 2003. "El presupuesto del sector defensa en el Perú: Gastos de 'cuartel' y gasto en armamentos." In Gustavo Suárez, Wilson Hernández, and José Robles, *Transparencia y eficiencia en gastos para la defensa*, 31–117. Ser. Democracia y Fuerza Armada. Lima: Instituto de Defensa Legal.

Herz, Monica, and João Pontes Nogueira. 2002. *Ecuador vs. Peru: Peacemaking amid Rivalry*. Boulder, CO: Lynne Rienner.

Hey, Jeanne A. K., and Thomas Klak. 1999. "From Protectionism towards Neoliberalism: Ecuador across Four Administrations (1981–1996)." *Studies in Comparative International Development* 34 (3): 66–97.

Hilbink, Lisa. 2007. *Judges beyond Politics in Democracy and Dictatorship: Lessons from Chile*. New York: Cambridge University Press.

Human Rights Watch. 2009. *Paramilitaries' Heirs: The New Face of Violence in Colombia*. New York: Human Rights Watch.

Hunter, Wendy. 1994. "The Brazilian Military after the Cold War: In Search of a Mission." *Studies in Comparative International Development* 28 (4): 31–49.

———. 1996. *State and Soldier in Latin America: Redefining the Military's Role in Argentina, Brazil, and Chile*. Peaceworks Ser. 10. Washington, DC: United States Institute of Peace.

———. 1997. *Eroding Military Influence in Brazil: Politicians against Soldiers*. Chapel Hill: University of North Carolina Press.

Huntington, Samuel. 1957. *The Soldier and the State: The Theory and Politics of Civil-Military Relations*. New York: Vintage.

Hurtado, Lourdes. 2005. "¿La educación militar como forma de educación superior en democracia?" In Felipe Agüero, Lourdes Hurtado, and José Miguel Florez, *Educación militar en democracia: Aproximaciones al proceso educativo militar*, 47–89. Lima: Instituto de Defensa Legal.

Informe Confidencial. Various years. Surveys. Quito and Guayaquil: Informe Confidencial.

Instituto Nacional de Estadística e Informática (INEI). 2005a. *Perú: Compendio estadístico 2005*. Lima: INEI.

———. 2005b. Statistics. Lima: INEI.

Inter-American Commission on Human Rights. 1999. *Report No. 42/99, Case 11.045 (La Cantuta)*. Mar. 11. Washington, DC: Organization of American States. www.cidh.org/annualrep/98eng/Admissibility/Peru%2011045.htm.

———. 2000. *Second Report on the Situation of Human Rights in Peru*. OEA/Ser.L/V/II.106. June 2. Washington, DC: Organization of American States. www.cidh.org/countryrep/Peru2000en/TOC.htm.

———. 2009. *Annual Report of the Inter-American Commission on Human Rights 2009; Chapter V; Follow-Up Report—Access to Justice and Social Inclusion: The Road Towards Strengthening Democracy in Bolivia*. OEA/Ser/L/V/II.135, Doc. 40. Washington, DC: Organization of American States. http://cidh.org/pdf%20files/CAP%20V%20BOLIVIA.Seguimiento.eng.pdf.

Inter-American Court of Human Rights (IACHR). 2007. "Case of Zambrano Vélez et al. *v.* Ecuador, Judgment of July 4, 2007." San José, Costa Rica: IACHR. www.corteidh.or.cr/docs/casos/articulos/seriec_166_ing.pdf.

International Committee of the Red Cross (ICRC). 2007. *ICRC Annual Report 2006—Colombia*. Geneva: ICRC. www.unhcr.org/refworld/docid/469378cc0.html.

International Crisis Group (ICG). 2004. "Colombia's Borders: The Weak Link in Uribe's Security Policy." ICG Latin America Report 9. Sept. 23. Quito and Brussels: ICG.

———. 2011. "Moving beyond Easy Wins: Colombia's Borders." ICG Latin America Report 40. Oct. 31. Bogotá and Brussels: ICG.

Isaacs, Anita. 1993. *Military Rule and Transition in Ecuador, 1972–92*. Pittsburgh, PA: University of Pittsburgh Press.

Isacson, Adam. 2009. "Enmendando el 'Pacto': El cambio en el equilibrio civil-militar en la Colombia de Álvaro Uribe." In Felipe Agüero and Claudio Fuentes, eds., *Influencias y resistencias: Militares y poder en América Latina*, 169–219. Santiago: FLACSO Chile and Editorial Catalonia.

Isacson, Adam, Joy Olson, and Lisa Haugaard. 2007. "Below the Radar: U.S. Military Programs with Latin America, 1997–2007." Mar. Washington, DC: Center for International Policy, Latin America Working Group Education Fund, Washington Office on Latin America.

Jameson, Kenneth P. 1997. "Crisis in Ecuador: Who's in Charge Here? (Fabian Alarcon's Succession to the Presidency following Abdala Bucaram's Removal from Office)." *Commonweal* 124 (7): 11–12.

Jarrín Roman, Oswaldo R. 2001. Directiva No. 2001-13 para el cumplimiento del Convenio de cooperación de seguridad militar entre el Ministerio de Defensa Nacional y las empresas petroleras que operan en la región amazónica. Quito.

Jaskoski, Maiah. 2012a. "Civilian Control of the Armed Forces in Democratic Latin America: Military Prerogatives, Contestation, and Mission Performance in Peru." *Armed Forces and Society* 38 (1): 70–91.

———. 2012b. "The Ecuadorian Army: Neglecting a Porous Border while Policing the Interior." *Latin American Politics and Society* 54 (1): 127–157.

———. 2012c. "Public Security Forces with Private Funding: Local Army Entrepreneurship in Peru and Ecuador." *Latin American Research Review* 47 (2): 79–99.

Kamps, Jaap, and Laszlo Polos. 1999. "Reducing Uncertainty: A Formal Theory of Organizations in Action." *American Journal of Sociology* 104 (6): 1776–1812.

Kay, Bruce H. 1996. "'Fujipopulism' and the Liberal State in Peru, 1990–1995." *Journal of Interamerican Studies and World Affairs* 38 (4): 55–98.

———. 1999. "Violent Opportunities: The Rise and Fall of 'King Coca' and Shining Path." *Journal of Interamerican Studies and World Affairs* 41 (3): 98–127.

Kimerling, Judith. 1991. *Amazon Crude*. Washington, DC: Natural Resources Defense Council.

———. 2006. "Indigenous Peoples and the Oil Frontier in Amazonia: The Case of Ecuador, ChevronTexaco, and *Aguinda v. Texaco*." *International Law and Politics* 38: 413–664.

Koberg, Christine S. 1988. "Dissimilar Structural and Control Profiles of Educational and Technical Organizations." *Journal of Management Studies* 25 (2): 121–130.

Lawrence, Paul R., and Jay W. Lorsch. 1967. *Organization and Environment: Managing Differentiation and Integration*. Cambridge, MA: Harvard University Press.

Leal Buitrago, Francisco. 1994. *El oficio de la guerra: La seguridad nacional en Colombia*. Bogotá: Tercer Mundo Editores.

Ledebur, Kathryn. 2005. "Bolivia: Clear Consequences." In Coletta A. Youngers and Eileen Rosin, eds., *Drugs and Democracy in Latin America: The Impact of U.S. Policy*, 143–184. Boulder, CO: Lynne Rienner.

Ledebur, Kathryn, and Coletta A. Youngers. 2006. "Bolivia's Coca Policy Walks a Tightrope." *NACLA*. Nov. 13. https://nacla.org/node/1423.

———. 2008. *Balancing Act: Bolivia's Drug Control Advances and Challenges*. May. Washington, DC: Washington Office on Latin America and Andean Information Network. www.idpc.net/sites/default/files/library/AIN_WOLA_BalancingAct.pdf.

Levitsky, Steven. 1999. "Fujimori and Post-Party Politics in Peru." *Journal of Democracy* 10 (3): 78–92.

Levitsky, Steven, and Lucan A. Way. 2002. "Elections without Democracy: The Rise of Competitive Authoritarianism." *Journal of Democracy* 13 (2): 51–65.

Linz, Juan J., and Alfred Stepan. 1996. *Problems of Democratic Transition and Consolidation: Southern Europe, South America, and Post-Communist Europe*. Baltimore: Johns Hopkins University Press.

Loveman, Brian. 1999. *For la Patria: Politics and the Armed Forces in Latin America*. Wilmington, DE: Scholarly Resources.

———. ed. 2006a. *Addicted to Failure: U.S. Security Policy in Latin America and the Andean Region*. Lanham, MD: Rowman and Littlefield.

———. 2006b. "U.S. Security Policies in Latin America and the Andean Region, 1990–2006." In Brian Loveman, ed., *Addicted to Failure: U.S. Security Policy in Latin America and the Andean Region*, 1–52. Lanham, MD: Rowman and Littlefield.

Lowenthal, Abraham F., ed. 1976. *Armies and Politics in Latin America*. New York: Holmes and Meier.

Lucero, José Antonio. 2001. "High Anxiety in the Andes: Crisis and Contention in Ecuador." *Journal of Democracy* 12 (2): 59–73.

Madrid, Raúl. 2011. "Bolivia: Origins and Policies of the Movimiento al Socialismo." In Steven Levitsky and Kenneth M. Roberts, eds., *The Resurgence of the Latin American Left*, 239–259. Baltimore: Johns Hopkins University Press.

Mainwaring, Scott. 2006. "State Deficiencies, Party Competition, and Confidence in Democratic Representation in the Andes." In Scott Mainwaring, Ana María Bejarano, and Eduardo Pizarro Leongómez, eds., *The Crisis of Democratic Representation in the Andes*, 295–345. Stanford, CA: Stanford University Press.

Marcella, Gabriel, ed. 1994. *Warriors in Peacetime: The Military and Democracy in Latin America—New Directions for U.S. Policy*. Portland, OR: Frank Cass.

Marcella, Gabriel, and Richard Downes. 1999. "Introduction." In Gabriel Marcella and Richard Downes, eds., *Security Cooperation in the Western Hemisphere: Resolving the Ecuador-Peru Conflict*, 1–19. Coral Gables, FL: North-South Center Press, University of Miami.

Mares, David R. 1999. "Political-Military Coordination in the Conflict Resolution Process: The Challenge for Ecuador." In Gabriel Marcella and Richard Downes, eds., *Security Cooperation in the Western Hemisphere: Resolving the Ecuador-Peru Conflict*, 173–194. Coral Gables, FL: North-South Center Press, University of Miami.

———. 2001. *Violent Peace: Militarized Interstate Bargaining in Latin America*. New York: Columbia University Press.

Mares, David R., and David Scott Palmer. 2012. *Power, Institutions, and Leadership in War and Peace: Lessons from Peru and Ecuador, 1995–1998*. Austin: University of Texas Press.

Masterson, Daniel M. 1991. *Militarism and Politics in Latin America: Peru from Sánchez Cerro to Sendero Luminoso*. Westport, CT: Greenwood Press.

Mauceri, Philip. 1996. *State under Siege: Development and Policy Making in Peru*. Boulder, CO: Westview Press.

Mayorga, Fernando. 2009. "Bolivia: Militares y política en tiempos de cambio." In Felipe Agüero and Claudio Fuentes, eds., *Influencias y resistencias: Militares y poder en América Latina*, 107–144. Santiago: FLACSO Chile and Editorial Catalonia.

McClintock, Cynthia. 1989. "The Prospects for Democratic Consolidation in a 'Least Likely' Case: Peru." *Comparative Politics* 21 (2): 127–148.

———. 1998. *Revolutionary Movements in Latin America: El Salvador's FMLN and Peru's Shining Path*. Washington, DC: United States Institute of Peace Press.

———. 2003. *The United States and Peru: Cooperation at a Cost*. New York: Routledge.

———. 2005. "The Evolution of Internal War in Peru: The Conjunction of Need, Creed, and Organizational Finance." In Cynthia J. Arnson and I. William Zartman, eds., *Rethinking the Economics of War: The Intersection of Need, Creed, and*

Greed, 52–83. Washington, DC: Woodrow Wilson Center Press; Baltimore: Johns Hopkins University Press.

———. 2006a. "Electoral Authoritarian versus Partially Democratic Regimes: The Case of the Fujimori Government and the 2000 Election." In Julio Carrión, ed., *The Fujimori Legacy: The Rise of Electoral Authoritarianism in Peru*, 242–267. University Park: Pennsylvania State University Press.

———. 2006b. "A 'Left Turn' in Latin America? An Unlikely Comeback in Peru." *Journal of Democracy* 17 (4): 95–109.

McCoy, Jennifer L. 1999. "Chávez and the End of 'Partyarchy' in Venezuela." *Journal of Democracy* 10 (3): 64–77.

Meznar, Martin B., and Douglas Nigh. 1995. "Buffer or Bridge? Environmental and Organizational Determinants of Public Affairs Activities in American Firms." *Academy of Management Journal* 38: 975–996.

Millett, Richard L., and Michael Gold-Biss, eds. 1996. *Beyond Praetorianism: The Latin American Military in Transition*. Miami: North-South Center Press, University of Miami.

Ministerio de Defensa, Colombia. 2010. *Protecting Rights: Actions and Outcomes of the National Security Forces in the Protection of Human Rights, 2002–2010*. Bogotá: Ministerio de Defensa. www.mindefensa.gov.co/irj/portal/Mindefensa?NavigationTarget=navurl://95c66dcdeb913584ob3d360e23426336.

Ministerio de Defensa Nacional, Ecuador. 2001. Convenio de cooperación de seguridad militar entre el Ministerio de Defensa Nacional y las empresas petroleras que operan en el Ecuador. Quito. Quito: Ministerio de Defensa Nacional.

———. 2002. *Política de la defensa nacional del Ecuador*. Quito: Ministerio de Defensa Nacional.

Ministerio de Defensa Nacional, Perú. 1989. *Manual del ejército guerra no convencional contrasubversiva ME 41-7*. Lima: CCAAE.

———. 2005. *Libro blanco de la defensa nacional del Perú*. Lima: Ministerio de Defensa Nacional.

Ministerio de Economía y Finanzas, Ecuador. n.d. Budget statistics. http://mef.gob.ec/40 (accessed 2007).

Ministerio de Economía y Finanzas, Perú. n.d. Budget statistics. http://ofi.mef.gob.pe/transparencia/default.aspx (accessed 2006).

Montúfar, César. 2003. "El Ecuador entre el Plan Colombia y la Iniciativa Andina: Del enfoque de los 'efectos' a una perspectiva de regionalización." In César Montúfar and Teresa Whitfield, eds., *Turbulencia en los Andes y Plan Colombia*, 205–234. Quito: Centro Andino de Estudios Internacionales, Universidad Andina Simón Bolívar Ecuador.

Montúfar, César, and Teresa Whitfield, eds. 2003. *Turbulencia en los Andes y Plan Colombia*. Quito: Centro Andino de Estudios Internacionales, Universidad Andina Simón Bolívar Ecuador.

Moreano, Hernán. 2010. Entre santos y "traquetos": El narcotráfico en la frontera colomboecuatoriana. *Colombia internacional* 71 (Jan.–June): 235–261.

Moser, Caroline O. N., and Cathy McIlwaine. 2004. *Encounters with Violence in Latin America: Urban Poor Perceptions from Colombia and Guatemala.* New York: Routledge.

Narcotics Affairs Section, U.S. Department of State (NAS). 2005. "Project Budgets, 2001–04." Quito: U.S. Department of State.

Norden, Deborah L. 1996a. *Military Rebellion in Post-Authoritarian Argentina: Between Coups and Consolidation.* Lincoln: University of Nebraska Press.

———. 1996b. "Redefining Political-Military Relations in Latin America: Issues of the New Democratic Era." *Armed Forces and Society* 22 (3): 419–440.

———. 1996c. "The Rise of the Lieutenant Colonels: Rebellion in Argentina and Venezuela." *Latin American Perspectives* 23 (3): 74–86.

———. 2003. "Democracy in Uniform: Chávez and the Venezuelan Armed Forces." In Steve Ellner and Daniel Hellinger, eds., *Venezuelan Politics in the Chávez Era: Class, Polarization, and Conflict*, 93–110. Boulder, CO: Lynne Rienner.

North, Liisa L. 2004. "State Building, State Dismantling and Financial Crises in Ecuador." In Jo-Marie Burt and Philip Mauceri, eds., *Politics in the Andes: Identity, Conflict, Reform*, 187–206. Pittsburgh, PA: Pittsburgh University Press.

Obando, Enrique. 1993. "El narcotráfico en el Perú: Una aproximación histórica." *Análisis internacional* (Lima) 2 (Apr.–June): 80–100.

———. 1994. "The Power of Peru's Armed Forces." In Joseph S. Tulchin and Gary Bland, eds., *Peru in Crisis: Dictatorship or Democracy?* 101–124. Boulder, CO: Lynne Rienner.

———. 1998. "Civil-Military Relations in Peru, 1980–1996: How to Control and Coopt the Military (and the Consequences of Doing So)." In Steve J. Stern, ed., *Shining and Other Paths: War and Society in Peru, 1980–1995*, 384–410. Durham, NC: Duke University Press.

———. 2006. "U.S. Policy toward Peru: At Odds for Twenty Years." In Brian Loveman, ed., *Addicted to Failure: U.S. Security Policy in Latin America and the Andean Region*, 169–196. Lanham, MD: Rowman and Littlefield.

Observatorio Internacional por la Paz (OIPAZ). 2001. "Informe preliminar: Testimonios de frontera—Derechos humanos y Plan Colombia." Quito: OIPAZ.

O'Donnell, Guillermo A. 1973. *Modernization and Bureaucratic-Authoritarianism: Studies in South American Politics.* Berkeley, CA: Institute of International Studies, University of California, Berkeley.

———. 1993. "On the State, Democratization and Some Conceptual Problems: A Latin American View." *World Development* 21 (8): 1355–1369.

———. 2001. "Democracy, Law, and Comparative Politics." *Studies in Comparative International Development* 36 (1): 7–36.

Ortiz B., Cecilia. 2006. *Indios, militares e imaginarios de nación en el Ecuador del siglo XX.* Quito: Ediciones Abya-Yala.

Otárola Peñaranda, Alberto. 2004. "El proceso de reforma del Ministerio de Defensa y el rol de las Fuerzas Armadas para la consolidación democrática: El caso peruano." In Rolando Ames Cobián, Alfredo Arízaga, Fernando Bustamante, Renzo

Chiri Márquez, Tomás E. Concha Sanz, Nelson Daniels, Francisco Gutiérrez, et al., *El control democrático de la defensa en la región andina: Escenarios para una integración civil-militar*, 165–180. Ser. Democracia 9. Lima: Comisión Andina de Juristas.

Oviedo, Jorge. 1991. *Nueva historia del Ecuador Vol. II: Época republicana V—El Ecuador en el último período*. Quito: Editor Enrique Ayala Mora.

Palmer, David Scott. 1997. "Peru-Ecuador Border Conflict: Missed Opportunities, Misplaced Nationalism, and Multilateral Peacekeeping." *Journal of Interamerican Studies and World Affairs* 39 (3): 109–148.

Palomino Milla, Fernando. 2004. *Economía de la defensa nacional: Una aproximación al caso peruano*. Ser. Democracia 10. Lima: Comisión Andina de Juristas.

Paris, Roland. 2001. "Human Security: Paradigm Shift or Hot Air?" *International Security* 26 (2): 87–102.

Parsons, Talcott. 1960. *Structure and Process in Modern Societies*. Glencoe, IL: Free Press.

Peceny, Mark, and Michael Durnan. 2006. "The FARC's Best Friend: U.S. Antidrug Policies and the Deepening of Colombia's Civil War in the 1990s." *Latin American Politics and Society* 48 (2): 95–116.

Peñaherrera, Blasco. 1989. "Algo le pasó al presidente." *Nueva sociedad* (Quito) 100 (Mar.–Apr.): 14–33.

Perelli, Carina, and Juan Rial. 1996. "Changing Military World Views: The Armed Forces of South America in the 1990s." In Richard L. Millett and Michael Gold-Biss, eds., *Beyond Praetorianism: The Latin American Military in Transition*, 59–82. Miami: North-South Center Press, University of Miami.

Pérez Enríquez, Diego. 2003. "La construcción del libro blanco de la defensa del Ecuador." Master's thesis, Universidad Andina Simón Bolívar Ecuador.

———. 2004. "Fuerzas Armadas ecuatorianas: 2004." *Ecuador debate* (Quito) 62 (Aug.).

Pérez, Orlando J. 2006. "U.S. Security Policy and U.S.-Venezuelan Relations." In Brian Loveman, ed., *Addicted to Failure: U.S. Security Policy in Latin America and the Andean Region*, 80–102. Lanham, MD: Rowman and Littlefield.

Permanent Mission of Colombia to the United Nations. 2008. Letter to Secretary-General of the UN. No. 553-F. May 28. New York: Permanent Mission of Colombia to the United Nations. www.un.org/en/ga/sixth/63/Addtl_Prot_TEXT/Colombia.pdf.

Perreault, Thomas. 2008. "Natural Gas, Indigenous Mobilization and the Bolivian State: Identities, Conflict and Cohesion." Programme Paper 12. July. United Nations Research Institute for Social Development.

Pion-Berlin, David. 1988. "The National Security Doctrine, Military Threat Perception, and the 'Dirty War' in Argentina." *Comparative Political Studies* 21 (3): 382–407.

———. 1989. *The Ideology of State Terror: Economic Doctrine and Political Repression in Argentina and Peru*. Boulder, CO: Lynne Rienner.

———. 1992. "Military Autonomy and Emerging Democracies in South America." *Comparative Politics* 25 (1): 83–102.

———. 1997. *Through Corridors of Power: Institutions and Civil-Military Relations in Argentina*. University Park: Pennsylvania State University Press.

———. 2005. "Political Management of the Military in Latin America." *Military Review* 85 (1): 19–31.

Pion-Berlin, David, and Craig Arceneaux. 2000. "Decision-Makers or Decision-Takers? Military Missions and Civilian Control in Democratic South America." *Armed Forces and Society* 26 (3): 413–436.

Pion-Berlin, David, and Harold A. Trinkunas. 2007. "Attention Deficits: Why Politicians Ignore Defense Policy in Latin America." *Latin American Research Review* 42 (3): 76–100.

———. 2010. "Civilian Praetorianism and Military Shirking during Constitutional Crises in Latin America." *Comparative Politics* 42 (4): 395–411.

Piscoya, Luis. 2004. "Inteligencia en el Perú: Conceptos organizativos y manejo de crisis." In *Apuntes para una nueva visión de la seguridad nacional*, 355–366. Lima: Instituto de Estudios Políticos y Estratégicos.

Policía Judicial, Ecuador. 2006. Statistics. Quito: Policía Judicial.

Policía Nacional, Perú (PNP). 2006. Statistics. Lima: PNP.

Posen, Barry. 1984. *The Sources of Military Doctrine: France, Britain, and Germany between the World Wars*. Ithaca, NY: Cornell University Press.

———. 2004. "The Sources of Military Doctrine." In Robert J. Art and Kenneth N. Waltz, eds., *The Use of Force: Military Power and International Politics*. 6th ed., 23–43 Lanham, MD: Rowman and Littlefield.

Postero, Nancy Grey. 2007. *Now We Are Citizens: Indigenous Politics in Postmulticultural Bolivia*. Stanford, CA: Stanford University Press.

Programa de Estudios Interamericanos, Pontificia Universidad Católica del Ecuador (PUCE), and Democracy Project, American University. 1997. *Diálogo civil-militar*. Quito: PUCE.

Quintana, Juan Ramón. 2001. "Gobernabilidad democrática y Fuerzas Armadas en Bolivia." In Martín Tanaka, ed., *Las fuerzas armadas en la región andina: ¿No deliberantes o actores políticos?* 31–94. Lima: Comisión Andina de Juristas.

———. 2004. "Bolivia—Militares y policías: Fuego cruzado en democracia." In Raynald Belay, Jorge Bracamonte, Carlos Iván Degregori, and Jean Joinville Vacher, eds., *Memorias en conflicto: Aspectos de la violencia política contemporánea*, 105–156. Lima: Embajada de Francia en el Perú, Instituto de Estudios Peruanos, Instituto Francés de Estudios Andinos, and Red para el Desarrollo de las Ciencias Sociales en el Perú.

Ramírez Lemus, María Clemencia, Kimberly Stanton, and John Walsh. 2005. "Colombia: A Vicious Circle of Drugs and War." In Coletta A. Youngers and Eileen Rosin, eds., *Drugs and Democracy in Latin America: The Impact of U.S. Policy*, 99–142. Boulder, CO: Lynne Rienner.

Red de Seguridad y Defensa de América Latina (RESDAL). 2007. *Atlas comparativo de la defensa en América Latina*. Buenos Aires: RESDAL.

Rengifo Ruiz, Marciano. 2001. Proyecto de ley que modifica plazo de intervención de las Fuerzas Armadas en las zonas no declaradas en estado de emergencia. Proyecto de Ley No. 1022/2001-CR. Oct. 19. Lima: Congreso de la República del Perú.

Rial, Juan. 1996. "Armies and Civil Society in Latin America." In Larry Diamond and Marc F. Plattner, eds., *Civil-Military Relations and Democracy*, 47–65. Baltimore: Johns Hopkins University Press.

Rivera Vélez, Fredy. 2005. "Ecuador: Untangling the Drug War." In Coletta A. Youngers and Eileen Rosin, eds., *Drugs and Democracy in Latin America: The Impact of U.S. Policy*, 231–261. Boulder, CO: Lynne Rienner.

Roberts, Kenneth M. 1998. *Deepening Democracy? The Modern Left and Social Movements in Chile and Peru*. Stanford, CA: Stanford University Press.

———. 2006. "Populism, Political Conflict, and Grass-Roots Organization in Latin America." *Comparative Politics* 38 (2): 127–148.

Robles Montoya, José. 2003. "Metodología de análisis para la asignación de recursos de la defensa: Presupuestos y adquisiciones." In Gustavo Suárez, Wilson Hernández, and José Robles, *Transparencia y eficiencia en gastos para la defensa*, 121–189. Ser. Democracia y Fuerza Armada. Lima: Instituto de Defensa Legal.

———. 2005. "Transparencia y control en la asignación de recursos para la defensa: Discurso y realidad." In Lourdes Hurtado, José Miguel Florez, César San Martín, Rossy Luz Salazar, José Robles, Gustavo Sibilla, Rut Diamint, and Ana María Tamayo, *Los nudos de la defensa: Enredos y desenredos para una política pública en democracia*, 123–152. Ser. Democracia y Fuerza Armada. Lima: Instituto de Defensa Legal.

Rochlin, James F. 2003. *Vanguard Revolutionaries in Latin America: Peru, Colombia, Mexico*. Boulder, CO: Lynne Rienner.

Rojas, Cristina. 2009. "Colombia's Neoliberal Regime of Governance: Securitization by Dispossession." In Laura Macdonald and Arne Ruckert, eds., *Post-Neoliberalism in the Americas*, 231–245. New York: Palgrave Macmillan.

Rojas, Isaías. 2005. "Peru: Drug Control Policy, Human Rights, and Democracy." In Coletta A. Youngers and Eileen Rosin, eds., *Drugs and Democracy in Latin America: The Impact of U.S. Policy*, 185–230. Boulder, CO: Lynne Rienner.

Rosen, Stephen Peter. 1991. *Winning the Next War: Innovation and the Modern Military*. Ithaca, NY: Cornell University Press.

Rospigliosi, Fernando. 1994. "Democracy's Bleak Prospects." In Joseph S. Tulchin and Gary Bland, eds., *Peru in Crisis: Dictatorship or Democracy?* 35–61. Boulder, CO: Lynn Rienner.

———. 2000. *Montesinos y las Fuerzas Armadas: Cómo controló durante una década las instituciones militares*. Lima: Instituto de Estudios Peruanos.

Rousseau, David L. 2005. *Democracy and War: Institutions, Norms, and the Evolution of International Conflict*. Stanford, CA: Stanford University Press.

Rozman, Stephen L. 1970. "The Evolution of the Political Role of the Peruvian Military." *Journal of Interamerican Studies and World Affairs* 12 (4): 539–564.

Sawyer, Suzana. 1997. "The 1992 Indian Mobilization in Lowland Ecuador." *Latin American Perspectives* 24 (3): 65–82.

———. 2004. *Crude Chronicles: Indigenous Politics, Multinational Oil, and Neoliberalism in Ecuador.* Durham, NC: Duke University Press.

Scott, W. Richard. 2003. *Organizations: Rational, Natural, and Open Systems.* 5th ed. Upper Saddle River, NJ: Prentice-Hall.

Secretaria Ejecutiva CONSEP, Observatorio Ecuatoriano de Drogas. 2004. *Estadísticas sobre oferta de drogas: Magnitudes y características de droga aprehendida, cultivada, fabricada y traficada según tipo.* Quito: Consejo Nacional de Control de Sustancias Estupefacientes y Psicotrópicos.

Selmeski, Brian R. 2002. "Democracy, Economic Development and the Ecuadorian Armed Forces: Blurred Lines between Defense, Civic Action and Institutional Enrichment." Paper presented at the Primer Encuentro de LASA sobre Estudios Ecuatorianos, Quito, July 18–20.

———. 2007. "Sons of Indians and Indian Sons: Military Service, Familial Metaphors, and Multicultural Nationalism." In A. Kim Clark and Marc Becker, eds., *Highland Indians and the State in Modern Ecuador*, 155–178. Pittsburgh, PA: University of Pittsburgh Press.

Simmons, Beth A. 1999. "Territorial Disputes and their Resolution: The Case of Ecuador and Peru." Peaceworks Series. No. 27. Washington, DC: United States Institute of Peace.

Simon, Christopher A. 1999. "Public School Administration: Employing Thompson's Structural Contingency Theory to Explain Public School Administrative Expenditures in Washington State." *Administration and Society* 31 (4) 525–541.

Soberón Garrido, Ricardo. 2001. "Corrupción asociada al tráfico ilícito de drogas (TID) y las fuerzas armadas, 1992–1996." Working paper. Lima: Proyecto Transparencia y Reforma en Políticas Fiscal, Social y de Justicia, Unidad de Coordinación de Préstamos Sectoriales.

———. 2005. "Narcotráfico y derechos humanos." In Hugo Cabieses, Baldomero Cáceres, Róger Rumrril, and Ricardo Soberón, *Hablan los diablos: Amazonía, coca y narcotráfico en el Peru—Escritos urgentes*, 185–246. Quito: Ediciones Abya-Yala.

———. 2006. "Listado de bases antisubversivas en el Perú." Inventory. Lima.

Sorenson, Olav. 2003. "Interdependence and Adaptability: Organizational Learning and the Long-Term Effect of Integration." *Management Science* 49 (4): 446–463.

Stanski, Keith. 2007. "'This Land Is Your Land / This Land Is My Land': Territory, Politics, and Irregular War along and across the Colombia-Ecuador Border, 1975–2003." MPhil thesis, University of Oxford.

Stepan, Alfred. 1971. *The Military in Politics: Changing Patterns in Brazil.* Princeton, NJ: Princeton University Press.

———. 1973. "The New Professionalism of Internal Warfare and Military Role Expansion." In Alfred Stepan, ed., *Authoritarian Brazil: Origins, Policies, and Future*, 47–68. New Haven, CT: Yale University Press.

———. 1978 *The State and Society: Peru in Comparative Perspective*. Princeton, NJ: Princeton University Press.

———. 1988. *Rethinking Military Politics: Brazil and the Southern Cone*. Princeton, NJ: Princeton University Press.

Sweig, Julia E., and Michael M. McCarthy. 2005. "Colombia: Staving off Partial Collapse." In Russell Crandall, Guadalupe Paz, and Riordan Roett, eds., *The Andes in Focus: Security, Democracy and Economic Reform*, 11–43. Boulder, CO: Lynne Rienner.

Tapia, Carlos. 1997. *Las fuerzas armadas y Sendero Luminoso: Dos estrategias y un final*. Lima: Instituto de Estudios Peruanos.

Thompson, James D. 1967. *Organizations in Action: Social Science Bases of Administrative Theory*. New York: McGraw-Hill.

Tickner, Arlene B. 2007. "U.S. Foreign Policy in Colombia: Bizarre Side Effects of the 'War on Drugs.'" In Christopher Welna and Gustavo Gallón, eds., *Peace, Democracy, and Human Rights in Colombia*, 309–352. Notre Dame, IN: University of Notre Dame Press.

Torres, Arturo. 2009. *El juego del camaleón: Los secretos de Angostura*. Quito: Eskeletra Editorial.

Trinkunas, Harold. 2002. "The Crisis in Venezuelan Civil-Military Relations: From Punto Fijo to the Fifth Republic." *Latin American Research Review* 37 (1): 41–76.

———. 2005. *Crafting Civilian Control of the Military in Venezuela: A Comparative Perspective*. Chapel Hill: University of North Carolina Press.

———. 2009. "Las Fuerzas Armadas Bolivarianas en los tiempos de Chávez ¿Desde el papel protagónico a la subordinación revolucionaria?" In Felipe Agüero and Claudio Fuentes, eds., *Influencias y resistencias: Militares y poder en América Latina*, 81–106. Santiago: FLACSO Chile and Editorial Catalonia.

United Nations Office on Drugs and Crime. 2007. *2007 World Drug Report*. Vienna: United Nations.

United Nations Office of the High Commissioner for Human Rights (UNOHCHR) Committee against Torture. 2005. *Consideration of Reports Submitted by States Parties under Article 19 of the Convention; Addendum: Peru*. CAT/C/61/Add.2. www.unhchr.ch/tbs/doc.nsf/898586b1dc7b4043c1256a450044f331/9b331d59b6315bc6c125714600518c83/$FILE/G0542145.pdf.

———. 2008. *Consideration of Reports Submitted by States Parties under Article 19 of the Convention; Addendum: Colombia*. CAT/C/COL/4. www2.ohchr.org/english/bodies/cat/docs/AdvanceVersions/CAT-C-COL4.pdf.

U.S. Military Group, Ecuador. 2009. "Info Paper—USG Security Cooperation with Ecuadorian Military." Updated Mar. 31. Quito: U.S. Military Group.

U.S. State Department Bureau of Democracy, Human Rights, and Labor. 2009. *2009 Human Rights Reports: Colombia*. www.state.gov/g/drl/rls/hrrpt/2009/wha/136106 .htm.

Valdivia, Gabriela. 2008. "Governing Relations between People and Things: Citizenship, Territory, and the Political Economy of Petroleum in Ecuador." *Political Geography* 27 (4): 456–477.

Vallejo, Margarita. 1991. "Los roles de las fuerzas armadas ecuatorianas en el post-retorno: Un acercamiento a su análisis." Master's thesis, Facultad Latinoamericana de Ciencias Sociales Ecuador.

Van Cott, Donna Lee. 2005. *From Movements to Parties in Latin America: The Evolution of Ethnic Politics*. New York: Cambridge University Press.

Vargas, Ricardo. 2004. "State, Esprit Mafioso, and Armed Conflict in Colombia." In Jo-Marie Burt and Philip Mauceri, eds., *Politics in the Andes: Identity, Conflict, Reform*, 107–125. Pittsburgh, PA: University of Pittsburgh Press.

Vélez, María Alejandra. 2001. "FARC-ELN: evolución y expansión territorial." *Desarrollo y sociedad* (Bogotá) 47 (Mar.): 151–225.

VI Conferencia de Ministros de Defensa de las Américas. 2004. *Declaración de Quito*. Nov. Quito: Ministros de Defensa de las Américas. www.idepe.org/pdf/VIConferenciaMinistrosDefensa.pdf.

Weeks, Gregory. 2003. *The Military and Politics in Postauthoritarian Chile*. Tuscaloosa: University of Alabama Press.

Wickham-Crowley, Timothy P. 1992. *Guerrillas and Revolution in Latin America: A Comparative Study of Insurgents and Regimes since 1956*. Princeton, NJ: Princeton University Press.

Yashar, Deborah J. 2005. *Contesting Citizenship in Latin America: The Rise of Indigenous Movements and the Postliberal Challenge*. New York: Cambridge University Press.

Youngers, Coletta A., and Eileen Rosin, eds. 2005. *Drugs and Democracy in Latin America: The Impact of U.S. Policy*. Boulder, CO: Lynne Rienner.

Yrigoyen Fajardo, Raquel. 2002. "Hacia un reconocimiento pleno de las rondas campesinas y el pluralismo legal." *Allpanchis* 59–60 (1): 31–81.

Zamosc, Leon. 1994. "Agrarian Protest and the Indian Movement in the Ecuadorian Highlands." *Latin American Research Review* 29 (3): 37–68.

Zisk, Kimberly Marten. 1993. *Engaging the Enemy: Organization Theory and Soviet Military Innovation, 1955–1991*. Princeton, NJ: Princeton University Press.

Newspapers and Magazines

Aguirre, Doris. 2009, May 17. "Fiscal dice que militares ultimaron a cuatro pobladores en el VRAE." *La República* (Lima).

Arauz Ortega, Marco. 1998, Nov. 7. "¿Desmilitarizar las conciencias?" *El Comercio* (Quito).

Arcaya, Eladio, and Elías Navarro. 2005, Dec. 25. "Cientos de efectivos se lanzan a la caza de Sendero en el Ene y el Huallaga." *La República* (Lima).

Ascue Sarmiento, Javier. 2003, Dec. 15. "Junín: El valor de la libertad." *El Comercio* (Lima).

———. 2005, Dec. 24. "Población de Aucayacu celebrará Navidad sin ninguna restricción." *El Comercio* (Lima).

———. 2005, Dec. 25. "Narcoterroristas prepararon emboscada a policías de Aucayacu desde noviembre." *El Comercio* (Lima).

Associated Press. 2000, Oct. 12. "Colombian Rebels Take Helicopter Crew Hostage in Ecuador." *CNN.com.*

Bachelet, Pablo. 2008, Mar. 28. "Uranium Cache in Colombia Poses Rebel Puzzle." *Miami Herald.*

Balbi, Mariella. 2006, Jan. 2. "Entrevista, Fernando Rospigliosi: Confusiones y recetas sobre Sendero." *El Comercio* (Lima).

Bazán Coquis, Adolfo. 2001, Aug. 20. "Entrevista Fernando Rospigliosi: ¿Se dividirá la lucha antisubversiva?" *El Comercio* (Lima).

BBC News. 2000, Nov. 2. "Bid to End Peru Rebellion Peacefully."

Caretas (Lima). 2008, Oct. 23. "La batalla de Vizcatán." No. 2050.

———. 2009, Apr. 16. "El calvario." No. 2074.

———. 2009, Apr. 30. "Los 'mochileros' del VRAE." No. 2076.

———. 2009. May 7. "Las trincheras del VRAE." No. 2077.

———. 2009, June 4. "Plan VRAE revisado." No. 2081.

Castillo, María Elena. 2005, Dec. 6. "Cinco policías mueren en emboscada en Ayacucho." *La República* (Lima).

———. 2005, Dec. 9. "Choque con senderistas en el Ene." *La República* (Lima).

———. 2008, Nov. 20. "Más celeridad al investigar muertes en Ríos Seco." *La República* (Lima).

Castillo, María Elena, Elías Navarro, and Manuel Tóvar. 2005, Dec. 7. "Diez minutos duró el criminal ataque." *La República* (Lima).

Cordero, Jaime. 2004, July 6. "No hay que bajar la guardia: Niegan rumores de cierre de más bases contrasubversivas." *El Comercio* (Lima).

Correo (Machala). 2009, Feb. 26. "Ejército libró dos enfrentamientos con las FARC en Putumayo."

Economist. 2003, Jan. 11. "Military Mutters: Politics in Peru."

El Comercio (Lima). 1992, May 16. "En mitín de oposición San Román insistió en Asamblea Constituyente."

———. 2000, Oct. 20. "Tarea disuasiva: Militares peruanos entrenan en el Putumayo."

———. 2000, Oct. 30a. "Amotinado cuestiona a mandos montesinistas."

———. 2000, Oct. 30b. "Comandante Humala combatió a las huestes de Sendero Luminoso."

———. 2001, Mar. 4. "La paz se abre paso: Terrorista 'Alipio' cayó en la selva de Cusco."

———. 2001, May 15. "Nuevo golpe al contrabando: Decomisan más de 800 galones de combustible ecuatoriano."

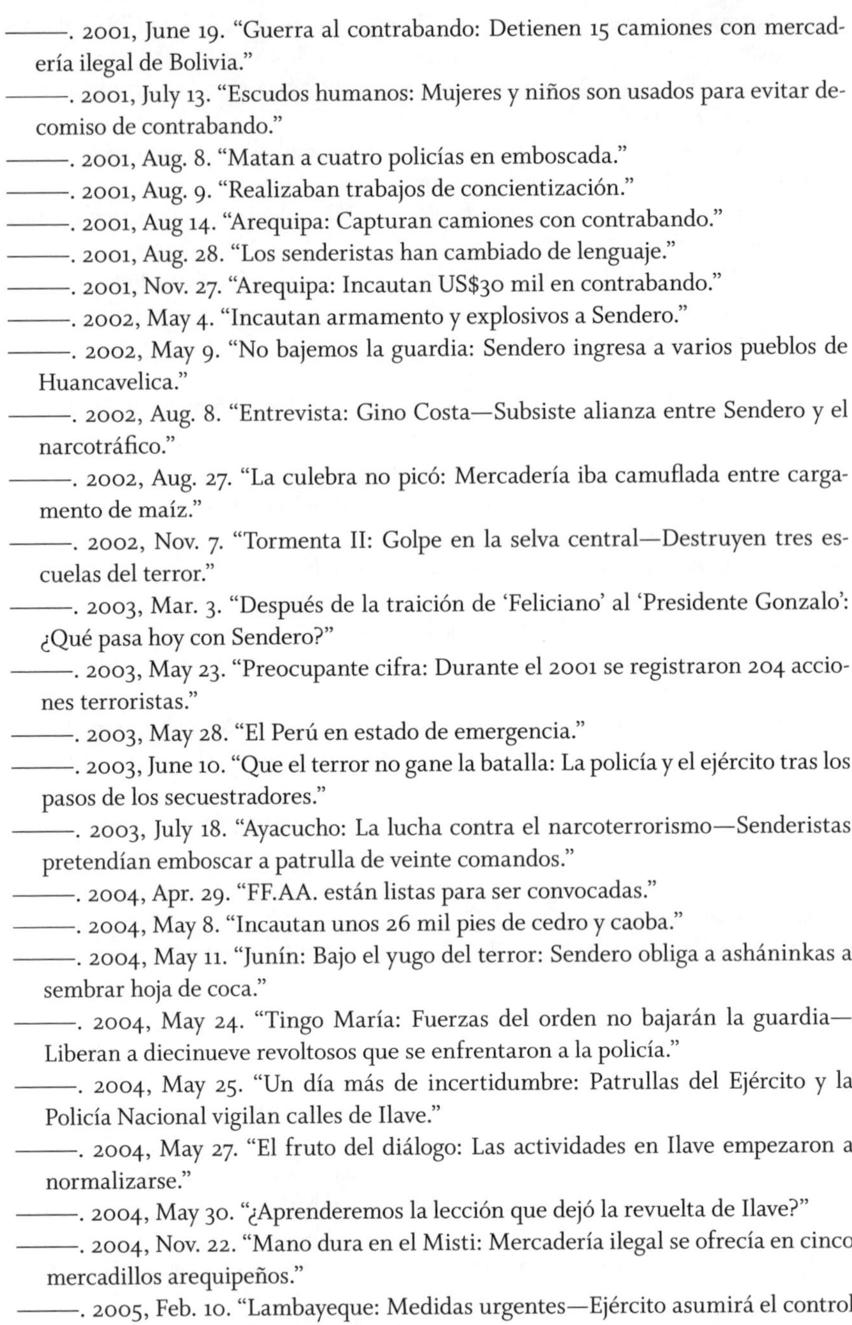

———. 2001, June 19. "Guerra al contrabando: Detienen 15 camiones con mercadería ilegal de Bolivia."
———. 2001, July 13. "Escudos humanos: Mujeres y niños son usados para evitar decomiso de contrabando."
———. 2001, Aug. 8. "Matan a cuatro policías en emboscada."
———. 2001, Aug. 9. "Realizaban trabajos de concientización."
———. 2001, Aug 14. "Arequipa: Capturan camiones con contrabando."
———. 2001, Aug. 28. "Los senderistas han cambiado de lenguaje."
———. 2001, Nov. 27. "Arequipa: Incautan US$30 mil en contrabando."
———. 2002, May 4. "Incautan armamento y explosivos a Sendero."
———. 2002, May 9. "No bajemos la guardia: Sendero ingresa a varios pueblos de Huancavelica."
———. 2002, Aug. 8. "Entrevista: Gino Costa—Subsiste alianza entre Sendero y el narcotráfico."
———. 2002, Aug. 27. "La culebra no picó: Mercadería iba camuflada entre cargamento de maíz."
———. 2002, Nov. 7. "Tormenta II: Golpe en la selva central—Destruyen tres escuelas del terror."
———. 2003, Mar. 3. "Después de la traición de 'Feliciano' al 'Presidente Gonzalo': ¿Qué pasa hoy con Sendero?"
———. 2003, May 23. "Preocupante cifra: Durante el 2001 se registraron 204 acciones terroristas."
———. 2003, May 28. "El Perú en estado de emergencia."
———. 2003, June 10. "Que el terror no gane la batalla: La policía y el ejército tras los pasos de los secuestradores."
———. 2003, July 18. "Ayacucho: La lucha contra el narcoterrorismo—Senderistas pretendían emboscar a patrulla de veinte comandos."
———. 2004, Apr. 29. "FF.AA. están listas para ser convocadas."
———. 2004, May 8. "Incautan unos 26 mil pies de cedro y caoba."
———. 2004, May 11. "Junín: Bajo el yugo del terror: Sendero obliga a asháninkas a sembrar hoja de coca."
———. 2004, May 24. "Tingo María: Fuerzas del orden no bajarán la guardia—Liberan a diecinueve revoltosos que se enfrentaron a la policía."
———. 2004, May 25. "Un día más de incertidumbre: Patrullas del Ejército y la Policía Nacional vigilan calles de Ilave."
———. 2004, May 27. "El fruto del diálogo: Las actividades en Ilave empezaron a normalizarse."
———. 2004, May 30. "¿Aprenderemos la lección que dejó la revuelta de Ilave?"
———. 2004, Nov. 22. "Mano dura en el Misti: Mercadería ilegal se ofrecía en cinco mercadillos arequipeños."
———. 2005, Feb. 10. "Lambayeque: Medidas urgentes—Ejército asumirá el control y vigilancia de Batangrande."

———. 2005, Feb. 23a. "Lambayeque: Medidas extremas—Cien soldados velarán por la intangibilidad de Batangrande."

———. 2005, Feb. 23b. "Peligrosa alianza: 'Artemio' y líderes cocaleros del Huallaga estrechan cooperación."

———. 2005, Aug. 20. "Tacna: Decomisan licores por US$100 mil."

———. 2005, Oct. 23. "Carlos Tapia, ex-integrante de la Comisión de la Verdad: 'Se debería mandar a un equipo de la Dircote para capturar a "Artemio." ' "

———. 2005, Nov. 15a. "Inaudita depredación del santuario histórico de Batangrande: Bosques fueron arrasados con cargador frontal y niveladora."

———. 2005, Nov. 15b. "Preguntas frecuentes sobre Convemar."

———. 2005, Dec. 4a. "Quince encapuchados emboscan a policías."

———. 2005, Dec. 4b. "Sendero aumenta su presencia y ofrece proteger cultivos de coca."

———. 2005, Dec. 11. "El informe del domingo: Vizcatán, zona liberada de Sendero Luminoso."

———. 2005, Dec. 20. "Respaldan gestión para la delimitación marítima."

———. 2005, Dec. 21a. "Dos semanas antes habían atacado Yaviro."

———. 2005, Dec 21b. "Hace menos de quince días otros cinco efectivos fueron asesinados."

———. 2005, Dec. 22. "Dircote detuvo a 'Clay' en 1989 pero fue liberado."

———. 2005, Dec. 23. "Pobladores de Aucayacu realizan multidunaria marcha por la paz."

———. 2005, Dec. 25. "Descuido que costó ocho valiosas vidas: Narcoterroristas prepararon emboscada a policías de Aucayacu desde noviembre."

———. 2005, Dec. 28. "Terroristas amenazan a los que hostigan a los narcotraficantes."

———. 2005, Dec. 29a. "La propuesta del presidente regional de Ayacucho: Valle de los ríos Apurímac y Ene no debe ser militarizado."

———. 2005, Dec. 29b. "Valle de los ríos Apurímac y Ene no debe ser militarizado."

———. 2006, Jan. 5a. "Kuczynski afirma que el Perú no es un narcoestado."

———. 2006, Jan. 5b. "La lucha antisubversiva contará con reasignación inicial de S/.50 millones."

———. 2006, Jan. 5c. "Mobilizan policías y equipos para luchar contra el narcoterrorismo."

———. 2006, Jan. 6. "Consejo de Seguridad y Defensa habría decidido pedir crédito suplementario por 50 millones de soles."

———. 2006, Jan. 18. "Primer jefe del Frente Policial del Huallaga asume su cargo."

———. 2006, Jan. 21. "Dinero fresco y nueva visión en lid contra narcoterrorismo."

———. 2006, Feb. 5. "Decomisan más de 99 galones de combustible al norte del país."

———. 2006, Feb. 20. "Policía abate a jefe militar de Sendero Luminoso."

———. 2006, Oct. 21. "Nativos achuares y empresa Pluspetrol logran acuerdos."

———. 2007, May 10. "Diálogo con los achuares está en espera."
———. 2009, June 6. "Bagua se desangra."
———. 2009, June 7. "Se enseñaron con 9 policías rehenes."
———. 2009, Nov. 17. "Invasores continúan atrincherados en Batán Grande, Lambayeque."
El Comercio (Quito). 1982, Oct. 19. "Protesta fue general ayer en el país."
———. 1982, Oct. 21. "Se declara emergencia nacional."
———. 1982, Oct. 22a. "La huelga paralizó a la capital ayer."
———. 1982, Oct. 22b. "Paralización e incidentes en el país."
———. 1982. Oct. 22c. "Protestas y violencia."
———. 1984, Mar. 13. "Napo analiza respuesta gubernamental y Esmeraldas anuncia adhesión al paro."
———. 1984, Mar. 14. "Fuertes pérdidas en el sector petrolero."
———. 1984, Mar. 15. "F.A. repelerán ataques contra instalaciones petroleras."
———. 1984, Mar. 16. "Buscan rentas para Napo y Esmeraldas."
———. 1984, Mar. 17. "En emergencia Napo y Esmeraldas."
———. 1984, Mar. 23. "Ministros justifican declaración del estado de emergencia nacional."
———. 1984, Mar. 28. "Terminó el estado de emergencia nacional."
———. 1988, May 28. "FF.AA. colaborarán en lucha contra delincuencia."
———. 1988, June 1. "Politización del movimiento gremial obligó a emergencia."
———. 1994, June 23a. "Se normalizó el transporte."
———. 1994, June 23b. "Vuelve la calma al país."
———. 1994, June 24. "Difícil reto para la Iglesia."
———. 1994, June 25. "Se asienta la normalidad."
———. 1994, Oct. 7. "Se reorganizan los operativos."
———. 1997, Feb. 10. "Arteaga: En 6 horas ocupó el solio."
———. 1997, Feb. 13. "Aduanas: La emergencia las paraliza."
———. 1997, Feb. 18. "El pueblo a la calle, los líderes a La Recoleta."
———. 1997, Feb. 19. ". . . Y los políticos se salieron con la suya."
———. 1998, Jan. 14. "La vigilancia militar vuelve a Guayaquil."
———. 1998, Feb. 16. "FF.AA.-Policía: Su fusión al debate en la Asamblea."
———. 1998, Feb. 17. "La Policía no quiere pasar a las FF.AA."
———. 1998, Feb. 18. "La Asamblea debatirá el plan de las FF.AA."
———. 1998, Feb. 22. "Fuerzas Armadas-Policía: Juntos pero no revueltos . . ."
———. 1998, Feb. 27. "Las FF.AA. en una sociedad moderna."
———. 1998, Mar. 12. "Policía-FF.AA.: Poca colaboración."
———. 1998. Mar. 21. "Una gresca alteró a la Asamblea."
———. 1998, Mar. 28. "Las FF.AA. tienen otra propuesta."
———. 1998, May 24a. "Fuerzas Armadas en el desarrollo nacional: Combate hombro a hombro contra el fenómeno de 'El Niño.'"
———. 1998, May 24b. "Fuerzas Armadas: Su papel en el siglo XXI."
———. 1998, May 24c. "Un sistema aduanero eficaz es responsabilidad de todos."

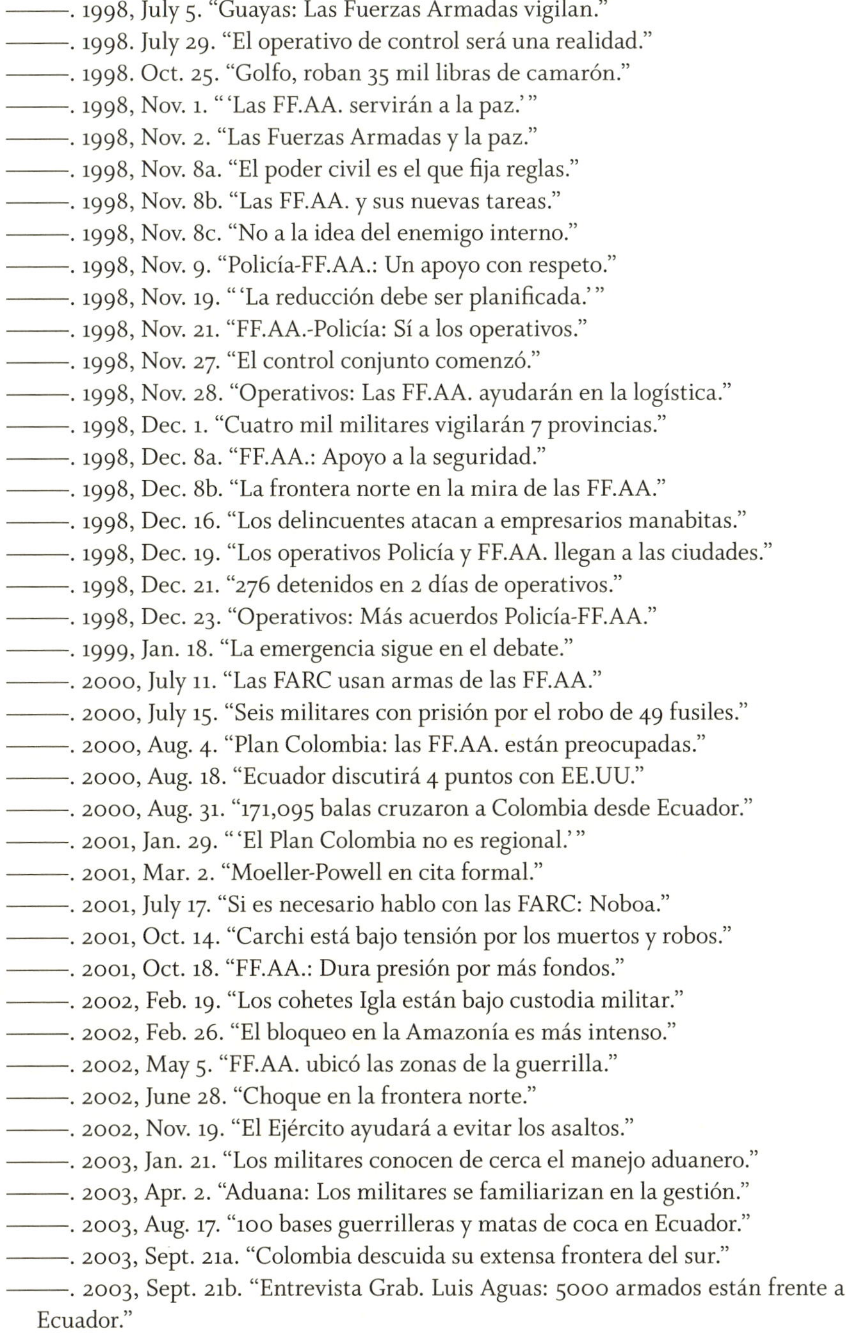

———. 1998, July 5. "Guayas: Las Fuerzas Armadas vigilan."
———. 1998. July 29. "El operativo de control será una realidad."
———. 1998. Oct. 25. "Golfo, roban 35 mil libras de camarón."
———. 1998, Nov. 1. " 'Las FF.AA. servirán a la paz.' "
———. 1998, Nov. 2. "Las Fuerzas Armadas y la paz."
———. 1998, Nov. 8a. "El poder civil es el que fija reglas."
———. 1998, Nov. 8b. "Las FF.AA. y sus nuevas tareas."
———. 1998, Nov. 8c. "No a la idea del enemigo interno."
———. 1998, Nov. 9. "Policía-FF.AA.: Un apoyo con respeto."
———. 1998, Nov. 19. " 'La reducción debe ser planificada.' "
———. 1998, Nov. 21. "FF.AA.-Policía: Sí a los operativos."
———. 1998, Nov. 27. "El control conjunto comenzó."
———. 1998, Nov. 28. "Operativos: Las FF.AA. ayudarán en la logística."
———. 1998, Dec. 1. "Cuatro mil militares vigilarán 7 provincias."
———. 1998, Dec. 8a. "FF.AA.: Apoyo a la seguridad."
———. 1998, Dec. 8b. "La frontera norte en la mira de las FF.AA."
———. 1998, Dec. 16. "Los delincuentes atacan a empresarios manabitas."
———. 1998, Dec. 19. "Los operativos Policía y FF.AA. llegan a las ciudades."
———. 1998, Dec. 21. "276 detenidos en 2 días de operativos."
———. 1998, Dec. 23. "Operativos: Más acuerdos Policía-FF.AA."
———. 1999, Jan. 18. "La emergencia sigue en el debate."
———. 2000, July 11. "Las FARC usan armas de las FF.AA."
———. 2000, July 15. "Seis militares con prisión por el robo de 49 fusiles."
———. 2000, Aug. 4. "Plan Colombia: las FF.AA. están preocupadas."
———. 2000, Aug. 18. "Ecuador discutirá 4 puntos con EE.UU."
———. 2000, Aug. 31. "171,095 balas cruzaron a Colombia desde Ecuador."
———. 2001, Jan. 29. " 'El Plan Colombia no es regional.' "
———. 2001, Mar. 2. "Moeller-Powell en cita formal."
———. 2001, July 17. "Si es necesario hablo con las FARC: Noboa."
———. 2001, Oct. 14. "Carchi está bajo tensión por los muertos y robos."
———. 2001, Oct. 18. "FF.AA.: Dura presión por más fondos."
———. 2002, Feb. 19. "Los cohetes Igla están bajo custodia militar."
———. 2002, Feb. 26. "El bloqueo en la Amazonía es más intenso."
———. 2002, May 5. "FF.AA. ubicó las zonas de la guerrilla."
———. 2002, June 28. "Choque en la frontera norte."
———. 2002, Nov. 19. "El Ejército ayudará a evitar los asaltos."
———. 2003, Jan. 21. "Los militares conocen de cerca el manejo aduanero."
———. 2003, Apr. 2. "Aduana: Los militares se familiarizan en la gestión."
———. 2003, Aug. 17. "100 bases guerrilleras y matas de coca en Ecuador."
———. 2003, Sept. 21a. "Colombia descuida su extensa frontera del sur."
———. 2003, Sept. 21b. "Entrevista Grab. Luis Aguas: 5000 armados están frente a Ecuador."
———. 2003, Oct. 19. "Ecuador no llevó un control eficaz de sus cohetes LAW."

———. 2003, Nov. 29. "El Consejo de Guerra dará su sentencia por el robo de armas."
———. 2004, Sept. 7. "Un grupo armado amenazó a tres poblaciones de la frontera."
———. 2004, Sept. 8. "Los grupos armados se filtran en Sucumbíos."
———. 2004, Nov. 13. "Puerto Mestanza teme la llegada de paramilitares."
———. 2004, Nov. 17. "'EE.UU. considera a Ecuador un amigo y aliado.'"
———. 2004, Nov. 22. "La cita de Defensa arrojó 46 acuerdos."
———. 2004, Dec. 3. "La cultura del silencio y el terror impera en la frontera: Iglesia."
———. 2005, Jan. 14. "'El Gobierno de Ecuador me invitó.'"
———. 2005, Jan. 27. "Los recursos para afrontar la emergencia aún no se definen."
———. 2005, Mar. 18. "Las infiltraciones de las FARC agitan a la frontera norte."
———. 2005, Apr. 21. "Herrera le dio el primer aviso a Lucio Gutiérrez."
———. 2005, Apr. 22. "El 'abandono del cargo' es un tema en discusión."
———. 2005, May 8. "La coca se cosecha y transporta en mayo."
———. 2005, May 17a. "La guerrilla profundiza sus redes en el Ecuador."
———. 2005, May 17b. "Las clínicas no reportan heridos de bala."
———. 2005, May 19. "Una columna de las FARC incursionó en Carchi."
———. 2005, June 25. "La Corporación Aduanera Ecuatoriana tiene una gerente temporal."
———. 2005, June 30. "Colombia plantea una fuerza conjunta."
———. 2005, July 25. "En General Farfán reina el miedo tras la incursión de 'los paras.'"
———. 2005, July 26. "La frontera teme un rebrote de violencia por la vuelta de los paras."
———. 2005, July 28. "El Jefe de las FF.AA. sobrevoló ayer la frontera."
———. 2005, Aug. 1. "La cercanía de la guerrilla alarma a Tufiño."
———. 2005, Aug. 15. "La gente enfermó y sus cultivos se perdieron por las fumigaciones."
———. 2005, Nov. 16. "EE.UU. insiste en la cooperación regional contra el terrorismo."
———. 2005, Dec. 19a. "2000 militares vigilarán el sistema petrolero."
———. 2005, Dec. 19b. "Siete meses más para el convenio del 2001."
———. 2007, Dec. 28. "Las FF.AA. ofrecen tres tipos de seguridad a las petroleras."
———. 2008, Mar. 6. "117 bases guerrilleras destruidas en el país."
———. 2008, Mar. 16. "Ecuador es un corredor de las FARC."
———. 2008, May 15. "Correa pidió que se controle el ingreso de subversivos: Cosena."
———. 2008, July 25. "Nuevas escaramuzas del Ejército con las FARC en la frontera."
———. 2009, Feb. 8. "El Ejército se potenció luego de Angostura."
———. 2009, Feb. 22a. "El Ejército puso una base en El Palmar."
———. 2009, Feb. 22b. "La Fiscalía indaga el nexo narcos-FARC."
———. 2009, Mar. 1a. "Los GIAC, la nueva amenaza a las FF.AA."
———. 2009, Mar. 1b. "Ninguna tolerancia habrá para los grupos armados."

———. 2009, Mar. 15. "Frontera: Guerrillera muere en combate."

———. 2009, Mar. 29. "El cuaderno secreto de Reyes."

———. 2009, Mar. 31. "2 oficiales de las FF.AA., indagados."

———. 2009, Apr. 16. "'50 miembros de la Policía y del Ejército han sido comprados por las FARC.'"

———. 2009, Apr. 29. "Fiscalización recibió a Hidalgo y a Silva."

———. 2009, May 11. "Colombia: Nuevos campamentos ecuatorianos impedirán santuarios de las FARC en frontera."

———. 2011, Jan. 19. "Crudo: Alto precio y baja producción."

El Deber (Santa Cruz). 2010, June 1. "Evo pide a FFAA entrar a la lucha antidrogas."

———. 2010, June 2. "Las FFAA apoyan lucha contra el narcotráfico, dicen en la Octava."

El Universo (Guayaquil). 2003, Feb. 9. "Mañana inicia plan combinado."

———. 2004, July 1. "La Policía y las Fuerzas Armadas realizaron ayer operativos a pie."

Expreso de Guayaquil. 2005, June 23. "Dos informes rechazan al glifosato."

———. 2005, July 6. "'Hay que poner un control, sea o no visa.'"

———. 2005, Aug. 10. "Las FF.AA. solicitan recursos."

Faiola, Anthony. 2000, Oct. 1. "Colombia's Creeping War: Neighbors Now Fear Spill-over of Violence." *Washington Post*.

Farnam, Arie. 2002, July 11. "Colombia's Civil War Drifts South into Ecuador." *Christian Science Monitor*.

Ford, Dana. 2009, May 18. "Peru Oil Pipeline Halted on Protests in Amazon." Reuters UK. http://uk.reuters.com/article/2009/05/18/uk-peru-energy-protests-idUKTRE54H6EN20090518?sp=true.

García Panta, Luis. 2003, May 17. "Aniversario del terror: Policía con orden de inamovilidad." *El Comercio* (Lima).

Gutiérrez R., Miguel, and Elízabeth Prado. 2009, Apr. 12. "Militares fueron dinamitados cuando realizaban patrullaje." *La República* (Lima).

Hidalgo Vega, David. 2005, Dec. 28. "Un diagnóstico del miedo." *El Comercio* (Lima).

Hoy (Quito). 2000, Aug 18. "Mayoría teme Plan Colombia."

———. 2000, Sept. 1. "Cuando lo militar opaca los temas de comercio."

———. 2000, Oct. 27. "Ecuador, con apoyo de EEUU."

———. 2001, Feb. 9. "Nativos amazónicos huyen por amenazas de grupos armados."

———. 2001, Aug. 31. "Guerrilla colombiana se camufla en Ecuador."

———. 2002, July 23. "'Ecuador no será parte de Ejército Andino.'"

———. 2003, Apr. 8. "Gutiérrez oficializa decreto para intervención de FFAA."

———. 2005, June 28. "Las FARC se aprovechan de la vecindad del Ecuador."

———. 2008, Mar. 2. "Llamada satelital, clave para dar con 'Raúl Reyes.'"

———. 2008, Mar. 16. "Correa reta a Bush a controlar frontera."

———. 2008, May 17. "'No sabíamos del campamento': Ponce."

La Hora (Quito). 2004, Jan. 29. "Plan Ecuador en la Frontera: Ejército será radical para mantener seguridad."

———. 2004, May 11. "Sucumbíos reclama a FFAA coordinación en planes."
———. 2005, Feb. 22. "Operativos: Militares y policías unen esfuerzos."
La República (Lima). 1983, Mar. 11a. "Más de 700 detenidos hay en Lima: Violencia durante el paro deja 4 muertos y 100 heridos."
———. 1983, Mar. 11b. "Mayoría acató paro en provincias."
———. 1984, Nov. 29. "Decretan emergencia y suspenden las garantías por paro nacional de hoy."
———. 1984, Nov. 30a. "500 detenidos por paro que afectó todo el país."
———. 1984, Nov. 30b. "Bloqueo absoluto de vía al centro."
———. 1984, Nov. 30c. "En Arequipa y Puno el paro fue total."
———. 1984, Nov. 30d. "Todos se unieron a la protesta."
———. 1984, Dec. 1a. "Gobierno levanta el estado de emergencia."
———. 1984, Dec. 1b. "La violencia nos envuelve a todos."
———. 1987, May 16. "Tropas patrullan la ciudad y controlan orden público."
———. 1987, May 17. "Más policías se pliegan a la huelga."
———. 1987, May 20. "Paro fue contundente en Cusco, Puno, Moquegua, Huancayo, e Ica."
———. 1987, May 21. "Se acabó la tensión y Lima volvió ayer a la normalidad."
———. 1988, July 19. "Trabajadores paran hoy en todo el país contra grave crisis económica."
———. 1988, July 20a. "Fue un día pacífico, sin acciones de violencia en Carretera Central."
———. 1988, July 20b. "Gobierno sostiene que el 69.4 por ciento acudió a su trabajo."
———. 1988, July 20c. "Mayoría de trabajadores acataron paro nacional."
———. 1988, July 20d. "Paro fue acatado masivamente en Arequipa, Cusco, Puno, Ayacucho . . ."
———. 1989, Aug. 13. "Detienen a 14 dirigentes mineros."
———. 1989, Aug. 17. "Casa por casa buscan a dirigentes mineros para hacer fracasar huelga."
———. 1989, Aug. 19a. "Denuncian secuestro de dirigentes mineros."
———. 1989, Aug. 19b. "Trabajadores irán a paro nacional si gobierno no soluciona huelgas."
———. 1989, Aug. 20. "Mineros harán marchas de sacrificio."
———. 2000, Nov. 6. "Antauro cuenta con más de 400 reservistas."
———. 2003, May 30. "Represión a estudiantes deja un muerto y 50 heridos en Puno."
———. 2004, Apr. 14. "Purgan a personal de la Dirección de Contrainteligencia del CNI."
———. 2005, June 3. "Fiscalizarán nueva central de inteligencia nacional."
———. 2005, Oct. 18. "Fallece coronel del Ejército."
———. 2005, Oct. 19. "Terroristas no mataron a coronel del Ejército."
———. 2005, Dec. 3. "Protestas por contaminación tras rotura de ducto de gas de Camisea."

———. 2005, Dec. 7a. "Diez minutos duró el criminal ataque."

———. 2005, Dec. 7b. "Ronderos advirtieron de la presencia de SL."

———. 2005, Dec. 15a. "Crean sistema de inteligencia."

———. 2005, Dec. 15b. "Ronderos culpan a SL de ataque a convoy policial."

———. 2005, Dec. 19. "Terroristas atacan patrulla EP en Satipo."

———. 2005, Dec. 20a. "Mandos militares critican juicios por DDHH."

———. 2005, Dec. 20b. "Nativa asháninka muere en ataque terrorista a base militar en Junín."

———. 2005, Dec. 21. "Senderistas asesinan a ocho policías en selva de Aucayacu."

———. 2005, Dec. 26. "PPK infla cifras de terroristas que han salido de las cárceles."

———. 2005, Dec. 28. "Continúan operativos en el Huallaga."

———. 2005, Dec 31a. "Alan García plantea: Frente común contra el terrorismo."

———. 2005, Dec. 31b. "Iberico insiste en impunidad para militares."

———. 2005, Dec. 31c. "Lourdes Flores promete indultar a militares condenados injustamente."

———. 2006, Jan. 5a. "PPK informó sobre el plan de desarrollo para el Huallaga."

———. 2006, Jan. 5b. "Unidad antisubversiva de la PNP instalarán en Yungay."

———. 2006, Jan. 19. "Crean Batallón Antiterrorista PNP."

———. 2006, Feb. 10. "La captura de 'Clay.' "

———. 2006, Oct. 11. "700 nativos toman el Lote 1AB de Pluspetrol."

———. 2008, Feb. 20. "Cuatro agricultures muertos en desbloqueo de carreteras."

———. 2008, July 10. "PNP detuvo a 216 durante paro de la CGTP."

———. 2008, Oct. 29. "Regulan la defensa legal de policías y militares."

———. 2008, Dec. 29. "Mesa Angosto judicializó casos de DDHH."

———. 2009, Jan. 13. "Ejército peruano prepara la ofensiva final en el Vizcatán."

———. 2009, June 7. "PNP y Ejército controlan Bagua."

la Rosa, Rocio. 2003, Aug. 6. "Cambio de estrategia: Comités de autodefensa fueron reactivados en Ayacucho." *El Comercio* (Lima).

Latin American Herald Tribune. 2009, Jan. 6. "Ecuador Military to Shed Stakes."

Latin America Weekly Report. 1992, Nov. 26. "The Coup Attempt That Wasn't Quite What Fujimori Made It Out to Be."

Los Angeles Times. 2010, Nov. 18. "Bolivia's Army Declares Itself 'Socialist.' La Plaza: News from Latin America and the Caribbean."

Lucas, Kintto. 2002, Mar. 1. "Politics—Ecuador: Protests and Repression Heat up the Northeast." *IPS-Inter Press Service*. Lexis Nexis Academic.

Mayo Filio. 2005, Feb. 6. "Grupo armado se oculta en la enmarañada selva: Sujeto conocido como 'José' sería nuevo líder de Sendero Luminoso." *El Comercio* (Lima).

———. 2005, May 10. "Junín: Cuenta regresiva—Patrullas de Satipo arrinconan a los senderistas en Vizcatán." *El Comercio* (Lima).

McDermott, Jeremy. 2009, May 7. "Toxic Fallout of Colombian Scandal." *BBC News*.

Meza, Robert. 2001, Sept. "Comienza a hacerse justicia en el caso Barrios Altos." *IDEELE*, no. 140. Lima: Instituto de Defensa Legal.

Navarro, Elías, and Eladio Arcaya. 2005, Dec. 24. "Otro enfrentamiento de la PNP con senderistas en Vizcatán." *La República* (Lima).

Neira, Mariana. 1994, Jan. 6. "La narcoguerrilla: El enemigo oculto." *Vistazo* (Quito), no. 633.

New York Times. 1992. Nov. 14. "Peru Says Loyal Forces Crushed Coup Attempt by Army Dissidents."

———. 2000, Nov. 26. "New Cabinet Installed in Peru: It Quickly Ousts Top Generals."

———. 2003, Sept. 28. "A Swirl of Foreboding in Mahogany's Grain."

———. 2005, Jan. 3. "After Standoff, Peru Rebels Offer to Give up Weapons."

Observatorio Político Defensa, Seguridad y Relaciones Civil-Militares. 2007–8, various months. "Resumen de noticias." Quito: Programa para la Administración Democrática de la Defensa, of the Proyecto Relaciones Civil-Militares PUCE/Democracia Seguridad y Defensa, and Fundación Conrad Adenauer Stiftung.

Páez, Ángel. 2005, Mar. 27. "Fujimori y su cúpula militar tramaron atacar a Ecuador." *La República* (Lima).

———. 2005, Nov. 14. "Peru-Chile: Armamentismo sin pausa." *La Insignia*. www.lainsignia.org/2005/noviembre/ibe_056.htm.

———. 2005, Dec. 5. "EEUU autorizó a Holanda vender a Chile 18 cazabombarderos F-16." *La República* (Lima).

———. 2006, Jan. 2. "Fondo de Defensa no cubrió las necesidades de Fuerzas Armadas." *La República* (Lima).

———. 2006, Feb. 21. "Marciano te llaman." *La República* (Lima).

Peruinforma.com. 2005, Oct. 12. "Campesinos piden intervenir en fideicomiso Las Bambas." www.peruinforma.com/imwebsite/article.php?sid=28767 (accessed 2006).

Potestá, Orazio. 2004, Oct. 2. "Para ser 'niños pioneros': Sendero Luminoso planeó secuestro de 50 escolares en Ayacucho." *El Comercio* (Lima).

Ramírez, Miguel. 2001, Sept. 2. "Cuidado con la selva central: Hijos salvan vida a gobernador." *El Comercio* (Lima).

Reuters. 2010, Aug. 6. "Bolivian Army Starts Training Militias." http://af.reuters.com/article/energyOilNews/idAFN0616063820100806?pageNumber=2&virtualBrandChannel=0&sp=true.

Rivadeneira, Miguel. 1998, Nov. 9. "El papel de las Fuerzas Armadas." *El Comercio* (Quito).

Robles, Frances. 2008, Mar. 4. "Colombia Wants Charges against Chavez." *Miami Herald*.

Robles Montoya, José. 2004, Mar. 19. "CNI: SIN inteligencia." *Ideele-mail*, no. 350. Lima: Instituto de Defensa Legal.

Rohter, Larry. 2003, Oct. 14. "Bolivian President Remains Defiant as Protests Intensify." *New York Times*.

Romero, Simon. 2009, Mar. 18. "Cocaine Trade Helps Rebels Reignite War in Peru." *New York Times*.

Salazar, Milagros. 2005, Dec. 8. "Sendero atacó a policías, lo tenía todo planificado." *La República* (Lima).
Servindi. 2005, Oct. 17. "Toman aeropuerto de Atalaya y anuncian ocupación de campamento de Camisea." Human Rights Watch. http://amazonwatch.org/news/2005/1017-toman-aeropuerto-de-atalaya-y.
Tamayo, Juan O. 2000, Nov. 18. "Ecuador Feels Fallout from Colombia's Narcotics War." *Miami Herold.*
Tobar, Hector. 2004, May 20. "A Mob's Lynching of Mayor Roils Peru." *Los Angeles Times.*
24 horas libre. 2009, Mar. 6. "Denuncias contra militares entorpecen acciones en el VRAE, advierte Flores-Aráoz." 24horaslibre.com.

Index

Alarcón, Fabián, 33, 34
Alfaro Vive ¡Caro! (AVC), 31, 47, 223n21
Amazonas, Peru, 38, 111, 112
Ancash, Peru, 40
Andoas, Peru, 174–175, 181
Angostura, Ecuador, 133, 158
Arequipa, Peru, 77, 110, 228n32
Argentina, 11, 13, 215–216n8
Arteaga, Rosalía, 34
Asháninka, 75, 227n23
Autodefensas Unidas de Colombia (AUC). *See* Colombian paramilitaries
Ayacucho, Peru, 39, 40–41, 42, 74, 79–80, 221n7

Bagua, Peru, 112
Banzer Suárez, Hugo, 198, 200
Barrios Altos, Lima, Peru, 84, 230n54
Basombrío, Carlos, 65, 76
Belaúnde Terry, Fernando, 24, 25, 40–41, 42
Bolivian military: antinarcotics efforts of, 199–200, 201, 202, 246nn16–18; civic-action projects of, 205, 247n25; crime fighting by, 200, 202; internal divisions within, 206; police rivalry with, 202, 205, 246n20; presidential control of, 202–203, 204–205; protest control by, 200–201
Brazil, 10, 11, 216n12
Bucaram, Abdalá, 33–34, 35

Camisea, 30, 60, 63–64, 169, 172–174, 181
Caracazo (1989), 9, 196
Carbajal, Julio, 44–45
Carchi, Ecuador, 120, 136–137; insurgent presence in, 117, 119, 121, 124, 134, 156–157; landowners in, 122, 176, 179, 238n45
Cenepa War (1995), 4, 19, 32, 38, 130, 221n2
Centro de Altos Estudios Nacionales (CAEN, Peru), 29, 219n17
Chapare, Bolivia, 199–200
Chávez Frías, Hugo, 198, 203, 204
Chavín de Huántar operation and trial, 44, 91, 231–232n68
Chiabra, Roberto, 68, 69, 97
Chile, 82, 201
civil-military relations, 11; in Bolivia, 204–205; in Ecuador, 17, 30–36; in Peru, 17, 24–30, 68–69, 97–99, 217n2; in Venezuela, 197, 203
client influence, 17–18, 181–183; in Ecuador, 165, 166, 168, 175–181; limits to, 17, 165, 181–183; in Peru, 18, 165, 168, 170–175, 243n9
Cobo, Fausto, 32
coca growers, 4, 119, 222n16, 234nn7–8, 235n17; protests by, 62, 64, 78–79
Cochabamba, Bolivia, 200–201
Colina Group, 84, 230n54
Colombia, 244–245n2; coca harvest in, 119, 234nn7–8; Ecuadorian government and, 127, 158, 241–242n86; and human rights, 189–190; insurgency in, 1–2, 54, 116–119, 153, 186; and Peru, 82; police of, 187, 245n3; and Venezuela, 195, 204
Colombian military: antinarcotics efforts of, 186, 188; budget, 187; counterinsurgency mission prioritized by, 185, 186–188; counterinsurgency strategy of, 188, 241n78; and false positives scandal, 192, 245n9; human rights abuses by, 185–186, 188–192; incursions into Ecuador by, 120, 126, 132, 158, 234n12, 241–242n86; and international

Colombian military (*continued*)
humanitarian law, 193, 245–246n10; justice system of, 189, 192; professionalism of, 187; size of, 187–188; ties to paramilitaries of, 234n12, 245n5; U.S. support to, 186, 187, 190
Colombian paramilitaries, 116, 119, 124–125, 188, 234n11, 245n6; and cocaine trade, 234–235n16; killings by, 121, 188; operations in Ecuador by, 120–121; size of, 117; ties to military of, 234n12, 245n5
Comisión de la Verdad y Reconciliación (CVR, Peru), 84, 91, 98, 104, 230n53, 230n57
Comisión Ecuménica de Derechos Humanos (CEDHU, Ecuador), 151
comités de autodefensa (CADs, Peru), 66–67, 222n14, 230n53; and Peruvian military, 52, 53, 74, 224n35
Confederación de Nacionalidades Indígenas del Ecuador (CONAIE), 34, 35, 49, 223n27
Confederación General de Trabajadores del Perú (CGTP), 111
Consejo de Seguridad Nacional (COSENA, Ecuador), 31, 126, 137, 162–163, 243n100
Consejo Nacional de Camélidos Sudamericanos (CONACS, Peru), 82, 175, 230n50
contingency theory, 15, 16, 216n13
contraband interdiction: by Ecuadorian military, 136–137, 238nn48–50; by Peruvian military, 80–81, 229n42, 230n46
Coordinadora Nacional de Derechos Humanos (CNDDHH, Peru), 60, 65–66, 84
Correa, Rafael, 35–36, 162; and FARC, 158, 241n85, 243n100
corruption, 28, 123, 156–157, 197, 218n11; in Peruvian military, 26–27, 29, 107, 185, 206, 218n8
Costa, Gino, 68, 69, 97, 98
counterinsurgency: civilian casualties in, 93–94, 96; Colombian military and, 185, 186–188, 241n78; in Latin America, 8–9, 215–216n8; and legitimacy, 64–68, 73, 105; and military autonomy, 15–16, 21, 58, 73–76, 84–86, 87–88, 102–103, 113; Peruvian bases and patrols for, 73–74, 75, 76, 102, 104–105, 171–172, 227nn17–19; Peruvian military's assertive, 40–44, 102–105, 113–114; Peruvian military's doctrine of, 41–42, 43, 46, 93, 221n9, 222n17; Peruvian police and, 71, 74–76, 86, 98, 104, 222n15, 226n13, 227n22, 232n77; and professionalism, 71–73; and resource maximization, 68–71; U.S. support for, 18, 55, 70–71, 93, 126, 188, 236n27; Venezuelan military and, 194, 195–196
Cuban Revolution, 8, 215n7
Cuenca, Ecuador, 136
Cusco, Peru, 40, 60, 172

drugs. *See* illegal drug trade
Durán Ballén, Sixto, 33, 49, 220n24, 224n30

economic development, 5, 8; Ecuadorian military and, 146, 217n21, 239n66; Peruvian military and, 42, 221n11; Venezuelan military and, 196
Ecuador: AVC insurgency in, 31, 47, 223n21; border with Colombia, 116, 119–121, 124–125, 233n2; civil-military relations in, 17, 30–36; Colombian citizens entering, 118, 137, 234n5, 238n51; Colombian insurgents as threat to, 1–2, 19, 117–118, 126; Colombian military incursions into, 120, 126, 132, 158, 234n12, 241–242n86; constitution of, 134–135, 240n75; coup of 2000 in, 32, 34–35, 220n27; crime in, 49, 121–123, 135, 148, 224n29, 234n15, 237n43, 240n73; FARC presence in, 117, 118–119, 121, 124, 153–154, 233n4, 234n6, 234n13, 241n79; and illegal drug trade, 122, 235n17, 235n19; indigenous movement in, 32, 34–35, 49; military regime in, 19, 217nn21–22; national police in, 55, 141, 147–150, 239n67, 240nn68–69; national security council in, 31, 126, 137, 162–163, 243n100; National Security Law of, 135, 147, 169, 223n25, 237n41; neoliberal economic reforms in, 33–34, 220n24; oil industry in, 33, 169, 217n20, 223n25; organic military and defense laws of, 36, 135, 237n41, 240n75; public opinion in, 125, 135, 224n29, 235n24, 237n42; states of emergency in, 135, 138, 148, 237n43, 240n73; and United States,

163, 243n101; wars with Peru, 4, 19, 31, 32, 38, 56, 130, 220n1, 221n2; and weapons trafficking, 123, 136
Ecuadorian military: antinarcotics work of, 139–140; autonomy of, 7, 31, 35, 36, 151, 241n77; avoidance of conflict with FARC by, 55–56, 133–134, 152–154, 155–156, 160, 161, 162, 182–183, 225n39; border defense prioritized over police work by, 48–50; branches of, 18; budget, 17, 31, 32, 128–129, 158, 159, 219n22, 242n91; civic-action projects of, 35, 144, 180, 220n28, 239n63; clashes with FARC by, 54–55, 134, 160–161; client influence on, 165, 166, 168, 175–181, 182; contraband interdiction by, 136–137, 238nn48–50; contradiction in sovereignty assignment of, 3, 22, 37, 54–56, 140, 150, 154–155, 156–157, 160, 163; corruption in, 123, 156–157; crime-fighting efforts by, 49–50, 130, 135–136, 148, 179–180, 224nn30–31, 237n43, 237–238n44, 240n70, 240n72; decentralized structure of, 17, 155; economic development work by, 35, 146, 217n21, 220n28, 239n66; and human rights abuses, 151, 240n74; immigration control by, 137; industries of, 33, 36; and internal security, 134–135; justice system of, 151, 160, 240–241n75; and legitimacy, 124–125, 150, 161–164, 184; Manta air force base of, 32, 158, 163; meetings with FARC by, 156–157, 160, 241n82; mission beliefs of, 14, 141–144, 145–147, 164, 182, 239nn64–66; mission neglect by, 2, 50, 55, 115, 154–155, 157, 241n81; mission overload of, 3, 16, 22, 23, 54–56, 115, 140, 150, 151–154, 163; and national police, 147–150, 205, 239n67, 240nn68–69; northern border defense mission of, 17, 50, 54, 55, 115, 127–128, 130, 131–132, 157, 159, 242n89; and oil companies, 138–139, 166, 169–170, 177–179, 182–183, 239n58, 244nn12–13; patrol tactics of, 48, 133–134, 155–156, 159, 160, 237n38, 237n40; and Plan Colombia, 22, 127, 151–154; police work as important to, 115, 141–142, 164, 184, 206; police work institutionalization by, 134–140, 147; policing assignments of, 2, 19, 47, 135–136, 137–138, 139–140, 142, 146, 237n43, 237–238n44; political role of, 30–31, 33–35, 164; post-Cenepa role shift of, 144–150; and predictability, 140, 164; and private security companies, 149, 182; and professionalism, 129–131, 150, 223n22; protest control by, 48–49, 137–138, 179, 223n23, 223n27; regions and divisions of, 148, 240n71; and resource maximization, 127–129, 150; southern border defense by, 14, 17, 47–48, 115, 130; sovereignty mission of, 7, 14, 19, 37, 115, 164; and subnational political officials, 176–177, 179–180; training of, 48, 148–149, 159, 242n92; units, poverty of, 167–168; U.S. support to, 128–129, 175–176, 179, 182, 236nn32–33, 243n10, 244n18; and wealthy landowners, 135, 176, 179, 238n45; weapons interdiction by, 136, 238n47
Ejército de Liberación Nacional (ELN, Colombia), 116–117, 237n40
Ejército de Liberación Nacional (ELN, Peru), 41–42
El Oro, Ecuador, 135, 237n43
Esmeraldas, Ecuador, 117, 121, 122, 133, 139, 237n44, 237–238n45
external defense: Argentine military and, 11; Ecuadorian army and, 47–48, 50, 54, 55, 115, 130, 131–132, 146, 240n68; Peruvian military and, 16, 38, 82–83, 221n10, 230n52; prioritization of, 8, 12; and professionalism, 7–8; Venezuelan military and, 195, 246n16

Febres Cordero, León, 31, 49
Francisco de Orellana (“Coca”), Ecuador, 131, 176, 243n10
Fuerzas Armadas Revolucionarias de Colombia (FARC), 54, 116, 153, 186; attacks initiated from Ecuador by, 119, 234n10; and cocaine trade, 234–235n16; Correa and, 158, 241n85, 243n100; Ecuadorian army avoidance of conflict with, 55–56, 133–134, 152–154, 155–156, 160, 161, 162, 182–183, 225n39; Ecuadorian army clashes with, 54–55, 134, 160–161; Ecuadorian army meetings with, 156–157, 160, 241n82; and Ecuadorian border communities, 118–119,

Fuerzas Armadas Revolucionarias de Colombia (FARC) *(continued)* 121, 124, 153–154, 234n13, 241n79; Ecuadorian government policy toward, 125–128, 158, 162–163; "terrorist" label of, 127; ties with Ecuadorian military by, 56, 123, 156–157, 225n41; training and recuperation in Ecuador by, 117, 119, 233n4, 234n6; and Venezuela, 195, 204; weaponry of, 153, 156–157
Fujimori, Alberto, 27, 28, 29, 38, 69, 219n18; *autogolpe* of, 26; military autonomy granted by, 26, 52–53; politicization of military by, 5–6, 25

Gallardo, José, 146
García, Alan, 24–25, 29, 43, 231n60; human rights policy during 1985–1990, 25, 51, 52
García Meza, Luis, 199
Gaviria Trujillo, César, 187
Gómez de la Torre, Oscar, 77
Guayaquil, Ecuador, 49, 135–136, 148, 179–180, 238n48, 244n15
Guayas, Ecuador, 148, 224n29
Guevara, Ernesto "Che," 215n7
Gutiérrez, Lucio, 33, 34, 35, 127, 237n43
Guzmán, Abimael, 39, 43

Huamán, Adrián, 42, 224n35
Huanta, Peru, 171–172; military killings in, 86, 221n8
Humala, Antauro, 30
Humala, Ollanta, 27
human rights abuses: Bolivian military and, 202; Colombian military and, 185, 188–190, 191–192; Ecuadorian military and, 151, 240n74; MRTA and, 230n53, 231n68; Peruvian military and, 25, 43, 51, 65–66, 67, 84–85, 86, 89, 91, 221n12, 230–231n57, 231nn64–66, 231–232n68; Sendero Luminoso and, 39, 60, 66, 84, 230n53
human rights policy, 11, 25, 84–85, 230–231n57; Peruvian army paralysis attributed to, 21, 51–52, 91–92, 99; U.S., 191, 245n8
Hurtado, Osvaldo, 31–32
hydrocarbon companies: Ecuadorian army security work for, 48–49, 138–139, 166, 168–170, 177–179, 182–183, 223n23, 239n58, 244nn12–13; Ecuadorian state oil company, 33, 217n20; Peruvian army security work for, 172–173, 243n7; popular protests against, 123–124, 138, 178, 179, 181, 235n22, 238–239n56

Ilave, Peru, 78, 228n33
illegal drug trade, 4; Bolivia and, 199–200, 201, 246nn16–18; Brazilian efforts against, 10; coca eradication efforts, 46, 64, 112–113, 199, 246n17; Colombia and, 187, 188, 234–235n16; in Ecuador, 122, 235nn17–19; interdiction efforts against, 46, 200, 246n18; in Peru, 62, 222n16, 225n4; Peruvian military and, 26–27, 44–46, 112–113, 218nn8–9, 233n87; Sendero Luminoso and, 44, 59, 62–63; U.S. efforts against, 46, 55, 64, 113, 187, 199, 200, 245n3, 246n17
Inter-American Court of Human Rights (IACHR), 84, 151, 190, 191, 230n56
International Committee of the Red Cross (ICRC), 193, 221n13
international humanitarian law (IHL), 96–97, 193, 232n76, 245–246n10
Iquitos, Peru, 167, 229n35

Jarrín, Oswaldo, 179
Junín, Peru, 39–40, 61, 243n6

kidnappings: by MRTA, 40; in northern Ecuador, 120–121, 122, 234n15, 235n21; by Sendero Luminoso, 60, 66, 226n9

land squatters, 79–80, 175, 229n40
Larrea, Gustavo, 120
Latacunga, Ecuador, 133, 180–181
Leahy Amendment, 190
Ledesma, Walter, 28
legitimacy, 2, 184; Ecuadorian military and, 124–125, 150, 161–164, 184; and mission performance, 6, 9–11, 57; Peruvian military and, 38, 64–68, 73, 76, 105
Lima, Peru, 64, 84, 111; Sendero Luminoso attacks in, 40, 50, 51, 67
Loret de Mola, Aurelio, 68, 87, 97

Macas, Luis, 223n27
Machala, Ecuador, 136, 180, 238n46
Mahuad, Jamil, 34, 38, 148, 240n73
Mendoza, Carlos, 34–35, 147
Mesa, Carlos, 199, 200
military autonomy: in Colombia, 189–192; and contradictions in sovereignty missions, 3, 15–16, 21, 37, 51–52, 83–86, 87–88, 90, 113; Ecuadorian military and, 7, 31, 35, 36, 151, 241n77; and mission constraints, 15–16, 21, 23, 24–30, 37, 86–87, 151; and mission performance, 6–7, 52, 87–88, 92–97, 102–103, 104, 202; Peruvian military increases in, 25, 52–54, 102–103, 104; Peruvian military reductions in, 3, 51, 83–85, 87–88
military budgets, 11–12, 18; Colombian, 187; Ecuadorian, 17, 31, 32, 128–129, 158, 159, 219n22, 242n91; Peruvian, 25, 29, 52, 70–71, 75, 76, 166, 219nn18–19, 226n15, 243n2
military politicization, 4, 5–6, 25, 26, 197
mining companies, 168, 169, 170–175, 243n7
mission beliefs, 184, 205; of Brazilian military, 216n12; of Ecuadorian military, 14, 141–144, 145–147, 164, 182, 239nn64–66; of Peruvian military, 14, 71–72, 105–107, 164, 181; and predictability framework, 13–14, 22
mission neglect, 3, 4, 5, 7, 15, 164; by Ecuadorian military, 2, 50, 55, 115, 154–155, 157, 241n81; by Peruvian military, 2, 19, 50, 58, 73–76, 83, 98
Moeller, Heinz, 127–128
Moncayo, Paco, 239n65, 239n67
Montesinos, Vladimiro, 218n13, 218–219n14; corruption of, 27, 28, 218n11; use of intelligence agency by, 26, 218n6, 232n68
Monzón Valley, Peru, 62
Morales, Evo, 199, 200, 204–205
Movimiento Bolivariano Revolucionario 200 (MBR-200), 198, 246n14
Movimiento de Izquierda Revolucionaria (MIR, Peru), 41–42
Movimiento Revolucionario Túpac Amaru (MRTA), 38–39, 40, 44, 45; and human rights abuses, 230n53, 231n68

Napo, Ecuador, 48–49, 137
Nariño, Colombia, 117
Noboa, Gustavo, 35, 127
Nueva Loja, Ecuador, 118–119, 122, 237–238n44

Occidental Petroleum, 124, 178
Oleoducto de Crudos Pesados (OCP) Limited, 123, 139, 177, 179
Operation Dignity, 199, 200
Orellana, Ecuador, 123–124, 138, 139, 178, 179, 238n55, 238–239n56
Organizations in Action (Thompson), 15, 216n14

Palacio, Alfredo, 35, 128
Paniagua, Valentín, 28, 84, 218–219n14
Partido Comunista de Venezuela Movimiento de la Izquierda Revolucionaria (PCV/MIR), 196
Pastrana, Andrés, 117, 187
Pérez, Carlos Andrés, 196
Pérez Jiménez, Marcos, 194
Peru: borders with Chile and Colombia, 82; civil-military relations in, 17, 24–30, 68–69, 97–99, 217n2; cocaine production and trafficking in, 62, 225n4; constitution of, 64–65, 169; economic growth in, 217n1, 217n4; Fujimori *autogolpe* in, 26; human rights policy in, 25, 51, 52; intelligence agencies in, 25, 26, 54, 85, 217n2, 218n6, 231n58; Japanese embassy hostage crisis in, 40, 44; justice system in, 28, 84–85, 87, 230–231n57, 231n62; Law of Repentance in, 94, 232n75; popular protests in, 47, 63–64, 78–79, 181, 222n18, 228n32; public opinion in, 67; Sendero Luminoso insurgency as threat in, 25, 39–40, 41, 44, 50, 59–62; states of emergency in, 40, 68–69, 77, 171; Velasco Alvarado government in, 19, 217nn20–21, 219n17; wars with Ecuador, 4, 19, 31, 32, 38, 56, 130, 220n1, 221n2
Peruvian military: amnesty for, 52, 84, 97–98, 99; antinarcotics efforts of, 44–46, 71, 81–82, 112–113, 206, 230n48, 233n87; assertive counterinsurgency by, 40–44, 102–105, 113–114; attempts to win local population, 44–45, 57, 206; autonomy

Peruvian military *(continued)*
increased for, 25, 52–54, 102–103, 104, 202; autonomy reduced for, 3, 15–16, 21, 23, 24–25, 28–30, 37, 51, 83–86, 88; autonomy seen as necessary for, 92–97; branches of, 18; budget, 25, 29, 52, 70–71, 75, 76, 166, 219nn18–19, 226n15, 243n2; centralized structure of, 16–17, 73, 75, 99–102, 109–110, 226–227n16, 228n25; civic-action work by, 26, 53; and civilian casualties, 93–94, 96; and civilian control, 17, 29, 68; on civilian-guerrilla distinction, 94–96; and civilian justice system, 28, 87, 231n62; client influence on, 18, 165, 168, 170–175, 181, 243n9; and cocaine trade, 26–27, 44–46, 218nn8–9; cohort differences in, 88–92, 95–96, 231n53; and *comités de autodefensa* (CADs), 52, 53, 74, 224n35; constitutional role of, 64–65, 169; contraband interdiction by, 80–81, 229n42, 230n46; contradiction seen in mission of, 3, 15–16, 21, 37, 51–52, 83–86, 87–88, 90–91; corruption in, 26–27, 29, 107, 185, 206, 218n8; counterinsurgency bases of, 73–74, 76, 102, 104–105, 227nn17–19; counterinsurgency doctrine of, 41–42, 43, 46, 93, 221n9, 222n17; counterinsurgency mission of, 15–16, 41, 42, 68–70; counterinsurgency patrols by, 74, 75, 102, 171–172; counterinsurgency prioritized over policing, 109; defense fund for, 30, 219n19; disappearances by, 85, 221–222n13, 230n55; and economic development, 42, 221n11; and external defense, 38, 42, 220n1, 221n2, 221n10; Fujimori supporters in, 28, 218–219n14, 219n15, 247n5; human rights abuses by, 25, 43, 67, 89, 91, 221n12, 221–222n13, 231nn64–66, 231–232n68; human rights policy seen as paralyzing counterinsurgency, 51–52, 91–92, 99; and international humanitarian law, 96–97, 232n76; justice system of, 86; and legitimacy, 38, 64–68, 73, 76, 105; massacres by, 41, 51, 52, 84, 221n8, 230n54; and mining and hydrocarbon companies, 170–175, 181, 243n6; mission beliefs of, 14, 71–72, 105–107, 164, 181; mission neglect by, 2, 19, 50, 58, 73–76, 83, 98; police relations with, 50, 88, 92, 104, 112, 224n32; politicization of, 5–6, 25, 26; and predictability, 83–84, 97, 102, 105, 113; and private security companies, 170, 181; and professionalism, 26, 28, 38, 71–73, 76; protest control by, 46–47, 77–79, 107–109, 111–112, 174, 222n19, 222–223n20, 228n33, 229n35, 233n86; rebellions and coup plot of, 25, 27–28, 30, 217n3, 218n12; *recursos directamente recaudados* (RDR) of, 166, 243n2; rejection of police missions by, 14, 44–47, 76–82, 105–107, 109–114, 184–185, 206; removal of land squatters by, 79–80, 175, 229n40; and resource maximization, 18, 68–71, 73; rules of engagement for, 103–104, 105, 110–111, 113, 233nn81–82; sovereignty mission of, 14, 37, 164; training and education in, 28–29, 82–83, 96–97, 219n17, 228n30, 232n76; transparency of, 29–30; units, poverty of, 166–167; U.S. support to, 46, 70–71, 81–82, 230n48

Peruvian police, 77; antinarcotics operations by, 64, 81, 230n48; in counterinsurgency operations, 71, 74–76, 86, 98, 104, 222n15, 226n13, 227n22, 232n77; insurgent attacks on, 43, 50, 74, 75, 98, 224n32, 232n77; and Peruvian army, 50, 88, 92, 104, 112, 224n32; protest control by, 112, 181, 228n32

Petroecuador, 33

Petróleos de Venezuela, S.A. (PDVSA), 203

Plan Colombia, 115, 118, 125, 188; alarm in Ecuador over, 124, 125, 235n24; Ecuadorian government response to, 125–128; Ecuadorian military and, 22, 127, 151–154

Plan Patriota, 118

Plan VRAE, 102–103, 111, 232–233n79, 233n82

policing missions, 5, 10, 12, 205; of Bolivian military, 199–202; of Colombian military, 185, 186; of Ecuadorian military, 2, 19, 47, 135–136, 137–138, 139–140, 142, 146, 237n43, 237–238n44; Ecuadorian military commitment to, 2, 115, 141–142, 164, 184,

206; Ecuadorian military institutionalization of, 134–140, 147; Peruvian military assignments to, 19, 73, 77–81, 174–175, 215n2, 228n33, 229n35, 229n40; Peruvian military rejection of, 14, 44–47, 76–82, 105–107, 109–114, 184–185, 206; and sovereignty missions, 9, 14, 48–50, 109, 185; and trauma to military organizations, 109, 184–185, 186, 194, 198, 199, 201, 205; of Venezuelan military, 194, 196
predictability framework, 3, 13–17, 183; and contradictions, 14–16, 83–84, 185; Ecuadorian military and, 140, 164; and mission beliefs, 13–14, 22; and mission performance, 17, 21, 56, 140, 216n17; Peruvian military and, 83–84, 97, 102, 105, 113; and uncertainty, 16–17
privatization, 4, 77, 110, 137, 228n31
professionalism: Ecuadorian military and, 129–131, 150, 223n22; and mission performance, 2–3, 6, 7–9, 14, 57; Peruvian military and, 26, 28, 38, 71–73, 76
protests, 4; Bolivian water and gas wars, 200–201; by coca growers, 62, 64, 78–79; Ecuadorian military control of, 48–49, 137–138, 179, 223n23, 223n27; against free trade agreements, 111, 235n22; against hydrocarbon companies, 123–124, 138, 178, 179, 181, 235n22, 238–239n56; by indigenous groups, 48, 49, 223n27; labor strikes, 47, 111, 222n18, 223n23, 233n86; over land use, 112, 174; Peruvian Arequipazo, 77; Peruvian military control of, 46–47, 77–79, 107–109, 111–112, 174, 222n19, 222–223n20, 228n30, 228n33, 229n35; by police, 222–223n20, 240n68, 246n20; against privatization, 4, 77, 110, 137, 200–201, 228n31; Venezuelan Caracazo, 9, 196
Puno, Peru, 80–81, 167, 230n46; protests in, 64, 77–78, 107, 109, 110
Putumayo, Colombia, 54, 117, 118

Quito, Ecuador, 49, 136

resource maximization: Ecuadorian military and, 127–129, 150; and mission performance, 2, 6, 11–13, 17–18, 56–57, 165, 183, 184; Peruvian military and, 18, 68–71, 73
Reyes, Raúl, 156, 158, 241n84
Robles Espinoza, Rodolfo, 218n6
role beliefs, 13–14
Rospigliosi, Fernando, 52, 54, 65, 68, 76
Ruiz, Rengifo, 87

Salinas Sedó, Jaime, 27
Samper, Ernesto, 191
Sánchez de Lozada, Gonzalo, 201
San Román, Máximo, 27
Sendero Luminoso, 2, 51, 170; armed attacks by, 41, 43–44, 50, 60, 75, 102–103, 221n7, 228n26, 232n78; and Asháninka indigenous group, 75, 227n23; declining power of, 43–44, 59–60, 61–62; and drug trade, 44, 59, 62–63; expansion of, 25, 39–40, 41, 50; human rights abuses by, 39, 60, 66, 84, 230n53; kidnappings by, 66, 226n9; new strategy of, 46, 61, 65; propaganda of, 60–61; splits in, 59, 225n1
Servicio de Inteligencia Nacional (SIN, Peru), 26, 54, 85, 218n6, 218n8
Solórzano, Carlos, 34
sovereignty missions, 5, 184, 206; of Bolivian military, 198; of Colombian military, 185; contradictions in, 23, 37, 164; of Ecuadorian military, 7, 14, 37, 115, 164; military neglect of, 3, 4, 7, 164; military preference for, 8, 12, 14, 37; of Peruvian military, 14, 37, 164; and policing missions, 9, 14, 48–50, 109, 185; of Venezuelan military, 194–196
Sucumbíos, Ecuador, 120, 122, 139, 238n55; FARC presence in, 118–119, 124, 234n9; military confrontations with FARC in, 54–55, 134, 160; oil protests in, 123–124, 138, 178, 238–239n56

Tacna, Peru, 82, 167
Techint, 60, 173
Texaco, 48, 177, 244n12
Tingo María, Peru, 78–79
Toledo, Alejandro, 29, 77, 98
Tulcán, Ecuador, 137, 237–238n44
Tumbes, Peru, 167

United States: antinarcotics efforts of, 46, 55, 64, 113, 187, 199, 200, 245n3, 246n17; and Bolivia, 199, 200, 246n17; and Colombia, 118, 126, 187, 190, 191, 236n27, 245n3, 245n8; and Ecuador, 55, 128–129, 158, 163, 175–176, 179, 182, 236nn32–33, 243n10, 244n18; human rights policy of, 191, 245n8; and Peru, 46, 64, 70–71, 81–82, 113, 221n13, 230n48; and Venezuela, 203
Uribe, Álvaro, 116, 191

Valle del Alto Huallaga (VAH), 44, 69, 86; coca growers in, 62, 64, 78–79; counterinsurgency efforts in, 45, 46, 222n17; Sendero Luminoso insurgency in, 44
Valle del Río Apurímac y Ene (VRAE), 79, 86; military counterinsurgency in, 68–69, 102–105, 172; Sendero Luminoso insurgency in, 44, 63, 66
Vargas, Antonio, 34
Vargas Pazzos, Frank, 32
Velasco Alvarado, Juan, 19, 217nn20–21, 219n17
Venezuela: anti-Chávez coup in, 198, 203, 206, 246n15; under Chávez, 198, 202–203, 246n22; Chávez coup attempts in, 198, 246n14; and Colombian insurgency, 117, 195, 204; national guard in, 196, 246n12
Venezuelan military: civilian control of, 197, 202–203; counterinsurgency mission of, 194, 195–196; dissent against Chávez within, 203, 246n23; economic development role of, 196; internal divisions within, 9, 197–198, 206; policing mission of, 194, 196; popular support for, 11, 196, 246n13; protest control by, 9, 194, 196–197, 198, 206; sovereignty missions of, 194–196
Vizcatán, Peru, 63, 104–105

Yacimientos Petrolíferos Fiscales Bolivianos (YPFB), 204